MICROSOFT CERTIFIED SYSTEMS ENGINEER GEAR

HARRISON

ASP/MTS/ADSI
WEB SECURITY

ISBN 0-13-084465-9

90000

Prentice Hall PTR
Upper Saddle River, New Jersey 07458
http://www.phptr.com

9 780130 844651

Library of Congress Cataloging-in-Publication Data

Harrison, Richard

    ASP/MTS/ADSI Web security / Richard Harrison.

        p.   cm.

    ISBN 0–13–084465–9

    1. Computer networks—Security measures.   2. World Wide Web
(Information retrieval system)—Security measures.   I. Title.

TK5105.59.H37   1999   99–18599

005.8—dc21   CIP

Acquisitions editor: Greg Doench
Cover designer: Anthony Gemmellaro
Cover design director: Jerry Votta
Manufacturing manager: Alexis R. Heydt
Marketing manager: Kaylie Smith
Developmental editor: Jim Markham
Compositor/Production services: Pine Tree Composition, Inc.

Prentice Hall books are widely used by corporations and government agencies for training, marketing, and resale.

The publisher offers discounts on this book when ordered in bulk quantities. For more information contact:

> Corporate Sales Department
> Phone: 800-382-3419
> Fax: 201-236-7141
> E-mail: corpsales@prenhall.com

> Or write:

> Prentice Hall PTR
> Corp. Sales Dept.
> One Lake Street
> Upper Saddle River, New Jersey 07458

Printed in the United States of America
10 9 8 7 6 5 4 3 2

ISBN: 0-13-084465-9

Prentice-Hall International (UK) Limited, *London*
Prentice-Hall of Australia Pty. Limited, *Sydney*
Prentice-Hall Canada, Inc., *Toronto*
Prentice-Hall Hispanoamericana, S.A., *Mexico*
Prentice-Hall of India Private Limited, *New Delhi*
Prentice-Hall of Japan, Inc., *Tokyo*
Simon & Schuster Asia Pte. Ltd., *Singapore*
Editora Prentice-Hall do Brasil, Ltda., *Rio de Janeiro*

CONTENTS

2

The Windows NT Security Environment *25*

3

Network Security   *65*

4

IIS Web Server Security   *101*

7

ASP Security Fundamentals   *231*

8

ASP Application-Level Security   *253*

9

Creating Our Own Public Key Infrastructure with Microsoft Certificate Server *295*

11

Web Database Security with MTS/ASP   *379*

14

Membership Server *487*

15

Active User Objects   *519*

ACKNOWLEDGMENTS

Writing this book has involved a great deal of work, and only with the help of many individuals was all this made possible. In particular, my thanks to:

You, for buying this book; I hope you enjoy it and find it useful.

Greg Doench, Anne Trowbridge, Mary Treacy, Patty Donovan, Dana Smith, Robert Milch, and the team at Prentice-Hall/Pine Tree Composition.

Mike Howard, Microsoft IIS Security Product Manager, for answering my questions in a timely manner

The numerous reviewers whose feedback made this a better book

Last but not least, Pam, and our children, Kirsty, Matthew, and Nathan, for their support and patience while I got lost in this project

Richard Harrison—rich@cyberdude.com

INTRODUCTION

Without doubt, the World Wide Web is currently causing major excitement in business, but the challenges that abound are also probably giving a lot of sleepless nights to many senior company personnel. The rapid changes in information processing and networking technology are compressing time—time that is desperately needed for businesses to adapt to the many opportunities offered by the new generation of Internet solutions. The speed at which companies adopt Internet technologies will dictate to what extent they thrive or survive.

The Web now offers business the opportunity to innovate and achieve exceptional growth by reducing costs, increasing sales, and improving customer services. But if businesses ignore the Internet now, they will definitely pay later. Large companies will widen their portfolio of services, and new startup companies will appear, perhaps halfway around the world and with a very small workforce, and these will poach upon the core business of the traditional, "stone age" companies. Customers will have little loyalty and will move to other companies that offer convenient, compelling, cost-effective services.

In addition, many organizations are now using Web technology over private internal networks to create *Intranets.* Senior managers have long recognized that an effective information technology strategy is required to provide productivity improvements, access to new and enhanced revenue streams, and increased customer satisfaction. A distributed computing framework based on Web technologies is now providing the key to fulfilling these requirements. The use of platform-independent browser technology accessing server-based applications avoids the costly and complex distribution tasks previously required with networked computers. The rapid adoption of Internet standards by every major IT vendor has made possible the integration of the various distributed environments and different infrastructures within organizations.

Forward-looking businesses now wish to automate and streamline their various business processes to reduce costs and provide new opportunities for marketing advantage. As an example, consider the manufacturing supply chain. Before the goods reach the end-customer, numerous organizations are involved along the chain, from handling the raw materials, through the manufacturing process, and on to distribution and retail. Each of these organizations can achieve faster delivery times and reduce inventory costs if it handles its business processes electronically. Business-to-business electronic commerce involves the secure trading of goods and information between partners, and this involves businesses opening up their networks to form *Extranets* that allow external organizations to integrate their systems to form virtual enterprises.

It is now expected that the next hugely successful companies will be the ones that quickly enable the next generation of business systems that exploit the convergence of computers and networking for business advantage. But what are the perils of working in this new Internet age?

Break-ins at high-profile Internet sites, attacks on vital Internet services, impersonation of important organizations, invasion of personal privacy, and tales of electronic commerce fraud produce attractive headlines and scare stories about Internet security for the computer industry press. From this it is not surprising that one of the biggest concerns businesses have about using Internet technologies pertains to the security of their systems.

Fortunately, many of these stories could have been avoided if the organization involved had not made elementary mistakes. Without doubt, the biggest security threat from the Internet comes from within—from organizations that do not fully understand how to use the available security software technology .

In this book we shall put the risks of using Internet technologies into perspective by investigating the various threats that abound and discussing what levels of protection are available. We shall then build on this knowledge to learn how to deploy a secure infrastructure for the Web.

How This Book Is Organized

ASP/MTS/ADSI Web Security is primarily for software developers and system architects who are building business-critical Web solutions where security is paramount. However, everyone involved in a Web solution must be fully aware of the security issues, and thus many parts of the book will be very useful to other members of the Web team, such as administrators, Web authors, systems support, and so on.

The book focuses on the comprehensive set of Web technologies from Microsoft that is enabling companies to build secure business applications for deployment over the Internet/Intranet/Extranet. The book has been divided into two distinct sections. These are: "Security Fundamentals and Core Technologies" and "Web Security Programming."

Before we dive into the design and development of any Web solution, it is vital that we fully understand the key issues. So in the first section of the

Introduction **xxiii**

book we shall discuss the fundamental concepts upon which Web security is based and the core security technologies that Microsoft has provided to enable us to create a secure infrastructure for our Web applications. In addition, we shall see that strong Web security is achieved with a combination of software technology and the consistent employment of a number of operating practices.

The second section of the book builds on this foundation to discuss building secure Web solutions using application-level security with the following Microsoft development technologies: Active Server Pages (ASP), Microsoft Transaction Server (MTS), and Active Directory Service Interface (ADSI). This section will enable the reader to explore the many hidden capabilities, and to fully exploit this new and exciting software technology. Lots of examples are provided to illustrate the various techniques, and they are written in a manner suitable for adaptation and inclusion in the reader's own Web projects.

A summary of the book's contents follows.

Security Fundamentals and Core Technologies

Chapter 1, "Security Is a Journey, Not a Destination," explains what we mean by security, the risks of operating with Internet technologies, and how to manage these risks. It shows that security has several facets and explains the issues that need to be addressed to create a trusted system. Security is not something that is turned on and then forgotten; it is an ongoing task to keep one step ahead of the Internet bandits.

Chapter 2, "The Windows NT Security Environment," investigates the security features that form the bedrock of Microsoft's Windows NT architecture. It shows that Windows NT security encapsulates the processes, algorithms, and techniques to provide a defense against unauthorized access to the system's resources, and it allows security to be applied in various combinations and layers to provide a flexible solution to address the different security requirements demanded by organizations.

Chapter 3, "Network Security," looks at the problems of networked computers and shows how to protect systems from malicious attacks. It includes discussions of firewalls, proxy servers, secure channels, and virtual private networks.

Chapter 4, "IIS Web Server Security," investigates the security features of Microsoft's latest standards-based commercial Web application server. It looks at the key concepts in the configuring of a IIS Web site to keep the content and applications secure, and it explains how to identify and authenticate Web users. It also discusses the security model offered by the server extensions used by the Microsoft development tools FrontPage and Visual Studio.

Chapter 5, "Secure Channels," expands on Chapter 3 to discuss secure channels in detail. It explains how to use them to establish a point-to-point network connection that offers end-point authentication, nonrepudiation, message encryption, and message authentication. It also discusses digital certificates and cryptography, which are fundamental in the operation of secure channels.

Chapter 6, "Establishing Trust . . . Protecting the Desktop," considers the issues of protecting client systems operating on the Internet from malicious code and distasteful Web content. It explains the risks of using downloaded code and investigates the mechanisms available to determine whether downloaded code can be trusted. It also discusses the differences between the Java and ActiveX approaches to security.

Web Security Programming

Chapter 7, "ASP Security Fundamentals," introduces application-level security and explains how such techniques must be used in combination with the core security offered by Windows NT and IIS. It takes the reader on a quick crash course in ASP and the key concepts needed for subsequent security-related topics. It also discusses how ASP handles sessions using cookies and the potential for an attack by someone hijacking an ASP session.

Chapter 8, "Application-Level Security with ASP," gets our hands dirty with lots of programming code and some examples of application-level security using ASP service-side scripting. It shows how to enable site access controls, enforce a user to register its personal details before being given site access, audit the Web site access, determine the information stored in a client's digital certificate, and provide additional assurances against an ASP session being hijacked.

Chapter 9, "Creating Our Own Public Key Infrastructure with Microsoft Certificate Server," investigates how to create and deploy an IT infrastructure that makes it possible to achieve high levels of security using strong authentication and encryption technologies, and discusses such issues as certificate hierarchy, certificate enrollment, and certificate revocation. It looks at the internal architecture of Microsoft Certificate Server and illustrates how to extend the base product to handle nonstandard requirements.

Chapter 10, "MTS Security Fundamentals," discusses how to integrate ASP with software components that are installed into the Microsoft Transaction Server (MTS) environment. It concentrates on the security implications of MTS and shows how security can be applied by either configuration or within the programming logic.

Chapter 11, "Web Database Security with MTS," shows how to protect a Web database so that access is provided at suitable levels appropriate to the particular Web visitor. It illustrates how to use the security features provided by MTS Roles.

Chapter 12, "Directory Services," discusses the fundamentals of directory services and shows the advantages they provide when managing a community of Web users. It investigates the industry standards and in particular discusses the increasingly popular Lightweight Directory Access Protocol that is used for accessing directory services over a TCP/IP network. It also introduces a programmatic interface called ADSI that makes it easy for application programmers to support a directory environment within their applications.

Chapter 13, "Implementing Membership with ADSI," puts together all of the pieces we have seen so far and illustrates how to use ASP, MTS, and ADSI in a comprehensive example that demonstrates a "members only" Web site.

Chapter 14, "Membership Server," focuses on the membership components provided by Microsoft Site Server. It shows how to build large-scale systems that use Membership Server to track and profile millions of users, automate the identification of users by means of cookies, and protect areas of the site that have subscription-only/confidential content.

Chapter 15, "Active User Objects," discusses a major element of Microsoft Site Server that can be used to automatically identify a Web user and provide easy access to its associated personnel attributes located in a number of different datastores. It also illustrates how to use the information in the user's profile in order to enable customized Web content and make the available information more fitting by providing personalized pages.

Appendix

The Appendix, "Microsoft and the Active Platform," focuses on the Microsoft platform, and through we assume that the reader understands Microsoft's Internet strategy and has a reasonable grasp of its software products. The appendix is provided for readers who are not fully up to speed with this topic, and it acts as a reference guide to key Microsoft software products and tools used to build multi-tier Internet and Intranet applications.

Support

Support and errata for this book can be obtained at: **http://surf.to/harrison**

Richard Harrison is a Microsoft Certified Solution Developer (MCSD) and a senior consultant for a major global IT services company. He has recently been specializing in Microsoft Internet technologies and helping organizations to use these technologies to build mission-critical Web solutions.

He is a co-author of the following successful books from Wrox Press (and parts have been reproduced on the Microsoft Developer Network):

Professional ASP 2.0
Professional IE 4.0 Programming
Professional ASP

To contact him, please e-mail **rich@cyberdude.com** or refer to the Web site **http://surf.to/harrison**

Security
Is a Journey . . .
Not a Destination

In days gone by, evil highwaymen patrolled the rough dirt tracks of old England. They preyed on wayfarers and their possessions, causing fear throughout the land. As the tracks improved, and hence became more widely traveled, crime escalated too. It was only when the protection of travelers and their goods could be ensured that these rough tracks were able to evolve into sensible highways, providing the essential transportation infrastructure for modern business and human lifestyle.

Today's so-called information superhighways are now going through a similar inaugural phase, with many individuals and organizations rushing to get some sort of online capability. However, only when business has confidence that the systems cannot be infiltrated, and that network information can pass unimpeded, will electronic business—on a worldwide scale—intensify.

A few commercial organizations may regard the risks of doing business in cyberspace as unacceptable; but the rapid expansion of this powerful delivery channel means that they make such decisions at their peril. The use of the Internet can no longer be considered an option in business activity; it is a necessity. If you hesitate, then your rivals will gain a considerable headstart in using this potent technology.

The unfortunate (and often ignorant) hype over Internet security doesn't help. The scare stories—often generated by people who will happily hand over a credit card in a store, but will not divulge the same details over the Web—are causing confusion and nervousness in the business community.

As with any commercial activity, the risks of using the Internet should be put into perspective. To perform accurate risk analysis, it is important to understand what levels of protection are available.

In this chapter, we'll preview the key concepts that you should be aware of as you design and develop a security system. As we go through the book, we'll have an opportunity to understand what these concepts mean. In particular we shall look at:

- What is security?
- The issues that need to be addressed to create a trusted system
- How to manage the risks by performing risk assessment
- Risks on the Internet
- Requirements for Web security

So let us start our journey by clarifying what we mean by security. Then we can discuss the need to apply appropriate levels of security for each particular situation.

What Does Security Mean?

Since **security** is a term that means different things to different people, and has both business and technical connotations, we shall use this first section to clarify what we mean by it. Typically developers, product vendors, organizations, and end users all have different points of view on the subject.

We shall start with a definition of security and then proceed to preview the key concepts that you should be aware of as you design and develop a security system. Many of these initial security topics are applicable to traditional systems as well as to more modern Internet/Intranet environments.

Trusted Systems

From the business perspective, security means implementing a system that can be **trusted**. This means that the system must be designed and correctly configured to provide:

- Legitimate access to the system
- Data confidentiality
- Protection against malicious codes
- Auditability of user access
- Data integrity
- High levels of availability
- Nonrepudiation of received information

Let us dig round each of these topics just a little and introduce some key terms.

Access Controls

A key task of any security subsystem is to restrict system access to a known group of users. Checking for the legitimate use of a system involves the following steps:

- Identify the user; this process is called **authentication**
- When the user attempts to perform a particular action (e.g., invoke an executable program), check that the user has been granted the appropriate **access rights** (or **permissions**)

Typically, there are various levels of access rights. For example, one user may be allowed to read and modify data, while another may only be allowed to read the data.

This topic will be frequently encountered in this book. In Chapters 2 and 4 we shall discuss Microsoft Windows NT and IIS and see how these products provide core facilities for user authentication and applying permissions. Then, throughout Section Two of the book, we shall see various mechanisms for identifying the user to determine what levels of functionality to provide for the user.

The application of access controls must also include physical access to the computing facilities. Physical security is discussed later in the chapter.

Data Confidentiality

Providing data confidentiality and protection against unauthorized modification can be partially achieved by applying authentication procedures.

We can gain additional confidence about the confidentiality of any data by using software services that provide **data encryption**. This is the process of applying an algorithm to a message, which scrambles the data it contains. Given only the encoded data, it is very difficult and time-consuming (if not practically impossible) to deduce the original message.

One way to circumvent the access controls is to trick a legitimate user or the system to invoke a malicious piece of code. Such a program could snoop around for interesting data (such as users' passwords) and then send the data electronically to the perpetrator. Sometimes such malicious code can be concealed within a standard program so that when it is invoked, both the normal and the rogue functionality are invoked and the user goes unaware of any security breach. Such a program is called a **Trojan Horse** (or just a **Trojan**) and can be very difficult to detect. In Chapter 6 we shall discuss how to establish levels of trust and see a mechanism for detecting the origin of software. In short, the indispensable message is, don't execute software from anyone you don't trust—especially if you are running with administrator's permissions.

One other scenario where your information could easily fall into the wrong hands is when it is traversing over a network and outside the security of your system. In Chapter 5 we shall discuss secure communication channels and see how network traffic can be encrypted (and deciphered) by the networking software.

Virus Protection

A Trojan is one type of malicious code, but there are others. Solutions are required to protect our systems against any software that contains hidden malicious functions and tries to spread onto as many other systems as possible. Such programs, macros, and scripts go under the generic name of **viruses**.

Many people are unaware that viruses are not restricted to executables. For example, Microsoft Word now has the ability to code macros using Visual Basic, and these can be invoked automatically when the document is opened. The power of Visual Basic means that such macros could easily perform some harmful actions. There have been numerous examples of Word documents with dangerous payloads being e-mailed to unsuspecting recipients. The latest versions of Word display a warning if the document contains macros, but this relies on the user's being aware of the possibilities of enabling the macros for documents from an unknown origin.

Unfortunately, many viruses are spreading more quickly than they can be detected and removed. Viruses generate a wide variety of symptoms, from an annoying repetitive message, to accessing and transmitting confidential data, to complete hard disk wipe-out. Never underestimate what might be lurking within a virus.

Even the most innocuous virus may carry serious consequences. Suppose a business-critical system was infected with a virus that puts up a "joke" message and then holds up further system processing until a user has responded. The impact of such a virus is potentially disastrous.

Virus detection software can be used for continual scanning of the hard disk(s), memory, and network interfaces for known viruses, and to treat the system by removing the malicious code. We shall discuss networking architectures in Chapter 3 and see how to protect internal systems from direct exposure to the Internet using a proxy server. Both proxy servers and e-mail systems should be running virus detection software.

Since new viruses are continually being developed, it is important to regularly update virus detection software to the latest versions to ensure detection of any recent additions to the list of known viruses.

Auditability

Auditability involves the generation and recording of all user actions and accessing of systems resources—and it must include enough information to identify the user who performed any given operation. Such information is often invaluable when trying to analyze the events leading to a security breach.

It is obviously important for these audit trails to be protected from unauthorized access or modification. Alerts can be triggered to warn administrators about security and access problems, which could mean that potential attacks are in progress.

We shall introduce the Windows NT Event Viewer in Chapter 2 and the standard IIS logging facilities in Chapter 4. We shall augment these facilities by using ASP to record user activity to provide an audit trail in Chapter 8.

Auditing works hand in hand with authentication. Once the user has been identified, his or her activity can be recorded and associated with the user identifier. However, it is common on the Internet to allow users to access Web sites anonymously. The activity for all such users will normally be associated with a single "anonymous" user identifier. However, while users may believe they are surfing anonymously, there are a number of other items that sometimes may be used to identify them; examples include cook-ies and IP address. We shall discuss this further in Chapter 6 when we ad-dress privacy.

Data Integrity

To trust our system we must be able to rely on our data. As mentioned above, we must protect the data from rogues and malicious attack . . . but we must also be able to protect it from operating failures.

Data integrity relies on software services that prevent files and data stores from being left in a corrupted state should system, network, or appli-cation failures occur. For example, if a failure takes place part-way through a series of database updates, the system will automatically roll back the data to the previous consistent state, and the user will be notified that the transac-tion did not complete successfully.

In Chapters 10 and 11, we shall discuss Microsoft Transaction Server and see how it greatly reduces the complexity of developing reliable database applications across a distributed computing environment.

Availability

With today's business-critical systems, it is vital to achieve high levels of availability. If a system failure occurs, then a backup system should be avail-able. Ideally, the backup system should detect that a problem has occurred and automatically take over as the primary system, leaving the user unaware of such events.

A major problem for important systems is **denial-of-service attacks.** In such an attack, a rogue user invokes some executable logic that deliberately uses up excessive system resources in order to leave none available for other users. Obviously, such attacks on business-critical systems can be very costly to organizations.

Some famous examples of attacks that have been targeted at Windows NT machines are:

• **Ping of Death Attack.** Here, the attacker sends a large ICMP packet. When the target machine attempts to reassemble the received packet, it overflows its internal buffers and causes the machine to become unsta-ble.

• **SYN Flood Attack.** The establishment of a TCP/IP connection involves a three-stage handshake, as follows. First, a SYN packet is sent from the client. Second, the server returns a SYN-ACK packet to the client. Fi-nally, the client responds to the SYN-ACK. A SYN Flood attack occurs when the client initiates a huge number of connections but never responds to any of the SYN-ACKs. Consequently, the server's TCP/IP stack runs outs of resources, causing the machine to have undesirable effects.

- **RPC Listener Attack.** Running the Telnet terminal emulator and connecting to TCP/IP port 135 and sending ten various characters causes the CPU utilization to hit 100%. We shall discuss TCP/IP in Chapter 3. Suffice to say here that port 135 is used for a special purpose and the designers never coded defensively the possibility of erroneous characters being received.

- **Teardrop (or Bonk) Attack.** In this attack, the TCP/IP header contains false information about the size of the subsequent information, and this causes the TCP/IP layer to become totally confused, resulting again in unpredictable results (including the blue screen of death).

- **Large URLs Attack.** Here, IIS would crash if it received an HTTP request that contained a URL that was abnormally large (i.e., 8K or more).

Like viruses, denial-of-service attacks can be invoked using a wide range of mechanisms; moreover, it's often difficult to prevent such an attack or to establish who is the instigator. Attacks of this type are evolving, and software vendors are consistently playing catch-up as they build defensive logic into their products to handle each known type of attack.

Attacks like those outlined above are continually being devised and are extremely hard to protect against, except by relying on software vendors to release updates to their products with defensive logic built in that prevents the attack from causing disruption.

Microsoft itself is frequently under attack and is often the first to know when a new type of attack has been contrived. On several occasions, Microsoft developers have had to work hard to release emergency patches. Toward the end of this chapter we give details of the Microsoft Security Advisor Service and the URL where emergency patches are made available. Web site administrators must monitor these facilities to immediately apply any recommendations from Microsoft.

Nonrepudiation

In many situations, it is very important that a message, once sent, cannot be disowned by its sender. Disownership of a message is referred to as repudiation; and **nonrepudiation** is a very important assurance, particularly in many areas of electronic commerce, where the ability to positively identify the source of a message or document means that the sender cannot deny involvement in creating the message.

For example, let us consider the purchase of some Microsoft shares via an online broker. What if the shares drop in price and the purchaser denies having purchased them? The broker needs the ability to prevent the purchaser from falsely claiming never to have sent the transaction. Similarly, consider the more likely event that the shares went up in price. The purchaser needs a cryptographic receipt that confirms that the broker processed the transaction.

Nonrepudiation is tackled with a branch of cryptography that creates digital signatures and digital certificates. We shall introduce these topics in Chapter 5 when we discuss secure communication channels and in Chapter 8 when we demonstrate ASP and client certificates processing. In Chapter 9 we discuss Microsoft Certificate Server and see how to create a secure infrastructure based on this technology.

Risk Management

As a rule, the first and most fundamental task when implementing security is **risk management**.

Risk management is not about taking no risks at all. If that were the case, our machines would be disconnected from the Internet and be set to standalone for good. Instead, as the name suggests, it is all about understanding the risks and controlling them.

Web security is not a matter of being implemented or not. Instead, it is a matter of its application to various degrees that are determined by an analysis of a number of factors, such as the perceived risks, the costs involved, and the ease of use.

Risk management can be considered as three tasks:

- Assessing the risks
- Implementation of a security policy
- Continual analysis of the risks involved

Risk Assessment

Risk assessment involves the process of:

- deciding what we need to protect and whom we are protecting it from
- analyzing the worst possible security breaches and their resultant costs (in both financial and nontangible forms)

Then, taking costs and usability into account, we can choose a security strategy and determine the optimum levels of security that must be applied. If an organization decides that the worst possible scenario is just too bad to contemplate, then it may be necessary to restrict the business functionality of the system or to impose limits so as to remain within an acceptable band where any loss can be absorbed.

Throughout this book we shall highlight the various issues that need to be considered, discuss the various threats that are lurking on the Internet and demonstrate the various tools in our arsenal so that appropriate Web security can be implemented.

Policy Definition

Stemming from the risk assessment is the task to create a clear and concise security **policy document**. The policy document defines the rules and guidelines for successful and secure operation of the system, and should include such issues as:

- Different types of users, and their responsibilities
- What access restrictions are implemented for different parts of the system
- Procedures for handling backups and other maintenance operations
- Testing strategies
- Procedures for handling security violation incidents
- Procedures for handling audit logs
- Password policy
- Procedures for guaranteeing privacy of information
- Rules and procedures to regulate software downloads from the Internet
- How to address breaches in security

Writing a policy document is not a trivial matter, and the list of contents given above is by no means exhaustive! It is important that the document be reviewed and made available to all members of staff.

The policy document is a vital tool in ensuring that potential problems are identified before it is too late and is essential for disseminating accurate information in large organizations or those with a high staff turnover rate. The design of any Web system will often assume that this security policy is being implemented, and any deviation may compromise the security of the system.

Ongoing Risk Assessment

Once the system has been implemented, it's important that the risk management continues to ensure that security mechanisms are kept up to date and use the latest technologies that are available.

To illustrate this, consider the following. The cost of high-performance computers is falling rapidly. This means that potential attackers are gaining access to increasingly powerful equipment, enabling them to attempt to break password and encryption mechanisms by trying every possible input value to the algorithms. Such techniques are called **brute force methods**.

There are always new types of attacks being devised. The solution is to keep up with the latest threats, technologies, and ideas by regularly monitoring security-related newsgroups and Web sites, by exploiting the latest powerful processors, and by using higher levels of encryption.

Perfect Security

Today's business demands force most software vendors to bring their software to market as soon as possible, and this often means that companies make compromises with their testing strategies. Any company that claims its products are unbreakable is suffering from an overdose of marketing hype. Vendors cannot guarantee that their software is bug-free; consequently, it is fair to say that no single security measure can guarantee a 100% secure system.

These days, security holes are frequently detected, highlighted, and discussed on Internet newsgroups, and then vendors quickly release emergency patches.

The brute force attack mentioned above highlights that it's not only bug-ridden software that can be broken through. Weak security mechanisms, while useful, cannot be relied upon in isolation.

It's possible to reduce the risks of being on the Internet by combining multiple security measures. If one security hole is found and breached, then the other measures are in place to protect the system. Obviously, the more security measures that are in place, the greater the reduction of risk of any complete security breach. In practice, when considering the appropriate number of security levels, it's necessary to balance costs (for items like software, hardware, and consultancy) and ease of use against potential risk exposure.

For example, very complex encryption algorithms could be implemented to ensure the privacy of data. However, such algorithms are likely to be very CPU intensive, so their cost must be reconciled with the cost of whatever additional hardware is required.

Furthermore, the application of excessive security can seriously affect a user's productivity. In some cases, a user will be tempted to cut corners, compromising security in the process. Consider, for instance, a password policy that forces a password to include both uppercase and lowercase characters, with at least one number and at least one nonalphanumeric character. A user who finds such a password difficult to remember may be tempted to write it down on paper. Such information is easily disclosed if the paper falls into the wrong hands.

Physical Security

Of course, if we are operating a business-critical system, then we will need to consider the **physical security** of the computer hardware. These considerations may seem obvious, but there are aspects of physical security that we must build into our plan *before* we build our system.

Ideally, our hardware must be located in a dedicated room, designed for delicate computer equipment. We need to consider temperature, humidity, dust extraction, etc. The computer room should have restricted and monitored access limited to the personnel who are needed to administer the system. Food and drink must be banned from the room; if someone spills a cup of coffee into the Web Server, and the staff loses access to data or applications as a result, then it will cost the organization greatly. This may seem an obvious point, but the service department of any large company has tall tales to tell about "liquid contamination"!

We will need to make sure that power switches and reset buttons are positioned so that they can't be activated accidentally. I once leaned on a big red button and immediately killed all of the machines in the machine room! We should consider using an **uninterruptible power supply** (UPS) and perhaps a backup generator, so that the system continues to run in the event of a power failure. Power conditioners should be used to prevent surges that can harm the delicate equipment.

In some circumstances, cabling may have to be passed through insecure areas. In this case it's worth considering fiber optic links as a way of avoiding the various techniques for tapping signals emitted from a twisted pair cable.

High Availability/Fault Tolerance

Highly available systems can be achieved using the latest clustering software, which allows two or more machines to be interconnected and to work as a single unit. In the simplest case, one machine is identified as the primary processing system, and the second acts at a hot standby system that automatically takes over (without user knowledge) if the first system fails. More powerful clustered installations allow multiple machines to cooperate and dynamically load balance the workload over the available resources. If one system fails, the load is rebalanced over the remaining machines.

Fault-tolerant disk systems, called **Redundant Array of Inexpensive Disks** (RAID), can be used to protect data if a single point of failure occurs. A RAID is manufactured by joining several disk units together and spreading the data, with redundancy, over the various units. Distributing the data over multiple disk spindles also increases disk performance, because data can be read from several points simultaneously. Various types of RAID exist, designated from 0 to 5: these types define characteristics that affect cost, performance, data redundancy, and ultimately suitability for a particular task.

Backing Up Your System

In order to protect the system against data corruption due to equipment failures and either accidental or malicious user actions, it's worth making regular backup copies of your data. The backed-up data should be kept offsite, to avoid data loss in the case of a major disaster at your premises (such as a malicious security breach). Of course, since backup files will contain significant company information, they must be safeguarded to ensure that they don't fall into the wrong hands.

Security and the Internet

So far we have introduced a number of key security concepts that are prerequisites for success. By implementing the appropriate security measures, we can defend our systems from both internal and external perils. Now, let us have a closer look at the sorts of threats that can arise from the Internet.

In this section, we will take a high-level view of how security affects Web architectures. We will assume that you already have a reasonable understanding of basic Internet technologies and concepts.

Threats on the Internet

The security needs of Internet-based systems are very different from those of traditional networking. For example, the Internet offers no centralized infrastructure to provide responsibility for network security.

The initial conception and implementation of the Internet was to provide openness and robustness, and to ensure availability of the network for all computers at all times. Even though the Internet was originally a network built for national defense, the security of confidential information was considered secondary because only trusted users had access to the network.

The Internet is on a huge global scale, with connected systems open to a user base of potentially many millions. Only a small minority of Internet users are interested in system security weaknesses (and probably only a small percentage of them have developed the capability to exploit such weaknesses). However, the huge volume of users means that the number of determined, skilled attackers out there is too significant to be ignored.

Talk of any newly found vulnerability travels quickly across the Internet. What may begin as an isolated finding can lead to massive worldwide problems if news of the vulnerability spreads rapidly—and it often does!

External Threats

In order for a business to access the full potential of the Internet and its huge user base, it must open its internal network, and provide a shop window to promote its affairs. Most visitors will be happy simply to look through this window; but there will always be a few Peeping Toms who will attempt to see things never intended for public scrutiny. Worse still, a small number of resourceful people will go one step further, by attempting to break the window, climb through, and (undoubtedly) cause concern and damage.

The bandits of today's superhighway can be classified into three groups:

- **Charlatans:** Those who impersonate an existing person or organization, or take on a false identity. For example, suppose that you're purchasing a book from a Web site, how can you be confident that the vendor is really a legitimate business? Can you be sure that you haven't sent your credit details to some impostor? Alternatively, suppose that you are the book vendor, how can you be confident that you're dealing with a legitimate customer? Impersonators aren't just a financial danger; they may also make harmful statements that damage your reputation.

- **Spies:** Those who access confidential information. For example, consider the transfer of your business plans via electronic mail. How can you be confident that these details are not being intercepted? Could they be passed on to your direct competitors?

- **Vandals:** Those who tamper with data. For example, consider the payment of your electric bill via an Internet home banking service. How can you be confident that your instructions will not be interfered with? Could the payment transaction be illegally redirected to someone else's account?

Of course, some loathsome rogues will be resident in more than one of these three groups. As Internet technology expands, the unscrupulous are able to find new and ingenious mechanisms for their attacks. Unfortunately, the severe damage they can cause is often not discovered until it is too late.

> The recent media hype about network security has referred to such individuals as hackers. This is a misnomer. A *hacker* is someone with expertise in exploiting holes in network security but never performs any malicious actions. A bandit who causes malicious actions is a *cracker*.

If Internet communications are to become a key component in the IT strategy of your organization, then you will need a set of technologies and standards to outmaneuver these bandits. The good news, as we shall see throughout this book, is that the protection mechanisms do exist.

Internal Threats

While the Internet is perceived to be a hostile place with thousands gunning for your system, most organizations believe that the biggest threat is internal. Statistical studies suggest that over 85% of computer crimes are carried out by individuals who are authorized to use the systems involved.

The people to watch inside your organization are:

- **Administrators:** Because responsibility for the system's security stops with the administrator, he is frequently the weakest link in security management. The security technologies that we shall discuss in this book are not easily mastered; they will only work if they have been configured correctly and *all* security holes are filled. If not, there is always one smart person who will find a way to get through.

- **Village Idiots:** Actions that lead to serious damage and severe consequences are not always malicious. For example, deleting a database will have the same impact whether it was deleted accidentally or deliberately. Appropriate security can ensure that inexperienced users do not perform unintentional operations.

- **Traitors:** It is quite possible that the spies and vandals we have already discussed are disgruntled staff members or associated with partner organizations that have been granted privileged access into your systems.

While threats could come from anywhere in the world, be aware that they may be coming from next door!

Web Security Requirements

Building a secure Web architecture needs careful design in a number of different areas, including:

- The Web Server
- The Network
- The User's Desktop
- The Corporate Enterprise System

These components and the interactions between them are illustrated in the diagram below:

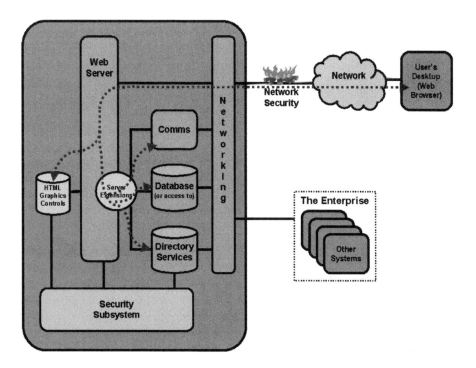

In this section we will discuss the requirements for each of these areas and summarize the topics that will be addressed throughout this book.

The Web Server

Early Web servers were designed purely to publish information, and as we have already suggested, security was often regarded as secondary. Nowadays, Web technology is being used to share sensitive key information and participate in high-value electronic commerce transactions. As a result, it is important to make certain that there are no security holes that can be exploited.

To achieve a secure solution, it is vital that Web applications run on a Web server that is tightly integrated with a secure networking operating system.

The security subsystem that must provide:

- Authentication of each user's identity
- Restrictions on accessing system resources (such as disk files, processes, etc.) to only those users who have permission to perform the action
- Auditing of users' actions
- A rich set of administrative tools

Furthermore, the operating system must be well proven and provide a robust, scaleable, and high-performance foundation.

Only with such an operating subsystem can we have the confidence to build a security subsystem that controls malicious hackers and reckless employees and ensures availability, confidentiality, and integrity.

The Network

The phenomenal growth of Web technologies has led to the general adoption of a family of protocols known as the **Internet Protocol Suite** (or more commonly as **TCP/IP**). All major software and hardware vendors now provide support for TCP/IP, and it has quickly become the *de facto* standard for networking across heterogeneous computing environments.

By putting a machine on a TCP/IP network, you are providing a channel by which other machines can communicate with systems services and resources on your machine. Likewise, your machine can use the same channel to interface with other systems.

Unfortunately, the same channel provides open access to your machine, for both well-founded and malicious uses. Furthermore, the information that passes over the network can easily be tapped, and captured for potentially unscrupulous use.

The wealth of information on the Internet means that giving Internet access to the desktops in your organization provides a great productivity tool. The downside, apart from the waste of working hours by employees surfing for private entertainment, is the danger generated by their bringing executables from unknown resources into your organization, which could include malicious code. We will return to this point in a moment.

The requirements for secure Web networking include:

- Protocol filters to:
  - prevent break-ins to any private areas of the Web system or other machines in the corporate enterprise
  - control internal users accessing the Internet
- Secure point-to-point communication channels ensuring:
  - encrypted data channels
  - message tampering detection
  - client and server authentication

We shall return to discussing TCP/IP networking and the associated security risks later in Chapter 3; we shall also see how to implement the filters that are listed in the above requirements. Then, in Chapter 5, we shall look at secure communication channels that address the remainder of the requirements listed above.

The User's Desktop

The proliferation of software executables that can easily be downloaded from the Web poses huge risks for most Web users. When software is downloaded from unauthorized sources, viruses with malicious code may be introduced, perhaps hidden within standard software, that can cause a wide variety of unwanted effects.

One commonly recited example is that of a Web site that offered free pornographic photographs. As part of the registration process, the user was required to download a special program for viewing the graphic files. Unbeknown to the user, the downloaded program also adjusted the user's dial-up networking properties so that all future calls to the user's ISP instead accessed the Internet via a long-distance premium charge call to Moldova. Such activity was unnoticed by users until their telephone bills arrived, and the caper was very profitable for the porn suppliers before it was tracked down.

In the next chapter we will see another dangerous example of this kind of Trojan. In this example, an administrator invokes a program from an unknown source, activating a hidden piece of logic within the program that e-mails the passwords database to a hacker—and all without the knowledge of the administrator.

Typically, when we purchase software in a shop, we know who published it (the name is on the box) and we can be sure that it has not been tampered with since it left the software publisher (if the box is sealed). While there is no absolute certainty that the software is free from viruses, we generally trust it. The same set of assurances is needed for downloaded software.

The requirements for the protection of a user's desktop are an electronic form of shrink-wrapping that provides, for any downloaded software,

- the name of the software publisher
- assurance that the software has not been tampered with since being published

Only if we fully trust the software publisher should we allow the software to be installed. We shall investigate trust and protecting the desktop in Chapter 6.

Additionally, the desktop can be protected from known viruses by using virus detection software on a proxy server. This is discussed in Chapter 3.

Corporate Enterprise Systems

It is often necessary to integrate a new Web solution with existing corporate systems; examples include mainframes (legacy systems), database servers, e-mail systems, and so on. Doing so enables the Web system to become a powerful customer-facing system for the delivery of existing and future business services. This approach enables the organization to modernize its infrastructure yet protect its typically huge investments in IT systems.

Every organization will have its own unique hodgepodge of different technologies, operating environments, and applications.

Some of the mechanisms that can be used to provide a seamless integration to external systems include:

- using a software framework that facilitates the interoperability of software components; an example is COM (or ActiveX), discussed in Appendix A
- using the Winsock 1.1 API; this provides a high-level, easy-to-use interface for writing applications that require TCP/IP communication; it also supports other protocols
- accessing a remote database directly using an interface like ODBC, OLEDB, or an API provided by a native client database driver
- invoking remote functions directly using DCE Remote Procedure Call (RPC)

- using LDAP protocols to interface with Directory Services, e-mail systems, and X500 compliant datastores
- implementing screen-scraping techniques whereby interface software becomes a virtual user; this involves: navigating the screens, entering data, and parsing the response screens to extract relevant data
- using a message-queuing product for transactions where delivery must be assured but they do not have to complete in real time—an example of this is Microsoft Message Queue Server
- using CICS API to invoke a transaction in IBM's CICS (Transaction Processing) Environment
- using middleware—a software abstraction layer that handles low-level protocol complexities and provides a simple API

Each interface to an external system will bring its own set of security requirements and problems. Different systems will require the application of different levels of security. We shall investigate interfacing ASP to different interfaces throughout Section Two of the book.

Microsoft Internet Security

In this book we shall focus on the comprehensive set of Web technologies from Microsoft that are enabling companies to build secure business applications for deployment over the Internet. Microsoft joined the Internet game relatively late but has rapidly gained momentum. Since 1996 it has released an incredible range of innovative Internet products, all embracing various industry standards. These products provide users with rich and compelling Internet experiences, and organizations with the mechanisms to develop business-critical Internet solutions.

A complete overview of Microsoft and its Internet products and strategies is included in Appendix A. The discussion in the main text is limited to security issues.

We shall see throughout this book that Microsoft's security strategy is based around three key objectives:

- Security must be tightly integrated into operating systems and services
- Security must be comprehensive and contain no holes
- Security must be easy to use and administer

The foundation of Microsoft's Web strategy is its **Windows NT** operating systems and its commercial Web server, **Internet Information Server**

(IIS). At the time of writing, IIS4 is supplied as part of the Windows NT 4.0 Option Pack.

Security was a paramount concern when Microsoft developed its vision of Windows NT for the enterprise, so security features were designed into the bedrock of the operating system. This enables any organization to layer its security options in an appropriate combination specifically suited to combat the perceived risk it faces. We shall discuss Windows NT Security in Chapter 2.

IIS was designed for ease of use, scaleability, portability, security, and extensibility, and is widely acknowledged to be superior to any of the alternatives. IIS version 4.0 is Microsoft's latest standards-based Web application server for Windows NT Server; it provides a powerful environment for the next generation of line-of-business applications. Because IIS and Windows NT are tightly integrated, they share the same security features and administration tools. We shall discuss IIS security in Chapter 4.

The capabilities of IIS are expanded with Microsoft **Site Server,** which is packaged as part of the BackOffice family of products. This provides a comprehensive set of components and management tools that makes it possible to reduce development time and costs when building and deploying secure lines of business Web sites. The membership components of Site Server provide additional user authentication mechanisms, as will be demonstrated in Chapter 14.

The Microsoft **Internet Security Framework** (ISF), a policy statement released at the end of 1996, explained Microsoft's strategy to support a set of security technologies designed for online communications and electronic business. Since this document was released, Microsoft has delivered an extensive public-key security architecture for the Windows platform based on industry standards. It includes certificates services, secure communication channels, payment protocols and cryptographic support. We shall discuss cryptography and digital certificates in Chapter 5, and show how to use them for accountability in Chapter 6. Then, in Chapter 9, we shall see how to use Microsoft Certificate Server to create a security infrastructure based on digital certificates.

Holes in Microsoft Security

Security is continually evolving, and problems with existing software are frequently encountered. Microsoft, like all other major software vendors, is often highlighted in the trade press and Internet newsgroups when security problems with its products are found.

One great site that monitors discoveries of new security flaws in Windows NT and associated products (not necessarily Microsoft's) can be found at

http://www.ntsecurity.net/

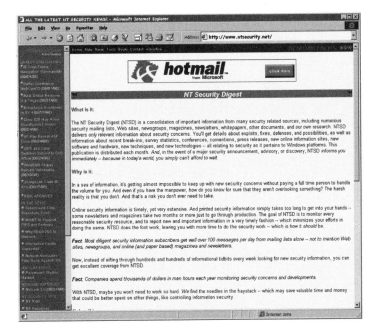

This site provides information that makes it possible to keep up to date on known security holes in Windows NT and provides advice on places to go for current information and updates.

Take a look and see what new discoveries have been posted in the last few days.

This site also provides details for subscribing to their NT Security Digest and NT Security Alert List.

The NT Security Digest consolidates important security information obtained from many related sources.

When the guys at this site learn of a new and important NT security issue, they notify all list members within the hour.

And the service is free!!

Once a security hole has been exposed, an educated administrator can patch it.

Microsoft's Support for Security Issues

Microsoft recognizes the importance of security and wants to ensure that everybody is comfortable using its products in environments where security is paramount. To this end it has implemented an area on its Web site called the **Microsoft Security Advisor**.

SECURITY ADVISOR

The Security Advisor Web site provides a forum for the latest security issues, press releases, and details/advice on any recently discovered security flaws.

The URL of the Security Advisor is:

http://www.microsoft.com/security

E-mail on security matters can be sent to the Security Advisor at

secure@microsoft.com

Service Packs/Hot Fixes

Microsoft maintains a large online database of fixes for its operating systems. These are available either as **service packs** (SP) or as **hot fixes**. Service packs are substantial operating system upgrades which apply numerous bug fixes that have undergone considerable regression testing. Hot fixes are individual bug fixes that are released between service packs; they are often released as emergency bug fixes and thus do not undergo the same stringent testing procedures that a service pack undergoes. Since service packs are cumulative, SP4, for example, will include all the latest fixes, as well as all earlier fixes from SP1, SP2 and SP3.

The latest service pack is always the one to be applied. Hot fixes should be carefully considered and only applied when the shortcoming has a serious impact or poses a major security risk. Service packs and hot fixes are available at

```
ftp://ftp.microsoft.com/
```

■ Summary

In this opening chapter we have discussed the basic concepts of security and have seen what to expect in the remainder of the book. Security is a huge topic and has many facets. Good security is achieved by formulating sound policies, employing appropriate security technologies, consistently monitoring all practices, and in general being aware of trends in the security arena.

The key points learned in this chapter are:

- The security needs of Internet-based systems are very different from traditional networking.
- Security is a huge, wide-reaching topic embracing such concepts as user authentication, access controls, confidentiality of data, and protection against malicious code.
- Security means implementing a system that can be trusted to provide availability, confidentiality, and integrity.
- The amount of technology to be applied to the problem is determined by balancing the business risk against cost and ease of use.
- Always apply the latest service packs and monitor the available hot fixes.
- There are many loathsome bandits lurking on the Internet (or perhaps your Extranet/Intranet) with the capability of exploiting any security weaknesses in your Web systems.

- The site administrator must be fully security-aware and have a full understanding of the security arsenal that is available. Acquiring advanced security tools is a waste of time if they are not properly implemented.
- The physical security of systems must not be ignored.

Finally, we must remember that security is continually evolving.

- New problems with existing software are frequently encountered.
- The bandits are getting smarter.
- Software and hardware technologies are rapidly getting more powerful.

So always keep in mind that:

Security is a journey, not a destination

Security is not something that is turned on and then forgotten. It entails the ongoing task of risk assessment to monitor the continual changes in order to keep one step ahead of the bandits.

We shall now take our next steps by investigating the security aspects of Windows NT.

The Windows NT Security Environment

The starting point for strong Internet security is the operating system that we build our solution on. Fortunately for organizations using Microsoft's commercial Web server, Internet Information Server (IIS), the Windows NT security environment has excellent security features that contrast sharply with the thin and weak security layers that are bolted onto the top of some other operating systems.

It is vital to design security functionality deep into the foundations of an operating system. Trying to add security features to a system is an impractical proposition, and ultimately such features will be susceptible to easy exploitation, as Microsoft found with its 16-bit Windows. Strong levels of security were built into the core of Windows NT in order to meet and exceed certifiable security standards (that is, the C2 security guidelines required by the U.S. Department of Defense's evaluation criteria, which we will discuss later in this chapter).

Windows NT Security encapsulates the processes, algorithms, and techniques to provide a defense against unauthorized access to the system's resources. Many parts of the base Windows NT operating system, plus other Microsoft components, such as BackOffice, and third-party software, can tightly integrate with the security features to provide consistent, flexible levels of protection.

Unfortunately, because one of Windows NT's primary objectives is to make resource sharing simple, a default out-of-the-box Windows NT system delivers a low-key security configuration. If such a machine is to be put into a high-risk Internet/Intranet environment, it must be configured to optimize security, thus minimizing any potential threats.

In this chapter we shall investigate:

- The security features that form the bedrock of Microsoft's Windows NT architecture
- How the Windows NT security model enables use of a granular set of rules for access controls over resources
- What the C2 level security is and how to configure our system to these guidelines
- The pitfalls associated with the use of passwords and a strategy for reducing any exposure to attack

So let us move swiftly on. First we will see how Windows NT provides a secure foundation by preventing uncontrolled access to the system resources.

Protecting the Windows NT System Resources

In most cases, the application of security is transparent to the user. Behind the scenes, however, there is a Windows NT Kernel component called the **Security Reference Monitor** that performs a security check whenever a system resource is accessed. On Windows NT, any access to system resources must go via a Win32 API function call which includes the logic to automatically invoke the built-in access security checks. This contrasts with DOS, 16-bit Windows, and Windows 98/95 (which provides backward compatibility to DOS and 16-bit Windows). These operating systems allow direct access to many system resources, making strong security impossible. While Windows 98/95 supports the Win32 API used by Windows NT, it ignores many of the security-related parameters to these functions.

Under Windows NT, no application program can access the memory space used by the operating system. The processor will provide this protection, and any violation will cause the application to be terminated. Each application runs in its own memory space and cannot access the memory of another application without authorization. These features are vital in making Windows NT a secure and robust operating system.

In order to enforce these strict user access controls, we use the Windows NT Directory Services.

Windows NT Directory Services

Windows NT Directory Services (NTDS) is one of the services provided by Windows NT. It enables a user (or the user context under which a process runs) to be identified, and provides access controls and auditing facilities to the various resources throughout the system and network. In addition, it allows a system administrator to manage the users and the network, from any system on that network.

User Accounts

Every user who has access to a Windows NT system is identified by a **user account.** The user account consists of a user name, a password, and a number of log-on parameters that are applied to that user (for example, the location of a script file that is automatically invoked at log-on). User accounts are stored in a datastore called the **Security Accounts Manager** (SAM), which is a secure part of the Windows Registry.

The management of user accounts is done using the User Manager utility that is usually found by selecting the Start|Programs|Administrative Tools|User Manager menu option, see figure on top of page 28.

The administrator's account is a special Windows NT user account. Initially this account is actually called Administrator, but it really should be renamed: there is no point in giving a potential hacker half the account details for free! We can rename an account using the User|Rename menu option.

A further trick is to create a new user account named Administrator, and give this account zero privilege. Then, any hacker trying to log on as the dummy Administrator would get feedback that Administrator exists, and might then waste time attacking this fruitless account.

[handwritten margin note: rename default Administrator. Create new Administrator with no privileges]

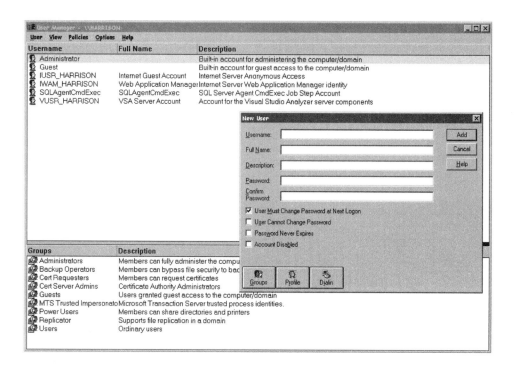

Note that the command **nbtstat—A** *<ipaddress>* will divulge a number of useful items of information to hackers, including the actual name of the Administrator account (and the Administrator does not have to be logged on for this to work!). This command is used to provide information about a protocol called NBT. In Chapter 3, we shall discuss what NBT actually is and see how it can (and must) be disabled when operating over the Internet. Later in this chapter we shall discuss how the password could be obtained using various attack mechanisms.

The "real" administrator has almost complete control over the system, including the ability to create, amend, and delete user accounts. For general activities, administrators should be assigned, and should use, a second account that gives them normal privilege levels; this will reduce the risk of mishaps causing major irreparable damage.

Another special user account created during Windows NT installation is the **guest account**. This account, initially called Guest, is designed for people who require temporary access to the system. For an Internet machine (and arguably for any machine), the guest account should *always* be disabled.

guest account should always be disabled

each user has a unique Security ID that cannot be replicated even if deleted from system.

Ideally, an administrator will assign meaningful names to user accounts. These names are only used externally, however. Internally, Windows NT identifies user account names by using a one-to-one mapping with a unique identifier, called the **Security ID** (SID). Note that *every* new account has its own unique SID. If a user account is deleted, an identical account cannot be recreated, even if we use the same name, password, and log-on parameters, the new account will have a newly generated, unique SID.

A logged-on user can inspect an external representation of their SID by looking at the system registry under the HKEY_USERS key. In the following screenshot, the user's SID is the 36-character string S-1-5-21-928664932-1139805398-1990678075-500.

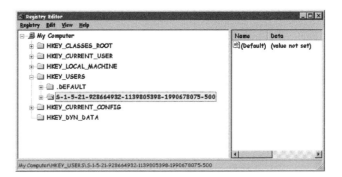

User Groups

A **user group** is a convenient collection of user accounts. It is a powerful mechanism for granting common capabilities to a number of accounts in a single operation.

When administrating systems with large numbers of accounts, or where users are being created and deleted all the time, it's a good idea to set up a number of user groups. New users are simply added to the group, and this avoids the time-consuming task of updating the permissions for each object on your system.

Creating new user groups and adding users to existing groups are integral parts of the job of managing user accounts. This task uses the User Manager utility that we saw a moment ago. Windows NT assigns a unique SID to each user group, in a similar way to its interpretation of user accounts.

There are a number of predefined groups, which include the following:

Group	Description
Administrators	Users having full system control
Users	Users who can perform tasks for which they have been granted rights
Guests	Users requiring temporary access to the system
Server Operators	Users who can manage server resources
Account Operators	Users who can manage user accounts
Backup Operators	Users who can back up and restore files
Print Operators	Users who can manage printers
Authenticated Users	Users who have been validated by the system

We can see the configured user groups in the bottom pane of the User Manager window; as administrator, we can amend the groups by adding and removing individual users.

Furthermore, Windows NT has a few built-in well-known SIDs that do not appear in the list of groups in the User Manager main screen. These include:

Group	Description
Authorized Users	Users who have been identified
Everyone	All users
Interactive	Users who have logged onto the system
Network	Users who are accessing the system remotely
System	The operating system

The members of these groups are set by the system, not the administrator, and that is why they do not appear in the User Manager dialog.

Workgroups and Domains

Windows NT machines can be grouped together in a peer-to-peer model called a **workgroup**, so that any machine in the workgroup can access the resources of another by specifying a user account/password configured on the remote machine. This simple model is useful in small offices, where the resource-sharing requirements are not complex.

When an NT Server is included in the network, a more powerful administrative model is available. The **domain** model is a logical group of computers that share a set of common user accounts and security information, which is stored in the central Directory Services datastore. A version of the User Manager, called the User Manager for Domains, is used to maintain the users and user groups in a domain.

[margin handwritten note: each domain must include at least one NT server as the PDC. A BDC may exist]

> The version of **User Manager** that is available is dependent on which operating system we are using.
>
> If we are using Windows NT Workstation, then we get the **User Manager** utility and can control the users on that machine.
>
> If we are using Windows NT Server, then we get the **User Manager for Domains** utility and can control the users for that machine plus those in a domain.

Each domain includes one Windows NT Server, which is designated as the **Primary Domain Controller** (PDC). The PDC is responsible for storing the master Directory Services datastore. In addition, one or more **Backup Domain Controllers** (BDCs) may exist. Each of these is able to maintain copies of the PDC's Directory Services datastore. The PDC and BDCs are continually involved in a replication process designed to ensure that the various copies of the Directory Services datastore remain synchronized.

A user may log on to a domain, using any connected computer, and is validated by either a PDC or a BDC. The BDCs share the workload in a heavily used network and provide redundancy in case a PDC becomes unavailable. A PDC and BDC can also be an application server; for example, it can also host the Internet Information Server.

[margin handwritten note: Domains can share resources across the network by setting up TRUST RELATIONSHIPS]

In large enterprises, multiple domains may exist to reflect the business or territorial structure of the organization. Resources (e.g., files, printers, etc.) can be shared across domains by setting up **trust relationships**.

Trust relationships can be either one-way or two-way. Consider the following example:

While resources in the YELLOW domain can trust users in the BLUE domain, the opposite is not true, because BLUE does not trust YELLOW. BLUE and RED have a two-way trust relationship, and users in either domain can access resources resident in the other. Note that trust is not transitive; e.g., in the above scenario RED cannot access the resources in YELLOW, and YELLOW must trust RED explicitly if it wants to allow RED to have access.

User Authentication

The typical method for handling user authentication is to get the user to log on to the system by supplying user account details plus a password. Alternative approaches, such as having to present a token (e.g., smart card, digital certificate) or biometrics (e.g., speech recognition, eye retinas), are likely to become more prevalent in the future as they provide stronger levels of authentication. We shall discuss the problems with traditional password mechanisms later in this chapter when we discuss passwords in detail.

One great feature of Windows NT security is its **single log on**. Once a user has logged onto a Windows domain, then their credentials are passed on to any accessed resources within a Microsoft distributed computing environment. The hassle of separate passwords for each networked machine is thankfully avoided.

NTLM

The standard user authentication protocol is called **Windows NT LAN Manager** (NTLM), and it undertakes checking the user's credentials in the Windows NT security database located on the PDC or BDC.

> This authentication mechanism is also called the Windows NT Challenge/Response. We are about to see why.

When a user accesses a service that requires the user to be authenticated, the protocol undertakes the following:

- The client sends the user's name, the computer name, and the domain to the service; the service passes this information on to a domain controller for processing
- The domain controller sends back a unique binary value (**the challenge**) to the service; this is then passed on to the client
- The client generates an encrypted value (**the response**) using its password and the challenge, and sends this to the service; the service passes this information on to a domain controller for authentication

- The domain controller compares the response with the value that it expected (it knows the user's password and challenge sequence and so can apply the same algorithm as the client); if the response value is as expected, the service is notified that the authentication was successful; if the response value does not match, then the user must be using a password different from the one known by the domain controller and so the service is notified that the authentication failed.

Note that throughout the authentication process, the user's password is never transmitted over the network.

The challenge/response processing is clarified by the following diagram:

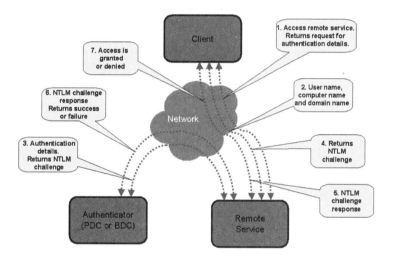

Delegation

One problem with NTLM authentication is that it does not allow your credentials to be **delegated** to a remote service and used in proxy, that is, when you access a network service that in turn requires access to other network service.

Consider the following example:

Here, the client accesses network service A. The Challenge/Response processing that we have discussed is undertaken, and the user at client A is authenticated. Network service A will run under the security context of this user.

Let us now suppose that network service A attempts to access network service B. B needs to authenticate A, so it will send the Challenge. But because A is running under the security context of the client, there is a problem. Remember that passwords are never sent over the network. Because A does not know the user's password, it cannot generate a suitable Response for the Challenge. Thus the authentication process breaks down.

Since Web servers are frequently required to access resources on other systems, we encounter this problem again in Chapter 4 when we discuss IIS Security and delegation.

For a complete solution to this problem, it is necessary to wait for a new authentication mechanism called **Kerberos** that will be delivered as part of Windows 2000 (NT 5.0).

Let us take a brief look into the future and see how Kerberos works and solves this problem.

Kerberos

Windows 2000 is designed to offer high levels of interoperability and so support multiple authentication mechanisms and security protocols. By means of the **Security Support Provider Interface** (SSPI), it is easy to plug additional authentication mechanisms into the Windows NT security infrastructure.

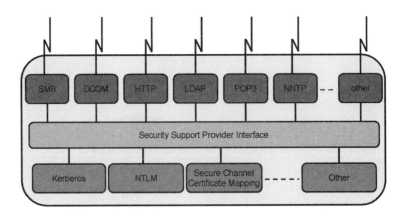

Microsoft has adopted Kerberos as the primary authentication system for Windows 2000, but the traditional NTLM mechanism will still be available for compatibility reasons. The above diagram also shows an authentication mechanism called **Secure Channel Certificate Mapping**; we shall discuss this in Chapter 5 when we discuss Secure Channels.

Kerberos is a shared-secret authentication protocol. In other words, both the user and the authenticating system can determine an encrypted hash version of the user's password. The protocol defines a series of messages that occur between the clients (to be authenticated), the service (doing the authentication), and the Kerberos central system (called a **Key Distributor Center** [KDC]).

The KDC is responsible for providing:

- Kerberos **tickets** which are used by an entity to identify itself to another entity
- Secret cryptographic keys for the secure transfer of information between entities

When a user logs on the Windows network, the Microsoft Kerberos security-support provider (shown in the above diagram) obtains a session ticket based on an encrypted hash of the user's password. This ticket is then stored in a ticket cache that is associated with the user on the client machine.

When the client accesses a network service, the ticket cache is checked for a bona fide session ticket that allows access to the service. If such a session ticket is not available, a request is made to the KDC for a suitable ticket. A returned session ticket will be added to the ticket cache and used for subsequent connections to the same server. A session ticket will have an expiration period that is configured as part of the local security policy.

When the client connects to the remote network service, the session ticket is sent as part of the protocol handshake. Parts of the session ticket are encrypted using a secret key shared between the service and the KDC (encryption with secret keys will be discussed in detail in Chapter 5 when we address Secure Channels). The network service can quickly authenticate the request since it will have a copy of the secret key in its own cache.

The following diagram clarifies this:

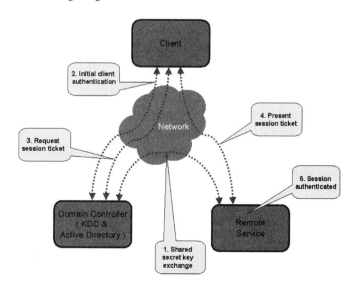

Session establishment with Kerberos is much faster than NTLM. With NTLM the service has to pass the user's credentials on to the domain controller for an additional authentication operation to occur.

Kerberos overcomes the NTLM problem with delegation. Kerberos delegation allows a service to impersonate a client, obtain a session ticket, and connect to another service on behalf of the client.

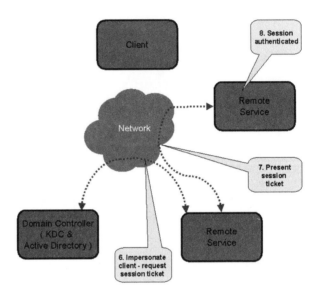

Object Security

The job of a Windows NT system involves access to many kinds of **Windows NT objects**: files, processes, threads, timers, devices, printers, registry keys, events, ports, application-specific private objects, and numerous types of resources. Each Windows NT object has its very own **Security Descriptor**, which contains the security information for that object.

The Security Descriptor

The Security Descriptor contains information defining the permissions, auditing and ownership of the object. Let us investigate each in turn:

PERMISSIONS

One of the basic principles of security involves authenticating the user and restricting access to system resources based on a **permissions** policy defined for that user. Typically, different levels of security are granted for different users.

The types of permissions that can be set for Windows NT objects are different for each object type. For example, for a file object we can specify which users can execute the file. But such a permission type would be inappropriate for, say, a printer object—we cannot execute a printer!

When a user attempts to access a Windows NT object, the security process checks whether the user has been granted or denied access to the resource. If there is no explicit grant or denial of access, the user is denied access.

AUDITING

By **auditing** users' access to systems resources, an administrator can track the activity of specific users. This provides an audit trail that is particularly useful for analyzing detected security breaches. Since security attacks cannot be prevented by auditing alone, it is necessary to employ additional, more defensive security techniques. However, if your system is being attacked, and the attacker discovers that he's being watched, he may be scared off.

Auditing can also track other problems, including hardware malfunctions and software errors/warnings. Furthermore, it can be useful in detecting actions that are not necessarily malicious but could cause serious damage.

Auditing, like access control, relies on the implementation of strong levels of authentication. If the audit trail says that a user performed a particular action, we need to be confident that it really *was* the person identified in the trail.

While auditing provides comprehensive and useful facilities, it does unfortunately consume both CPU and disk space, and so it must only be configured to appropriate levels.

OWNERSHIP

An object owner can control the level of access that every other user/user group may have to the object. If an object owner gives another user full control over an object, that user then has the right to alter the access permissions of the object.

Configuring the Security Descriptor

The mechanisms used to apply security to a Windows NT object are dependent on the object type. This is shown in the table below that details the common object types:

Object Type	Mechanism used to configure security
Directories and files	Windows Explorer
Registry keys	Registry Editor (`regedt32.exe`)
Printers	The security tab of the printer's property sheet. The list of printers can be accessed a number of ways including the Start|Settings|Printers menu option.

We shall demonstrate applying security with the Windows Explorer and the Registry Editor later in this chapter, but there is a bit more groundwork to do first.

Access Control Lists

The security descriptor contains two items of information, each called an **Access Control List** (ACL). The ACL is a list of name-permission pairs in which each name is the name of a user account or group, and the permission describes the kind of access permitted to that user or group. Each name-permission pair in the ACL is called an **Access Control Entry** (ACE).

The differences between the ACL and ACE are clarified by this screenshot of the dialog that is used to set the permissions on the file.

This dialog is taken from the File Permissions configuration dialog accessed through Windows Explorer. We shall investigate this facility later in the chapter.

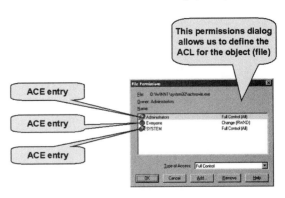

As was mentioned above, the security descriptor contains two types of ACLs:

- The discretionary ACL (DACL) regulates who can access the object
- The system ACL (SACL) regulates who can audit the object

We shall now investigate how the Windows NT security subsystem utilizes the ACLs to perform its checks when a user accesses an object.

ACL Processing

The Windows NT security subsystem dictates the security policies that are applied to each user on the domain. This control is undertaken by a part of the Windows NT Kernel called the **Local Security Authority** (LSA).

When the user's log on has been validated, the LSA produces a **Security Access Token** (SAT) that identifies the user's credentials. The SAT is attached to any process invoked by the user. Then, when the user's process tries to interact with an object, the SAT is checked against each ACE in the object's DACL. Access to the object is only permitted when an ACE for the user is located and has the appropriate permissions granted for the required action.

If object auditing has been enabled at the system level, the SAT is also checked against each ACE in the object's SACL. A log message will be generated if an ACE for the user is located and the ACE specifies that the type of action invoked by the user's process is one that is to be audited. We shall see later in this chapter how to enable auditing at both the system level and on a specific object.

With all of these TLAs (three-letter acronyms!) floating around, this becomes extremely hard for most readers to absorb first time. Hopefully, the following diagram will clarify a few things:

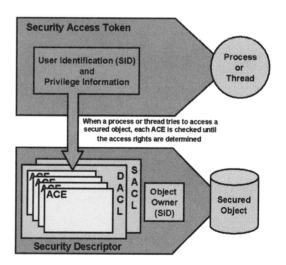

Auditing the System

By default, most auditing facilities are disabled when Windows NT is first installed.

To enable auditing, perform the following:

- Log-on as an administrator and invoke the User Manager
- Select the Policies|Audit menu option
- On the Audit Policy dialog, select the Audit These Events checkbox
- Select the audit options required by checking the Successful and/or Failure checkbox. The options available are:
  - Log on and Log off—audit when a user is logged on/off or a network connection is made
  - File and Object Access—audit when an object is accessed if that object has been enabled for auditing (we shall see how this is done later in this chapter)
  - Use of User Rights—audit when a user exercises a user right (we shall investigate what the user rights policy is shortly)
  - User and Group Management—audit when a user account/group account is created, amended, or deleted; or when a user account is disabled, enabled, or renamed; or when a password is amended or set

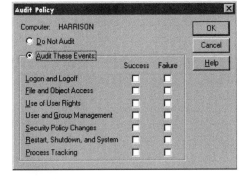

  - Security Policy Changes—audit when a change is made to user rights policy, audit policy, or trust relationship policy
  - Restart, Shutdown, and System—audit when the system is restarted or shut down; or when a system event occurs
  - Process Tracking—audit detailed process tracking information.

Let us now see how to retrieve the information that we are recording

Windows NT Event Viewer

The primary mechanism for reading the audit trail is the **Windows NT Event Viewer**. This is invoked from the Start|Programs|Administrative Tools|Event Viewer menu option.

Once this has been instantiated, the viewer shows one line per event message recorded. The log is actually partitioned into the following groups:

- System events logged by the Windows NT System components
- Security events logged by the security system; these can only be viewed by an administrator
- Application events logged by an application.

We can switch between the groups by means of options available from the Log menu.

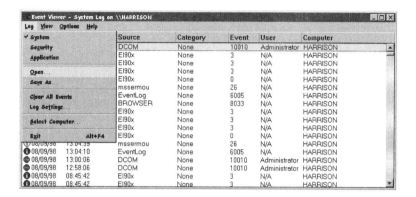

The information displayed in the event log is:

- Source—the software that generated the event
- User—the user associated with the process that generated the event
- Category—classification of the event; the categories are defined by the software that generated the event
- Computer—the name of the computer from which the event was generated
- Event Id—number to identify the event
- Type—icon that indicates Information, Warning, Error, Success Audit, or Failure Audit
- Date/Time—timestamp for when the event was generated

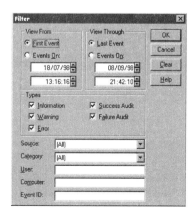

Events are typically ordered with the most recent at the top of the window, but this can be toggled by means of the View|Oldest First (Newest First) menu option.

We can also restrict the amount of information displayed by applying a Filter. These can be set by dialog obtained from the View|Filter menu option.

By clicking on an entry in the event log, we can get the details of the event, in particular:

- Description—a text description of the event
- Data—optional additional information; often contains low-level debug-type information that is used by developers/technicians to diagnose problems

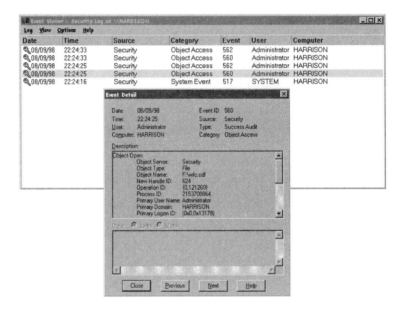

In the Event Viewer, select Log|Log Settings. The Event Log Settings dialog allows you to specify what to do if the log files get full. If auditing is considered vital, then you should enable the Do Not Overwrite Events so that the log file has to be manually cleared down, but make sure you set the log files big enough!

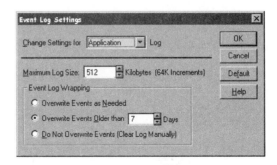

Privileges/User Rights

As was explained earlier, restrictions can be placed on users accessing individual Windows NT objects (such as a file or printer) by applying permissions.

Similarly, we can place restrictions on what system functions (or **privileges**) a particular user can undertake. Such controls are called **user rights**.

Many different privileges can be set; examples include:

- Access this computer from network
- Back up files and directories
- Change the system time
- Debug applications
- Log on locally
- Manage auditing and security log
- Shut down the system

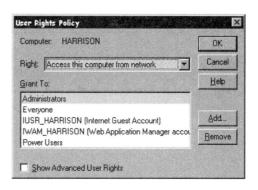

The User Rights Policy dialog is accessed from within the User Manager, using the Policies|User Rights menu option. It is used to assign the privileges granted to groups and user accounts. The security system will block any action by a user that does not have the appropriate user rights.

From the earlier diagram showing object security, it can be seen that the information about privileges is encoded into the Security Access Token assigned at log on. The Windows NT security environment checks that the user can perform specific actions by examining this token.

C2 Evaluation

In the introduction to this chapter, it was mentioned that the security in Windows NT meets the C2 security guidelines required by the U.S. Department of Defense. Now is the time to see what this really means.

Compliance with the C2 security standard was originally only required of governmental organizations. However, many commercial organizations demand the same level of security and recognize the value that such standards offer. The main requirements for C2 compliance are:

- **User identification and authentication.** Before gaining access to the system, users must prove their identity. This is typically done by providing a user name/password combination (e.g., by entering the details via a keyboard or by presenting a device such as a smart card which stores such information).

- **Discretionary access control.** Each object within the system (e.g., files, printers, and processes) must have an owner who can grant or restrict access to the resources at various degrees of granularity.

- **Auditing capabilities.** The system must provide the ability to log all user actions and object access, and include enough information to identify the user who performed any operation. Such information must only be accessible by system administrators.

- **Safe-object reuse.** The system must guarantee that any discarded or deleted object cannot be accessed, either accidentally or deliberately, by other entities.

- **System integrity.** The system must protect resources belonging to one entity from being interfered with by another entity.

The C2 guidelines are applicable to standalone systems and are specified in the **Trusted Computer System Evaluation Criteria** (TCSEC). To make life simpler, this document is often referred to as the **Orange Book**, thanks to the color of its cover.

One of the requirements of the Orange Book is that networking is disabled, and this is obviously not very practical for client/server and Internet systems in the real world. Various specifications expand on the Orange Book. These include the Red Book, which is an interpretation of the Orange Book for application to the networking components of a secure system.

Obtaining C2 certification is a long and complex task, and Microsoft is pushing hard for complete certification. Windows NT has passed the Orange Book certification process and is on the DOD's official list of evaluated products. At the time of writing, the Windows NT 4.0 evaluation was entering a further phase to address the Red Book guidelines.

There is a program on the Windows NT Resource Kit called C2Config.exe that identifies tasks that need to be applied to make a configuration conform to C2 guidelines. The C2 Configuration checklist is shown in the following screenshot.

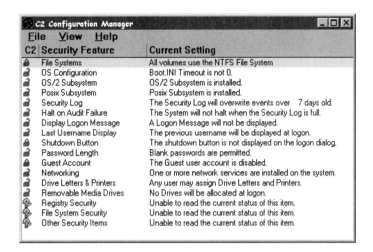

Protecting the File System

Now that we understand the concepts of Windows NT Directory Services, we shall proceed to investigate how this security is applied to the file system.

NTFS vs FAT

From version 4.0 of Windows NT, hard disks are formatted as either:

- **NTFS (NT File System)**
- **FAT (File Allocation Table)**

FAT is the simpler of the two formats and has been around since the early days of DOS. Information stored on FAT disks cannot provide access controls using standard security features (although network shares to these disks can have permissions configured).

FAT has now been superseded by NTFS because it offers far superior levels of performance, reliability, and security. With NTFS, files and directories can be treated as individual objects, and this allows their own specific permissions to be assigned.

Since NTFS offers many advantages, there are few reasons to use it; two exceptions are:

- For RISC-based computers; the hardware specification requires drive C to be a FAT-formatted drive and have at least 2Mb of disk space free. Of course in such a configuration, there is no reason why a second partition couldn't be formatted as NTFS and used to locate confidential and business-critical files

- For floppy disks; FAT uses very little overhead for file management and so is recommended as a better choice for partitions under 200Mb

FAT partitions can be converted to NTFS using the convert.exe utility from the command prompt.

A problem with both NTFS and FAT is that the files stored are not protected at the physical level; that is, the bits on the disk sectors could potentially be read directly, enabling any files to be restored. Someone who steals your computer disk drives could easily get access to any sensitive information by using various utilities for other operating systems that would read the disks (ignoring any of the usual NT Security checks).

A solution to this will be **EFS (Encrypted File System)**, which is targeted for release in Windows 2000. EFS will operate in a similar fashion to NTFS, but the files will be encrypted on the disk; this will happen transparently to the user.

File and Directory Permissions

Earlier in this chapter we briefly mentioned that the Windows Explorer is used to apply or change the permissions of NTFS directories and files for individual users and groups. We are now in a position to consider this further.

Permissions are set from the Windows Explorer by right-clicking on the file or directory and selecting the Properties menu option. Then, from the property sheet, select the Security tab, followed by the Permissions button.

This displays the Permissions dialog allowing the required security settings to be applied.

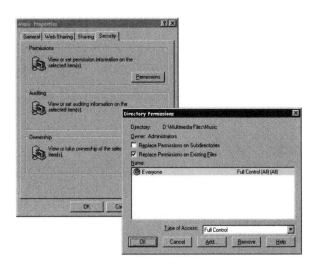

The following permissions can be specified for the object:

Permission	Functionality allowed
Read (R)	Allows viewing the names of files and subdirectories/file data
Write (W)	Allows adding files and subdirectories/changing the file data
Execute (X)	Allows running the file if it is a program file
Delete (D)	Allows the deleting of a directory/file
Change Permissions (P)	Allows changing the directory/file permissions
Take Ownership (O)	Allows taking ownership of the directory/file

When setting permissions on a directory, we must enable the Replace Permissions on Subdirectories checkbox if we want the settings to be applied to subdirectories and their files.

When files and subdirectories are created, they take on by default the permissions that are applied to their parent directory.

Standard combinations of these permissions can be selected using the Type of Access drop-down menu.

Directory Permissions

For directories, the following Type of Access are available:

	Permissions on directory	Permissions on files in directory
Full Control	All	All
Change	RWXD	RWXD
Add & Read	RWX	RX
Add	WX	Not Specified
Read	RX	RX
List	RX	Not Specified
No Access	None	None
Special Directory Access	See below	
Special File Access	See below	

Most users only deal with the standard options, but a customized configuration can be defined by selecting Special Directory Access or Special File Access. This displays a dialog allowing us to select any of the permissions.

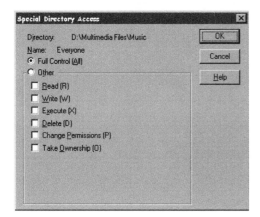
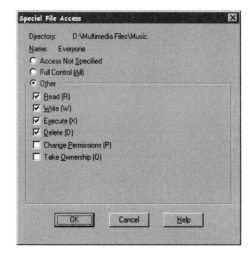

File Permissions

For files, the following types of access are available:

	Permissions on file
Full Control	All
Change	RWXD
Read	RX
No Access	None
Special Access	See below

In a manner similar to what was described for directories, by selecting Special Access we can specify a nonstandard combination of permissions.

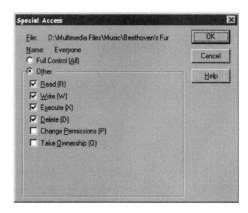

File and Directory Auditing

We shall now discuss how to enable an audit trail for users accessing our files and directories.

As was explained earlier in the chapter, the default installation of Windows NT disables security-event logging. Before the access of files and directories can be audited, the administrator must enable File and Object auditing using the User Manager. How this is done was shown in our earlier discussions.

Once it is done, file and directory auditing can be enabled on an individual basis.

Auditing is enabled from the Windows Explorer by right-clicking on the file or directory and selecting the Properties menu option. Then, from the property sheet, select the Security tab, followed by the Auditing button.

This displays the Auditing dialog, allowing the required security settings to be applied.

From this dialog we can enable events that succeed or fail that we wish to be included in the audit trail.

We can then use the Windows NT Event Viewer utility to view the generated audit logs to look for any abnormal activity and detect any security breaches.

File and Directory Ownership

There is one more button on the Security tab of the file/directories property sheet that we have not yet investigated; it is used to view or take ownership of the item. Recapping from earlier, the owner of a file or directory controls the level of access to it that others may have. The owner may elect to give other users Full Control permission, in which case these users may also control the access rights.

To take ownership of a file or directory, one of the following conditions must be in place:

• We are a member of the Administrators group
• The owner of the object has granted us the Take Ownership (O) permission

To take ownership, from the property sheet, select the Security tab, followed by the Ownership button.

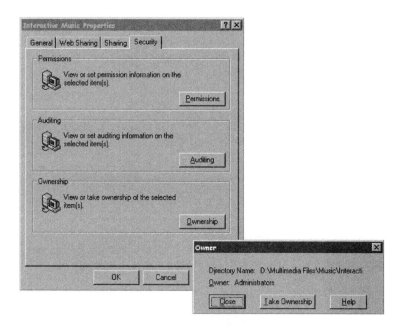

That completes our examination of applying Windows NT security to the file system. Next on our agenda is how to apply the same security controls to another crucial datastore, the Windows Registry.

Protecting the Windows Registry

The **Windows Registry** is a large repository, organized into a hierarchical structure, containing information about the current user and the machine's hardware and software configuration, including the SAM database and other security information. All software information that used to be resident in .INI files is now located in the Registry. The information can be inspected and amended using the Registry Editor (regedt32.exe).

> Extreme care must be taken when editing the Registry because it is very easy to set invalid values, corrupt the configuration, and make the system inoperative; no warnings are given! You are strongly advised to back up your Registry file before editing it.

As an example to illustrate how important it is to protect the Windows Registry, consider the following commonly attempted attack:

- First, access to an unsecured network share is obtained; we shall see in Chapter 3, when we discuss networking security, how such security holes are frequently left open.
- A Trojan executable is planted on the share that (a) changes the administrator's password to a value known by the attacker and (b) invokes Notepad or some similar program
- The Registry is amended so that the association between .TXT files is the planted Trojan.
- The next time the administrator clicks on a .TXT file, the Trojan will be activated and the password will be amended to the attacker's known value, without the administrator knowing.

The hacker then has a password providing great power to snoop or cause mayhem.

To protect the Registry, ACLs are applied to all Registry items (called **Keys**) in a similar fashion to NTFS files. The access permissions, auditing policies, and ownership for each item in the Registry can be set using the Security menu option in the Registry Editor.

Registry Permissions

Permissions are set from the Registry Editor by right-clicking on the Key and selecting the Security|Permissions menu option.

This displays the Registry Key Permissions dialog allowing the required security settings to be applied.

The permissions dialog looks similar to one we saw when working with NTFS files, but the permissions that can be set are different; namely:

Permission	Functionality allowed
Query Value	Allows key value to be read
Set Value	Allows key value to be set
Create Subkey	Allows new key to be created
Enumerate Subkeys	Allows all keys to be identified
Notify	Allows receipt of audit notifications
Create Link	Allows symbolic links to be created
Delete	Allows keys to be deleted
Write DAC	Allows permissions to be changed
Write Owner	Allows take ownership
Read Control	Allows security information to be read.

The standard combinations of permissions that can be selected using the Type of Access drop-down menu are as follows:

	Permissions on file
Full Control	All
Read	Read Control
Special Access	See below

By selecting Special Access we can specify a nonstandard combination of permissions.

Because of the nature of the Registry, it is a prime target for hackers. The default installation of Windows NT allows the user group Everyone access to most of the Registry using the remote access feature of the Registry Editor—and by definition, Everyone includes *any* remote user.

The screenshot shows the default permissions given to Everyone, and we see that the Set Value permission is granted, enabling a potential attacker to create havoc!

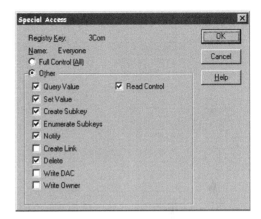

The Windows NT security system restricts network access to the Registry to specific users. These users are configured by granting Full Control access to the following Registry key:

**HKEY_LOCAL_MACHINE\System\CurrentControlSet\Control\
SecurePipeServers\winreg**

The danger here is that if this key is hacked (perhaps by a Trojan), the Registry and thus the whole system becomes insecure.

Registry Auditing

Auditing of a Registry key is enabled from within the Registry Editor by right-clicking on the Key and selecting the Security|Audit menu option.

This displays the Registry Key Auditing dialog allowing the required security settings to be applied.

From this dialog we can enable events that succeed or fail that we wish to be included in the audit trail.

If we wish to enable auditing on the SAM database,

we have a small problem, since the SAM and SECURITY items are secured and therefore do not allow access to the keys below. One small trick is to invoke the Registry Editor to run under the context of the user **system** by using the Windows NT Scheduler as follows:

At a command prompt, enter the following:

at <time> /interactive "regedt32.exe"

where **<time>** is set to the current time plus one minute (this assumes that the scheduler service is running as LocalSystem). The Registry Editor will soon appear, but this time the SAM and SECURITY items are no longer grayed out and can be explored—but take care not to corrupt anything! Auditing can now be enabled on the SAM database.

To audit the complete SAM database, select the SAM key and the Security|Auditing menu option. To select the entire set of keys, check the Audit Permissions on Existing Subkeys checkbox.

Registry Ownership

The final security option for the Registry is to take ownership of a key.

This is done from within the Registry Editor by right-clicking on the Key and selecting the Security|Owner menu option.

This displays the Owner dialog allowing the action to be invoked.

System Key

The System Key (provided from Windows NT Service Pack 3 release) is a mechanism for providing strong encryption on the SAM database to provide additional levels of protection. It will also protect copies of the SAM database that could be found on a backup tape and a repair disk. We shall see shortly how important this is.

The syskey.exe executable is used to apply the encryption and initialize/amend the master key. There are three options for managing this key:

- Use a system-generated key and hide it on the system using an obfuscation function. This method allows unattended system restart.
- Use a system-generated key and store it on a floppy disk. The floppy disk must be inserted when requested during a system reboot; future versions are expected to store the keys on more secure devices, such as smart cards.
- Use a system key derived from a password chosen by the administrator. The password must be entered when requested during a system reboot; the system key is not stored anywhere, this mechanism allows an administrator to use the same key on several machines.

> If your system is configured for auto-restart on a system crash (blue screen), then only the first option will be suitable. And if you forget your password or lose the floppy disk, your system will be unable to start!

Passwords

Standard Windows NT Security relies on users identifying themselves by specifying their account name and a password. We discussed earlier how, after a successful log on, Windows NT security assigns an SAT to all processes that are executed under the user's context, and how this is used to validate and audit access to the system resources.

One of the first targets of a hacker is to steal passwords in order to gain full access to a system.

Let us now see what tools we have to defend our systems and the security holes that hackers can exploit to get hold of users' passwords.

Account Policies

Policies for handling accounts and passwords can be selected using the Policies|Account menu option in the User Manager.

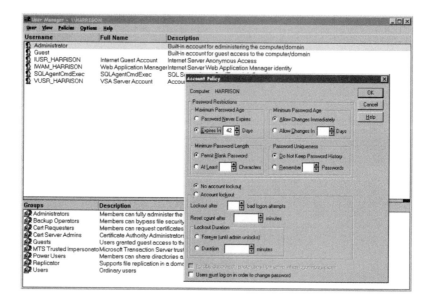

The password options are:

- **Maximum Password Age.** This forces users to change their passwords regularly; it is possible to override this by specifying that the password never expires for a particular account.

- **Minimum Password Age.** This prevents a user, when forced to change its password, from changing to a new password and then immediately reverting back to its favored password.

- **Minimum Password Length.** This prevents users from using blank passwords (length equal to zero). Longer passwords are harder to crack, since it is necessary to use a brute force attack where every potential value is tried.

- **Password Uniqueness.** This prevents users from cycling through a small list of favored passwords.

It is also possible for the system to lock out accounts when there are a number of failed log-on attempts during a short period of time. This can severely disrupt anyone trying to break into the system. Obviously, you should cater for the situation when a user miskeys his password. Remember from earlier that it is possible to configure the auditing policies to enable log-on failures to be tracked, so that an administrator can monitor any attempts at misuse.

Suggested values are shown in the previous screenshot.

Users with accounts in a Windows domain can be restricted to only having access during certain hours of the day. This is set using the Log-on Hours dialog box accessed via the Users properties.

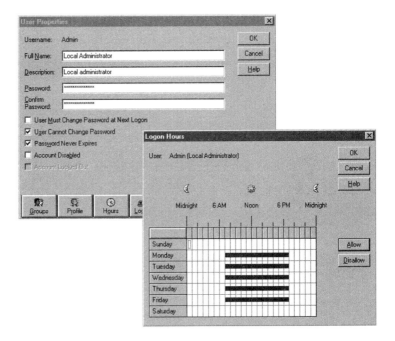

The security policy for an organization should ensure that only valid users have accounts in the system. Procedures should be in place to immediately disable and ultimately delete the user's account of a person who leaves a company.

Password Cracking

Of late there has been much media coverage about security flaws in the way Windows NT handles passwords. This has been generated by several tools designed to detect user accounts and passwords. Such password-cracking programs rely on the following password mechanism used by Windows NT:

Windows NT Domain Controllers do not actually store user passwords. Instead they store a value that is mathematically calculated using the password as an input to the algorithm. Such values are stored in the SAM database located in the Registry.

The calculated value is called a **cryptographic hash** and has the following properties:

- It is impossible to calculate the original value from the hash value
- It is unlikely that any other original value would evaluate to the same hash value

When a user logs on to the system, it is the hash value that is sent over the network to the Domain Controller. This compares the received hash value to its known hash value and determines whether the user has entered a valid password.

A **password cracker** operates by working through a large number of potential passwords, applying the cryptographic hash algorithm (which is a well-documented function) and comparing the result with a captured password's hash value. When a match is found, the password has been found. With today's processors working at blistering speeds, password crackers can try a huge number of passwords in a short time and quickly deliver a result.

L0phtCrack

An example of a password cracker is L0phtCrack 2.0, available from http://www.l0pht.com/

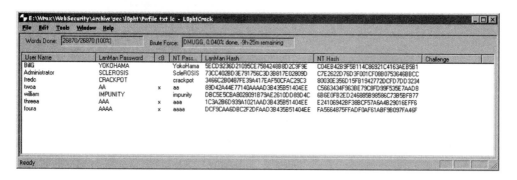

L0phtCrack uses two methods to crack a password. First it performs a **dictionary attack** in which it attempts to find a match by using the words that are in a dictionary file. For each word the hash algorithm is applied and then matched with the captured password's hash value. This method is very fast and can check through a large dictionary in a matter of minutes. The L0phtCrack download comes with an English dictionary containing over 26,000 words. Much larger dictionaries containing words from many languages, plus commonly used terms, such as names, abbreviations, football teams, etc., are generally available for download off the Web.

If L0phtCrack fails to find the password using a dictionary lookup, it moves into brute force mode. This involves trying every possible permutation of a series of characters. The larger the character set, the longer the process takes. Using the latest Pentium processors, and restricting the characters from A to Z, it is estimated that the process will take up to 24 hours. Including digits and punctuation will further increase this and could take a matter of days.

Obtaining Password Hashes

L0phtCrack suggests/provides three methods to obtain password hashes. The first two methods will not work if the Syskey functionality that we met earlier has been used to encrypt the SAM files, but there are many crackers currently trying to break the algorithms used.

The three methods suggested are:

- L0phtCrack provides a menu option to load the SAM information from a remote Registry (if the user has permissions)
- L0phtCrack provides a menu option to import the SAM information which can be retrieved from
  - the \winnt\system32\config directory; this is normally locked but can be accessed by booting the machine with a DOS floppy disk
  - the \winnt\system32\repair directory; the file is called sam._ and must be uncompressed using **expand sam._ sam**
  - Emergency Repair Disk; as above, this must be uncompressed.
  - backup tape
- L0phtCrack provides another mechanism that overcomes Syskey being installed or the user not having permissions/access to the SAM information. The solution is **network sniffing**. Provided that you are resident on the same network segment as the user, you can run a L0pht utility to tap the network and capture the user's account and password as they log on. Running the utility for several hours can capture many user passwords.

The first two mechanisms highlight how important it is to have correct permissions applied to the Registry, have NBT disabled (as discussed in

Chapter 3), have the correct ACLs applied to the mentioned \winnt directories, and to physically protect any backups/Emergency Repair Disks. However, even this will not deter a cunning hacker. Consider the following:

Another utility that can walk through a SAM database and obtain a list of user accounts and password hash values is pwdump.exe, available at

ftp://samba.anu.edu.au/pub/samba/pwdump/pwdump.exe

The generated list can be cracked using L0phtCrack. A hacker could easily incorporate pwdump into a program, so that, when someone with administrative privileges innocently executes the Trojan, the password information is gathered and perhaps e-mailed or left in a public location. Such a program could easily be delivered to the unsuspecting administrator via a Web page. All so simple! This highlights a simple rule:

> **Administrators must never invoke software from an untrusted source**

To help protect our systems we must implement passwords that cannot be found by dictionary attacks and are complex enough to make brute force attacks too time-consuming. Such passwords are called **strong passwords**.

Strong Passwords

Tools like L0phtCrack are ideal for administrators to use in order to monitor the passwords of their users and ensure that they are not easily cracked.

Password strength can be enforced using a password filter that was introduced by Microsoft in Windows NT Service Pack 2. Whenever a user changes his password, the filter ensures that:

- It is least six characters long
- It does not contain the user's name or part of the name
- It contains characters from at least three of the following groups:
  - English upper-case characters (i.e., A to Z)
  - English lower-case characters (a to z)
  - Digits 0 to 9
  - Nonalphanumeric (e.g., ,.<>;:'%)

To enable the password filter, the following Registry setting must be made on the PDC and BDCs: add passfilt.dll to the list of items in the following key:

**HKEY_LOCAL_MACHINE\System\CurrentControlSet\Control\LSA\
Notification Packages**

One-time Passwords

A password mechanism that is very popular in organizations using systems with high-value financial transactions is **one-time passwords**.

This involves using an electronic device that generates a new password at very brief intervals (e.g., every 60 seconds). Such devices are made to be small and convenient, often supplied to resemble a credit card or as a key ring fob.

When the system prompts a user for his password, he must first give the device a PIN value. If the PIN is accepted, the device will display the password to be used. The user then has a limited time to provide the password to the system.

The authentication system uses a clock synchronized with the clock on the device; this means that it knows what password to expect for any moment in time.

This system provides higher levels of authentication than the standard password mechanism because:

- The user must possess a physical item to gain access to the system
- If anyone intercepts the password used (perhaps by looking over the user's shoulder or by network sniffing), the password is useless within a very short time

There are several suppliers of such technology; one example is Security Dynamics Technologies, Inc.

Secure Dynamics

The solution from Secure Dynamics involves three separate items:

- The electronic device; this is called a **SecurID token**
- The authentication process; This is called **ACE/Server**
- The client interface; This is called **ACE/Agent**

The following diagram shows where these components are placed in a Microsoft Web environment.

When the user navigates to a Web page that requires authentication, the ACE/Agent will intercept the request and display a Web page requesting the user's password. Providing that the password is entered correctly and within the time limit, the ACE/Agent will redirect the user to the Web page that was originally requested. We shall discuss how to protect Web pages and enforce authentication when we discuss IIS security in Chapter 4.

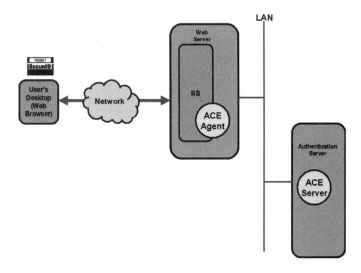

IIS is supplied from Microsoft with the ACE/Agent software.
Look for the installation file **aceclcab.exe**. It should be located in the **%SystemRoot%\system32** directory.

For more information about obtaining SecurID tokens, visit the Security Dynamics Web site at:

http://www.securid.com

■ Summary

In this chapter we have seen that Windows NT is designed with security in mind and contains numerous security-related features. It allows security to be applied in various combinations and layers to provide a flexible solution to address the different security requirements that organizations demand.

While Windows NT offers advanced security technology, it is vital that administrators be fully security-aware and understand the implications of the issues we have discussed.

The key points in this chapter are:

- Windows NT security encapsulates the processes, algorithms, and techniques to provide a defense against unauthorized access to the system's resources.
- Windows NT security is designed to meet and exceed the C2 security guidelines required by the U.S. Department of Defense.
- Object security provides a fine-grain set of controls on system resources; this involves setting access permissions, auditing policies, and ownership.
- User rights enforce restrictions on what privileges (i.e., system functions) a particular user can undertake.
- The Syskey utility to provide strong encryption of the SAM database.
- Administrative privileges must be restricted to a small number of trusted individuals; the administrator account should not be used for casual purposes.
- Administrators must never invoke untrusted software.
- Users must choose strong passwords; this should be enforced by the administrator.
- Use NTFS disk partitions rather than FAT.

Up to now, our discussion has made very few references to a key element in the title of this book, i.e., the Web. But at this point, it is important to appreciate that:

> Microsoft has ensured that security is an integral part of its Internet products and that these are tightly coupled with Windows NT security

We shall now move on to discuss security issues that are applicable to networking infrastructures.

Network Security

The Internet grew out of a U.S. Department of Defense (DOD) project called ARPANET (Advanced Research Projects Agency Network) that was developed in the late 1960s. The motivation was the DOD's concern that its communications infrastructure could be wiped out by a single nuclear strike on its central systems. It created a research project to address the development of a decentralized computer network, such that each node would be of equal importance and the resilience of the network would not be affected by an unexpected malfunction or deletion of a node. If a node was taken out of service (for whatever reason), the network would automatically adjust to use alternative routes, thereby guaranteeing the delivery of all information to its intended destination.

Subsequently, a series of protocols were defined that could operate simultaneously on the network. These protocols were known as the **Internet Protocol Suite**, or more commonly as **TCP/IP**.

When we put our machine on a TCP/IP network, we provide an easy route for external access. In the previous chapter we saw how to use the Windows NT security features to protect our files and systems resources. But that is by no means the end of the story. In this chapter we shall see that there are some networking issues that must be addressed.

In this chapter we shall discuss:

- An overview of TCP/IP networking
- How to get our systems connected to the Internet
- How to protect Internet-networked systems from malicious attacks

So let us proceed, and see how we need to change our view of network security when we come to connect to the Internet. We start with a TCP/IP primer.

An Overview of TCP/IP Networking

In order to understand Web security and the various topics covered in this book, it is important to have a grasp of the basic concepts and terminology of the Internet Protocol Suite. It is only with this understanding that we can appreciate why the Internet, by default, is insecure. Furthermore, many of the Web products and security mechanisms that we shall discuss assume that the reader has this knowledge.

> The first section of this chapter is sparse on direct security advice. Its purpose is to lay down a brief but thorough grounding on the TCP/IP concepts so as to provide the knowledge needed to address the later security topics.

We mentioned in the opening to this chapter, that the Internet Protocol Suite includes a number of protocols. The two most common protocols are:

- **Internet Protocol (IP)**—this is used to route a packet of data from node to node across the network
- **Transmission Control Protocol (TCP)**—this is used to create a point-to-point communication channel and ensures that the information is

delivered error-free and in the same order in which it was originally transmitted

It is these two main protocols that give the suite its more common name, TCP/IP.

The TCP/IP protocol maps onto the following layers, sometimes referred to as the **TCP/IP stack**:

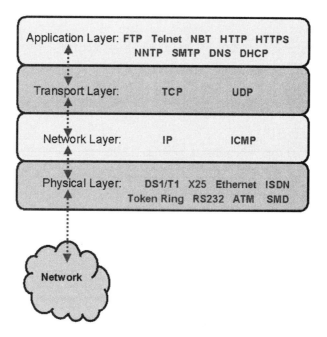

Readers who are familiar with OSI will see that TCP/IP does not strictly conform to the OSI seven-layer model.

The diagram shows a few of the more common application protocols included in TCP/IP. We will summarize the meanings of some of these in the table below.

Full name	Acronym	Purpose
HyperText Transfer Protocol	HTTP	Provides access to Web resources
HyperText Transfer Protocol over Secure Sockets Layer (SSL)	HTTPS	Provides secure access to Web resources (adds encryption, end point authentication, protection against message tampering)
File Transfer Protocol	FTP	Provides file transfer service
NetBIOS over TCP/IP	NBT	Implementation of an early Microsoft networking protocol
Telnet	Telnet	Provides terminal emulation facilities
Network News Protocol	NNTP	Provides service for discussion groups
Simple Mail Transfer Protocol	SMTP	Provides service for sending and receiving electronic mail
Domain Name System	DNS	Provides service for mapping logical machine names to physical addresses
Dynamic Host Configuration Protocol	DHCP	Provides service for assigning an IP network address, from an available pool, to a machine when it boots up
User Datagram Protocol	UDP	Provides a connectionless, unreliable transport service
Internet Control Message Protocol	ICMP	Provides maintenance functions such as maintaining routing tables and provides diagnostic facilities

TCP/IP can be implemented over many different types of physical communications channels, such as Ethernet, T1, X25, etc. This is one reason for TCP/IP's popularity.

Network Addresses

Each machine that is resident on an IP network is uniquely identified by a value known as its **IP address.** An IP address is written and spoken as a sequence of four 8-bit decimal numbers, separated by the dot character, like this:

193.25.255.190

In many cases, an IP network (such as the Internet) is an interconnected set of autonomous networks. The IP address must uniquely identify both the network and the machine within the network. There are four different ways in which this 32-bit block can be broken down into the **network address** and the **host address**. These four decompositions are defined by the **class types** A, B, C, and D, as shown in the table below:

Class type	Range of available network addresses xxx can be any integer value between 0 and 255 (represented by an 8-bit decimal)	Number of available host addresses	Example
A	1 to 126	16,777,216	Network | Host — 100 | 25 | 255 | 190
B	128.xxx to 191.xxx	65536	Network | Host — 129 | 25 | 255 | 190
C	192.xxx.xxx to 223.xxx.xxx	255	Network | Host — 193 | 25 | 255 | 190
D	224.xxx.xxx.xxx to 254.xxx.xxx.xxx	N/A	

As can be seen, it is the value in the first byte that dictates the class type. Thus, the example given above, **193.25.255.190**, is a class C address whose network address is **193.25.255**, and whose host address is **190**.

Since class C addresses allow a maximum of just 255 machines on the network, they are intended for small organizations. Larger organizations, which support more machines, would ideally use class A or class B addressing.

Class D addresses are used for **multicasting**. This is where information is broadcast to a group of hosts and an individual machine does not need to be identified. Conventional push technology is wasteful of bandwidth because the content is sent many times—once for each target machine. Multicasting allows the data to be transmitted once, and for the data to be delivered to each target machine that has subscribed to the service.

Hostnames and the Domain Name System

While IP addresses are convenient for computers to handle, they are difficult for us humans to remember and use. As an alternative, we can use a more friendly **hostname** which is a hierarchical naming convention that comprises of a series of labels separated by a "." character. Applications and networking software can use **Domain Name System** (DNS) servers to translate between hostnames and IP Addresses.

For example, **204.244.193.12** might be the IP address of www.harrison.net.

Subnet Masks

To provide greater flexibility, it is possible to alter the number of bits used for the network address and the host address by specifying a **subnet** mask in the TCP/IP configuration. The bits in the mask indicate those bits in the address that should be considered for the network component.

For example, an IP address of **129.25.255.190** and a subnet mask of **255.255.255.0** would mean that the network address is **129.25.255** and a host address of **190.**

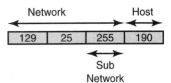

Allocation of IP Addresses

The allocation of IP addresses is centrally controlled by the **Internet Assigned Numbers Authority (IANA);** more information can be found at:

http://www.iana.org/

The majority of the Internet's class A and B IP addresses have now been fully allocated. As a result, some companies with more than 255 machines are forced to make use of multiple class C network addresses. One way to overcome this limitation is for IP software to use **supernetting**. This technique involves using subnet masks to consolidate several class C addresses into a single logical network.

> **Supernetting is also called CIDR (Classless Interdomain Routing) Block Addressing.**

Another approach is to apply an internal addressing scheme and use Internet gateway software to convert between the internal addressing scheme and real allocated IP addresses in the class C range when communicating externally.

A new version of the IP protocols, called **IPv6**, is currently under development. It will use an address space of 128 bits, allowing a potential of around 3.4×10^{38} interconnected machines.

Port Numbers

Typically, TCP/IP services are based on a client/server approach. As an example, consider an FTP server that waits for the moment when a connection is required to be established. When an FTP client establishes a link, it communicates with the FTP server via a series of request and response messages; and finally the link is disconnected.

In this example, how does the FTP client specify the link? In fact, the client must supply *two* pieces of information. The first is the IP address of the machine upon which the FTP server is running. The second specifies that the connection should be made with the *FTP service* (rather than any of the other TCP/IP services that might be awaiting a client connection)—this is called a **port number**.

A port number is used to distinguish between the individual network services that are running simultaneously above a TCP/IP protocol stack.

An individual TCP/IP connection can be uniquely identified by the following collection of items:

- Server machine IP address
- Server application port number
- Client machine IP address
- Client application port number

Server processes are associated with a fixed port number, and the client must know this port in order to connect with the service.

The client itself communicates using a random port number from a restricted range on its own local TCP/IP stack—the actual client port number used is usually unimportant. Our FTP example is illustrated on the following page.

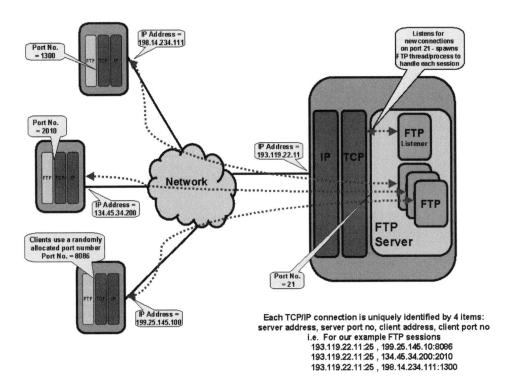

Each TCP/IP connection is uniquely identified by 4 items:
server address, server port no, client address, client port no
i.e. For our example FTP sessions
193.119.22.11:25 , 199.25.145.10:8086
193.119.22.11:25 , 134.45.34.200:2010
193.119.22.11:25 , 198.14.234.111:1300

Port numbers for standard TCP/IP services are controlled by the IANA and are often referred to as **well-known** ports; here are some examples:

Port No.	Protocol
21	FTP—File Transfer Protocol
23	Telnet—Terminal Emulation
25	SMTP—Simple Mail Transfer Protocol (e-mail)
70	Gopher—navigation and file transfer of internet resources
80	HTTP—Hypertext Transfer Protocol (WWW)
119	NNTP—Network News Transfer Protocol (newsgroups)
194	IRC—Internet Relay Chat (conferencing)
443	HTTPS—Hypertext Transfer Protocol over a Secure Channel

TCP/IP services do not have to use these port numbers, and most applications can be configured to use alternative numbers. However, since the client needs to know the port number to establish a connection, these standards make sense for normal use.

There are times when using a different port number can be useful. As an example, consider the need to run two independent Web servers on the same machine. This can be achieved by assigning a nonstandard port number to the second Web server. Doing this can be a useful security measure, since unauthorized users need to obtain this number to access the service. This approach is used by Microsoft IIS with its Web-based administration functions; these run on a second Web server and use a port number that is randomly generated when IIS is installed.

While using nonstandard ports can hide services from the average user, this procedure will not deter the experienced attacker. Programs called **port scanners** are available that will test each port on a target machine and list those port numbers detected to have a service that will accept a connection.

> **Do not rely on security by obscurity**

There are numerous port scanners available on the Web; one example is at:

http://www.ce.net/users/frankd/download.html

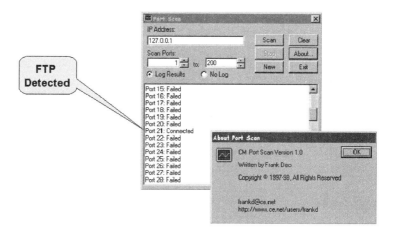

IP Routing

Routing is the primary task of the IP protocol. At this layer, packets of information called **datagrams** are received in one of two ways:

- From over the network, when they are passed up from the physical layer (i.e., modem/network card).
- From the applications, when they are passed down from the higher layers in the protocol stack.

There are three possible actions for each datagram:

- Pass it up to a higher level in the protocol stack
- Pass it on to a network via a local network card or modem (a machine with multiple cards is called **multi-homed**)
- Discard it

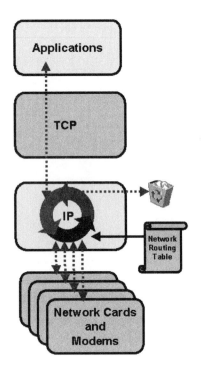

For security reasons, most TCP/IP stacks allow multi-homed routing to be disabled. This means that datagrams received from one network cannot be passed through the stack and onward to another network. For example, if one network card was connected to the Internet, and the other was connected to the corporate network, then it is likely that you would not want Internet TCP/IP traffic to freely access your corporate resources.

Each datagram includes a source IP address, and a destination IP address. The IP protocol uses a **network routing table** to determine the actions for each datagram. When a datagram is received, the table is searched, looking for an entry that matches information in the target IP address.

The table is searched for a match on one of the following items (the list is given in the order of precedence):

- Host machine
- Subnet
- Network
- Default

Having found a suitable entry in the network routing table, the IP layer can then decide which network card or modem to use, or whether to pass the datagram upward.

As an example, consider the following route table, which is for a machine with one network card and one modem:

```
Network Address           Netmask  Gateway Address         Interface  Metric
            0.0.0.0       0.0.0.0         10.22.3.1        10.22.3.97     2
            0.0.0.0       0.0.0.0     158.152.170.1    158.152.170.148     1
           10.22.3.0 255.255.255.0        10.22.3.97        10.22.3.97     2
          10.22.3.97 255.255.255.255        127.0.0.1         127.0.0.1     1
     10.255.255.255 255.255.255.255        10.22.3.97        10.22.3.97     1
           127.0.0.0     255.0.0.0         127.0.0.1         127.0.0.1     1
        158.152.0.0   255.255.0.0   158.152.170.148   158.152.170.148     1
    158.152.170.148 255.255.255.255        127.0.0.1         127.0.0.1     1
           224.0.0.0     224.0.0.0   158.152.170.148   158.152.170.148     1
           224.0.0.0     224.0.0.0        10.22.3.97        10.22.3.97     1
    255.255.255.255 255.255.255.255        10.22.3.97        10.22.3.97     1

Ethernet adapter CE31:

        IP Address. . . . . . . . : 10.22.3.97
        Subnet Mask . . . . . . . : 255.255.255.0
        Default Gateway . . . . . : 10.22.3.1

Ethernet adapter NdisWan4:

        IP Address. . . . . . . . : 158.152.170.148
        Subnet Mask . . . . . . . : 255.255.0.0
        Default Gateway . . . . . : 158.152.170.1
```

The network routing table can be displayed by the following instruction from the command prompt:

> route print

In this table we see that there are a number of special IP addresses:

IP address	Purpose
0.0.0.0	This designates the **default route**. The default route is a useful feature, which means that a given machine does not need to know how to reach every other machine on the Internet—if the destination is unknown, the machine can pass the message on to a default router for handling.
127.0.0.1	This is the **loopback address**, which always maps on to the local machine—it's useful for testing purposes where client and server logic is invoked on the same machine.
224.0.0.0	This is a class D address, used for multicasting purposes.
255.255.255.255	This is a **broadcast address** which means it is targeted at all machines on the network.

The network routing table shown above was for the following network topology:

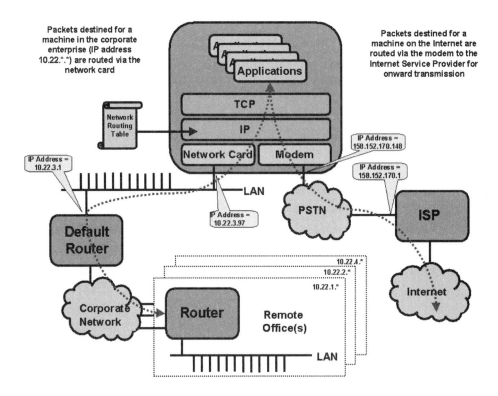

This concludes our overview of TCP/IP. We shall now look at how TCP/IP networking is used to get our systems onto the Internet.

Connecting to the Internet

To set up a basic Web site of our own, we could rent some Web space from one of the numerous (and relatively new) companies that now offer such services.

However, we shall consider the security issues involved in setting up a dedicated high-speed Internet link into your own premises. This is an expensive approach, but it provides much greater flexibility and control, and enables integration with other systems in our enterprise.

For the majority of organizations, the most cost-effective method for connecting to the Internet is to obtain access from an **Internet Service Provider** (ISP). Each ISP runs an autonomous network that interconnects with other ISPs to form the mesh of networks known as the Internet; this is illustrated below. Large organizations may choose the more complex and costlier option of connecting directly to a **Network Access Point** (NAP). NAPs are the main Internet hubs, interconnected by very high-speed network connections called **backbone links**.

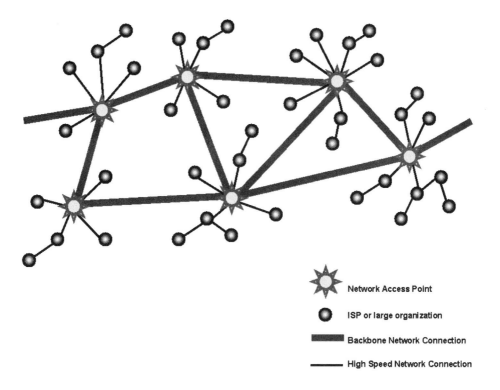

Network Access Point

ISP or large organization

Backbone Network Connection

High Speed Network Connection

Choosing an ISP

Choosing an ISP can be a daunting task, because so many companies all claim to offer the best services around. In reality, the performance offered by the different ISPs vary greatly—and so do their costs! The Internet is a network of networks, so the performance achieved will be dependent on the places you're trying to communicate with, and the number of hops via other networks that the traffic has to go through. (Note that the networking protocols insulate us from the decisions made in routing network traffic).

A slow node *en route* will affect the overall performance, because a chain is only as strong as the weakest link. It makes sense, therefore, to choose an ISP that offers a high-speed direct link to a NAP (thus reducing the number of network hops), and has several alternative routes available for contingency purposes. While it is sensible to choose those ISPs that offer the highest bandwidth links to a NAP, bear in mind that this bandwidth has to be shared with all of the ISP's customers—and that the large ISPs have many customers.

The physical connection between your premises and the ISP is usually subcontracted out to one of the major telecommunications companies that have, in the past few years, developed large and sophisticated data communication infrastructures. The type of connection that you choose will depend on your bandwidth requirements (and your budget, of course). For example, you could choose a dialup link, but it is often more cost-effective and reliable to have a permanent leased line installed. Several different technologies are used for providing leased lines, each with a different bandwidth capacity, and the exact offerings differ from one telecommunications supplier to another.

Establishing the Link

In the early days of Web computing, it was common to have a single dedicated Internet connection to a Web server that was isolated from the organization's internal networks. By implementing this arrangement, a company could avoid any security concerns about external parties having access to the internal computer's systems. The absence of any link between the Web server and the internal network is sometimes called an **airwall**—it represents optimum security!

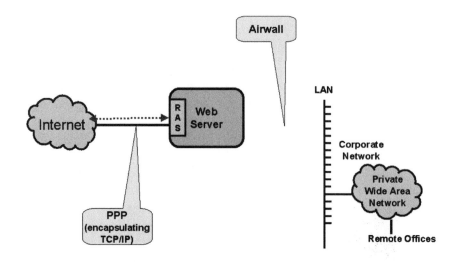

The layer of Microsoft software that can be used to interface with remote networks, such as an ISP, is the **Remote Access Service** (RAS).

Remote Access Service

RAS can act as either:

- Remote Access Client; also called **Dial-up Networking** and enables a machine to initiate connection to remote network
- Remote Access Server; allows remote systems and workers to connect to our networks

RAS operates over dial-up links or permanent leased-lines and supports communications using the following physical layers:

- asynchronous modem communication
- ISDN
- X25

In addition, RAS supports a number of protocols at the network layer including TCP/IP. The TCP/IP datagrams are carried over the physical wire using an industry standard protocol called **Point-to-Point Protocol** (PPP). The RAS support for PPP enables interoperability in multi-vendor heterogeneous environments and allows for integration to the ISPs networks.

PPP supports a number of authentication protocols including **Challenge-Handshake Authentication Protocol** (CHAP). This operates in a similar way to the challenge/response processing that we saw in Chapter Two for the NTLM authentication. As with NTLM, this has the advantage over the alternative PPP authentication mechanisms in that the password is not sent over the wire. The authentication mechanism used is configured on the PPP server (i.e., the end that receives the connection request).

If we ever fancied going into business as an ISP, we could use a RAS Server configuration connected to the Internet with a large modem bank. There is a component with the Windows NT 4.0 Option pack called **Internet Connection Services for RAS** (ICS). This is a collection of software applications designed to help organizations implement remote Internet access solutions. For example, there is facility to create a 'Connection Wizard', branded for our ISP company, that would assist a user to set its dial-up networking to access our RAS Server.

Linking to the Internet via the LAN

Today's Web systems require access to data sources located within the organization's enterprise, and so alternative networking strategies to the "airwall" are needed.

One common solution is for an Internet connection to be made to the organization's **local area network** (LAN). This bandwidth is then shared between the Web server and any other systems that use the Internet (such as e-mail). In addition, users within the organization can use their desktops to access the Internet via the same Internet connection.

The LAN is connected to the Internet via a **router**, which is a device with multiple network connections. The router analyzes the destination-addressing information in the network packets and decides when to pass traffic on from one network to another.

For small networks, Windows NT can now compete with traditional hardware routers by acting as a server-based router using a service called the **Router and Remote Access Service** (RRAS) which is an extension of RAS.

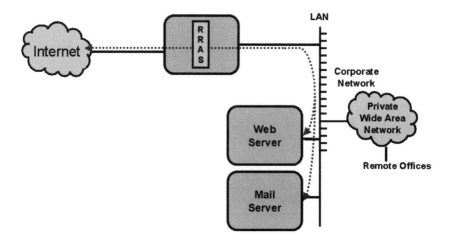

Connecting to the Internet via the LAN is very cost-effective but poses additional challenges in terms of security management. In particular, it is vital that external Internet users be able to access *only* those systems intended for external use. Later in this chapter, we shall examine how we can create secure routers/gateways (between the LAN and the Internet) using **firewall** technologies.

In order to address the business demand for the secure exchange of information over a public network like the Internet, a series of standard Internet protocols have evolved that ensure the confidentiality and integrity of data, and provide assurances over the identity of the parties in involved. These secure protocols are implemented using:

- **Secure Channel Services**
- **Virtual Private Networks**

We shall now take a look at these two technologies:

Secure Channel Services

Secure Channels Services is a software technology that provides a higher level of networking security by enabling additional endpoint authentication, message encryption, and message authentication. Secure Channels slots transparently into the TCP/IP protocol stack, as shown in the diagram.

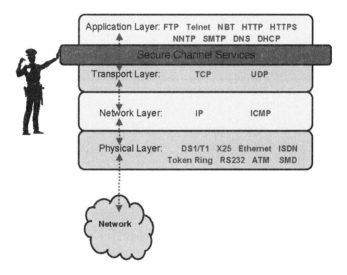

Secure Channels relies on **cryptography**, the ancient mathematical science of coding messages so that only authorized personnel can decipher them. In recent developments, cryptography has been applied to mechanisms for authenticating users on a network, ensuring the integrity of transmitted information, and preventing users from repudiating their transmitted messages.

Secure Channels is implemented as part of Microsoft's Internet Security Framework and is shipped with IIS and IE. While these are Microsoft products, Secure Channels provides support for several industry-standard security protocols and so can interoperate with products from alternative vendors:

- **Secure Socket Layer** (SSL 2.0/SSL 3.0), developed by Netscape
- **Private Communications Technology** (PCT 1.0), developed by Microsoft
- **Transport Layer Security** (TLS; targeted for Windows NT 2000 release), which is intended to provide a simpler and more robust solution by using the best parts of SSL and PCT

Secure Channels provides the following features:

- Privacy—datagrams cannot be examined
- Integrity—datagrams cannot be tampered with
- Authentication—enables client and server to request identification of one other

We shall discuss these topics in greater depth in Chapter 5, which is dedicated to Secure Channel Services issues.

Virtual Private Networks

Virtual Private Networks (VPNs) are networks that appear to be private but are in fact carried over a public network, so that participants on the private network benefit from the same levels of security achieved using an exclusive (but expensive) private network. The private network is called a **tunnel** because the VPN payload is encapsulated within public network packets and traverses the network transparently to those operating on the public network. The VPN payload is encrypted such that only the end-points can comprehend the contents and it would be meaningless to anyone on the public network who intercepted the information.

The public network referred to above could be the Internet, and it is frequently used as a low-cost mechanism for linking multiple remote offices together. As an example, consider the problem of a business having one office in the United States and another in the United Kingdom. The high costs of a private leased line between the two sites would be prohibitive for most small organizations. As an alternative, a VPN carried across the Internet would be a cost-effective and ideal solution

There are other VPN examples where the public network might be a corporate network. Consider a project working on a secret defense project with restricted LAN segments in two geographically separated operations. The two physically separated LANs could be logically linked together by tunneling over the unrestricted corporate network.

Another example might be two or more companies that are working in collaboration with an Extranet over an independent network that has been outsourced to a specialist telecommunications company. Should this company have full responsibility for the implementation and management of the network, it could gain full access to the network traffic and could potentially analyze the information that flows. By tunneling across this network, the companies in the alliance would have the confidence that their information remained confidential.

Microsoft and VPNs

Microsoft has extended the RAS and Dial-up Networking software in its operating systems to provide a VPN implementation that facilitates the secure transfer of information over the Internet, using a tunneling technology called **Point-to-Point Tunneling Protocol** (PPTP). PPTP encompasses several protocols, including TCP/IP, and provides an encrypted channel through the public networks.

PPTP is supported on both Windows NT 4.0 and Windows 95, and the later equivalents.

There are two primary scenarios for using PPTP:

- A client to remote network connection
- A LAN to LAN connection

This is shown in the diagram below:

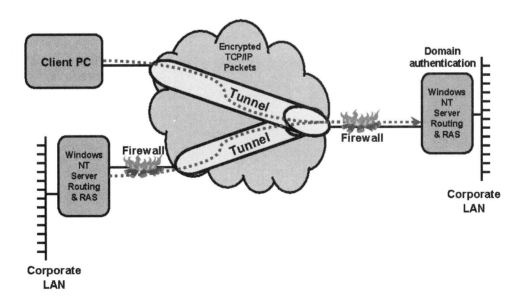

The client can use its Dial-up Networking facility to dial an ISP, and then use PPTP over the Internet to connect to a remote RAS server. RAS is responsible for authentication of the client by checking the users security credentials using one of the supported authentication mechanisms (e.g., CHAP as described above).

In a similar fashion, multiple LANs may be interconnecting using the tunnel. However, additional protocol routing logic is required to ensure that packets destined for the local machines are not sent over the network, which would of course waste the valuable bandwidth. This functionality can be achieved using RRAS whose routing functionality was explained earlier.

> There are two more tunneling protocols that are expected to become industry standards and will be supported by Microsoft at some time in the future; these are:
> - Layer 2 Tunneling Protocol (L2TP)—this combines the best features of PPTP and another tunneling protocol from Cisco
> - Internet Protocol Security (IPSec) Tunnel Mode—designed by the IETF

Protecting the Windows NT Server from Network Attacks

In this next section we shall investigate the strategies required to protect networks from attack. The knowledge of TCP/IP gained at the start of this chapter will be used to investigate the various firewall technologies that are available.

Blocking Nonessential TCP/IP Ports

With version 4.0 of Windows NT, Microsoft introduced the ability to block IP protocol packets by enabling/disabling network traffic on particular IP port numbers. This can be used to configure Windows NT to act as a simple firewall.

> This is a useful approach in low-risk environments, but many systems will require more advanced protection. For example, it is not able to protect against machines that impersonate another machine's IP addresses (such impersonation is called **IP Spoofing**). To guard against more subtle threats of this kind, it is necessary to implement the true firewall technology that will be discussed later in the chapter.

Let us consider an example. Windows NT could be configured with two network cards: one to connect to the Internet, and the other to our LAN. The Internet services on the Internet network card could be restricted to, for example, port **80** (HTTP). External access to any other port numbers would be denied. To allow a Web server extension full access to resources on the corporate LAN, all ports on the LAN network card would be enabled. This is illustrated in the diagram below:

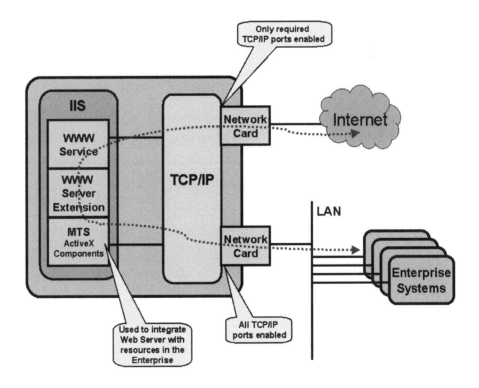

IP port blocking is enabled by means of the Network Control Panel. Select TCP/IP Properties on the Protocols tab. This provides an Advanced button, which displays a dialog including the Enable Security checkbox and a Configure button. This button finally produces another dialog where you can specify the ports that are permitted.

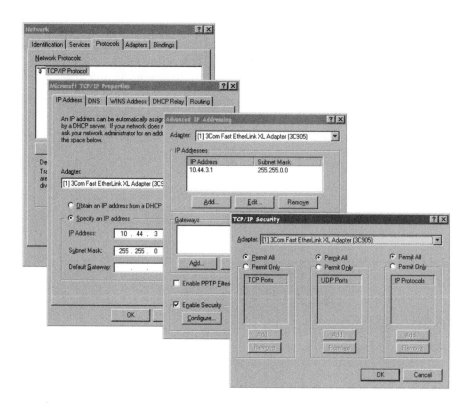

IP Forwarding

To ensure that the TCP/IP stack does not automatically route packets between the two network cards, the Enable IP Forwarding option on the TCP/IP properties must be unchecked:

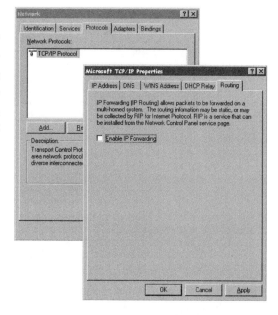

Firewalls

A **firewall** is used to protect a private network (such as a corporate network) from a connected untrusted public network (such as the Internet) by regulating the traffic that passes from one network to another and enforcing advanced network security policies. Firewalls are universally recognized as a fundamental component in a strong network security solution.

There are many types of firewalls, but they basically fall into two camps, **packet filtering** and **application proxy servers**. Advanced firewalls that use a combination of these mechanisms are considered to be the ideal protective solution.

Let us consider these two approaches with TCP/IP in mind, but remember that some firewalls can provide support for multiple networking protocols.

Packet Filtering

Earlier in this chapter we discussed devices called routers that are used to interface networks together, and to decide when to pass network traffic from one network to another. They do this by analyzing the IP addresses in the network packets and using a table of routing information to determine the destination of the packet.

Packet filtering routers can also examine information in the transport (TCP) layer. They can be configured to filter out certain types of traffic, preventing it from being passed between networks.

More specifically, such a router can disable external access to network services that are known to be vulnerable to abuse and capable of leaking system information, giving clues to potential attackers. It can provide controlled systems access by granting access to specific systems that provide external services (e.g., a Web Server), and sealing off all others.

A router can also provide additional checks over the origination of a message, denying (or granting) access from specific IP addresses. However, this is of minimal value, because it is very easy for an attacker to transmit network traffic that pretends to come from another IP address (i.e., spoofing another machine's address).

Packet filtering allows for two strategies. The first option is to enable all network traffic unless blocked. The second option, which is more popular and less risky, is to block all traffic unless enabled.

Here is a simple example to illustrate the second of these options. An organization could configure a packet-filtering router so that it allows network traffic to enter the organization's network from the Internet *only if:*

- The traffic type is on port 80 (HTTP) *and* the destination IP address matches the Web server address
- The traffic type is on port 25 (SMTP) *and* the destination IP address matches the e-mail server address *and* the source IP addresses matches the ISP's e-mail system

This is illustrated below:

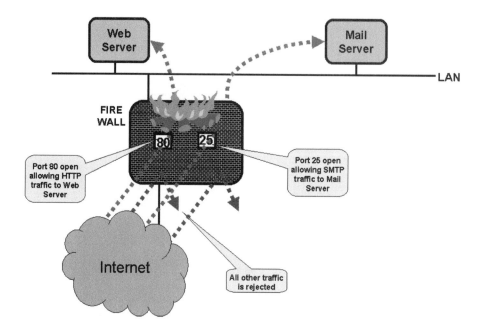

All other unwanted traffic, which might include potential attacks and break-ins, would be filtered and discarded.

Security rules (such as those in the example) would be defined in the security policy discussed when we addressed risk management in Chapter 1.

Packet filtering routers operate very quickly and are cost-effective. However, their filtering options are usually quite limited and often lack auditing facilities. Many organizations now also include **packet-filtering firewalls** to provide higher levels of granular control and better monitoring services.

Application Proxy Servers

The highest levels of control are provided by **proxy services**. Proxy services run at the application level (i.e., via HTTP, FTP, Telnet, and so on).

A separate proxy program is installed for each application protocol that requires support, and is used to relay messages between the entities on the two networks. To the client, the proxy acts as the server; and to the server, the proxy acts as the client. This is illustrated below:

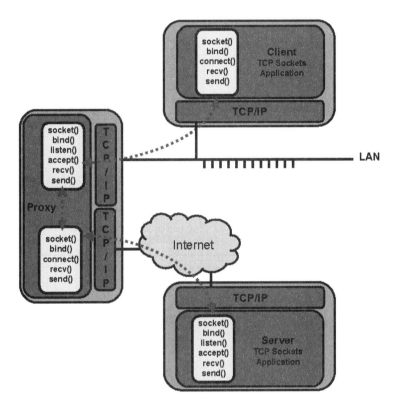

Each proxy program contains logic that understands the specifics of the protocol and knows how to defend against attacks. When a packet of information is received, either from an external entity or a user accessing the Internet, the contents are analyzed to enforce the security policies.

As an example, any inbound SMTP e-mail message with attachments could be scanned for known viruses; and any outbound SMTP e-mail message could be scanned for offensive words and forwarded to senior management for inspection and consideration.

The external machines do not see the actual IP addresses assigned to internal machines. Instead, they see some address that is substituted by the proxy. There are two immediate advantages to this. First, it helps to thwart hackers who monitor the network traffic, collecting information that might be useful for a potential attack. Second, an organization can allow Internet access to each desktop, even if it does not have enough real IP addresses for every machine in the enterprise. When a user accesses the Internet, the proxy swaps the user's internal IP address to a real Internet IP address.

HTTP proxy applications can provide further advantages. Pages retrieved by internal users can be cached in the proxy server, and when another internal Web user subsequently requests the same page, the cached page is retrieved. This can greatly improve the perceived performance, free up server resources, and save valuable Internet bandwidth. Various caching strategies are implemented by proxy servers to ensure that the pages returned to the user are up-to-date. We shall discuss this when we investigate Microsoft Proxy Server.

Locating a Firewall/Web Server

There are several options available when considering the optimum location for a public Web server in relation to a firewall. In this section we will discuss the possibilities.

WEB SERVER BEHIND THE FIREWALL

The first possibility is to place your public Web server behind the firewall: Of course, it is necessary to allow for external HTTP traffic targeted for the Web server machine. Therefore, the firewall must be configured to allow such traffic through.

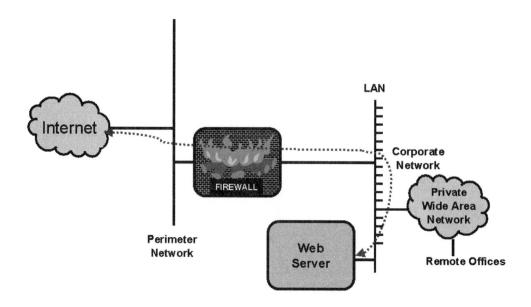

The potential problem here is that external access to the corporate LAN is allowed. Depending on the organization's security policy, this might be considered an unnecessary risk. Others might feel that HTTP is relatively safe, and the potential for any risk very small.

WEB SERVER OUTSIDE THE FIREWALL

If the public Web server is placed outside a firewall, any public access to the organization's LAN is avoided. Isolating the LAN within the firewall reduces any potential risk and avoids the external HTTP network traffic that might affect the performance of internal systems. This configuration requires that the Web server be properly secured, because it is fully exposed to any attacker:

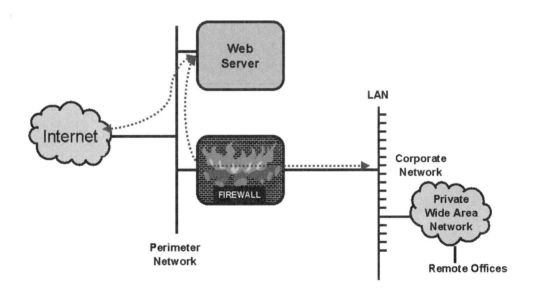

It is likely that the Web server will need to generate dynamic content by integrating with databases, legacy systems, and so on. Therefore, the firewall will need an appropriate configuration to allow Web server extensions to securely access such components behind the firewall.

WEB SERVER ON A PERIMETER NETWORK

The optimum strategy for placement of the Web server is to combine the ideas outlined above, using a perimeter network and two firewalls:

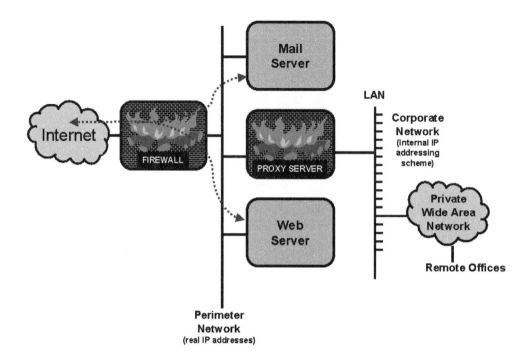

All externally accessed Internet servers (such as Web, e-mail, and so on) are located on the perimeter network, which uses real Internet allocated IP addresses. Proxy services, located in the internal firewall, are then used to convert between the real IP addresses and the internal IP addresses.

> Finally, remember that a firewall cannot protect a network if somebody goes around it. If an internal network user uses a modem to dial-out onto the Internet, then all security checks will be bypassed. This must be written into the security policy document and staff made aware that any breach is a serious offense.

Microsoft Proxy Server

Microsoft Proxy Server is a component with the BackOffice portfolio that enables an organization to securely provide Internet access to the corporate desktop. This provides a powerful solution by combining content caching and firewall technologies into a single product.

By caching content, such as Web pages and graphics, it is able to reduce the consumption of valuable network bandwidth, curtail the workload of the server, and improve response time to the user.

The firewall support provides a multilayered defense mechanism that includes:

- Packet filtering—to block packets at the IP level
- Application proxy—acts on behalf of the client to interact with the remote resource located on the Internet; understands fully the message interactions for various standard Internet protocols; can be used to implement filters, e.g., to prevent viruses and Java applets from entering the corporate network
- Hidden internal network addresses—this ensures that the outside world cannot access the organization's resources; also, organizations typically use an internal addressing scheme with IP addresses that are not valid on the Internet
- Extensive logging facilities and mechanisms to generate alerts for security and protocol violations
- Site filtering—this makes it possible to restrict/deny access to specific network addresses
- Reverse proxy/virtual hosting—this makes it possible to publish content to the Internet without compromising the security of the internal corporate network; the proxy server impersonates a Web server, as illustrated in the following diagram.

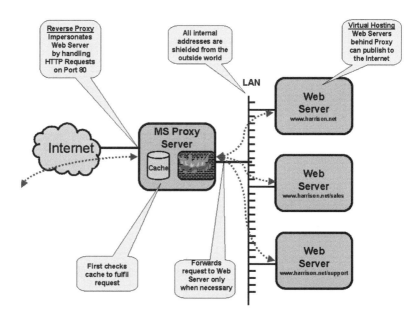

From the desktop's point of view, the Microsoft Proxy Server contains two distinct types of Proxy Servers:

- **Web Proxy Server**—this provides Internet access to applications that support the standard proxy protocol (known as the CERN standard, after the organization that devised it).
- **Winsock Proxy Server**—this provides Internet access to applications that do not support the standard proxy protocol.

Web Proxy Server

The **Web Proxy Server** is used to provide Internet access to Web Browsers (i.e., handle the HTTP, HTTPS, FTP, or Gopher protocols). When a browser is configured to use the Proxy Server, any request for Web content is passed to the Proxy Server to action the request.

The Proxy Server will first authenticate the user and check that the requested URL is acceptable for the policy that has been defined by the administrator. Subject to these details being acceptable, the request is serviced by either passing it on to the appropriate Web server or using local cached content (greatly increasing the user's perceived performance), and returning the information back to the Web browser. The user's request can be optionally logged for later analysis.

This is illustrated below:

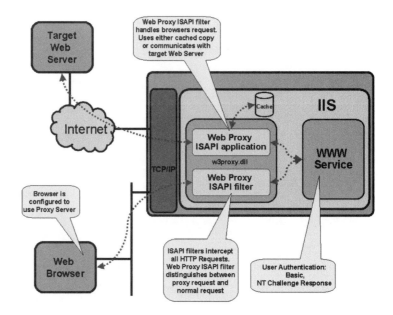

The Proxy Server is responsible for replacing the client's internal IP address and replacing it with the Internet IP that has been assigned to the Proxy Server.

The logic used by the Web proxy to determine how to process an HTTP request and return the requested object is illustrated below:

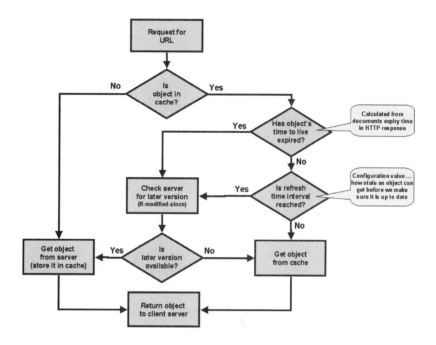

Winsock Proxy Server

The **Winsock Proxy Server** is used as a proxy for the industry standard Winsock 1.1 API. It provides a high-level API for various communications protocols, including TCP/IP. It enables desktop applications that invoke this API to communicate with remote applications.

When the Proxy Server is installed, special client software is made available on a network-shared directory; this must be installed on every desktop machine that needs to use the Winsock Proxy Server. The normal Winsock DLL is called wsock32.dll (32 bit environments); the setup process will rename this and install a new Proxy Server version that takes on the wsock32.dll name. These changes are transparent to the user and their desktop application

The setup process will also examine the network configuration and determine which IP addresses are local and which are remote, thus requiring the services of the Proxy Server to communicate with. When the desktop calls on Proxy version Winsock API, the target IP Address is checked to see if the subsequent actions are to act on a local or remote address.

If the request is to communicate with a local machine, it simply relays this request and all subsequent calls on to the authentic Winsock API.

If the request is to communicate with an external machine, it remotes this request and all subsequent calls on to the Proxy Server; this in turn is communicating with the target Internet application.

This is illustrated below:

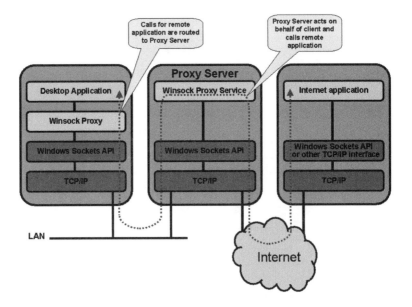

As before, the Proxy Server will shield the client's internal IP address by replacing it with the IP address that has been assigned to the Proxy Server.

Windows Networking and SMB

Windows Networking allows Windows NT to manage a number of important tasks: sharing directories and printers, logon to systems, enabling remote access to the Registry, performing remote administrations, and exchanging data between applications. For Windows Networking, Windows NT uses an industry standard client/server networking protocol called **Server Message Block** (SMB).

The latest version of Microsoft's SMB implementation has been named the **Common Internet File System Protocol (CIFS)**.

SMB can be encapsulated and transmitted using several transport-layer protocols, including TCP/IP and NetBEUI. If SMB is used over TCP/IP or NetBEUI, then NetBIOS is also required, as shown in the diagram below:

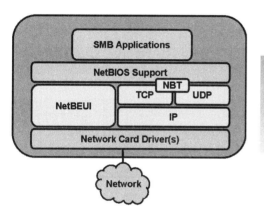

NetBEUI is a LAN protocol designed for small networks. It cannot be used with routers and so is not suitable for enterprise networks over multiple offices.

NetBIOS is an application programming interface, not a protocol.

Usually, the default installation of Windows NT is to enable NetBIOS operating on both TCP/IP and NetBEUI.

A Windows NT machine that uses **NetBIOS over TCP/IP** (NBT), and is bound to the network card that is connected to the Internet, poses a *huge* risk from hackers, as it provides an open door to many Windows NT resources.

For example, once an attacker has gained access to a network's shared directories, he can snoop around or cause malicious damage to our data. There have also been examples of denial-of-service attacks using remote SMB connections.

Safe SMB

Fortunately, it is possible to have NetBIOS, TCP/IP, and NetBEUI all installed and to disable the NetBIOS-to-TCP/IP binding. The Windows NT machine can still participate in Windows Networking by using the NetBEUI channel, which is not routed over the Internet.

Disabling Windows Networking over TCP/IP is done using the Bindings tab of the Network Control Panel. The bindings to disable are:

- NetBIOS → WINS Client (TCP/IP) → Ethernet
- Server → WINS Client (TCP/IP) → Ethernet
- Workstation → WINS Client (TCP/IP) → Ethernet

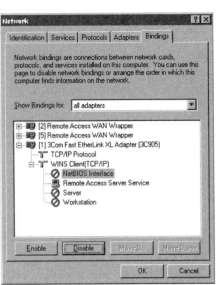

For larger organizations, the approach of disabling NBT and relying on NetBEUI will probably be unsuitable because:

- NetBEUI has performance limitations and is really only suitable for small networks
- NetBEUI is not a routable protocol; it therefore cannot be used for corporate enterprises with networking topology that is distributed over multiple sites using routers

The alternative defense mechanism for disabling Internet users accessing NBT is to block all external TCP/IP traffic received on ports 137, 138, and 139. It is also recommended that port 135 be blocked to prevent a number of NT services being remotely invoked.

This can be done using either a firewall or IP port blocking, as discussed earlier in this chapter.

> **Port 135 is used for the RPC (remote procedure calls) listener**
> **Port 137 is used for NetBIOS name resolution**
> **Port 138 is used for NetBIOS messaging**
> **Port 139 is used for NetBIOS sessions**

There is one other issue that should be considered to protect our system. To access Windows Networking services, a user must have the **Access this computer from network** privilege. By default, Windows NT grants this privilege to the **Everyone** group, which includes every remote user (even those who have not been authenticated). A safer configuration is to remove this privilege from this unconditional group, and replace it with the new group called **Authenticated Users**, which was introduced as part of Service Pack 3.

NetBIOS Auditing Tool

A tool that can perform various security checks on systems offering NetBIOS file-sharing services is the NetBIOS Auditing Tool (NAT), available from

http://www.secnet.com/ntinfo/ntaudit.html

NAT retrieves various items of useful information that are exposed by a remote SMB compliant server and then attempts to access any available services. It starts by performing a dictionary attack to get authenticated, and then lists any remote SMB connections that can be established.

Any shares that can be written to are vulnerable to attacks, such as planting a Trojan executable, and are highlighted in the audit.

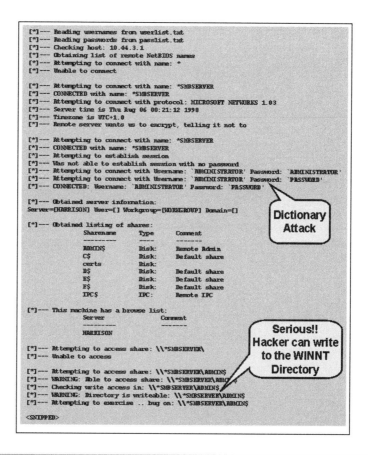

Service Pack 3 provides some protection from the above attacks. For optimum security, however, the recommendations in this section should be applied.

■ Summary

In this chapter we have looked at basic Internet networking. Once our Web solutions are connected to the Internet, we can protect ourselves from network attacks, as has been discussed here. The key points in this chapter are:

- TCP/IP (as used over the Internet and many corporate networks) has now become the *de facto* standard for interconnecting computer systems.
- The simplest method for interfacing to the Internet is via an ISP. However, there are several issues to consider when selecting a suitable ISP.
- Secure Channels Services enable secure transfer of data by enabling endpoint authentication, message encryption, and message authentication.
- VPN Services provide secure and reliable connections to allow mobile workers and organizations to interoperate with remote offices or to other companies over public networks.
- Firewalls should be implemented to protect networks by enforcing advanced network security policies.
- SMB/Windows Networking should be disabled from external access via the Internet.

We have looked at some of the problems and made some recommendations. Unfortunately, that is not the end of the story. Remember: no networked system can ever be 100% secure! Before long someone will devise a new type of attack, and for a short time, until a solution is made available, will have many systems in peril.

IIS Web Server Security

We shall now turn to the Web server that is the natural choice for the Windows NT platform: **Internet Information Server** (IIS). IIS version 4.0 is Microsoft's latest standards-based commercial Web application server. It is designed for ease of use, scalability, portability, security, and extensibility, and it provides a powerful environment for the next generation of line-of-business applications.

IIS4 builds on the success of its predecessor to provide organizations with a powerful platform for the publishing of information and the delivery of business applications over both the Internet and corporate Intranets. The key objective of this latest version is to supply an integrated platform offering comprehensive Web services, and easy-to-develop and reliable Application Services.

IIS provides the highest levels of integration with the Windows NT Server operating system and many Microsoft server products, including Transaction Server, Message Queue Server, Index Server, Certificate Server, and Cluster Server; these products are described in the Microsoft Internet strategy overview in Appendix A.

In addition, IIS easily integrates with the Microsoft BackOffice portfolio to leverage:

- The data storage facilities of SQL Server
- The Web site life-cycle management facilities of Site Server
- The messaging and groupware facilities of Exchange
- The host connectivity facilities of SNA Server

At the time of writing, IIS is supplied as part of the Windows NT 4.0 Option Pack. It will also be supplied as a base component of the Windows 2000 (NT 5.0) operating system, when released. The discussion in this chapter assumes that you are familiar with the installation of IIS and the basic administration of Windows NT.

In this chapter we shall be focusing on the security issues of IIS, namely:

- The different mechanisms available to administer the Web server settings.
- The key concepts in configuring an IIS Web site to keep the content and applications secure.
- How to identify and authenticate users; how this is tightly integrated with Windows NT security.
- The different types of authentication and when each should be used.
- How to create an audit trail of user activity.
- The security model offered by the server extensions used by the Microsoft development tools FrontPage and Visual Studio.

By the end of this chapter, we will have a comprehensive understanding of the core features provided by IIS security. But first, let us look at the different options available for administering the IIS environment.

IIS Administration

There are several mechanisms for managing the IIS Web server and its applications. IIS offers us the choice of:

- Internet Service Manager (MMC)—a Windows based administration utility

- Internet Service Manager (HTML)—a Web-based administration application
- Developing our own applications/scripts to interface to the IIS Administration Objects via COM.

The different layers of software that are involved for each of the above options are shown in the following diagram.

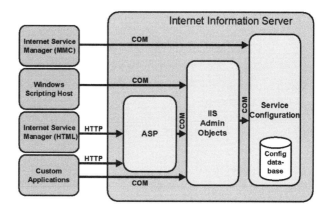

Let us start our investigations with a look at the first option, the Windows-based Administration facility.

The Microsoft Management Console . . . Windows-based Administration

The **Microsoft Management Console** (MMC) provides a single application in which you can perform the various administration tasks for your enterprise. It enables the different management tools and system-status views to be integrated into a single common-management console.

It is part of Microsoft's management strategy that all Windows NT and BackOffice administration tasks will eventually be controlled from within the MMC. In addition, other software vendors can easily develop their own administration programs to reside within this environment. Such programs will interface with the MMC container using COM.

COM provides software interoperability at the component level. Readers who are unfamiliar with COM are referred to Appendix A.

MMC container

snap in
administration
com control (3S) Internet Service Manager

In fact, the MMC is not actually responsible for handling any of the administration logic. Instead, it simply acts as a container for various administration programs that perform such tasks. These programs are called **snap-ins**. A snap-in is just a COM control and can be written in any language that supports COM; examples include VB, VC++, or VJ++.

A system administrator can group a number of snap-ins together to create a **tool**, which can be saved as a `.MSC` file. Tools with a limited number of snap-ins can be created and their use delegated to less-experienced operators; this gives the operator a more manageable view of the tasks to be performed and avoids giving access to functions not needed.

One example of an MMC snap-in is the **Internet Service Manager**, one of the tools used to administer IIS.

The MMC is shown in the following screenshot; this example shows snap-ins for:

• Internet Service Manager (IIS)

• Transaction Server

• Index Server

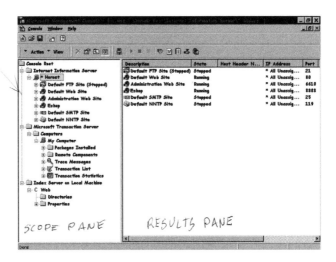

SCOPE PANE   *RESULTS PANE*

Each console in the MMC contains two panes. The left-side pane is called the **scope pane,** and the right-side pane is called the **results pane**. The scope pane shows the hierarchy of all items that can be managed; these items are collectively known as the **namespace**.

Each item in the namespace can be selected, and the corresponding information is displayed in the results pane in an appropriate format. Items in either pane can be administered using functions accessed from the toolbars, the main menu, and the right-click context menu.

Once a snap-in has been installed on a machine, it can be included in the namespace by means of the Console|Add/Remove Snap-in menu option.

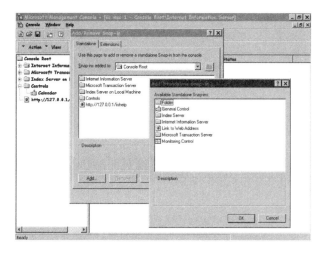

When a snap-in is added to the console, it adds items to the namespace. The namespace can be further customized by adding folders, ActiveX controls, and Web links.

The amended namespace definition can be saved to create a tool using the Console|Save As menu option; this prompts for the name of a management console file, which has a .MSC. Opening a .MSC file will instantiate the MMC with the appropriate set of snap-ins.

Internet Service Manager

The Internet Service Manager allows the administration of a number of Internet-related services:

- WWW (HTTP)—Web Server
- FTP—File Transfer
- NNTP—Newsgroups
- SMTP—Electronic Mail
- Proxy Server

In this chapter and throughout this book, we shall be focusing on the security-related property sheets for the Web server.

The MMC allows remote administration over a LAN. A connection can be made to another networked computer by right-clicking on the Internet Information Server folder and selecting the **Connect** menu option.

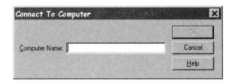

As an alternative to the MMC, IIS4 can be administered using an HTML version of the Internet Service Manager via a Web browser; we shall now take a look at this alternative.

Web-based Administration

The Web-based Internet Service Manager has the advantage that administration tasks can be handled remotely using HTTP. This can be used to administer the Web server over the Internet. A good example of when this approach is advantageous is a situation where an ISP hosts multiple sites for external organizations. Responsibility for many of the administration tasks can be delegated to the organization's own personnel.

The Administration Web site is kept separate from the main Web sites and is installed on a random port number. This will prevent most people from knowing the exact Administration URL; however, recapping from Chapter 3, it is easy to do a port scan to find any ports in use.

On my machine the URL for the Administration Web site is:

http://harrison:6610/iisadmin

You will need to replace the machine name and the port number with values suitable for your environment.

When IIS is installed, the following menu option is set up to access the correct URL:

Start|Programs|Windows NT 4.0 Option Pack|Microsoft Internet Information Server|Internet Service Manager (HTML).

The installation of IIS will configure the system so that the Administration Web can only be accessed from the same machine as the Web server. The configuration is set to grant access only to users on the TCP/IP loopback address 127.0.0.1. We shall see later how this security setting can be amended.

The Administration Web has a dual-screen layout displaying a context-sensitive menu list of options on the left-hand side of the browser and a **tree view/administration form** on the right-hand side of the browser.

The tree view shows the entities that can be administered. This is accomplished by clicking on an item, which then appears highlighted, and then selecting one of the following menu options:

- New
- Delete
- Rename
- Properties
- Start
- Stop
- Pause
- Resume

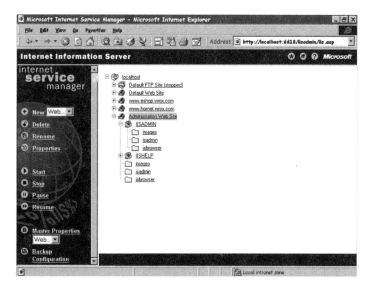

If the current item selected is the root (i.e., the machine name), the New option will either create a new Web site or a new FTP site, depending on the current value in the associated checkbox. If the current item selected is a directory, then the New option will create a new virtual root.

A virtual root is a pointer to a physical disk location; this will be fully explained, later in the chapter.

By selecting the Properties option, the list of menu options is updated and an administration form is displayed on the right-hand side of the browser.

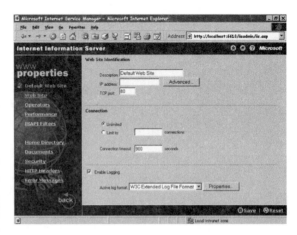

Access to the administration facilities is protected using Windows NT security and is limited to a defined group of users called **Web Site Operators**; we shall discuss this shortly. Furthermore, the use of Windows NT security enables administration facilities to be given to external organizations and protected so that no operator can interfere with another organization's configuration.

IIS Administration Objects

The **IIS Administration Objects** (IISAO) exposes a COM interface allowing IIS to be administered from external software components. This allows developers to create their own customized administration programs using either a Windows-based application or a script language.

The IIS Admin Objects are namespace providers in support of the **Active Directory Services Interface** (ADSI). We shall delve into directory services and ADSI in Chapter 12 when we investigate how to use them in Web applications to implement access controls. Until then we shall keep things simple with an example that assumes minimal knowledge of such topics; hopefully, this will whet your appetite for our later ADSI discussions.

A **directory service** is part of a distributed computing environment that provides a simple-to-use and high-performant mechanism to enable finding and locating resources and users. An example is the Windows NT Directory Services discussed in Chapter 2.

A **namespace** is a bounded area that contains a group of common objects; for example, **files** reside with the **file system** namespace. ADSI provides a set of interfaces enabling the administration of a directory service namespace.

The IIS Admin Objects expose a hierarchical namespace of objects. Each IISAO object has a unique identifier that resembles a URL; it consists of **IIS://** followed by the machine name followed by the path object in the IIS configuration.

For example, the object identifier for the first (default) Web server is:

IIS://localhost/w3svc/1

The machine name `localhost` is defined in the TCP/IP configuration to have an IP address of 127.0.0.1; in the TCP/IP overview in Chapter 2 that this is the special "loopback" address and refers to the local machine. We can replace `localhost` with the name of any networked computer; this allows us to operate on a remote machine.

IISAO and VB

OK, so let us see this in action. We shall now study an example that uses IISAO/ADSI under the control of a simple VB application. The application will provide an operator with a single button to start and stop the Web server. The color of the form will change between green and red to highlight the state of the server.

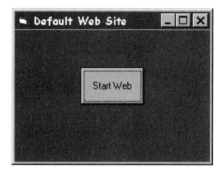

To get a reference to the object, we use the VB **GetObject** statement. To call the IIS Admin Objects we must execute the program under a user that has the IIS administrator privileges; Windows NT security will enforce this.

```
Dim objWebServer As IISNamespace

Set objWebServer = GetObject("IIS://localhost/w3svc/1")
```

We have assigned the object to the variable **objWebServer**, which is of type **IISNamespace**. This is made known to the project by setting a reference to the Active DS IIS Namespace Provider type library.

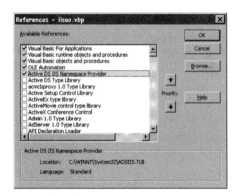

When the program is invoked, we can use the **ServerComment** property to set the window title bar.

```
Form1.Caption = objWebServer.ServerComment
```

Furthermore, we use the **ServerState** property to ascertain whether the Web server is currently started or not; the form can then be initiated appropriately.

```
Select Case objWebServer.ServerState
    Case MD_SERVER_STATE_STARTING, MD_SERVER_STATE_STARTED
        bStarted = True
    Case Else
        bStarted = False
End Select
```

When the user clicks on the button we can start and stop the Web server using the **start** and **stop** method calls.

```
Sub StopWeb()
    Call objWebServer.stop
End Sub
```

```
Sub StartWeb()
    Call objWebServer.start
End Sub
```

SOURCE CODE

Here is the source code, listed in its entirety:

```
Option Explicit
Const MD_SERVER_STATE_STARTING = 1
Const MD_SERVER_STATE_STARTED = 2

Dim bStarted As Boolean
Dim objWebServer As IISNamespace

Private Sub Command1_Click()

    If bStarted Then
        Call StopWeb
    Else
        Call StartWeb
    End If

    bStarted = Not bStarted
    Call UpdateForm

End Sub

Sub UpdateForm()

    If bStarted Then
        Form1.BackColor = vbGreen
        Command1.Caption = "Stop Web"
    Else
        Form1.BackColor = vbRed
        Command1.Caption = "Start Web"
    End If

End Sub

Sub StopWeb()
    Call objWebServer.stop
End Sub

Sub StartWeb()
    Call objWebServer.start
End Sub
```

(continued)

```
Private Sub Form_Load()
    Set objWebServer = GetObject("IIS://localhost/w3svc/1")

    Form1.Caption = objWebServer.ServerComment

    Select Case objWebServer.ServerState
        Case MD_SERVER_STATE_STARTING, MD_SERVER_STATE_STARTED
            bStarted = True
        Case Else
            bStarted = False
    End Select

    Call UpdateForm
End Sub
```

IISAO and Windows Scripting Host

By using the **Windows Scripting Host** we can invoke scripts at the command line to automate many standard administration tasks.

The Windows Scripting Host is a low-memory scripting host that conforms to the ActiveX Scripting architecture discussed in Chapter 7. This enables IIS administration scripts to be written in any ActiveX script language and includes VBScript, ECMAScript (JavaScript) plus a number of other languages developed by third parties. Such scripts can be invoked from the command prompt or the Start|Run menu.

A number of sample administration scripts are provided with IIS; these are located in the following directory:

%SystemRoot%\system32\inetsrv\adminsamples

There are many examples, but let us consider the two scripts called **startWeb.vbs** and **stopWeb.vbs**; these, unsurprisingly, can be used to start and stop one or more IIS Web servers. The following command-line arguments can be passed to the scripts:

Switch	Parameter
–computer or –c	machine_name [, machine_name2, . . . etc . . . .] This specifies the names of the computers (separated by commas) on which the Web servers are running. If the machine name is missing, the local machine is used.
–adspath or –a	server_no [, server_no2, . . . etc . . . .] This specifies the metabase index numbers (separated by commas) of the Web servers.
–verbose or –v	*None* This specifies that information messages about the actions being invoked are required.

For example, to start the two Web servers on a machine called harrison, we would invoke the command as shown below:

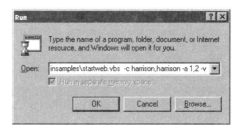

Because we specified the verbose parameter, we see the following messages:

If we examine, the **startWeb.vbs** and **stopWeb.vbs** files, we see that the main logic is similar to the VB version.

First the IISAO object identifier name is established, using the parameters passed; the name is shown in the above information messages, i.e., **IIS://harrison/W3vc/1** and **IIS://harrison/W3vc/2**.

Next, a reference to the object is established using the **GetObject** command and assigned to a local variable.

Finally the **Start** (or **Stop**) method is called on the object to invoke the required action.

Metabase

The configuration information for IIS4 is stored in a specially formatted file called the **Metabase**. This is different from its predecessor, IIS3, which stored the complete Web server configuration in the Windows Registry. The file is structured so that the IISAO object identifiers are keys to the various configuration items.

Microsoft has moved the configuration from the Registry to the Metabase for two key reasons: the need for speed and to support the large volumes of data that are now stored.

The Metabase is, at installation, called **metabase.bin** and located in the **%SystemRoot%\system32\inetsrv** directory.

The name and location of the Metabase can be amended from the defaults by adding the following Registry item to specify the completely new path and file name:

Local_Machine\Software\Microsoft\INetMgr\Parameters\MetaDataFile
(type RegSZ)

The Metabase should be located on an NTFS partition and have file permissions applied to protect it from direct and unwanted access.

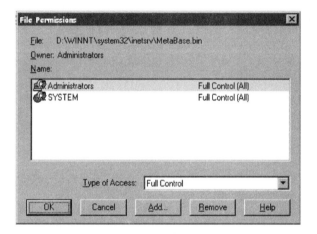

The Metabase must never be copied from one computer to another. To replicate changes from one computer to another, use the tool called **IISSync**, which is installed as part of IIS; it is located in the **%SystemRoot%\system32\inetsrv** directory. To replicate the Metabase to machine called harrison2, we would invoke the following instruction from a command prompt:

> IISSYNC harrison2

Metabase Backup

The Metabase should be regularly backed up. This can be done using facilities with the Internet Service Manager (MMC) by right-clicking on the computer and selecting the Backup/Restore Configuration menu option.

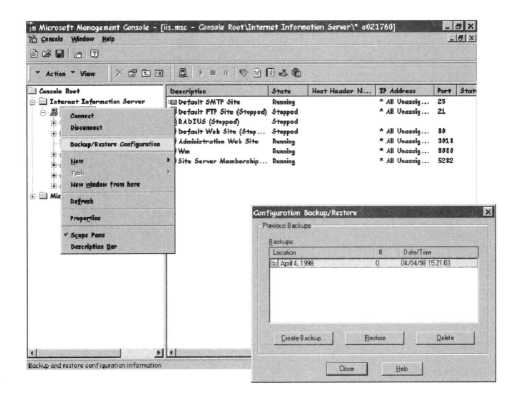

We could use IIS Admin Objects to create our backup/restore utility. Here 's a simple example:

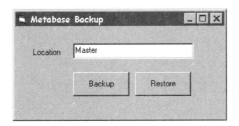

```
Option Explicit
Const MD_BACKUP_NEXT_VERSION = &HFFFFFFFF
Const MD_BACKUP_OVERWRITE = 1
Const MD_BACKUP_HIGHEST_VERSION = &HFFFFFFFE


Dim objComputer As IISComputer
```

(continued)

```
Private Sub butBackup_Click()
    On Local Error Resume Next

    Screen.MousePointer = vbHourglass
    objComputer.backup txtLocation.Text, _
                    MD_BACKUP_NEXT_VERSION, MD_BACKUP_OVERWRITE

    If Err Then
        MsgBox "Restore failure"
    End If

    Screen.MousePointer = vbDefault
End Sub

Private Sub butRestore_Click()
    On Local Error Resume Next

    Screen.MousePointer = vbHourglass
    objComputer.Restore txtLocation.Text, _
                    MD_BACKUP_HIGHEST_VERSION, 0

    If Err Then
        MsgBox "Restore failure"
    End If

    Screen.MousePointer = vbDefault
End Sub

Private Sub Form_Load()
    Set objComputer = GetObject("IIS://localhost")
End Sub
```

This time we create a reference to the **IISComputer** object and invoke the two methods, **backup** and **restore**, to manage the metabase.

```
Set objComputer = GetObject("IIS://localhost")
```

The metabase is backed up into a file located in the **%SystemRoot%\system32\inetsrv** directory. The name of the file is as entered by the user in the **txtLocation** field.

```
objComputer.backup txtLocation.Text, _
                MD_BACKUP_NEXT_VERSION, MD_BACKUP_OVERWRIT
```

The Web-based Internet Service Manager can also be used to save the metabase, but it does not have any facility to restore the configuration. The problem is that the **restore** method starts by shutting down all IIS services; then, after the metabase is restored, it restarts the services. Any Web server extension that invoked the **restore** method would be terminated in mid-flight.

Having seen the different ways of administering the Web Server, we shall round the section off by investigating how to control the groups of individuals allowed do the administering.

Web Site Operators

Web Site Operators are a group of Windows NT user accounts that are granted operator privileges for a specific Web site. Such a group is specified in the Internet Service Manager (MMC) via the Operators property sheet, which is opened by selecting the Web site in the MMC and then clicking on the Properties button.

Users can be added and deleted from the group by means of the Add and Remove buttons

Such operators have limited privileges and can only perform activities related to the individual Web site. Examples of tasks that can be performed include:

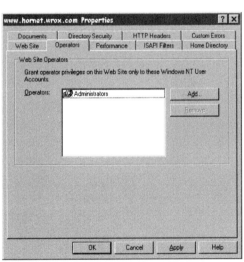

- Setting access permissions

- Enable/disable logging

- Setting the default document

- Setting content expiration

- Setting content ratings features

- Setting custom headers

A Web site operator cannot perform activities that would have global implications, i.e., affect IIS, the network, or Windows NT. Tasks that cannot be performed include:

- Changing or creating virtual roots
- Amending bandwidth throttling
- Changing the anonymous access configuration
- Changing the IP address or port number of the site
- Manipulating SSL connections or working with certificates

The Web site property sheets adjust themselves accordingly to match the user's level of privilege; any prohibited options are grayed out.

Accessing the Web Server

Like any Web server, the IIS Web service is responsible for handling an HTTP request, mapping the specified URL onto the server's file system, and obtaining the data to be sent back in the HTTP response. The URL may specify the name of a file (e.g., HTML, Graphics, Java Class, etc.), in which case the file is used in the response as is. Alternatively the URL may reference executable logic to be invoked e.g., an ASP page, an ISAPI extension, or a CGI process; and this enables response data to be generated dynamically.

In this section, we shall investigate the mechanisms provided by the Web server to control which users can access the resources on the system.

Web Directories

A Web surfer accessing our site cannot trawl across all files on the system. Files can only be exposed to remote Web browsers via HTTP if they appear in the directories configured for Web access. There are three different types of directories that can be configured for Web access:

- Home Directory
- Virtual Directory
- Subdirectory

We shall consider each type in turn.

Home Directory

An HTTP URL that contains just the domain name or an IP address actually references a document known as the **default document**, which is located in a directory called the **home directory**.

As an example, the URL

http://www.harrison.net/

would map to the default document located in the home directory on the server **www.harrison.net**. The default document is usually `default.htm` or `default.asp`, and typically provides the Web site's home page or index page.

A Web site administrator must map the home directory onto a physical file directory. For example:

http://www.harrison.net/

might map onto

`c:\inetpub\wwwroot`

Virtual Directory

To allow access to information not in the hierarchy beneath the home directory, a **virtual directory** must be configured. This is an alias that forms part of the URL and maps onto another physical file directory.

As an example, the URL

http://www.harrison.net/ecomm

might map onto `d:\commerce server`, and since no document is specified, the browser would again access the default document.

Virtual directories may also point to networked directories using the UNC naming convention (e.g., `\\harrison2\commerce server`).

A virtual directory does not give any clues to the user of the internal physical location of the files and directories. Furthermore, it can have its own set of properties that are independent from the remainder of the Web site.

Subdirectory

A **subdirectory** in a URL maps onto the corresponding item in the physical file structure. Expanding on the above example, the URL

http://www.harrison.net/ecomm/stores

would map onto

`d:\commerce server\stores`

In contrast to previous versions of IIS, the latest version allows subdirectories to have different properties than their parent directory. For example, a home directory only allowing read access could have a subdirectory called **scripts** with contents allocated to execute permissions. This greatly simplifies the configuration; in many IIS3 configurations, numerous virtual directories were often defined with no purpose other than to overcome this limitation.

Creating Directories

Using the Internet Service Manager (MMC), we can add a new site and configure the home directory.

This is done by selecting the server, right-clicking, and choosing the Create New|Web Site menu option, which invokes the New Web Site Wizard. The wizard dialogs request:

- The Web site description
- The TCP/IP address/port number (usually port 80)
- The physical path name for the home directory
- The directory access permissions (to be explained shortly)

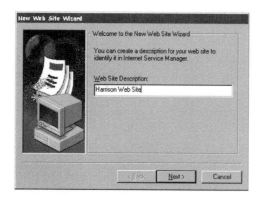

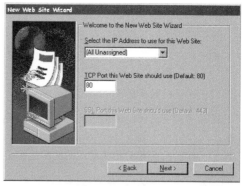

In a similar manner, we can use the MMC to configure a virtual root.

This is done by selecting the Web site/directory, right-clicking, and choosing the Create New|Virtual Directory menu option, which invokes the New Virtual Directory Wizard. The wizard dialogs request:

- The virtual directory alias
- The physical path name for the home directory
- The directory access permissions

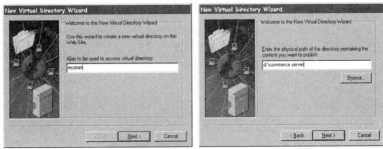

Subdirectories need not be defined in the IIS4 configuration. If we create a subdirectory within the physical directory it will appear in the MMC namespace (after selecting the Action|Refresh menu option).

Note in the following screenshot the different icons for a subdirectory (script) and a virtual directory (ecomm).

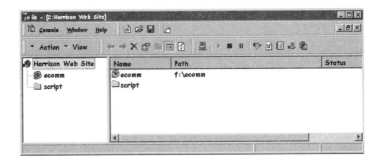

Access Permissions

The IIS Web service facilities are built upon the Windows NT security model. This means that all files and directories are protected by ACL permissions, as described in Chapter 2. All users accessing the Web service are either given guest access or are authenticated against the Windows NTDS database (as we will see below), and then given appropriate access to the various objects.

Further to this, additional security can be applied to a Web directory by means of the Internet Service Manager (MMC). We first select the property sheets by right-clicking on the directory and selecting the properties menu option; then we select one of the following tabs: Home Directory, Virtual Directory, or Directory, depending on the type of directory we are working with.

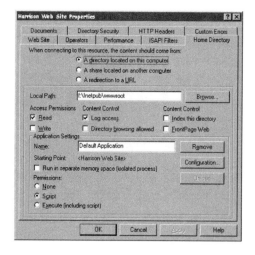

The Web Directory's Access Permissions allows Read and Write permissions to be applied to the contents of IIS directories. Enabling these checkboxes allows:

- Read—when enabled, Web users may read or download files located in the directory
- Write—when enabled, Web users may upload files or change the content of files located in the directory

Furthermore, the Application Settings Permissions specify whether applications located in this directory may be executed. IIS enforces this security in addition to the NT security. The options are:

- None—no items located in this directory may be invoked
- Script—only scripts, such as ASP documents, located in this directory may be invoked
- Execute—any application (with appropriate Execute NTFS ACLs) located in this directory may be invoked. Enabling this is not advised, although the level of risk exposed by this option is dependent on the executables in the directory.

> We shall see below how to use Windows NT Security to control access to files and directory. At this stage, we must appreciate that IIS Security works in combination with Windows NT Security.

Content Control

There are several other properties on the Directory property sheet that specify how the IIS handles the Web content. The Log Access and FrontPage Web checkboxes will be considered later in this chapter. The Index this directory notifies Index server to include the content in its search indexes; since this has no relevance to security, it will not be considered further in this book.

The Directory Browsing Allowed checkbox means that a hypertext directory listing is generated if the user navigates to the directory by specifying a URL without a filename and if there is no default document. This enables a user to navigate through the directory structure by clicking on the filename and directory names.

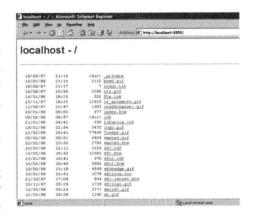

Because directory browsing acts a bit like Windows Explorer and discloses the structure of the Web site, we would generally leave this option disabled.

IP Controls

The Web service can be configured to either allow or deny access from machines in a range of IP addresses or from a particular domain name (e.g., harrison.net). This can be useful for restricting access to particular organizations or making access difficult for competitors.

> **Restricting access by a domain name requires a lookup on every request; this will have a dramatic impact on performance.**

It is not always possible to restrict access to specific users using this technique. The lack of available IP addresses means that many networks use techniques for randomly allocating IP addresses from an available pool when the client first starts; if this is done, it would not be possible to guarantee the identity of the user from the IP address.

The configuration of allowed/denied IP addresses uses the IP Address and Domain Name Restrictions Manager section of the Directory Security property sheet.

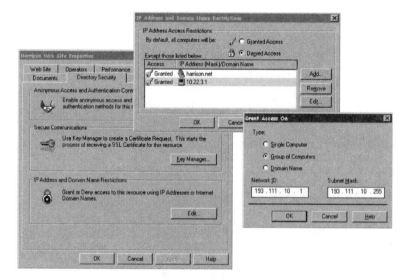

In Chapter 3 we learned that TCP/IP services, such as a Web Server, can be configured to operate on any port number that is not used by another service. If we have a known set of approved users, or a **closed user group** (CUG), we can use this to good effect.

By changing the port number of our WWW service to something other than the normal port 80, we can make life awkward for casual surfers. All we need to do is notify all site members of the URL plus port number to use.

The port number is configured using the Web Site property sheet.

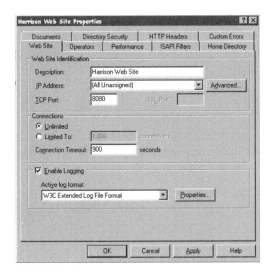

Users can access the HTTP service on a specific port by specifying the number as part of the URL. For example,

http://www.harrison.net:8080/

would initiate an HTTP request on port **8080**.

If the port number is not specified, the browser will default to port 80. Anyone attempting to access the site without knowing about its CUG port number would get a failure.

This technique cannot be relied upon in isolation to keep people out. In Chapter 3, we saw that some hackers will attack a Web site using a port scanner on the site. Recapping, this is a program that attempts to establish a TCP/IP connection on every port in a specified range. All established connections are reported and a complete list of ports for a potential attack found.

User Authentication by the Web Server

In Chapter 2, we discussed how Windows NT resources are protected using permissions and that all users accessing the resource were first authenticated and then their permissions checked to either grant or deny the access.

IIS Security works in a similar manner and is tightly integrated with Windows NT Security. All Web resources (e.g., HTML files) are protected using permissions and can only be accessed by users who have the correct permissions granted. All users browsing on the Web site are associated with a Windows NT user account. Once a user has been identified, IIS runs under the security context of that user—this is called **impersonation.**

Authentication

IIS supports several mechanisms for authenticating the user. These are configured by means of the Authentication Methods dialog, which is accessed using the Anonymous Access and Authentication Control button on the Directory Security property sheet.

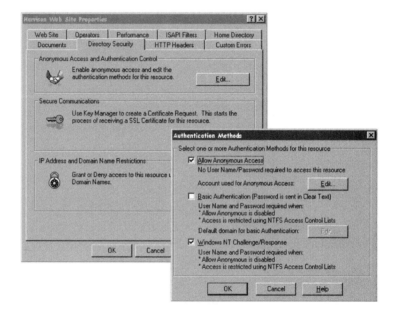

The authentication methods available are:

- **Anonymous**—if enabled, users may browse the site anonymously using a guest account; this means that they do not supply any credentials that identify themselves.

- **Basic Authentication**—if enabled, users are authenticated using the method defined in the HTTP specifications from the World Wide Web Consortium (W3C).

- **Windows NT Challenge/Response**—if enabled, users are authenticated using the Microsoft NTLM authentication method discussed in Chapter 2.

The checkboxes for all of these methods work independently, meaning that it is possible to enable multiple authentication mechanisms, and the appropriate one is then automatically used for a request.

We shall now discuss how anonymous users are handled, following this with an investigation on the key differences between Basic Authentication and Windows NT Challenge/Response.

The IUSR Account—Anonymous Authentication

When IIS is installed, it creates a user account called **IUSR_sysname** where **sysname** is the computer name of the Windows NT system, as specified in the Identification tab of the Network Control Panel. The **IUSR_sysname** account is assigned to the Guests account group, allocated a random password, and given the user right to Log On Locally, which is a prerequisite to access the IIS WWW services.

A user who accesses our site anonymously will operate under the security context of the **IUSR_sysname** account. This means that access is restricted to resources with the permissions allocated to the **IUSR_sysname** account.

The Edit button on the Authentication Methods dialog allows the configuration of the Anonymous user account.

The Enable Automatic Password Synchronization means that you don't have to enter the anonymous password in both the Internet Service Manager (MMC) and the User Manager.

Basic and Windows NT Challenge/Response Authentication

The Basic Authentication and Windows NT Challenge/Response mechanisms work in similar fashions. If the user requests a resource for which the **IUSR_sysname** user account does not have the appropriate permissions, the request is rejected with a 401 Access Denied message, and the browser is informed through HTTP what authentication methods the server will support.

Provided that a least one of these two authentication methods has been enabled at the server, most modern browsers will then prompt the user for a user name and password, and submit these details with another request for the same resource. IIS will then validate the user account details supplied, and if successful will invoke the request under the identity of this user rather than the **IUSR_sysname** account. If this new user account has been granted suitable permissions to access the resource, the resource will be returned; otherwise the process is repeated and the user is again prompted for a set of user credentials.

The difference between Basic Authentication and Windows NT Challenge/Response is that the latter does not send the password across the wire (this was explained back in Chapter 2). In contrast, Basic Authentication sends this information in a format called Base64 that is very easy to decipher. At the time of writing, the only browser to support Windows NT Challenge/Response was Microsoft's Internet Explorer.

> The undesirable transmission of user names and passwords in Base64 format can be overcome using Secure Channel Services encryption, which we will meet in Chapter 5. When Basic Authentication has been used, the user name/password is included in every subsequent HTTP request—thus the encryption must be used for the complete session and not just for the authentication stage.

There is another advantage to using Windows NT Challenge/Response authentication methods and Internet Explorer in an Intranet environment where a user has already logged on to a Windows domain. In this case, the browser will automatically attempt to use the user's domain credentials in the authentication process. This will happen automatically and transparently to the user, thus improving the user's experience and providing seamless integration with the existing infrastructure.

We shall now look at these authentication mechanisms in further detail by studying some HTTP trace files.

> More information about HTTP, including the protocol specification, can be found at:
>
> http://www.w3.org/Protocols/

Authentication in Action

The following trace files are from an example scenario that shows in detail the different processing for each of the authentication mechanisms supported by IIS.

> In this example, the machine name is **harrison**.

ANONYMOUS AUTHENTICATION

First, let us study an HTTP trace file for **Anonymous Authentication**; here the user account **harrison\IUSR_harrison** has Read permission for a file called **/rich/rhnav.htm**:

29/06/98 23:40:23 Sent	*GET/rich/rhnav.htm HTTP/1.0* *Accept: image/gif, image/x-xbitmap, image/jpeg, image/pjpeg,* *application/vnd.ms-excel, application/msword,* *application/vnd.ms-powerpoint, */** *Accept-Language: en* *User-Agent: Mozilla/2.0 (compatible; MSIE 3.0B; Win32)* *Host: 194.1.1.32* *Connection: Keep-Alive*	This is the request message sent from the browser to the Web server, to request the resource.

29/06/98 23:40:23 Received	*HTTP/1.0 200 OK* *Server: Microsoft-IIS/4.0* *Connection: keep-alive* *Date: Mon, 29 Jun 1998 23:40:23 GMT* *Content-Type: text/html* *Accept-Ranges: bytes* *Last-Modified: Sun, 28 Jun 1998 19:34:16 GMT* *Content-Length: 1653* *<html>* *. . . . etc . . . .* *</html>*	This is the response message, including the contents of the requested HTML file.

Here, the request contains no account information about the user, just the user's Host IP Address. The Web server accesses the requested file by impersonating the **IUSR_harrison** account; Windows NT security ensures that it can access the file, and then IIS returns it to the requestor.

BASIC AUTHENTICATION

Next, we will see how Basic Authentication works. Both Anonymous Authentication and Basic Authentication have been enabled in the Authentication Methods dialog. The difference this time is that:

- The **harrison\IUSR_harrison** account *does not* have Read permission for the file
- The **harrison\rich** account *does* have Read access

30/06/98 14:52:49 Sent	*GET/rich/rhnav.htm HTTP/1.0* *Accept: image/gif, image/x-xbitmap, image/jpeg, image/pjpeg,* *application/vnd.ms-excel, application/msword,* *application/vnd.ms-powerpoint, */** *Accept-Language: en* *User-Agent: Mozilla/2.0 (compatible; MSIE 3.0B; Win32)* *Host: 194.1.1.32* *Connection: Keep-Alive* --	This is the request message sent from the browser to the Web server, to request the file. It is the same as the last time, of course, with no user account information.

30/06/98 14:52:49 Received	*HTTP/1.0 401 Access Denied* *WWW-Authenticate: Basic realm="194.1.1.32"* *Content-Length: 24* *Content-Type: text/html* *Error: Access is Denied.* --	This is the response rejecting access, as the **IUSR_harrison** account does not have appropriate permissions. In the second line it informs the browser that Basic Authentication is enabled.

The browser then prompts for the account name and password. The account name can be fully qualified with a preceding domain name, e.g., **harrison\rich**

30/06/98 14:53:23 Sent	*GET/rich/rhnav.htm HTTP/1.0* *Accept: image/gif, image/x-xbitmap, image/jpeg, image/pjpeg,* *application/vnd.ms-excel, application/msword,* *application/vnd.ms-powerpoint, */** *Accept-Language: en* *User-Agent: Mozilla/2.0 (compatible; MSIE 3.0B; Win32)* *Host: 194.1.1.32* *Connection: Keep-Alive* *Authorization: Basic YWRtaW5pc3RyYXRvcjpob3JuZXQ=* --	This is the new request message (now including the account information) sent from the browser to the Web server to request the resource. Though the account information looks encrypted it is in fact only Base64 encoded. The account name and password can easily be deciphered.

> **Base64 encoding is explained in Chapter 8.**

30/06/98 14:53:23 Received	*HTTP/1.0 200 OK* *Server: Microsoft-IIS/4.0* *Connection: keep-alive* *Date: Tue, 30 Jun 1998 14:53:23 GMT* *Content-Type: text/html* *Accept-Ranges: bytes* *Last-Modified: Mon, 29 Jun 1998 09:18:08 GMT* *Content-Length: 909* *<html>* *. . . . . . etc . . . . . .* *</html>* --	The account details sent from the browser have been successfully validated. This is the response message including the contents of the file.

This process allows the Web server to retrieve files by simply passing on the user's account and password. Because the Web server is impersonating the user, Windows NT security will allow access to the file if the user has the correct permissions.

WINDOWS NT CHALLENGE/RESPONSE (NTLM)

Last, let us look at the most complex of the three methods, **Windows NT Challenge/Response** (NTLM). This time, all three types of authentication have been enabled in the Authentication Methods dialog, and again the **harrison\IUSR_harrison** does not have Read permission for the file but the **harrison\rich** account *does*.

This trace should be studied in conjunction with the diagram provided in Chapter 2 that illustrates the messaging involved in the NTLM authentication process.

30/06/98 11:28:50 Sent	*GET/rich/innav.htm HTTP/1.0* *Accept: image/gif, image/x-xbitmap, image/jpeg, image/pjpeg,* *application/vnd.ms-excel, application/msword,* *application/vnd.ms-powerpoint, */** *Accept-Language: en* *User-Agent: Mozilla/2.0 (compatible; MSIE 3.0B; Win32)* *Host: 194.1.1.32* *Connection: Keep-Alive*	This is the request message sent from the browser to the Web server, to request the resource.
	--	
30/06/98 11:28:50 Received	*HTTP/1.0 401 Access Denied* *WWW-Authenticate: NTLM* *WWW-Authenticate: Basic realm="194.1.1.32"* *Content-Length: 24* *Content-Type: text/html* *Error: Access is Denied.*	This is the response rejecting access, as the **IUSR_harrison** account does not have appropriate permissions. This time it informs the browser that both Basic Authentication and Challenge/ Response (NTLM) are enabled.
	--	The browser will now attempt
30/06/98 11:28:51 Sent	*GET/rich/innav.htm HTTP/1.0* *Accept: image/gif, image/x-xbitmap, image/jpeg, image/pjpeg,* *application/vnd.ms-excel, application/msword,* *application/vnd.ms-powerpoint, */** *Accept-Language: en* *User-Agent: Mozilla/2.0 (compatible; MSIE 3.0B; Win32)* *Host: 194.1.1.32* *Connection: Keep-Alive* *Authorization: NTLM TlRMTVNTUAABAAAA7IAAAMAAwAn* 　　　　　*AAAABwAHACAAAABBMDIxMjgwQUNMAAAA* 　　　　　*QAAAAAAAABAAAAAclAAA==*	authentication using the same account information that the user is currently logged onto the Windows network with. This all happens transparently to the user. 　This message is the client submitting: • the user name • the computer name • the domain
	--	This information is sent on by IIS to the authenticator (PDC or BDC) and is used to generate the **Challenge**.

30/06/98	HTTP/1.0 401 Access Denied	This message contains the
11:28:51	WWW-Authenticate: NTLM TlRMTVNTUAACAAAAAAAA	**Challenge**.
Received	CgAAAABwgAAFoycWyKaYbMAAAAAkJMVAE==	

HTTP/1.0 401 Access Denied
WWW-Authenticate: NTLM TlRMTVNTUAACAAAAAAAA
CgAAAABwgAAFoycWyKaYbMAAAAAkJMVAE==
Connection: keep-alive
Content-Length: 24
Content-Type: text/html
Error: Access is Denied.

30/06/98
11:28:51
Sent

GET/rich/innav.htm HTTP/1.0
Accept: image/gif, image/x-xbitmap, image/jpeg, image/pjpeg,
application/vnd.ms-excel, application/msword,
*application/vnd.ms-powerpoint, */**
Accept-Language: en
User-Agent: Mozilla/2.0 (compatible; MSIE 3.0B; Win32)
Host: 194.1.1.32
Connection: Keep-Alive
Authorization: NTLM
TlRMTVNTUAADAAAAAAAAEAAAAAAAAAQ
AAAAAAAABAAAAAAAAAEAAAAAAAAAQ
AAAAAAAABAAAAAClAAA==

The browser then uses the password and the Challenge to calculate the **Response** which is seen in this message.

This information is sent on by IIS to authenticator, which knows the user's password and the Challenge. It too can calculate the expected Response and compare it with the actual Response received, thus determining whether the user has the correct credentials.

The password is never sent over the wire.

At this point, IIS will run under the security context of the currently logged Windows domain user account. If the user has permission for the file, it will now be returned—just like Basic Authentication.

For our example scenario, to keep it interesting, we shall not make things so simple!

Let us assume that this Windows NT user account does not have Read permission for the requested file. Windows NT security, and therefore the IIS, will deny the request:

30/06/98
11:28:51
Received

HTTP/1.0 401 Access Denied
WWW-Authenticate: NTLM
WWW-Authenticate: Basic realm="194.1.1.32"
Content-Length: 24
Content-Type: text/html
Error: Access is Denied.

This is the response message that rejects access because the user account currently logged on does not have the appropriate permissions.

The browser now prompts for the user's account name and password.

30/06/98 11:29:38 Sent	GET/rich/innav.htm HTTP/1.0 Accept: image/gif, image/x-xbitmap, image/jpeg, image/pjpeg, application/vnd.ms-excel, application/msword, application/vnd.ms-powerpoint, */* Accept-Language: en User-Agent: Mozilla/2.0 (compatible; MSIE 3.0B; Win32) Host: 194.1.1.32 Connection: Keep-Alive Authorization: NTLM TlRMTVNTUAABAAAAA5IAAAMAAwAgAAAAAAAAAAAAA BBQ0wAAAAAAAAAAAAQAAAAAAAABAAAAAclAAA==	This is the new request message, which now includes the newly entered user name plus the machine name/domain name. This information is included in another request for the Web resource.
30/06/98 11:29:38 Received	HTTP/1.0 401 Access Denied WWW-Authenticate: NTLM TlRMTVNTUAACAAAAAAAACgAAAABgg AA5oKRq7FlM0QAAAAAAAAAA== Connection: keep-alive Content-Length: 24 Content-Type: text/html Error: Access is Denied.	This is the **Challenge** message that is sent back from the server.
30/06/98 11:29:38 Sent	GET/rich/innav.htm HTTP/1.0 Accept: image/gif, image/x-xbitmap, image/jpeg, image/pjpeg, application/vnd.ms-excel, application/msword, application/vnd.ms-powerpoint, */* Accept-Language: en User-Agent: Mozilla/2.0 (compatible; MSIE 3.0B; Win32) Host: 194.1.1.32 Connection: Keep-Alive Authorization: NTLM TlRMTVNTUAADAAAAGAAYAHYAAAAYABgAjg AAAA4ADgBAAAAAGgAaAE4AAAAOAA4AaAAAAAAAAACm AAAAAYIAAEEAMAAyADEAMgA4ADAAYQBkAG0AaQBu AGkAcwB0AHIAYQB0AG8AcgBBADAAMgAxADIAOAAw AByc4FDb+4fwflx6Qtntd5lrkgegMrMWjacvu349PykEav Y87CleD/lbMq4KSTedMg==	Here is the **Response** to the Challenge, calculated using the entered password.
30/06/98 11:29:38 Received	HTTP/1.0 200 OK Server: Microsoft-IIS/4.0 Connection: keep-alive Date: Tue, 30 Jun 1998 11:29:38 GMT Content-Type: text/html Accept-Ranges: bytes Last-Modified: Mon, 29 Jun 1998 09:18:08 GMT Content-Length: 909 <html> . . . . . etc . . . . . </html>	**Hurray!!** The entered account details have now been successfully validated and our user identified. The entered user has suitable permissions to read the requested resource; it is returned appended on the end of the response message.

It is only after the Web browser provides details of a valid user account with suitable permissions granted for the requested file that the Web server is allowed to retrieve the file and return the contents back to the desktop.

This allows the administrator to effectively divide up the resources on the site. Some can be available to individual users, who have to supply the relevant passwords before they can access them, while others can be freely available to everyone. The use of virtual roots and subdirectories helps facilitate this and makes the application of permissions simpler (i.e., easier than applying permissions on an individual file basis).

Delegation

We shall now turn to a security pitfall often encountered by IIS Web site designers and first mentioned back in Chapter 2: the problem with the delegation of security credentials.

As was seen in the preceding discussion, when a Web user is authenticated using the Windows NT Challenge/Response mechanism, IIS does not actually receive a copy of the user's password. Instead IIS4 receives a hash of the username/password which it passes on to the domain controller for verification.

This can cause a problem if there is any ASP logic that requires access to a resource on another Windows NT machine. The remote machine will initially challenge IIS for proof of identification, but IIS will be unable to participate in this authentication protocol because it does not have a copy of the user's password and so cannot generate the appropriate messages.

This problem does not occur for Basic or Anonymous authentication. In both cases the server has the password for the account being impersonated.

When we originally mentioned this problem in Chapter 2, we discussed a solution expected in the near future. This solution is **Kerberos** security and is targeted for release as part of Windows 2000.

Password Expiry

A facility is built into the IIS authentication processing to automatically notify the user if the password for its Windows NT user account is about to or has expired.

This feature also gives the user the opportunity at this stage to change its password.

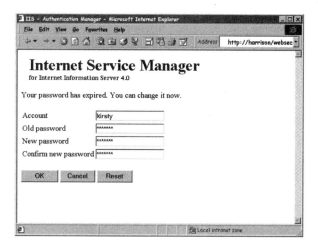

Note the padlock icon on the window's status bar. It indicates that the browser is using a security protocol called SSL that encrypts messages, prevents message tampering, and enables authentication. We shall explain SSL in Chapter 5.

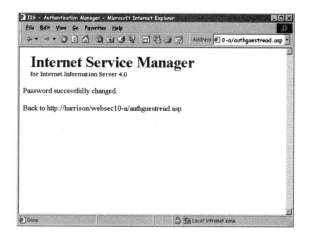

The following metabase properties control this feature:

PasswordCacheTTL specifies how frequently the user is notified that its password is about to expire. The default setting is 600 (in seconds).

PasswordChangeFlags is a bit map specifying the processing mode for the password change and notification. Values are:

- 0—Password change must operate on a secured channel. This is the default.

- 1—Password change may operate on an unsecured channel.
- 2—Password change notification is disabled.
- 4—Advance notification of password change is disabled.

PasswordExpirePrenotifyDays specifies the time remaining before the client's password will expire, and is used to indicate when an advance notification of password change will be sent. The default setting is 14.

Unfortunately, there is no user interface to change these values, so we must resort to a small Visual Basic routine. In the following program the configuration is changed to allow the password change to be done on a normal unsecured channel.

```
Private Sub butGo_Click()
Dim IIsObj, vDay

Set IIsObj = GetObject("IIS://LocalHost/W3SVC")

Cls
Print "PasswordCacheTTL=" & _
    IIsObj.PasswordCacheTTL
Print "PasswordChangeFlags =" & _
    IIsObj.PasswordChangeFlags
Print "PasswordExpirePrenotifyDays =" & _
    IIsObj.PasswordExpirePrenotifyDays
Print

'Allow password update to occur over an unsecured channel
IIsObj.Put "PasswordChangeFlags", 1
IIsObj.SetInfo

Print "Updated: PasswordChangeFlags =" & _
    IIsObj.PasswordChangeFlags
End Sub
```

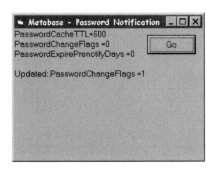

Now, because the padlock icon is no longer present, we can confirm that the password was updated over an unsecured channel

IIS Logging

IIS provides facilities to record the user's Web site activity by logging information in ASCII text files or an ODBC-compliant database. This information can be used to:

- Audit visitors who have accessed the site
- Troubleshoot security problems (used in conjunction with NT Object auditing, discussed earlier)
- Analyze the amount of traffic in order to capacity plan for future growth
- Spot the popular areas of the site and detect trends in the way users navigate through the site

IIS logging is enabled from the **Web Site** property sheet for the Web server. From here, we can select from the following formats:

- **W3C Extended Log File Format**—a customizable ASCII format that allows us to choose from a list of items those we need and wish to be included; this format has been defined by the World Wide Web consortium
- **NCSA Common Log File Format**—a fixed ASCII format that has been defined by the National Center for Supercomputing Applications
- **Microsoft IIS Log Format**—a fixed ASCII format ... compatible with earlier versions of IIS
- **ODBC Logging**—a fixed format logged to a database

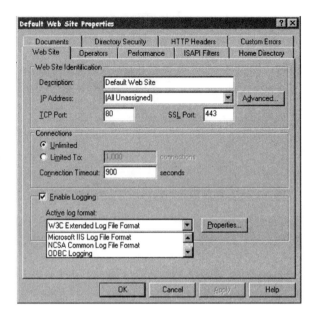

By selecting the **Properties** button, we can set various configuration values for the logging process. The dialog that is displayed will differ for each type of log format. The following screen dumps show the properties for the W3C Log File Format

The General Properties sheet allows us to specify the folder where the log files are generated.

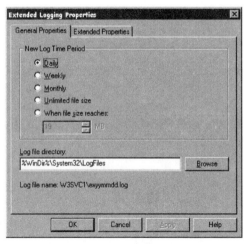

We can also specify either the time period that elapses or the maximum the file size can reach before the logging cuts over to a new file.

This sheet is similar for the other two ASCII logo formats. For ODCB Logging, this sheet requests the ODBC Data Source Name, the table name, and a user's name/password.

The Extended Properties sheet is only applicable for the W3C Log File Format. It enables us to select the items we wish to be included in the log file.

If the machine runs out of disk space, then IIS logging will shut down and a warning will be generated in the Windows NT Event log.

Interpreting the ASCII Log Files

ASCII Format log files can be inspected using a text editor, such as Notepad. There will be one entry for each HTTP request received.

The following example is from the top of a W3C Extended Log File Format, and the entries included match those in the previous screen dump that were selected for inclusion. The #Fields entry in the header lists those items that will be logged and is used by analysis tools to know how to interpret the subsequent data.

When an item is not available, a dash character is used as placeholder. In this example, there are several entries that the Referrer item is not available.

```
#Software: Microsoft Internet Information Server 4.0
#Version: 1.0
#Date: 1998-09-01 19:23:36
#Fields: time c-ip cs-method cs-uri-stem sc-status cs(Referer)
19:23:36 127.0.0.1 GET/iisHelp/iis/misc/default.asp 200 -
19:23:36 127.0.0.1 GET/iisHelp/iis/misc/navbar.asp 200
        http://localhost/iisHelp/iis/misc/default.asp
19:23:36 127.0.0.1 GET/iisHelp/iis/misc/contents.asp 200
        http://localhost/iisHelp/iis/misc/default.asp
```

(continued)

```
19:23:36 127.0.0.1 GET/iisHelp/iis/htm/core/iiwltop.htm 304
         http://localhost/iisHelp/iis/misc/default.asp
19:23:36 127.0.0.1 GET/iisHelp/iis/misc/Cont.gif 304
         http://localhost/iisHelp/iis/misc/contents.asp
19:23:36 127.0.0.1 GET/iisHelp/iis/misc/NoIndex.gif 304
         http://localhost/iisHelp/iis/misc/contents.asp
19:23:36 127.0.0.1 GET/iisHelp/iis/misc/NoSearch.gif 304
         http://localhost/iisHelp/iis/misc/contents.asp
19:23:36 127.0.0.1 GET/iisHelp/iis/misc/print.gif 304
         http://localhost/iisHelp/iis/misc/contents.asp
19:23:36 127.0.0.1 GET/iisHelp/iis/misc/synch.gif 304
         http://localhost/iisHelp/iis/misc/contents.asp
19:23:36 127.0.0.1 GET/iisHelp/iis/misc/ismhd.gif 304
         http://localhost/iisHelp/iis/misc/navbar.asp
19:23:36 127.0.0.1 GET/iisHelp/iis/misc/navpad.gif 304
         http://localhost/iisHelp/iis/misc/navbar.asp
19:23:36 127.0.0.1 GET/iisHelp/iis/htm/core/opgstop.asp 200 -
19:23:36 127.0.0.1 GET/iisHelp/iis/misc/MS_logo.gif 304
         http://localhost/iisHelp/iis/misc/navbar.asp
19:23:36 127.0.0.1 GET/iisHelp/iis/misc/cohhc.hhc 304 -
19:23:36 127.0.0.1 GET/iishelp/common/coua.css 304
         http://localhost/iisHelp/iis/htm/core/opgstop.asp
```

There are several tools available that generate sophisticated reports from the information stored in these log files. Microsoft has included such a tool in Microsoft Site Server and a reduced functionality version in Site Server Express (supplied as a component in the Windows NT 4.0 Option Pack).

FrontPage/Visual InterDev Security

We shall now look at an addition security model for IIS that is implemented by the two Microsoft Web development tools: **FrontPage** and **Visual Inter-Dev**. Both of these products use what is known as **FrontPage Server Extensions** to apply file permissions for accessing and amending Web content.

Up to now, to control Web access we have been using the Windows Explorer to manually apply appropriate Windows NT permissions directly to the files/folders. By using tools that support the FrontPage Server Extensions, we have a more appropriate mechanism to apply Web permissions and one that ensures they are applied in a manner both consistent and error-free.

With FrontPage security there are three types of users:

- **Browsers**—end-users who may view content.
- **Authors**—users who may add/delete/modify Web content. Also assigned **Browsers** permissions.
- **Administrators**—high-privilege users who may create/delete Web sites and change permissions. Also assigned Authors and Browsers permissions.

FrontPage Server Extensions, when installed, are applied to the root directory of a Web site. All content in this directory and subdirectories will be protected using the Browsers, Authors, and Administrators security model. This security will be applied uniformly to all items. Specific permissions cannot be applied on an individual file or directory basis.

In addition, a named subdirectory off the root directory may be created to contain an independent Web; Visual InterDev calls this a **Web Application,** and FrontPage calls this a **Sub-Web**. By default, a Web Application will inherit the permissions applied to the root Web; any changes made to the root permissions will be automatically applied to those that are inheriting permissions from it. Alternatively, a Web Application can be configured to exercise its own independent permissions.

When we set/amend the permissions for a user or a group, behind the scenes the FrontPage Server Extensions are modifying the ACLs on the directories. From then on, the security implemented is the standard IIS/Windows NT Security to which we are now (hopefully!) accustomed.

Within the Web directory hierarchy, FrontPage creates a number of directories beginning with **_vti_ . . .** which are used to store FrontPage configuration data and some software extensions that implement Web server extensions. The FrontPage Security is implemented by a number of ISAPI DLLs located in the **_vti_ . . .** directories as shown below:

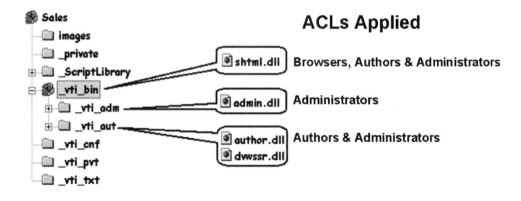

The development tools communicate with the following ISAPI DLLs by using HTTP POST messages:

- **admin.dll**—is used to implement administrative functions, e.g., change permissions. FrontPage will apply NT security permissions such that Administrators can invoke this.

- **author.dll** and **dvwssr.dll**—are used to implement authoring functions, e.g., open a Web for editing, get file for editing. FrontPage will apply NT security permissions such that Authors can invoke this.

The FrontPage Server Extensions also use the following ISAPI DLL at run-time:

- **shtml.dll**—is used to handle FrontPage functions that dynamically generate HTML at run-time (called **WebBots**). FrontPage will apply NT security permissions such that all Browser users can invoke this.

If we inspect the IIS properties for the **_vti_bin** node, we see that the software beneath the node has been given IIS execute permissions.

Setting Permissions

Permissions on a Web with FrontPage Server Extensions are configured using a dialog that is instantiated using the Project|Web Project|Web Permissions menu option in Visual InterDev, or the Tools|Permissions menu option in FrontPage. The two products use similar dialogs, but each uses its own terminology within the screen text.

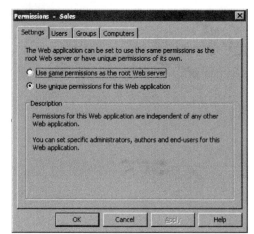

The Settings property sheet will only be displayed if the Web is not the root Web.

This allows us to specify whether the permissions are to be inherited from the root Web or we are to set our own.

If the permissions are the same as the root Web, then the other property sheets can only be used to view the permissions.

The Users property sheet allows us to define the permissions for individual users, i.e., whether they can Administer, Author, and/or Browse.

The radio buttons toggle between enforcing all end-users to be defined and allowing unrestricted access to all (i.e., providing access to the **IUSR_sysname** anonymous user account)

We can add a user by means of the **Add** button. This displays all users configured with the NT Security database and allows names and granted permissions to be selected.

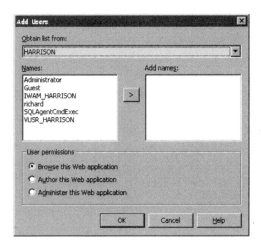

We can edit the permissions by clicking on the name and selecting the **Edit** button. The displayed dialog allows the required permissions to be chosen.

The groups property sheet allows us to define the permissions for groups of users.

We can add a group by means of the **Add** button. This displays all user groups configured with the NT Security database and allows groups and granted permissions to be selected.

Note that when FrontPage Server Extensions are installed, the Windows NT Security Administrators group is given by default FrontPage Administer, Author, and Browser access rights.

Similarly, we can edit the permissions by clicking on the group and selecting the **Edit** button. The displayed dialog allows the required permissions to be chosen.

The **Computers** property sheet allows us to define the permissions for users accessing from a particular computer. These permissions work in combination with the user/group permissions, with the more restrictive of the two taking precedence.

We can add a computer by means of the **Add** button. This allows the IP address of the computer and granted permissions to be selected.

Multiple computers within a range of IP addresses can be set using the "*" wildcard.

By clicking on the computer and selecting the Edit button, we can change the permissions assigned to the computer. The displayed dialog allows the required permissions to be chosen.

■ Summary

In this chapter we have investigated the core features provided by IIS and seen how it is tightly integrated with the Windows NT security model.

The key points in the chapter are:

- IIS can be administered using the supplied tools or by homegrown scripts/programs.
- The IIS configuration is now stored in a file called the Metabase; this has been optimized to achieve speed and to support the large volumes of data that are required.
- The use of virtual roots and subdirectories helps organize a site and simplifies the security configuration, since the permissions can be applied on a directory basis rather than an individual file basis.
- The Windows NT Challenge/Response authentication mechanisms do not send the password over the wire and so can be regarded as a more secure solution than the alternative Basic Authentication; in addition they enable seamless integration across an existing Windows NT networking infrastructure.
- Windows NT Challenge/Response authentication cannot be used when IIS has to access external resources under the user's security context.
- Audit trails of user activity can be used for various tasks, including tracking down security breaches, billing, capacity planning, and determining the most popular areas of the site.

• Setting the permissions across a Web site can be simplified using FrontPage server extensions; this facility ensures that security permissions are applied in a consistent and error-free manner.

The discussion in this chapter shows that Microsoft considers the security offered by IIS to be of paramount importance and has delivered an excellent solution.

In the preceding chapters we several times hinted at the advantages offered by Secure Channels; the time has now come to visit this topic.

Secure Channels

Our next task is to investigate in detail a security technology, first introduced in Chapter 3, which provides a further level of security that can be used in conjunction with the measures we have seen so far. This security technology is called **secure channels** and is provided by a layer of networking software known as the **secure channel services**.

A secure channel is a point-to-point network connection that provides end-point authentication, nonrepudiation, message encryption, and message authentication—in fact, all the weapons needed to defeat the charlatans, spies, and vandals first encountered in Chapter 1.

Secure channels rely on another security technology called **digital certificates.** Today, we frequently need to identify ourselves, using passports, credit cards, driver's licenses, identity cards, and so on. The next generation of equivalent assurance

149

mechanisms suitable for the digital age is likely to employ digital certificates stored on portable media, such as smartcards.

In this chapter we shall discuss:

- What is provided by secure channels services
- The common protocols used to implement a secure channel
- The benefits that implementing secure channels provides
- The ancient mathematical science of cryptography, which is at the foundation of most of the topics in this chapter
- The different techniques for encryption and when each should be used
- How secure channels actually work
- How a user can be authenticated using a digital certificate and its session run under the security context of a user account in the Windows NT security database.
- How to configure IIS and IE to use digital certificates and implement secure channels

Let us first put secure channels services under the microscope and see what they actually consist of.

Secure Channel Services

Secure Channel Services comprises a layer of networking software shipped with various products (including Windows NT4.0 and IE4.0) as a dynamic-link library called `schannel.dll`.

This software provides the support for a number of industry standard security protocols:

- SSL 2.0/SSL 3.0—**Secure Sockets Layer,** developed by Netscape and Consensus.
- PCT 1.0—**Private Communications Technology,** developed by Microsoft.
- TLS (Available in Windows NT 2000)—**Transport Layer Security**, intended to provide a simpler and more robust solution by using the best parts of SSL and PCT.

All of these protocols provide high levels of security by providing the following features:

- **Authentication**—one end-point of an established communications session can request information to identify the other end-point
- **Nonrepudiation**—a message sender cannot falsely claim that they did not send the message
- **Privacy**—messages in transit are encrypted; the contents cannot be inspected if intercepted
- **Integrity**—messages in transit cannot be tampered with; otherwise protocol violation will occur

In Chapter 3, we saw that application protocols (such as HTTP and FTP) provide the specific application data transfer logic using the lower levels for the actual delivery. Secure Channel Services transparently slots into the TCP/IP protocol stack, as shown here:

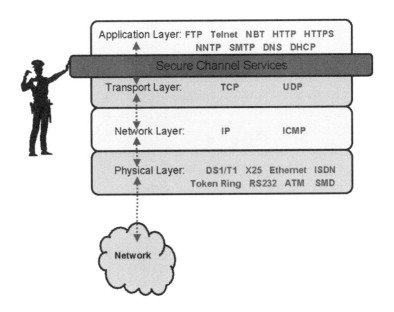

Before we can really understand how Secure Channel Services works, we first need to investigate the cryptography that is used. Once we understand these basics, we shall proceed to master the tasks required to get secure channels working on our systems.

A Simple Guide to Cryptography

Cryptography is an ancient mathematical science that provides a number of techniques for keeping information secure from prying eyes. The first serious application of cryptography was for military communications, and was used to conceal the contents of a message should it fall into the hands of the enemy.

Recent developments in cryptography have added additional uses, including mechanisms for authenticating users on a network, ensuring the integrity of transmitted information, and preventing users from repudiating (i.e., disowning ownership of) their transmitted messages.

In today's world of business-critical systems using numerous networks, the need for secure communications is obviously crucial. Cryptographic technologies provide enterprises with the best mechanisms for protecting their information, without putting the business at risk by exposing it on the network.

What Is Encryption?

Encryption is the process of applying an algorithm to scramble the data in a message, thereby making it very difficult and time-consuming, if not practically impossible, to deduce the original given only the encoded data. Inputs to the algorithm typically involve additional secret data called **keys**, which prevent the message from being decoded even though the algorithm is publicly known.

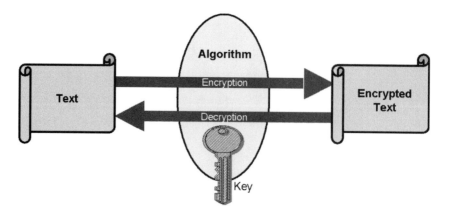

The safekeeping of keys—in other words their generation, storage, and exchange—is of paramount importance to ensure the security of the data. There is no point in applying the strongest levels of cryptographic algorithms if your keys are stored on a scrap of paper and left unsecured in your in-tray.

Encryption Strength

The strength of an encryption is dependent on two fundamental factors: the nature of the mathematical algorithm and the size of the keys involved. Under U.S. arms regulations, the length of the keys that can be used in exported software is limited. However, there is no limitation on the level of encryption used *within* the United States or sold in Canada.

Unfortunately the 40-bit encryption limit, which was in force up until recently, has been proven to provide little security from directed attack. Today's powerful processors, costing just a few hundred dollars, can crack such a message in a few hours by using brute force—that is, by trying every possible key until the decrypted message has been found. More expensive supercomputers can crack such messages in subsecond times! Each extra bit in the key doubles the time needed for the brute force attack, and most experts now claim that 128-bit keys are required to ensure confidence, and are vital for markets such as electronic commerce.

Many non-U.S. companies have developed add-on cryptographic products, using 128-bit key technology, to fill the vacuum left by the U.S. software industry's inability to compete in this market. Naturally, there is a lot of discussion between concerned parties, and the future of these export restrictions is unclear.

> Microsoft has now obtained export licenses for 128-bit encryption technology that is deployed in some of its specialized financial software; e.g., Microsoft Money.

While there are many different encryption algorithms, the ones used for secured channels fall into two distinct groups:

- Symmetric cryptography (also called secret key cryptography)
- Asymmetric cryptography (also called public key cryptography)

Let us see what the differences between the two types are.

Symmetric (Secret Key) Cryptography

In **symmetric cryptography**, the encryption algorithm requires the same secret key to be used for both encryption and decryption. Because of the type of key, this is sometimes called **secret key encryption**; it is illustrated in the diagram below:

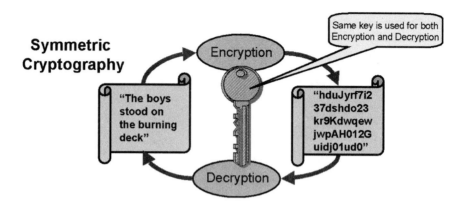

There are many different symmetric algorithms used in today's security software. Public examples include: DES, Triple-Des, RC2, RC4, RC5, and IDEA. The exact mechanics of the algorithms are extremely complex; fortunately, as Web developers we do not have to burden ourselves with the low-level details.

The advantage of these algorithms is that they are fast and efficient. However, the problem is key exchange—the mechanism for safely ensuring that both parties, the sender and the receiver, have the secret key. This is one of the weakest areas of symmetric cryptography. How do you send the key to your partners? You cannot just send it in an e-mail message, because it could be intercepted and possibly be used to compromise your security. Furthermore, how can you be confident that your partners will keep your key secure?

Asymmetric (Public Key) Cryptography

One solution to the problem of key security is **asymmetric cryptography**. This uses two different keys that are mathematically related. One key is called the **private key** and is never revealed; the other is called the **public key** and is freely given out to all potential correspondents. This type of cryptography is also known as **public key cryptography**.

The complexity of the mathematical relationship between the public key and the private key means that, provided the keys are long enough, it is practically impossible to determine one from the other.

With this type of encryption, the sender encrypts the message using the receiver's public key (which is known by everyone). The receiver is the only one who can decipher the message because no one else has his private key. This is illustrated in the diagram below.

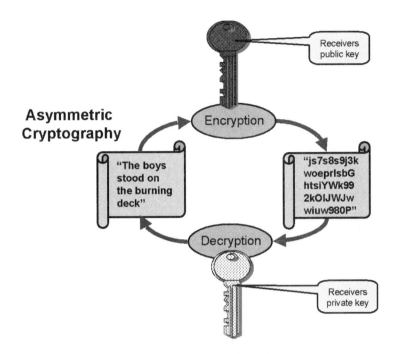

The almost universal public/private key algorithm is named RSA after its creators (Ron Rivest, Adi Shamir, and Len Adleman), and was patented by RSA Data Security in 1977. A sender uses the receiver's public key to encrypt the message. Only the receiver has the related private key to decrypt the message.

A major problem with asymmetric cryptography is that the processing required is very CPU intensive. This can cause potential performance problems on a heavily hit site when many simultaneous secure sessions are required. The need for excessive processing has led to the market for hardware cryptography devices that can offload this workload from the main CPU.

A further application for asymmetric algorithms is **digital signatures.** We shall now see how these are created and what benefits they provide in our secure infrastructure.

Digital Signature Encryption

The generation of **digital signatures** involves swapping the roles of the private and public keys. If a sender encrypts a message using his own private key, everyone can decrypt the message using the sender's public key because the public key is publicly known. A successful decryption implies that the sender, who is the only person in possession of the private key, must have sent the message.

This ensures **nonrepudiation**; that is, the sender cannot disown a message once it has been sent. The piece of data encrypted with a private key is called a **digital signature**. Common practice is to use a message digest as the item of data to be encrypted.

The nonrepudiation process relies on our certainty that the public key is valid. An evil person masquerading as the sender could create a public/private key pair and post the public key, saying it is the key for the sender. We shall see below how this problem is solved with trusted third parties and digital certificates.

In practice, the digital signature is obtained by encrypting (with the private key) a small value derived from the message rather than the complete message; this derived value is called the message digest.

Using a Message Digest

A **message digest** is a digital fingerprint of a message. It is the result of applying a mathematical algorithm (called **hash functions**) on a variable-length message, as illustrated below:

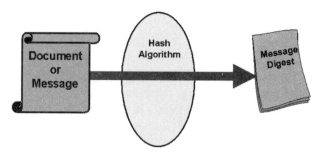

There are a number of relatively simple (and so not CPU-intensive) algorithms that can be used to create message digests suitable for digital signatures.

These algorithms have the following special properties:

- The original message (the input) is of variable-length
- The message digest (the output) is of a fixed-length and is smaller (often considerably) than the item it represents
- It is impossible to determine the original message (the input) from the message digest (the output); this is known as being a **one-way hash function**
- It is practically impossible to find two different messages (the inputs) that derive to the same message digest (the output); this is known as being a **collision-free hash function**.

Message digests can be used to guarantee that no one has tampered with a message during its transit over a network. Any amendment to the message will mean that the message and digest will not correlate.

Message digests can also be used to supply proof that an item of information, such as a password, is known—without actually sending the password or information in the clear. A practical example of this is the Windows NT Challenge/Response authentication mechanism that we met in Chapters 2 and 4.

The most common message digest algorithms designed for 32-bit computer systems are called MD4, MD5, and Secure Hash Algorithm (SHA-1). They offer, in that order, increasing levels of security, and therefore CPU usage.

Signing the Document

The next diagram illustrates the processes required to digitally sign a document. First, a digital signature is generated. This involves calculating the message digest for the document and then encrypting this value with the private key. The digital signature is then appended to document.

Note that in the diagram, the document is signed (i.e., its integrity and origin are assured) but is not **encrypted**, and thus anyone could look at the original document included with the signed digest. If required, we could encrypt the document as well; this would be done, of course, with the receiver's public key.

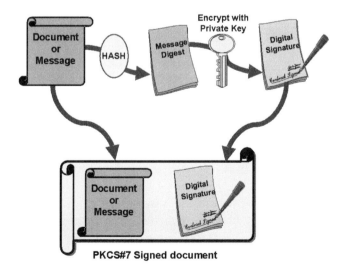

PKCS#7 Signed document

A signed object is normally formatted to a standard known as PKCS #7.

Validating the Document

The next diagram shows how the receiver of a signed document validates that the document really did originate from the person who claims to have signed the document.

After any encryption has been deciphered, the message digest is calculated twice as follows:

- The hash function is applied to the document
- The digital signature is decrypted using the public key of the document signer

Checking that the two calculated message digests are the same then validates the document. An impersonator would not have a private key related to the used public key and so could not have generated a digital signature that we would believe.

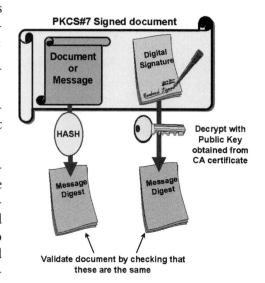

Validate document by checking that these are the same

Digital Certificates and Certificate Authorities

Earlier, when discussing nonrepudiation, we raised a possible doubt about the integrity of a public key. We shall now discuss the mechanisms that provide high levels of assurance that a public key really does belong to the claimant. This is achieved using **digital certificates** and **trusted third parties.**

A digital certificate is an item of information that binds the details of an individual or organization to a public key. If we can obtain access to someone's certificate, we have his public key, and can therefore get involved in the secure communications already discussed.

But what stops anyone from creating a false certificate, and pretending to be someone else? The solution to this problem is **Certificate Authorities** (CAs) responsible for the issuing of digital certificates. A CA is a commonly known, trusted third party, responsible for verifying both the contents and the ownership of a certificate.

There is an ever-increasing number of CAs. Examples include VeriSign, MCI, AT&T, GTE, Entrust, and Thawte. Different CAs will employ different amounts of effort in their verification processes, and must publicly divulge what checks they perform. Then users can apply the appropriate levels of trust for each CA they encounter. Also, different classes of certificates are available that reflect the level of assurance given by the CA. A certificate for a user who just surfs the Web requires less verification than a certificate for a serious business application.

If two entities trust the same CA, they can swap digital certificates to obtain access to each other's public key, and from then on they can undertake secure transmissions between themselves.

Digital certificates include the CA's digital signature (i.e., information encrypted with the CA's private key). This means that it is not feasible to create a false certificate. The public keys of trusted CA's are stored for use by applications like IE and IIS, as we will see later in this chapter.

X.509

The most widely accepted format for digital certificates is the **X.509 version 3** standard, and it is relevant to both clients and servers. The following diagram illustrates the fields in such a certificate:

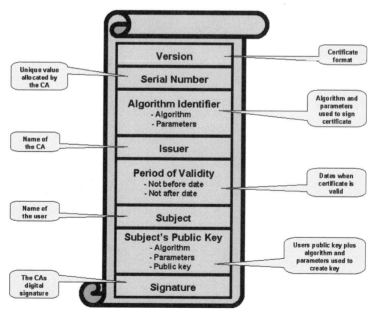

How Secure Channels Work

Now that we have a good understanding of some basic cryptographic concepts, we will move on and see how they are actually put into practice. We learned earlier that secure channels provide support for a number of security protocols. Each of these has its own specific low-level operation and complexities that we do not intend to cover. Instead we will investigate how all such protocols solve the general problem of connection, negotiation, and key exchange; and how this software technology protects us against the spies, vandals, and charlatans out there in the big wide world beyond our Internet connection.

Client-Server Authentication

We will first look at how a client and a server negotiate a secure communications link. The following table shows the messages that pass between client and server. The server has to prove that its certificate is valid by showing that it has the private key to encrypt a message digest:

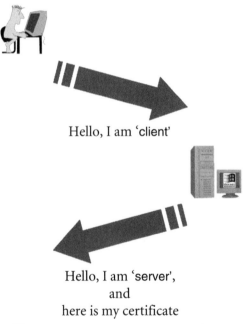

Hello, I am 'client'

Hello, I am 'server', and here is my certificate

The client *can verify the certificate by using the CA's public key to decrypt the digital signature in the* server's *certificate. If the computed hash of the* server's certificate *matches the hash in the certificate, then the* client *will proceed and extract the public key of the* server.

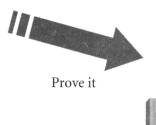

Prove it

The server *sends a random block of data plus a message digest of this data encrypted with the* server's *private key (digital signature).*

The client *can verify that the user is the* server *by recalculating the message digest, decrypting the digital signature, and checking for a match*

But what if an impostor was trying to impersonate the server?

Hello, I am 'client'

The server's *certificate is freely available, and so the* impostor *can quite easily send a message containing it.*

Hello, I am 'server',
and
here is my certificate

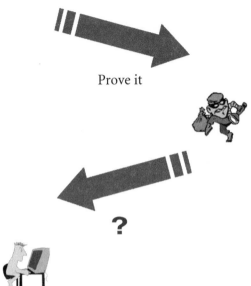

Prove it

?

The impostor *does not have a copy of the* server's *private key and so cannot construct a message that the* client *will believe.*

From this we can see how a user can be confident that the remote server is who it claims to be. The example also highlights the importance of protecting private keys.

Encrypting and Sending Messages

Now that the client has the server's public key from the server's certificate, it can send a message that only the server can decipher. This is because a prerequisite of the decrypting process is knowing the server's private key. However, we learned earlier that asymmetric cryptography is much more CPU-intensive than symmetric cryptography and not ideal for a busy site. What happens is that the client generates a random secret key and informs the server of its value, using asymmetric cryptography. From then on, encryption is done by symmetric cryptography, with only the client and the server knowing the secret key.

Here is the secret key

The secret key is encrypted with the server's *public key. Only the* server *can decode it, because doing so requires knowing the* server's *private key.*

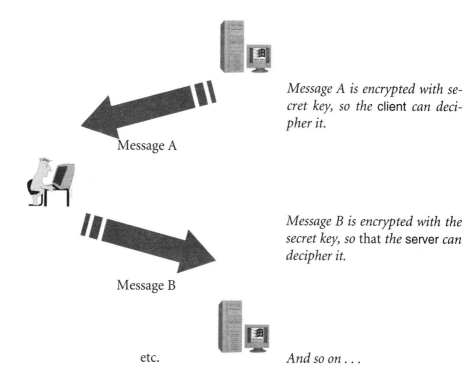

Message A is encrypted with se-cret key, so the client can deci-pher it.

Message A

Message B is encrypted with the secret key, so that the server can decipher it.

Message B

etc.

And so on . . .

Authenticating Messages Against Tampering

Now let us consider another bad guy, who eavesdrops on the network, and could intercept and tamper with messages en route to their destinations.

Message is encrypted with the secret key, and intercepted by the eavesdropper

The eavesdropper *tampers with the message and sends it on to* server.

Tampered Message

Because the message is encrypted, it is unlikely that tampering with it will create a valid message—but who knows, he might get lucky?

The solution is to attach a **message authentication code** (MAC) to each message. The MAC is a message digest value, calculated by applying a hash function on the message contents and the secret key. The message receiver calculates the MAC value for the message and checks for a match with the attached MAC value. Since eavesdropper does not know the secret key, it is extremely unlikely that he could evaluate the correct MAC for the new tampered message.

Implementing Secure Channels

We now know what Secure Channel Services is, and how it works in outline. The next step is to see how to configure IIS Web services and Internet Explorer to use Secure Channels.

Because of the extra cryptography processing required by secure channels, their use imposes a performance penalty on the Web server. Thus a thorough analysis of Web applications is recommended, so that the use of secured channels can be limited to areas where security is critical. It is usual to separate the content that needs secure transfer from standard content by placing it into a separate Web directory. Then secure channels can be applied to that one "secure content" directory. Content in this directory must be plain and small; keep images to a minimum, no sounds and definitely no movies!

Configuring and Using Certificates in Internet Information Server

Enabling SSL security on IIS requires first a **server certificate** that contains the details of our organization and is verified by a CA. The configuration of certificates with IIS is handled by the Key Manager utility, which can be found by selecting the key manager tool button within the Internet Service Manager (MMC).

To create a new public/private key pair, click on the Web service and then select the Create New Key option from the Key menu; this invokes the Create New Key wizard.

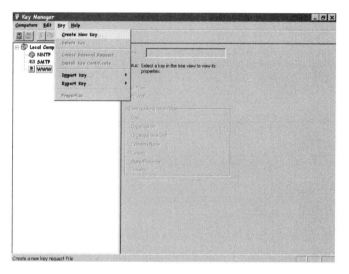

The wizard will generate a key pair and a certificate request message. The certificate request message is then sent to a CA for it to generate a signed digital certificate containing the information about our organization/Web server.

Using a series of wizard dialogs, we have to enter information about our organization and the key requirements.

The information we shall enter is:

- **Request File**—a file to be generated by the Key Manager and used to store the information sent to the CA for the certificate to be generated.
- **Key Name**—name given to identify the key on our system
- **Password**—password used to protect the private key
- **Bits**—key size: 512, 768, 1024 (large keys are more secure; export versions are restricted to 512, see note below)

- **User Details**:
  - **Organization**—company name (e.g., Harrison Associates Inc.)
  - **Organization Unit**—unit name within company (e.g., Hornet)
  - **Common Name**—TCP/IP domain name of server (e.g., `www.hornet.harrison.net`); if the server is on the Intranet you may use the NetBIOS name of the server
  - **Country**—two character ISO code (e.g., US)
  - **State/Province**—state name of address (e.g., Illinois); make sure you use the full state name, not an abbreviation
  - **City/Locality**—city name of address (e.g., Chicago)
- **Contact Details:**
  - **Name**—contact name (e.g., Richard Harrison)
  - **E-mail Address**—e-mail address of contact (e.g., rich@cyberdude.com)
  - **Phone Number**—phone number of contact (e.g., 1234567890)

> To clarify the export restrictions, the limits are:
> - 40 bits for secret keys
> - 512 bits for public keys

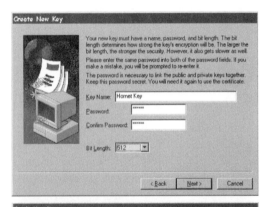

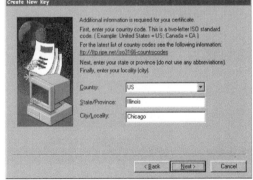

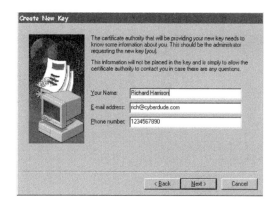

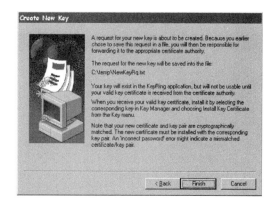

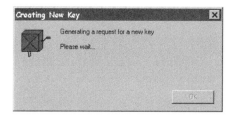

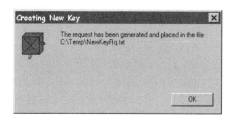

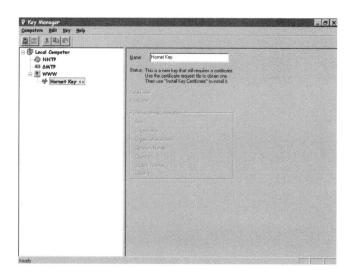

At this stage, we must enforce the changes we have made by selecting the Commit Changes Now option from the Computers menu.

Sending the Certificate Request

Once the wizard has created the key pair, we must send the generated Certificate Request details to our CA for the digital certificate to be generated. The request file generated for the information entered in the previous screen shots is given below:

```
Webmaster: rich@cyberdude.com
Phone: 1234567890
Server: Microsoft Key Manager for IIS Version 4.0

Common-name: www.hornet.harrison.net
Organization Unit: Hornet
Organization: Harrison Associates Inc
Locality: Chicago
State: Illinois
Country: US

-----BEGIN NEW CERTIFICATE REQUEST-----
MIIBMDCB2wIBADB2MQswCQYDVQQGEwJVUzERMA8GA1UECBMISWxsaW5vaXMxEDAO
BgNVBAcTB0NoaWNhZ28xEzARBgNVBAoTC1dyb3ggUHJlc3MxDzANBgNVBAsTBkhv
cm51dDEcMBoGA1UEAxMTd3d3Lmhvcm51dC53cm94LmNvbTBcMA0GCSqGSIb3DQEB
AQUAA0sAMEgCQQCKMk2YPhZC10L4wAa5MdUHw85DgUGHExtIk/m43j1kuCfv1Sa7
GkfBwG2X2FpJerhFrmHz1081NhPr6WK9nhyNAgMBAAGgADANBgkqhkiG9w0BAQQF
AANBAFxwC8ST08adPnc5g/M1KW3DGcOhOpw8JAdiHuuFjAt46bQzg73JIIu1AqZC
4FOHtTu1e1vgcUQ8MMtxK6D8Fgk=
-----END NEW CERTIFICATE REQUEST-----
```

> The format of this Certificate Request is defined by a standard known as PKCS #10.

A useful CA for the creation of certificates that can be used for demonstration and testing purposes is Entrust (`http://www.entrust.com/`); at the time of writing, it provides the service free of charge.

By navigating through the hyperlinks promoting demonstration certificates, we get to a screen where we can input our generated Certificate Request details.

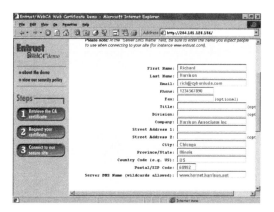

Installing the New Certificate

The response screen generated from Entrust for the above request is as follows: selecting the Display Certificate button displays the CA-generated X.509 digital certificate containing our details plus the CA's digital signature.

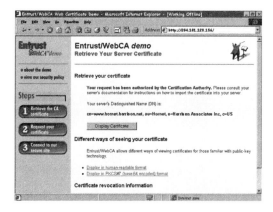

We simply copy the section between, and including the `-----BEGIN CERTIFICATE-----` and `-----END CERTIFICATE-----` lines from the e-mail message, paste it into a standard text file using, for example, **NotePad**, and save it on the server's hard disk.

To install the digital certificate, right-click on the key identifier in the Key Manager and select the Install Key Certificate menu option. A standard File Open dialog will now request the name of the file we have just created and will then request the key's password.

> It is this password that protects the certificate information even though it was received over the insecure Internet

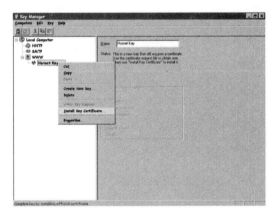

The next dialog allows us to specify on which Web server IP address the digital certificate is to be applied. Note that multiple IP addresses can be assigned to a certificate, but a maximum of one certificate can be applied to a single IP address/port number combination. In our case, we shall keep things simple and assign all addresses to our digital certificate.

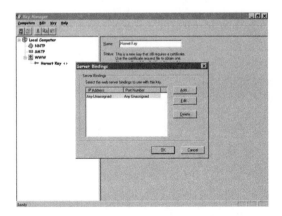

Finally, we must enforce the changes by selecting the Commit Changes Now option from the Computers menu. If the key installation has been completed successfully, Key Manager will show the key as being installed, and display the certificate details.

Enabling SSL

Once the certificate has been installed, we can enable SSL (one of the security protocols within Secure Channel Services) on any directory using Internet Service Manager. This is done by selecting the Secure Communications option on the Directory Security property sheet within the WWW Properties dialog. On the Secure Communications dialog we must check Require Secure Channel.

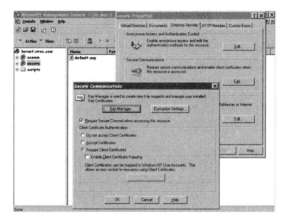

Up to now we have been discussing server certificates. In the next section we shall consider the other end of the network connection and look at **client certificates**. Secure Communications dialog provides the Require Client Certificates checkbox. When this is checked, IIS will instruct the browser to send a copy of its client certificate. Later, in Chapter 8, we shall learn how to develop server extensions with Active Server Pages to access the user's details stored in the client certificate.

Let us recap. What we have done so far is:

• Created a digital certificate containing our organization's public details

• Had our details endorsed by the Entrust digital signature

• Installed the digital certificate into IIS

• Enabled IIS to use SSL for content located in a directory, subdirectory, or virtual root

Configuring and Using Certificates in Internet Explorer

A Web browser can only decode and verify digital certificates generated by a particular CA if it has a digital certificate containing the details (including the public key) of the CA installed. This certificate is called a **CA Certificate**.

All Web browsers that wish to communicate using SSL with the IIS Web server that we configured above, must first install the Entrust CA Certificate. That is our next task.

> Adding a CA Certificate to a client application should not be done without due consideration. In doing so you are making a *serious trust decision* about the CA; in other words, you are confident that the CA will make sufficient effort to ensure the trustworthiness of the details in the certificate.

Then we will learn how to install a client certificate that contains information about the user; a CA will have verified the user's details. At the end of the previous section, we saw the option to configure IIS so that it requires the client browser to supply a certificate when a SSL session is established.

Installing the CA Certificate from Entrust

The Entrust CA certificate is installed on the Web browser by accessing its Web site at **http://www.entrust.com/** and following the instructions to the certificate demonstration pages—in particular, the option to import the CA Certificate.

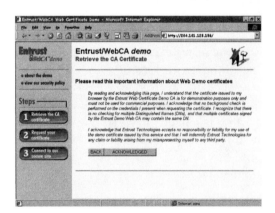 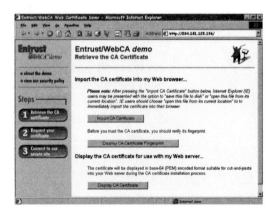

Selecting the Import CA Certificate button initiates the process. Using IE, we then get a confirmation message and can choose whether to accept and enable the site certificate or cancel the operation.

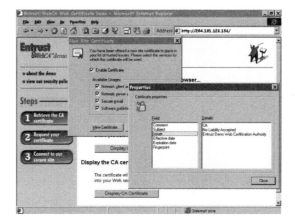

Inspecting the Installed CA Certificates

We can also inspect the CA certificates currently installed in IE by selecting Internet Options from the View menu, opening the Content tab, and clicking the Authorities button. Here, we can see that the Entrust demo CA certificate has been successfully installed.

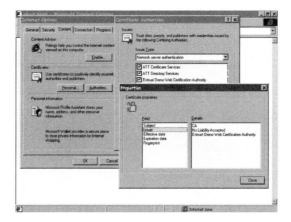

Now, when we establish an SSL connection to a Web site that uses the Entrust demo CA for its server's digital certificates, our browser will understand the contents of the certificates. In other words, we are telling the Web browser that we trust any sites that have this certificate.

> Since no verification of the server's credentials is done for the generation of Entrust demo certificates, we suggest that you normally have the Entrust demo CA certificate disabled in your browser when surfing around the Internet. If you arrive at a site that claims it needs this CA certificate enabled, be fully aware that this is not really a secure site that you can trust!

We have now done the minimum needed to establish an SSL session. While the Web server must have a server certificate, it is up to the server to mandate whether a client certificate is required. We saw earlier the server configuration option that dictates this, i.e., has the Require Client Certificates checkbox in the Secure Communications dialog.

Our next task is to install a client certificate in IE.

Installing a VeriSign Client Certificate

At the time of writing, VeriSign was providing client certificates free of charge for IE users. These can be obtained from the VeriSign Web site at

http://digitalid.verisign.com/class1MS.htm

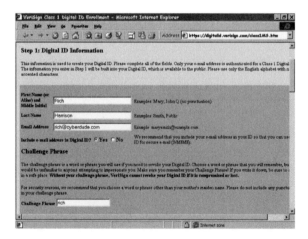

To create a client certificate, we will be required to provide our:

- First Name
- Last Name
- E-mail address
- Option to include or omit our e-mail address in the certificate
- Password, this can later be used to revoke the certificate

On submission, private key information is stored on our computer and any public information is sent to VeriSign.

Once the details have been submitted, a confirmation screen is received informing us to expect an e-mail message with further details for installing the digital certificate.

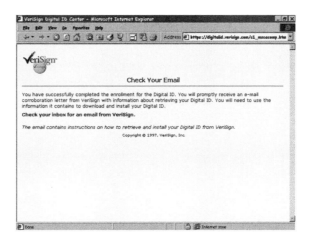

Using my details, as shown in the screen shot above, the following e-mail message was received.

```
To: rich@cyberdude.com
From: VeriSign Digital ID Center <onlineca@verisign.com>
Subject: Trial Class 1 VeriSign Digital ID
Reply-To: ID-Center@verisign.com
Errors-To: onlineca-errors@verisign.com
Sender: ID-Center@verisign.com
MIME-Version: 1.0
Content-Type: text/plain; charset=us-ascii
Content-Transfer-Encoding: 7bit


QUICK INSTALLATION INSTRUCTIONS
-------------------------------


To assure that someone else cannot obtain a Digital ID that contains
yourname and e-mail address, you must retrieve your Digital ID from
VeriSign's secure Web site using a unique Personal Identification
Number (PIN).
```

(continued)

```
Be sure to follow these steps using the same computer you used to
begin the process.

Step 1: Copy your Digital ID PIN number.
Your Digital ID PIN is: 2a9fd0346062cddf99253a26b15a77dd

Step 2: Go to VeriSign's secure Digital ID Center at
https://digitalid.verisign.com/mspickup.htm

Step 3: Paste (or enter) your Digital ID personal identification
number (PIN), then select the SUBMIT button to install
your Digital ID.

That's all there is to it!
```

So if we follow the instructions in the e-mail message, our personal digital certificate is installed into our Internet Explorer configuration. This involves navigating to **https://digitalid.verisign.com/mspickup.htm** and entering the Personal Identification Number (PIN) specified in the e-mail message.

> The digital certificate that is to be received is related to the private key information that was originally generated and stored on the computer. Thus the certificate retrieval procedure must be undertaken on the same machine and with the same logged-on user.

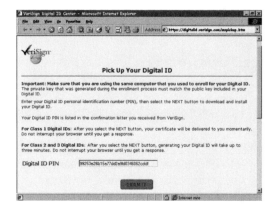
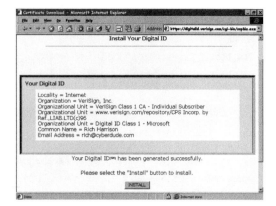

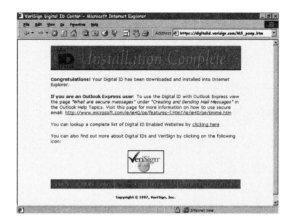

Now we can inspect the browser's personal certificates by selecting Internet Options from the View menu, opening the Content tab, and clicking the Personal button. Here we can see that the client certificate has been successfully installed.

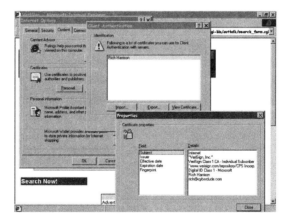

Deleting Personal Certificates

IE4 does not include a mechanism to delete an installed personal certificate (this oversight has been addressed in IE5).

The solution is to use a tool called **CERTMGR.EXE** which is available from numerous sources, including the Platform SDK, Internet Client SDK, and Java SDK. This tool provides many facilities for viewing, adding, and deleting certificates.

A personal certificate is deleted by invoking the following from the command prompt:

certmgr -del -c -n *SubjectField* **-s my**

A full list of options is available using:

certmgr -?

Accessing the Secured Content

To access content protected by SSL, we must use the protocol HTTPS in the URL. For example,

https://harrison/ssl

When we access Web content on a site that has **Require Client Certificates** enabled, IE will present the user with a list of installed personal certificates; the user can then select the one it wishes to be submitted to the Web server.

When the Web page is displayed, we can be assured that the connection to the Web server is protected using SSL by:

- The protocol **HTTPS** in the browser's address field
- A padlock icon appearing on the browser's status bar.

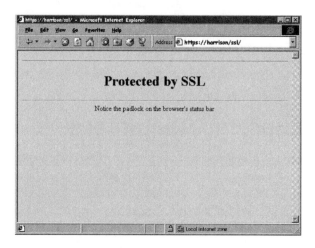

When we see the padlock we know that the communication is protected by encryption and message-tampering detection. We also know that the server has a certificate signed by one of the CAs we have approved (i.e., we have installed its CA Certificate in our browser).

We can inspect the server certificate details by selecting first the File|Properties menu option and then the Certificates button.

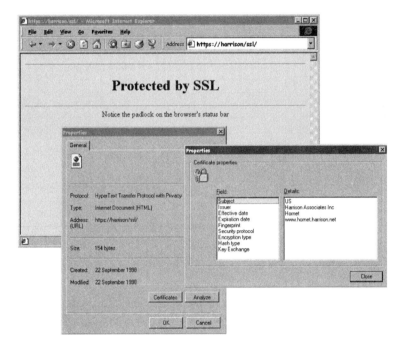

The Web server can interrogate the contents of our client certificate and be programmed to generate appropriate content for the information detected; but we will have to wait until Chapter 8 to see how this done with ASP.

We shall wrap up this chapter by looking at another useful employment of client certificates. With IIS we can optionally map certificates with specific credentials onto specific Windows NT user accounts—all done without any programming.

Client Authentication Using Certificates

Let us take another look at a diagram that we saw in Chapter 2, which showed how Windows NT security accommodates the different authentication mechanisms by means of plug-ins for the Security Support Provider Interface.

One of the plug-ins was Secure Channel Certificate Mapping. Now that we are up to speed with certificates, we are in a position to investigate this further.

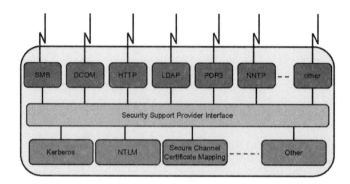

As an alternative to the Basic Authentication and Windows NT Challenge/Response Authentication mechanisms, IIS is able to use **Certificate Mapping** to authenticate a Web site visitor by analyzing the contents of its certificate and then impersonating a user account from the Windows NT security database.

Certificate Mapping

Certificate Mapping is enabled by means of the Enable Client Certificate Mapping checkbox on the Secure Communications dialog.

The Edit button allows us to define the rules by which client certificates get mapped onto particular user accounts. The Account Mappings dialog provides the following two tabs:

- Basic—this allows an individual certificate to be selected
- Advanced—this allows a series of rules on fields within the certificate to be specified

The screen shots are shown below:

BASIC

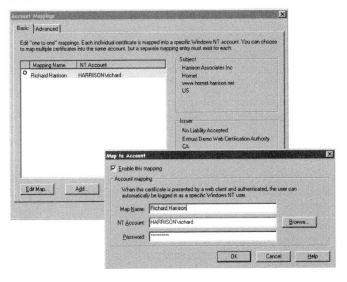

A certificate is selected by means of a standard **Open** dialog box.

Then the Windows NT user account is specified.

ADVANCED

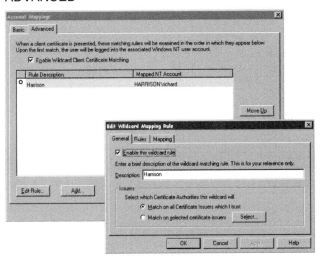

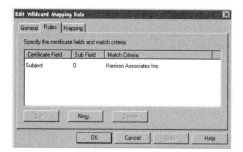

A list of certificate fields and the criteria for a match are specified.

By clicking the **New** button, the **Edit Rule Element** dialog is displayed, enabling another field/criterion to be added.

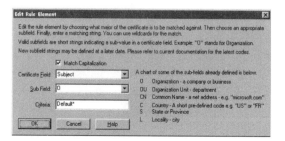

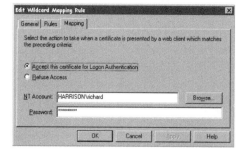

Then the Windows NT user account is specified.

When an SSL session is established, the certificate mappings are scanned until a match is found; IIS will then impersonate the mapped Windows NT user account.

■ Summary

In this chapter we have looked at the public-key-based security protocols implemented by Secure Channel Services. Web browsers and Web servers use these protocols to provide mutual authentication, message integrity, and message privacy.

We have seen in detail how these protocols work and learned how to configure IIS and IE to participate in the secure transfer of information.

The key points in this chapter are:

- Secure channels provide point-to-point networking protocols that enable the secure transfer of data; they reside transparently between the application protocol and TCP/IP.

- Secure channels require the use of digital certificates to provide both client-side and server-side authentication; they also encrypt and decrypt the message flow of the application protocol and ensure against message tampering.

- Secure channels create a series of mapping rules to check whether client certificate fields match predefined criteria; if a match is found, then IIS will impersonate an assigned Windows NT user account.

- Programmatic logic on the server can use the client certificate content to decide how to generate the returned Web content; this will be demonstrated in Chapter 8.

- Secure channels have a performance impact and should only be applied to Web content that really needs to be protected.

In this chapter we used trusted third parties to generate our certificates. In Chapter 9 we shall see how to use the Microsoft Certificate Server to implement a public key infrastructure of our own that involves the generation, management, and deployment of certificates.

In the next chapter, we shall consider the issues of trust and protecting the desktop. We shall meet certificates again when we use them to provide accountability for the download of software components from the Internet.

As you will see, the topics using certificates that are discussed in this and other chapters are going to be fundamental tools in our security toolbox.

Establishing Trust ... and Protecting the Desktop

In the opening chapter of this book we discussed the threats lurking on the Internet, looked at the basic requirements of Web security, and saw how to manage risk. Then, in the subsequent chapters we concentrated on the security issues and technologies that effect the Web server and the network. In this chapter we shall consider desktop security and see how a Web user can protect their client systems when operating on the Internet.

In the early days of the Web, everything was very safe and there was little cause for real concerns. When we requested a URL or clicked on a hyperlink, the browser would retrieve the associated HTML file and render it on the screen. If any graphics were referenced these too also retrieved and displayed appropriately.

Nowadays, life is quite different. The Web has now become "active," and accessing Web content can result in an avalanche of executables being automatically downloaded and arriving on your desktop. This executable logic can be delivered in a

185

variety of different forms, such as browser scripts, ActiveX controls, Java applets, batch files, macros attached to documents from office suite products, and normal .EXE executables. Because this logic can originate from an unknown source, there is obviously an opportunity for something really malicious to be downloaded and to cause irrevocable damage.

When we purchase software at a shopping mall—let's say the Microsoft Flight Simulator—we are confident that it is safe to install the product on our machines for two reasons. First, it has been developed by a vendor that we trust, and second, it is shrink-wrapped, and so we believe that it has not been tampered with since leaving the manufacturing site. For Web executable logic we need similar protection, i.e., **accountability** and **electronic shrink-wrapping**.

If we can accurately identify the origin of any downloaded logic, we can start to distinguish between that which we trust and that which we will not trust. Microsoft has now delivered a comprehensive solution to determine levels of trust and to provide a Web security solution for the desktop. In this chapter we shall discuss many of these features. In particular we shall look at:

- How to apply different levels of trust for the different systems that we encounter; such systems may reside both internally and on the public Internet
- How to deploy IE throughout the corporate enterprise with fixed security settings
- The issues that effect the users privacy of system and personal data
- How to protect a user from unknowingly accessing distasteful Web content
- The differences between the Java and ActiveX approaches to security
- The risks of using downloaded code and the mechanisms available to help the user decide whether downloaded code can be trusted
- An example of how to distribute code that gives a user high levels of confidence that it is safe to invoke

So, without further ado, let's start by considering how IE considers trust.

Levels of Trust

Prior to the release of Internet Explorer 4.0, Web users and corporate systems administrators had to configure the security options for their browsers with settings that made no allowance for the trustworthiness of the site being visited. For example, the use of ActiveX Control would be either enabled or disabled irrespective of whether it was being delivered from a trusted site (e.g., an Intranet) or from a site which there was no reason to trust.

Microsoft's solution to this is to divide the Web into **security zones**, so that a dynamic configuration can be enabled that adjusts automatically to a suitable level for the level of risk perceived to be appropriate for the current site being visited.

Security Zones

There are in fact five different security zones, and each corresponds to a level of trust that can be configured as required. The zones are:

- Local intranet zone
- Trusted sites zone
- Internet zone
- Restricted sites zone
- My Computer zone

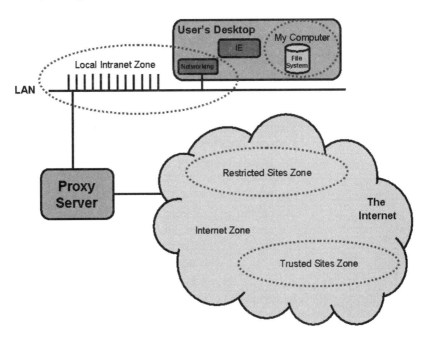

The **My Computer zone** refers to all content that is on the machine and accessed directly (i.e., not using HTTP). This is assumed to be safe and the options cannot be configured.

The four other zones can be seen on the Security property sheet accessed by selecting the View||Internet options menu option.

This property sheet allows us to configure each zone and define the security policies to be used.

The **Trusted sites zone** contains all the sites that we believe we can download and invoke active executable content without incurring any nasty effects.

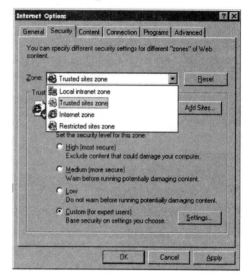

The **Restricted sites zone** contains all the sites we do not trust.

Subject to a site not being explicitly added to another zone, the **Local intranet zone** contains those sites that—

- have IP addresses that are configured to not be accessed via a proxy server (see below)
- are referenced using UNC filenames, e.g., **\\harrison\certdata**
- do not have dots within the domain name, e.g., **http://harrison/**

The **Internet zone** is the default bucket that contains all the sites that do not reside in one of the other zones.

As we navigate around the Web, the right-hand side of the IE status bar will be updated to reflect the security zone we currently inhabit

Sites can be added to a Local intranet zone, Trusted sites zone, or Restricted sites zone by means of the Add Sites button.

Take care where sites can be accessed using both a domain name and an IP address. In this case both entries should be added to the list. If only the domain name is specified, and the user accesses the site using the IP address, the browser will not recognize the site and assume it resides in the default Internet zone.

The machine in the Local intranet zone is specified using the Proxy Settings dialog accessed from the Connection property sheet.

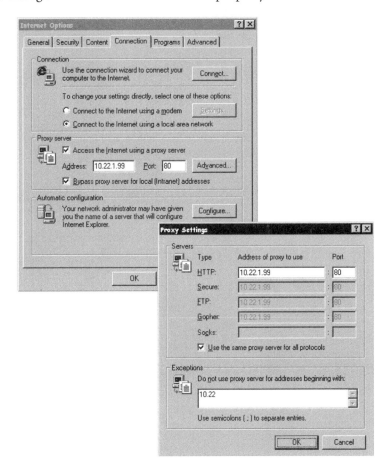

Security Levels

Each of the four security zones can be set to one of following security levels:

- High—excludes all content that could damage our computer
- Medium—warns us before invoking any content that could damage our computer
- Low—automatically, without warning, invokes any executable content
- Custom—allows us to set various individual security settings

The default security levels for the security zones are:

Local Intranet zone . . . . .Medium

Trusted sites zone . . . . .Low

Internet zone . . . . .Medium

Restricted sites zone . . . . .High

We set the specific security setting by clicking on the Settings button aligned with the Custom option.

The full list of settings is:

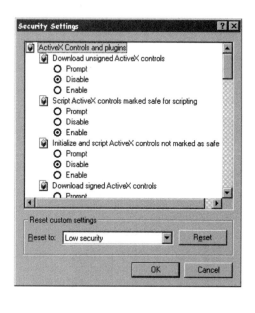

With these settings, users and corporate systems administrators have full control over the security settings that are applied to each security zone. For most individuals, however, the concepts behind Web security are either not of interest or far beyond their capabilities. They need such security measures to be installed for them. The solution in such instances, even where there may be hundreds of desktops to manage, is the Internet Explorer Administrator Kit.

Internet Explorer Adminstration Kit

The **Internet Explorer Administration Kit** (IEAK) enables the corporate systems administrator to handle the deployment of Internet Explorer across the enterprise with a specific configuration that meets the specific needs of the organization.

With this facility, we can:

- Customize the setup program to allow certain types of installations (e.g., Full, Minimal) and include additional (possibly internal) scripts and programs
- Customize the browser's configuration (e.g., start/search/support pages, quick links, title bar, animated busy logo, etc.)
- Customize the Windows Desktop Update, including Active Desktop items and Active Channels (e.g., to apply the corporate identity/branding to the desktop)

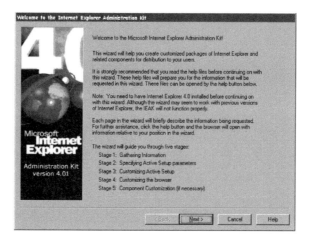

Among the various customization choices is the ability to manage the security options to be deployed—in particular specifying:

- The security settings to be applied to the different security zones
- The proxy settings, including addresses of machines, that are considered to be in the Local intranet zone and low-risk
- Any required digital certificates to be installed and blocking the downloading of any other certificates
- Any corporate standard disclaimer for newsgroup postings
- Any policies for the type of content that can be downloaded (how this works will be explained later in the chapter)

The **IEAK Wizard** provided by the kit leads the administrator through the various options available in order to create an IE setup package that when installed adopts the required configuration.

Because some options are liable to change in the future, IE can be installed to take its configuration from a central location.

The IEAK also includes a **IEAK Profile Manager** that enables such configuration options to be specified. This will be used to create an automatic configuration (.ins) file.

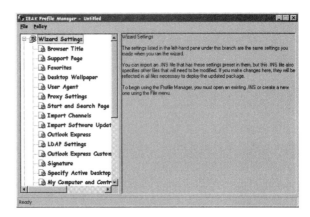

With the IEAK Wizard, the administrator must:

- Enable automatic browser configuration
- Specify the automatic configuration URL

The deployed IE installation will be configured with an **automatic configuration URL** that is used to access this centrally stored configuration.

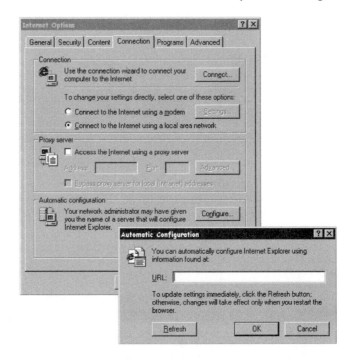

Privacy

Most Web users believe that they are operating anonymously when they surf the Internet. However, every time they navigate to a site they leave a calling card that reveals a number of items of personal information. This is illustrated by a demonstration located at the following URL:

http://www.anonymizer.com/snoop.cgi

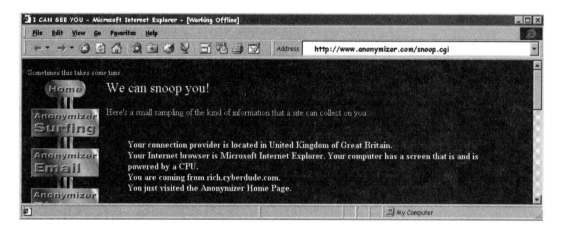

One piece of information that is sent to the server as part of the HTTP protocol is the client's IP address. In the above screen dump, the IP address underwent a reverse DNS lookup and determined the domain name to be rich.cyberdude.com. By using such information, multiple sites working together can track your activity. The HTTP protocol also gives information about the client's hardware/software, and a hacker can use such knowledge to exploit the known security holes for that particular system setup.

The **http://www.anonymizer.com** site provides a truly anonymous facility to browse the Web without revealing any HTTP user details (of course, this relies on you trusting this site to keep your details confidential). This facility also disables any client-side script logic sent to the client, because it is possible that this can access and reveal items stored by the browser that are not for public consumption. An example would be a list of sites you have recently visited.

Since many items of desired personal information (e.g., name, e-mail address, etc.) are not included in the HTTP protocol, Web surfers are frequently encouraged to reveal personal information as they register for subscriptions, downloads or site access, enter competitions, or sign guestbooks. One expects to have a right to privacy and assumes that this information will only be used for the purpose for which it was given. However, in reality, this personal information is worth a lot of money to marketing companies, and very often your details are captured to be sold to such an organization.

The solution is simple: Don't talk to strangers. Life is not so simple, however; many sites of this kind offer tempting services and downloads, and the only way to get the goodies for free is to divulge your information. If this is the case, then remember to only give information you are happy to become public. Also, if you can trust the site, then check to see if it has declared policy statement about what it will do with your personal data.

Personal and System Data

As the use of Web technologies proliferates, the privacy of the information stored on a Web user's systems is increasingly being examined. Fortunately, the vast majority of Web developers will respect the confidentiality of data belonging to other people that has not been willingly donated. The discovery of any breach of ethics in this area would rightly leave them open to attack—both morally and legally.

However, as we know, there are many loathsome bandits lurking, and compromising of stored personal and system data is difficult to detect. When data is tampered with, the damage that is done frequently has a severe impact and visible evidence. In contrast, a rogue program that is reading your confidential data may give no visual indication and so is very difficult to discover. It might even remain unearthed for a very long time.

A popular yarn that frequently roams the Internet has it that a certain major software vendor has developed a software component that can do an audit of the software installed on a user's desktop. Once the scan has completed, it sends the discovered information electronically and secretly to the vendor. This ascertained data identifies all of the products installed, including both its own products and those of its competitors.

This tale has never been proved, and it is very unlikely that a major vendor would stake its reputation on such a unscrupulous trick. Technically, though, it would be very easy to implement! Once software arrives onto your desktop and is invoked under your security context, there is very little to stop it from snooping into (or even tampering with) any of the data stored on your system.

It is therefore vital not to allow software from an unknown/unreputable source to be installed on your machines. Only deploy software from a known and trusted source.

Profiling

As a Web user, you should be aware of the possibility that much of the activity undertaken from your browser is being recorded. Such activity may be recorded at either a Web Server or a Proxy Server.

Many analysis tools are now very sophisticated and can generate detailed reports on your activities. This information can be used to determine your interests and, in effect, profile you. Your profile is highly salable because it provides very useful knowledge for organizations to use in direct marketing campaigns, making it possible to correctly target their advertising (or junk) mail. As another example of use, an insurance company could decide whether you are a good risk by examining your character from an obtained profile.

Several organizations, working in partnership, could pool their captured user knowledge together. This would enable them to obtain a larger and more accurate picture of their potential targets.

Web Servers

In Chapter 4 we investigated the audit facilities provided by IIS. These facilities are not unique to IIS, and every Web server has the ability to log various items of interest for every HTTP request/response pair.

Such log files may record the URL requested along with your IP address, and, if you have been authenticated, your username. To get a user to reveal its name (rather than remain anonymous), many sites offer extra services to users who are "registered members" and present their credentials each time they access the site.

One item that many Web Servers can record for each HTTP request is the **Refer Link**. This is the URL that refers to the item being requested. For example, if a user clicks on a hyperlink, the Refer Link that is logged is the URL of the page that contained the hyperlink. This is illustrated on the above anonymizer snoop screen dump; note that it identifies the page we previously visited.

Some tools that analyze Web log files (e.g., Microsoft Site Server Usage Analysis) use this field to detect trends in the way people navigate through a site. Organizations that place banner ads on other sites can use the Refer Link to detect those sites which are generating the most traffic. With this information, decisions on where to place future advertising campaigns can be made more wisely.

The problem with the Refer Link is that some people could feel that revealing the site from which they navigated is a breach of their privacy. Here is a scenario where this could cause a serious problem: If the Refer Link URL contains confidential parameters, such as a user account or password, this private information would be revealed to the administrators at the site the user has navigated to. So in short, do not pass confidential information as parameters in a URL to a Web page that has hyperlinks to an external site.

Proxy Servers

Many ISPs also offer Proxy Servers to provide better performance by caching frequently accessed pages. A Proxy Server can generate an audit trail of all your activity and will have knowledge of *every* site and URL you have visited; thus this single point can over time provide a complete profile of your character and interests.

Web users should also take care when accessing a Web via a Corporate Proxy Server. Any confidential information could be stored in the cache and viewed by system administrators. Also, remember that such products keep an audit trail, which may be used to report the various sites you have accessed. So don't spend your supposed working hours either reading the sports pages or accessing any naughty sites; your employer may be watching you!

Cookies

A cookie is a small item of coded information that a Web Server can permanently store on a Web user's machine. It records various attributes about the user—such values are ascertained on a previous visit to the site. At a later time, when the user visits the site again, the Web Server automatically retrieves this information and identifies the user and his preferences, all resulting in a good user experience.

This is similar to you walking into a shop for the first time and the salesperson asking your name. The next time you enter the shop, the salesperson recognizes you and greets you in an appropriate manner.

Cookies are also frequently used to overcome the hurdle that the HTTP protocol is stateless; i.e., all HTTP requests are received independently, and the protocol does not provide an easy mechanism to match multiple requests from the same user and share context information across these requests. Most Web applications require multiple interactions with the server. The use of cookies enables information to be carried across multiple requests. The Web server determines the current context by examining the information stored in the cookie. Typically, the cookie is kept small and is just a session identifier; this is used to look up the context information stored on the server.

The benefits to Web developers are obvious. They help build better Web applications. However, some users do not like cookies because they have no control over them.

Concerned users will set their Web browsers to either reject cookies or display a Security Alert to prompt the user as each cookie is received. This allows the user to examine where the cookie originated from and decide whether to accept it.

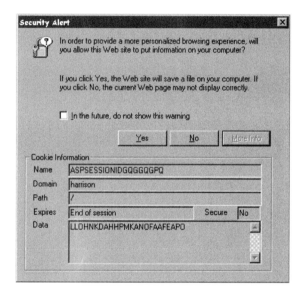

A Web server writes a cookie to a Web browser by sending a Set-Cookie message in the header of the HTTP response message, and this includes the cookie name plus its value. In addition, a domain name and path can be de-fined; any request to a machine with this domain name and with a URL that is within or beneath the path will trigger the cookie to be appended to the HTTP request.

For example, consider the Security Alert screen dump shown above. Here the domain name was set to harrison and the path was set to / (i.e., the top level). This means that any HTTP request to the machine harrison would include this cookie. From this dialog we can see that the cookie information also includes an expiry time to specify when the cookie will be deleted from the client system and a flag to mandate that the cookie must only be sent over an SSL connection.

The problems users cite about cookies include:

• An external system is writing information to their hard disk. This should not be perceived as a serious problem since cookies are stored in a predefined area, limited to 4K, and cannot be executed.

- They can be used to perform functions transparently without the user knowing. This is true, but to most Web users the advantage of personalization and rich interactivity far outweighs any concerns.
- They can be used to track the user as he navigates around the Web and so compromise his privacy. This is probably the most reasonable concern of the three, so let us investigate whether it is possible

"Stealth" Cookies

Because a cookie defines a single domain name of the site that can receive the cookie, and cannot be shared over multiple sites, it might initially seem that user tracking across the Web is not possible. However, there are some subtle tricks that can achieve this.

For example, consider the Microsoft enterprise that now offers several different types of services distributed over multiple Web sites each using a different domain name (Microsoft Site, MSN, MSNBC, Hotmail, Expedia Travel, Internet Gaming Zone, etc). Microsoft is reputedly able to identify every Web user using a single cookie that works across all the sites. How is this achieved if a cookie can only be accessed from a single site?

It's simple. When a user accesses any one of the Web sites, the server redirects the user to a master site that can read the cookie containing the user's unique identifier. The master site then redirects the user back to the original site and passes the user identifier back in the URL. This can all happen transparently to the user.

An example of User Activity Tracking is the DoubleClick advertising network, which does some clever tricks with cookies, again all happening transparently to most users.

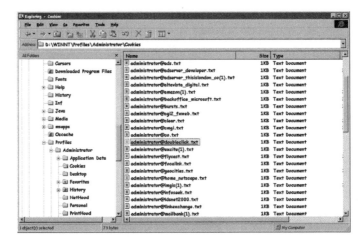

To illustrate this, first check your cookie jar, located in the folder: %SystemRoot%\profiles\%UserName%\cookies

There will be one file for each Web site that has sent one or more cookies to your browser.

If you frequently roam around the Web, it is highly likely that you will have cookies sent from the domain DoubleClick.

But did you ever visit this site? I have not knowingly visited it, yet this screen dump from my machine shows that they have sent me a cookie. How did they do it?

The objective of DoubleClick is to provide marketing banners for Web sites that are targeted at the interests of the user and issued in such a manner that a user does not normally see an ad twice in the same session.

Web sites are paid to host the DoubleClick ads. They do this by including an HTML image tag in their Web pages that refers to the image to be retrieved from the DoubleClick site. When the DoubleClick Web server receives a request for the ad image, it also receives the DoubleClick cookies. If the DoubleClick cookies do not exist on the client, they will be created.

As we browse around the Web, sites that support DoubleClick can pass information about the user's activity to a URL located on the DoubleClick server. One site that hosts DoubleClick ads is the Altavista Search Engine.

When I tried searching for the keyword "Volvo," I received a response that included a DoubleClick ad for Volvo. That's very clever, but there's more!

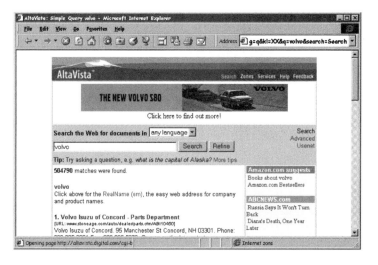

When we inspected the HTML, we found the following HTML statements:

```
<iframe src="http://ad.doubleclick.net/adi/altavista.digital.com/
layout2;kw=volvo;ord=1446294063" width=470 height=84 marginwidth=0
marginheight=0 hspace=0 vspace=0 frameborder=0 scrolling=
no bordercolor="#000000"></iframe>
```

See how Altavista has passed in the URL to DoubleClick the fact that I am interested in Volvos. DoubleClick will identify me as the user by inspecting a unique identifier stored in the DoubleClick cookie and will record my interest in my profile.

Subsequent requests for ad images will enable DoubleClick to identify me and respond with a suitable ad based on my profile. Given what they know about me so far, any ads to do with cars would seem a good bet.

We see from this that as users surf through the numerous DoubleClick-supported sites, information about their activities can be passed to DoubleClick, building up a very comprehensive profile of the user's interests without the knowledge of most users.

How offensive this is varies from one individual to another. I personally have no major problem with DoubleClick's tactics because their policy statement says that they do not know the name, address, phone number, or e-mail address of any user and do not sell or rent such information.

If, however, you object to DoubleClick's monitoring, then the following is suggested: edit the file containing the DoubleClick's cookies and corrupt their value; then make the file read-only.

Content Protection

One of the great concerns about the Internet is the amount of offensive information that is freely flowing around. However, because of the nature of the Internet, with no one in overall control, it is impossible to impose any level of censorship. Furthermore, with such a wide user base, and the variety of nationalities, cultures, and age groups, what may seem acceptable to some could be very distasteful (or even illegal) to others (or their parents!).

There are a number of software solutions that prevent the distribution of indecent material to minors. These use mechanisms such as:

• Scanning all received information and ditching any text that contains offensive words

- Disabling navigation to sites known to be suspect and included on a blacklist or whose domain names contain offensive words

The last mechanism is very hard to effectively implement, because it is difficult to keep the list up to date and some offensive sites use innocuous names or just IP addresses. In some cases, such software blocks access to perfectly harmless sites; for example, would such software prevent access to the Web site of a local utility like Wessex Water

(http://www.wessexwater.com/)?

As a result, a better mechanism was required to keep undesirable content off the client computer. A solution came from the World Wide Web Consortium; it is called the **Platform for Internet Content Selection** (PICS).

PICS labels (metadata) are inserted into a document and contain a value that rates the content to a level dependent on the label itself. For example, a Skill Level label may contain a value that defines the type of reader the document is targeted at: beginners, competent users, or experts.

The ratings are established either by the document publisher or by an independent third party (with or without the publisher's consent). The ratings may be embedded into the Web document or retrieved from a separate server.

Using these labels, filtering rules can be built into software to only allow documents to be viewed if they meet specified criteria; e.g., no documents to be accessed if they contain either violent content or offensive language. However, this all relies on you trusting the rater to have the same levels of personal taste.

RSACi

One implementation of PICS is from the Recreational Software Advisory Council, which has adapted its computer-game rating system for the Internet—hence the name **RSACi**. Each RSACi label has four numbers, indicating levels of violence, nudity, sex, and offensive language.

Microsoft Internet Explorer implements the RSACi ratings so that a user (or more likely the user's parent) can set maximum acceptable levels of language, nudity, sex, and violence. This filtering is accessed from the Content property sheet from the Internet Options menu option.

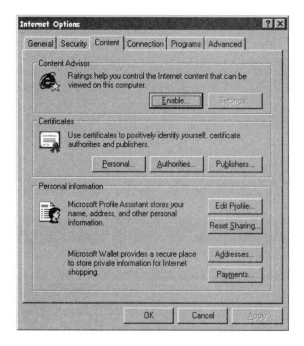

The facility is password protected, so that the minor cannot alter any of the protection settings.

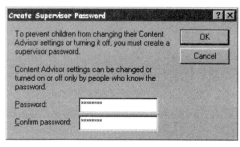

The Content Advisor dialog allows the acceptable levels to be set.

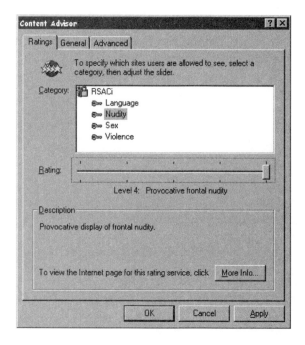

Once the Content Advisor has been enabled, if the user navigates to a Web page that has content with rating exceeding what is permitted, a dialog is displayed.

This dialog prevents the minor from proceeding but allows the parent to continue and see the content if they enter their password.

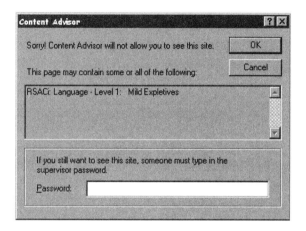

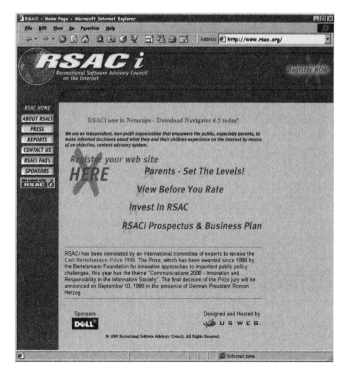

Document publishers register their Web site and establish their own RSACi ratings by using a facility at:

http://www.rsac.org/

After answering a number of questions about the Web site content, an HTML **Meta** tag is generated which can be pasted and copied into the Web pages.

For example,

```
<META http-equiv="PICS-Label" content='(PICS-1.1 "http://www.rsac.org/
ratingsv01.html" 1 gen true comment "RSACi North America Server" for
"http://surf.to/harrison" on "1998.08.31T18:30-0800" r (n 0 s 0 v 0 1
1))'>
```

This tag should be placed between the **<HEAD>** & **</HEAD>** tags.

Accountability/Electronic Shrinkwrapping

As we suggested in the introduction to this chapter, executing software that has been downloaded across the Internet from unknown sources exposes our systems to huge risk. Examples of the malicious activities that such code could perform include:

• Corruption of data
• Theft of information
• Unauthorized utilization of system resources

There are several ways that such potentially dangerous software can arrive at one's desktop. It could arrive as an attachment in an e-mail message or be downloaded (perhaps in a zipped/compressed format) using either FTP or a Web HTTP hyperlink.

In addition, a popular mechanism for achieving functionality too complex to implement using standard HTML and client-side scripting is **ActiveX Controls** or **Java Applets**. These small programs are either invisible or are responsible for the visuals within an area of the Web page, and they may be automatically downloaded along with the HTML and associated graphics. ActiveX Controls or Java Applets are included into an HTML document using the **<object>** and **<applet>** tags respectively.

ActiveX and Java come from two competing camps in the Internet technology wars, and as a result, there has been much scrutiny and a huge amount of debate over the merits and tradeoffs of the two technologies. Much of this discussion concerns security issues.

ActiveX Controls and Java Applets

Although ActiveX Controls and Java applets are used for similar purposes, they handle security using different approaches

Java

Java applets are developed using the Java programming language, and this offers good protection against poorly written code. However, when Java was originally devised, security issues were never considered, as the objectives at that time were somewhat limited to developing platform-independent code for embedded devices. Once Java was repositioned for the Web, this thinking had to be revised, as security became most people's immediate concern, and protection had to be provided against downloading and invoking malicious code.

The solution was to provide protection by limiting the scope to what a downloaded Java applet could actually do. In particular, applets must not be allowed to access the operating systems or any of the system's resources, such as the file system, to ensure the integrity of the system and privacy of the user's data. This protection is called the Java **sandbox** and comes from the idea that a child in a sandbox is in a safe environment—he cannot break things outside of the sandbox or be hurt from the outside.

The Java sandbox is implemented by the Java **SecurityManager**, which is called whenever any potentially dangerous operation is invoked and will prevent any downloaded applet from invoking such operations.

In a networked computer environment, the ability to communicate with the outside world is rather fundamental. Most people need Java to do more than just animate a penguin in a Web page! To achieve this, a set of special Java classes exists to allow external communication.

Two additional security components within the Java environment are the **Class Loader** and the **Bytecode Verifier**. The Class Loader is used to manage the execution of Java code in manner controlled from the region where it originated (i.e., from the same computer, from a machine on the firewall-protected network, or from the Internet). It will never allow a Java class to be replaced by one from a higher-risk region. The Bytecode Verifier performs a series of checks to validate the integrity of any downloaded code and that the code was generated by a trustworthy compiler.

With all these security measures, it is easy to think that any downloaded Java code can be considered safe. However, recall that in the first chapter we said that no system can be considered 100% secure. Java is no exception. Like many other technologies, Java has a history of security problems being identified and has gone through a series of iterations to address the problems. So while today's Java is theoretically safe, who knows whether there may not be some bug lurking and waiting to be exploited?

While the sandbox architecture does protect the host system from attacks on the system, it is still easy to create Java applets that do nasty things. There are many examples of hostile Java applets on the Internet that implement:

- Nuisance attacks—these do not damage data but are just annoying, such as threatening messages or repetitive sounds
- Denial-of-service attacks—these consume excessive system resources and either grind a system to a halt or cause a system crash
- Impersonation—for example, sending a forged e-mail message that appears to originate from the client user

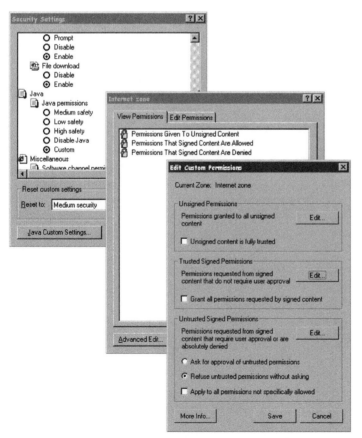

With the standard Java sandbox, functionality is either enabled or disabled depending on whether the applets originate from across the network or directly from the user's machine. The latest version of Microsoft's Java implementation has overcome this limitation by establishing a trust-based security system that provides for finer granularity over the privileges granted to a Java applet.

The Java code is digitally signed along with a specification of the privileges that it requires to be enabled in order to function.

When downloaded, these requirements are checked against the Java permissions configured in the appropriate Security Zone.

This allows greater control as appropriate security levels can be applied based on the origin of the applet; i.e., those that come from trusted hosts can be granted higher privileges.

The only real danger with Java security is that it relies on the integrity of the software that implements the sandbox. If a flaw is detected in this, the security hole could be exploited. If an organization perceives this as too much of a risk, the only solution is to apply a security level that completely disables Java applets.

ActiveX Controls

ActiveX has to be one of the most misunderstood and ambiguously used expressions in the Internet technology arena. Many people get confused because ActiveX actually encompasses a number of technologies and is not just one thing.

When Microsoft released its first set of Internet tools in March 1996, it announced **ActiveX** technology, which in all truth was just a new marketing name for Microsoft's existing **OLE** technology. ActiveX (or third-generation OLE technology) is a framework that allows software components to cooperate even if they were written by different vendors, at different times, using different tools, and if the objects are located in the same process or the same machine, or distributed over multiple machines. Put simply, ActiveX provides *software plumbing* between software objects and insulates the component developer from such complexities.

One of the ActiveX technologies is ActiveX Controls. Microsoft positions this as an alternative to Java Applets. Whereas a Java applet is downloaded for each user session, an ActiveX Control is typically only downloaded once and installed on the target client computer. A subsequent new download will only occur if the HTML specifies that a newer version of the control has been made available.

ActiveX Controls can be written in several high-level languages, including Visual Basic and Visual C++. In addition, Microsoft has packaged its Java VM so that it appears as an ActiveX Control to other external entities. For this reason, while many people debate how ActiveX and Java compete, Microsoft claims that the two technologies complement each other!

ActiveX Controls are not restricted by a sandbox and provide greater functionality than is possible with a Java applet. For example, it can create and modify files on the client's file system. While this "no limits" provides great power, it also opens up numerous possibilities for misuse. Once an ActiveX Control is installed, it can do anything, including corrupting your hard disk or disclosing confidential information.

ActiveX Controls relies on a user's judgment as to whether the control can be trusted. It is vital that the user be supplied with the appropriate information about a control so that a suitable decision can be made. To achieve this, Microsoft has implemented a digital signature technology called **Authenticode.**

Authenticode

Authenticode is a security mechanism that enables users and software developers (software publishers) to create a trust relationship between themselves. By using Authenticode, a software publisher can digitally sign the code when it makes it available for downloading.

Such code may be downloaded if referenced in an `<OBJECT>` tag or if assigned to a hyperlink that the user clicks on. How Internet Explorer handles the download of this code will be dependent on the security level applied to the security zone from which the code originates. If the setting is Exclude content that could damage your computer, the download will be not be allowed to proceed. At the other extreme, if the setting is Do not warn before running potentially damaging content, the download will occur without any user intervention. The alternative security level is Warn before running potentially damaging content, and in this case the Authenticode checks are invoked.

The Authenticode logic within Internet Explorer uses the digital signature to ascertain the author of the code, which it then notifies to the user. The user is given the option of either accepting the code or canceling the operation. If the user does not trust the origin of the code, then he should, without hesitation, reject the code.

This screen dump shows the Security Warning dialog that is displayed identifying the author of the code and a hyperlink to a URL giving more information about the author and the control.

Note, too, that the user can enable the checkbox to trust all future downloads from the same author (i.e., the Security Warning dialog would not be displayed).

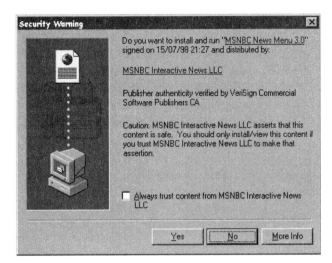

Another feature of Authenticode checks is that they will detect whether the code has been tampered with since being published by the software developer. If such a problem is detected, the user will be presented with a Security Warning dialog that asks if he wishes to proceed.

The latest version, Authenticode 2.0, provides further assurance by doing online checks on the status of the digital certificates and ensuring that the software was signed during the lifetime of the software publisher's certificate. Software developers can have their certificates revoked (i.e., made invalid) by their CA if it is believed that they have been abusing their code-signing agreements. A typical example would be if they were found to have deliberately created a malicious executable.

How Safe Is Authenticode?

One very important thing to remember is that signed code is not necessarily safe code, i.e., free of bugs or malicious code. There is little to stop some idiot from creating a malicious program, signing it, and then distributing it over the Internet. What Authenticode does provide is **accountability**: if a signed program misbehaves, then you can identify the source of the code and possibly take legal action.

Accountability relies on the software publisher's certificate containing valid credentials. This means that you must only have CA certificates installed for those trusted third-party organizations that you believe will take appropriate measures to ensure the integrity of the software publishers for whom they create certificates.

An example of a malicious signed ActiveX Control was the "Exploder Control" written by one Fred McLain. When this was downloaded to a PC that had a power conservation BIOS facility, the control shutdown the machine. Further information about this control can be found at **http://www. halcyon.com/mclain/ActiveX/welcome.html**.

One of the requirements for obtaining a software publisher's certificate is a pledge not to *knowingly* develop and distribute software containing malicious logic that could harm a system. Microsoft and Verisign were very upset by the Exploder because this pledge had been broken, and their lawyers forced the Exploder Control to be removed from the Web site. Verisign also revoked Fred McLain's certificate, which Authenticode 2.0 can determine during the code download.

The key lessons to the Exploder Control are:

- Appropriate security levels must be applied to the Internet zone; i.e., a minimum level of Warn before running potentially damaging content.

- When informed that a control was developed by an unknown or suspicious publisher, the user must decide whether this individual/organization can be trusted. If there are any doubts, the installation must be aborted. The biggest danger with Authenticode occurs when a user does not understand these simple concepts or the consequences of downloading untrustworthy code. For example, suppose the user gets fed up with the Security Warning dialogs and enables the security level for the Internet zone to be Do not warn before running potentially damaging content. The protection is disabled and gates are open for malicious code to freely enter the system. The use of IEAK enables the corporate system administrator to permanently define the security levels and trustworthy software publishers, so that employees do not have to make such decisions.

How to Distribute Safe Code

We shall now illustrate code signing with an example and see how easy Microsoft has made it for a software developer to provide users with assurances of the authenticity and integrity of downloaded code.

Code is normally distributed with a Cabinet (.cab) file which contains multiple files and applies a compression algorithm to reduce the total size. Compression is obviously important when downloading over the Internet. It is possible to distribute code directly as a single file (i.e., file types of: .exe, .dll, .ocx, and .vbd). With all of these file types, it is possible to sign the file.

Creating Our Control

For our example, we shall consider a simple ActiveX control that displays a face that switches between being happy and sad when clicked on. We shall create the control using VB and the functionality is deliberately trivial, as our purpose is to consider the code signing procedure—not the development of such controls.

> **This program is available on the CD-ROM.**

When we invoke VB, we are given the option of creating a new project from which we elect to create a project of type **ActiveX Control**.

Once this is selected, VB creates a suitable project that enables us to develop our control. Fortunately, VB insulates us from the complex COM interfaces that a VC++ programmer would need to support for visual ActiveX Controls. Life is just so easy for VB programmers!!

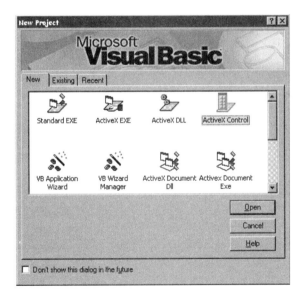

The program will use two Image controls. The first, **Image1**, is assigned a bitmap for a happy face and the second, **Image2**, is assigned a bitmap for a sad face. When the code is initialized, we make the first image visible and the second image invisible. When events are fired for a user clicking on the control, we switch the visibility of the two images. The code is very simple, as shown in the following screen dump.

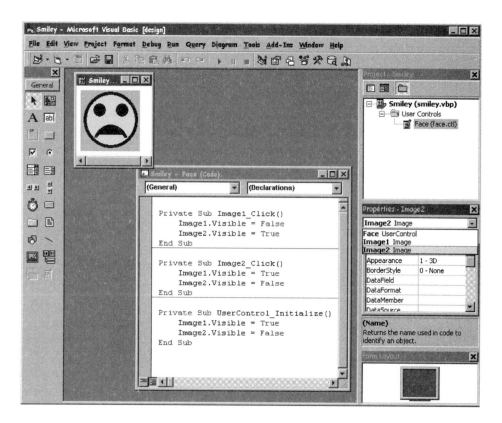

Packaging Our Control

To package our control into a cabinet file we use the Package and Deployment Wizard. This is located within the Add-ins menu. If this menu option is missing, use the Add-in Manager to enable it.

From the first dialog screen we select the Package option to create our distributable package. Such a package can contain multiple software components for installation either by:

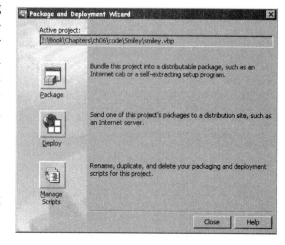

• the download component of IE

• or by self-extracting setup program

It is this package that we shall later sign with our digital signature.

When we build a package, the settings chosen are saved as a script. This screen allows a previous script to be recalled to take on the previous settings.

In our case we do not require an existing script, so select the Packaging Script to None.

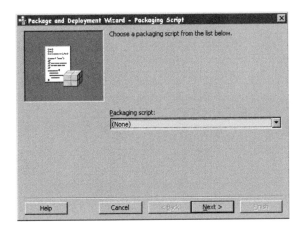

Next we choose the type of package we want to create. Since we are creating a package for an ActiveX Control that we want IE to automatically install, we choose the Internet Package option. This will generate our package as a cabinet file.

The Standard Setup Package is used to create the self-extracting setup program.

The Dependency File is used to generate a file containing a list of software items that are required for the application.

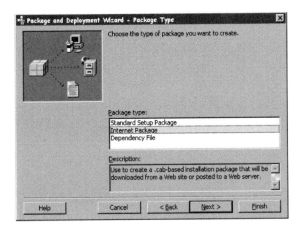

- a

We now move on to specify the directory where we want the package to be built. In this case, we have chosen a folder called **package** in the VB project folder.

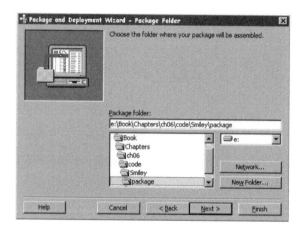

The next dialog allows us to specify the components that are needed by the control. The screen defaults to specify the ActiveX Control itself (smiley.ocx) plus the VB Runtime and OLE Automation.

The msstkprp.dll file is also present because it provides the design-time support needed to allow other software developers to create their own applications using our control. We don't need this, so the checkbox for this file is disabled.

Other components can be added using the Add button, but this is not required for our example.

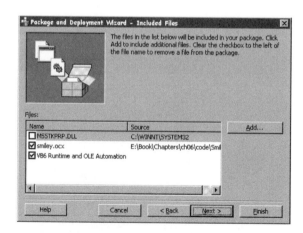

We now need to specify where the components specified in the previous screen are to be found. As we click on each item (on the left), the File source updates to show where the item will be found. We can change this source if required.

When we click on smiley.ocx it shows the item as included in the cabinet file.

When we click on VB Runtime and OLE Automation it shows the item as being Downloaded from the Microsoft Web site. As part of the installation of our smiley control, the VB Runtime would only need to be downloaded if the machine did not have this item already installed.

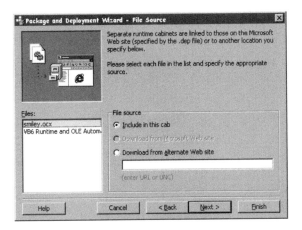

It is possible that an ActiveX Control could have the ability to do something nasty if used by a rogue user in a malicious fashion. In the next dialog we have to specify Safety Settings for our control

If we state that our component is Safe for Scripting, we are claiming that, irrespective of how the control is scripted, it will not create, change, or delete any files, change any system setting, or misuse any user information.

Similarly, if we state that our component is Safe for Initializing, we are claiming that, irrespective of how the control is initialized, it will not create, change, or delete any files, change any system setting, or misuse any user information.

Since our control does nothing dangerous, we set both of these settings to **Yes**. Note that when we do this we are accepting liability that the control is safe, and so we must be vigilant that there are no nasty capabilities lurking within.

The use of controls not marked as safe must be restricted by applying custom security levels and ensuring that they are not used from untrusted security zones.

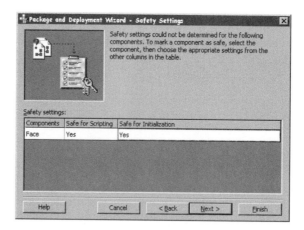

And finally we have finished and our cabinet file is created, containing our Smiley control and the installation information.

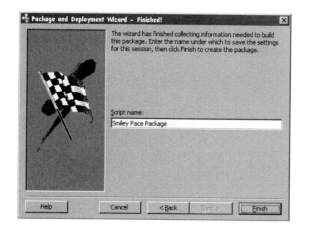

The cabinet file generated contains:

- smiley.ocx—our Smiley Face ActiveX Control
- smiley.inf—information needed by the installation process (such as dependency on other code libraries)

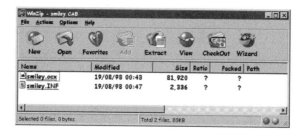

Getting a Software Publishing Certificate

The first thing to be done before we can sign our package is to obtain a **Software Publishing Certificate** (SPC) from a Certificate Authority, such as Verisign. An SPC can be regarded as a statement from a CA that the software publisher is approved.

There are two types of SPC:

- Commercial SPC—for businesses that develop software for other businesses
- Individual SPC—for noncommercial/non-profit-making people and organizations

For both types of SPC, applicants must provide their details (i.e., name, address, etc) plus make a pledge that they will not knowingly distribute code that could contain malicious actions or harm a computer system.

For a commercial SPC, the Certificate Authority will also check the financial stability of the company and ensure that it is still in business. This is done using recognized companies such as Dun & Bradstreet.

The CA will return two files: the SPC file and a Private Key file. It is vital to keep these files safe and not let them fall into the wrong hands. If this happened, there is the potential that someone could distribute malicious code that would be associated with us (although, as we shall see, a password is also required to sign the code).

The CA will charge for the approval process and for supplying the required files, but there will be no limit to the number of times we can use it to sign our code.

Using Microsoft Certificate Server

For our example, we shall generate the SPC and Private Key files using Microsoft Certificate Server. This is a product that enables us to act as our own CA and create an infrastructure based on public-key cryptography using digital certificates.

This use of Microsoft Certificate Server is OK to illustrate the code-signing procedure, but remember that a user who receives downloaded code should have confidence in both the software publisher *and* the CA. In the real world, since users are unlikely to have heard of our CA, it is improbable that they will trust our control. However, Microsoft Certificate Server is useful for Intranets/Extranets where our employees and business partners would certainly trust certificates issued by our CA.

So let us generate our SPC and Private Key file. Don't worry too much about the details of Microsoft Certificate Server yet; this product will be discussed in detail in Chapter 9.

To create the files we navigate to the Certificate Enrollment Form. It is accessed using the following URL:

http://harrison/CertSrv/CertEnroll/ceenroll.asp

where harrison is the name of the machine where my installation of Microsoft Certificate Server resides. You should replace this part of the URL with one appropriate for your machine.

On the first screen we fill in the organization details. For the sake of this example, we have called ourselves Smiley Software.

By selecting the Advanced button we can specify the following:

- Enable Export Private keys to File
- Enable Create an SPC file
- Set the Usage to Code Signing

 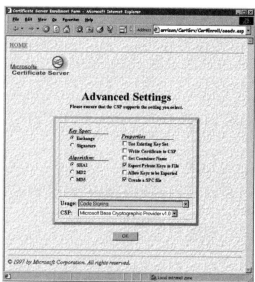

When we select the OK button, a dialog is displayed that requests a name for the Private Key file.

Once this has been entered, we return back to the Certificate Enrollment Form. We can now select the Submit Request button for our files to be generated.

On submission, we are requested for a password which is required whenever we use the Private Key file to sign code. It is vital that this password be kept safe and confidential in case the Private Key file mistakenly falls into the wrong hands.

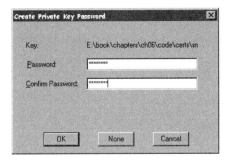

The next message, hopefully, tells us that our certificate has been successfully generated. We can now download the SPC file by selecting the **Download** button

A dialog is then displayed that requests a name for the SPC file.

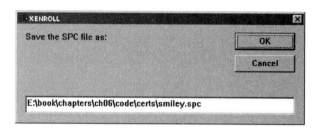

And that's all from Microsoft Certificate Server until Chapter 9. We now have our SPC and Private Key files.

Signing the Code

The final thing to do is sign the package to identify us as the author. This is so that when the control is downloaded, the user will see our credentials and identify us as the software publisher. Hopefully they will trust us and thus have the confidence in our software to allow the installation to proceed. Remember that the user being alerted to the download is subject to having appropriate security levels applied, i.e., medium level.

The tool used to sign the code is a utility called SignCode (executable name is signcode.exe). This utility is available with Visual Studio, IEAK, and the Microsoft Platform SDK.

When we sign our code, the following actions are undertaken:

- A hash algorithm is applied to the code package; the resulting digest is then signed using the private key
- The certificates in the SPC file plus the signed digest information are used to create a PKCS #7 formatted object
- A timestamp is obtained from a timestamping server, such as the one provided by Verisign
- The PKCS #7 object, the code package, and the timestamp are processed to form the signed code package.

These actions are illustrated in the following diagram:

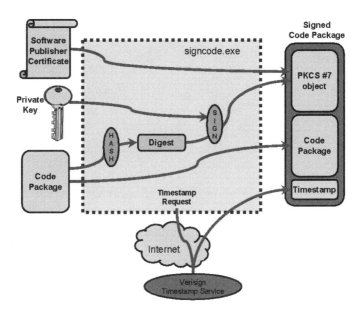

The SignCode utility is invoked with a series of parameters that conforms to the syntax below:

signcode [options] filename

The command option toggles that we shall use are as follows:

Toggle	Parameter
-spc	The name of the SPC file
-v	The name of the Private Key file
-n	Friendly name for the package
-i	URL of Web site where user can get more information about the package and software publisher
-t	URL of timestamp service e.g. Verisign at **http://timestamp.verisign.com/script/timstamp.dll**

Because the command is quite long and complex, it is best to key it into a batch file. This can then be invoked from the command line.

In the example shown here, the batch file is called sign.bat.

To sign the code, we must be online to the Internet so that we can communicate with the Timestamp Service

When we invoke the command, we are prompted for the password for the Private Key file.

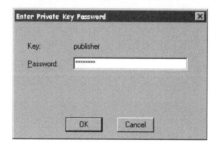

When the command in invoke, we are prompted

Deploying the Control

Let us now try to deploy our code. We shall create a simple Web page that displays our control and encourages users to click on it.

To create a Web page that incorporates our control we must use the HTML <**OBJECT**> tag as follows:

```
<OBJECT id="SmileyFace" name="SmileyFace"
    classid="clsid:250BDADA-368C-11D2-B99D-0080C74763E3"
    codebase="smiley.cab#version=1,0,0,0"
    border="0" width="99" height="98">
</OBJECT>
```

The **codebase** attribute points to the location of our signed package and gives the version of the control that is required. If the control is either not installed or is installed but out of date, the component download process will be invoked. The location may be a complete URL; for example, to access the standard ActiveX Controls available from the Microsoft Web site—in our example, the cabinet file is located on the same folder as the Web page.

The **classid** attribute contains the global unique identifier (GUID) for the control. This is a unique number generated by VB when the control is built.

Since such a number is not easy to remember, it is best to use one of the Microsoft development tools to insert the control into the HTML.

The following screen dumps show how this can be done using Front-Page Express (supplied with IE4).

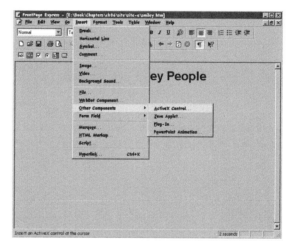

We can get a list of the installed ActiveX Controls by selecting the Insert|Other Components |ActiveX Control menu option.

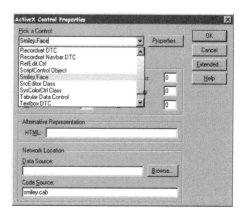

We select our Smiley Face control from the list of controls.

The **<OBJECT>** tag for the control is then inserted into the HTML.

The full HTML code for the page is as follows (some of the unnecessary HTML "noise" that FrontPage likes to insert has been deleted for clarity).

```
<HTML>
<HEAD>
<TITLE>Smiley Face</TITLE>
</HEAD>
<BODY bgcolor=silver>
<FONT FACE="Arial">
<CENTER>
<H1>Happy Smiley People</H1>

<OBJECT id="SmileyFace" name="SmileyFace"
    classid="clsid:250BDADA-368C-11D2-B99D-0080C74763E3"
    codebase="smiley.cab#version=1,0,0,0"
    border="0" width="99" height="98">
</OBJECT>

<H4>Click Me</H4>
</CENTER>
</FONT>
</BODY>
</HTML>
```

Our page is now ready for the Web. All we need to do now is create an IIS virtual root that points to a folder containing our Web page and signed code package.

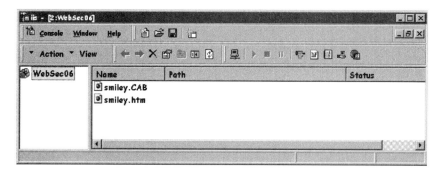

The User's Experience

When the user navigates to our Smiley Web page, IE will detect the `<OB-JECT>` tag and look in the Windows Registry for a component associated with the specified `classid`. If the component has been installed, then IE4 will check that the version is the one required.

If the component is either not installed or not up to date, IE will proceed to download the component from the location specified in the `code-base` attribute.

If the user has its security level (for the zone that our Smiley Web page is located within) to Warn before running potentially dangerous content, then the following screen will be seen:

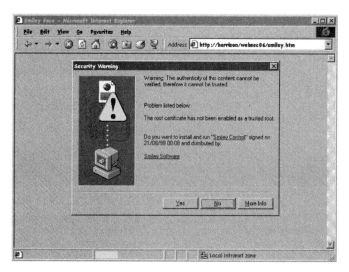

Once the package has been downloaded, the details of the PKCS #7 object are displayed for the user to decide whether they trust the control.

This Security Warning dialog warns us that the root certificate for the CA that generated the SPC file has not been installed on the browser (i.e., our Harrison CA is not a trusted CA).

This highlights why using Microsoft Certificate Server is not suitable for creating our own SPC files if we are deploying our software over the Internet. Instead we would need to get our SPC file from a recognized CA that everyone trusts, such as Verisign.

To continue, we shall assume we are working in an Intranet/Extranet environment where all our staff and business partners trust us and will accept code signed by our Harrison CA. To install the root certificate for our CA, we navigate to a Web page provided by our installation of Microsoft Certificate Server. Again, don't worry too much about the details of this, as we shall discuss Microsoft Certificate Server later in Chapter 9.

The Web page to access the CA certificate is:

http://harrison/CertSrv/CertEnroll/cacerts.htm

To install the certificate, click on the hyperlink. When asked to Open or Save the certificate file, select the Open option.

Finally, a dialog allowing the certificate details to be examined. Select the OK button to accept the certificate.

Now that the CA certificate has been installed, let's try to access our Smiley Web page again.

This time, the Security Warning dialog informs us that the CA has verified the software publisher.

By clicking on the hyperlink "Smiley Control" we access the Web site that gives us more information about the package and software publisher. This is the URL we specified when we signed the code using the –i option toggle.

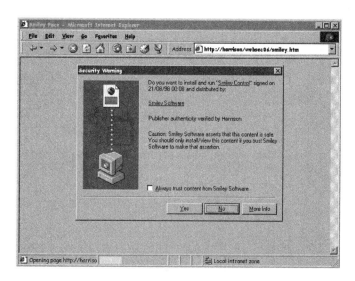

By clicking on the hyperlink "Smiley Software" we access detailed information about the certificate properties, i.e., the information stored in the PKCS #7 object that was generated when we signed the code.

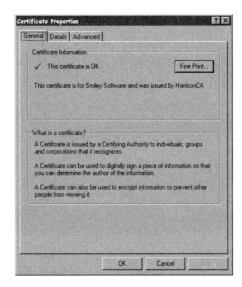

Finally, if we accept the code download, our ActiveX Control will be installed and its functionality becomes part of our Web page.

■ Summary

In this chapter we have seen how Microsoft has delivered a comprehensive Web security solution for the desktop.

The key points to this chapter are:

- When IE accesses a machine in a particular security zone it will automatically adjust the security settings to a suitable level that matches the perceived level of risk; appropriate security levels must be configured for the Internet zone.

- The IE Administration Kit helps an organization deploy of IE across the enterprise with a specific security and cosmetic configuration.

- Whilst Web users may believe that they are operating anonymously, there are mechanisms available to profile and track the activities of the user. Further exploitation can be undertaken if certain details about the user (e.g., name, email, etc.) can be captured.

- The user of RSACi ratings enables a desktop to be configured that protects a user from receiving unexpected offensive content.

- ActiveX and Java have very different security models:

- ActiveX Controls relies on trust and uses Authenticode sign-coding to provide the user with accountability and electronic shrink-wrapping; as a result ActiveX is powerful but potentially dangerous.

- Java Applets are sandboxed which often imposes severe limitations but makes them much safer.

- Never run "untrusted" software. Users must be trained to fully understand the dangers of running such software.

This concludes Section One of the book.

Now get ready to get your hands dirty . . . the programming starts now!

ASP Security Fundamentals

Up to now we have studied the core security technologies that Microsoft has provided to enable us to create a secure infrastructure for our Web applications. The second section of the book builds on this foundation to discuss building secure Web solutions using application-level security. Over the next two chapters we shall look at **Active Server Pages** (ASP), the key programmatic method for building IIS applications, and investigate how Web security is enhanced using application-level control.

Active Server Pages is Microsoft's compelling server-based technology for building dynamic and interactive Web pages, and it is fundamental for programming the new generation of IIS Web solutions.

In this chapter we shall:

- Take a quick crash course and undertake some ASP groundwork to discuss the key concepts; this will get us ready for the security-related demonstrations in the next chapter
- Discuss how ASP handles sessions using cookies to highlight the risks of a potential attack by someone hijacking an ASP session and invoking logic under another user's context; we shall consider the options available to protect against such attacks.

While we study application-level security levels, it is vital to appreciate that such techniques must be used in combination with the core security offered by the Windows NT operating system or the IIS engine, and not as a direct replacement.

We begin with an overview of how ASP helps us to quickly build great Web applications.

ASP Overview

Today's Web sites have moved well beyond the delivery of static HTML files, and users demand services which dynamically generate Web pages with content based on the identity of the user, the state of back-end components/databases, and any previously entered data. To enable such functionality, a Web server must provide extensions allowing integration to software components, databases, and legacy systems. IIS supports the Common Gateway Interface (CGI), which is the industry standard, and is supported by nearly every Web server implementation.

A CGI application is a program and is invoked when an HTTP request references the executable file name as part of the URL. For example:

http:/www.harrison.net/_vti_bin/search.exe?info=Internet

The CGI specification details how such a program accesses any input information and generates the output HTML file. The problem with CGI is that each invocation of a process is very resource intensive, and a busy Web server could have severe performance problems.

The alternative approach adopted by IIS is the open **Internet Server Applications Programming Interface** (ISAPI) standard. Microsoft has implement its **ISAPI extension** as a Dynamic Link Library (DLL), which means that it is loaded only once, on first demand, and then stays resident in the same process as the IIS Web server. Although the development and internals of ISAPI extension differ from those of a CGI program, the way they are referenced externally within a URL is similar. For example:

http:/www.harrison.net/_isapi/search.dll?info=Internet

In addition to server extensions, the ISAPI specification also provides for Web Server **ISAPI filters**. These are used to intercept and optionally process every HTTP request. Filters can be used for such tasks as additional security measures, auditing, redirecting requests, etc., but because they act on every message, they should be used sparingly (otherwise severe performance problems may occur). The simplest method for the development of ISAPI extensions and filters is to use the ISAPI wizard supplied with Microsoft's Visual C++. This wizard leads the developer through a number of dialogs to capture the various options available, and then it generates the skeleton code for the ISAPI application. Comments are inserted where the developer's code needs to be added. CGI and ISAPI are shown in the diagram below.

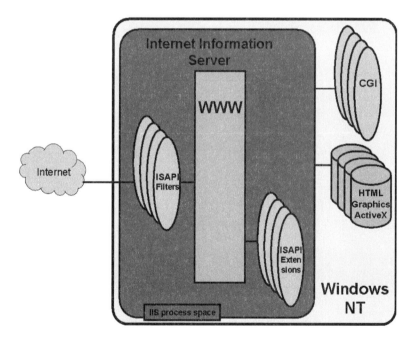

The latest version of IIS now offers process isolation, which means that ISAPI applications can be identified to run in a separate process space from the main Web server. This increases the robustness of the Web server by avoiding the potential for a misbehaving section of the code to bring down the whole server and all Web applications.

Active Server Pages (ASP) builds on top of the ISAPI infrastructure to provide a server-side application framework making it even easier than using high-level languages like VC++ to build dynamic Web applications.

An Active Server Page is a file with an `.ASP` suffix that contains both HTML syntax and server-side script logic. When the Web server receives an HTTP request for the ASP document, an output HTML file is generated for the response using a combination of both the static HTML information plus HTML that is generated by the scripting. The URL reference for an ASP page is similar to those for ISAPI and CGI. For example:

http://www.harrison.net/_asp/search.asp?info+Internet

As might be expected, ASP security is tightly integrated with Windows NT and IIS security. For an ASP to be invoked, the following conditions must be satisfied:

- The ASP file must have permissions applied which grant read access to the Windows NT user account associated with the Web user's session; if the `IUSR_sysname` account has read access, then the user may remain anonymous

- The IIS Application Settings for the directory in which the ASP file resides must be set to Script

Configuring the system to satisfy such conditions was discussed back in Chapter 3.

Rather than just develop script processing for ASP, Microsoft has used ActiveX to provide a flexible architecture for adding any scripting language to any application. So let us start by looking at ActiveX Scripting:

ActiveX Scripting

ActiveX Scripting allows **script hosts** to invoke scripting services within **script engines**. Because COM handles the *software plumbing* between the two, the hosts and engines can be from different software vendors.

The ActiveX Scripting specifications define the interfaces that a script host and script engine must support. The vendor of the script engine defines the script language, syntax, and execution rules. All script logic is interpreted on the fly by the script engine, and there is no concept of compiling the scripts. This is shown in the following diagram:

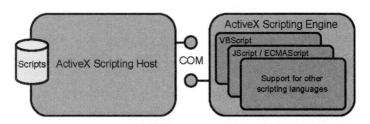

Internet Explorer, ASP, and the Windows Scripting Host are all examples of script hosts, but you can now use the framework to add scripting to your own applications.

Scripting Languages

Visual Basic Script (VBScript) and **JScript** are examples of scripting languages, but you can also develop your own. There are now several other scripting languages available from third parties (e.g., Perl, Python, Awk, etc.). VBScript is a subset of the Visual Basic for Applications (as used by Microsoft Office Products) which in turn is a subset of the popular Visual Basic. JScript is Microsoft's implementation of Netscape's JavaScript language. It was recently standardized by ECMA (European Computer Manufacturers Association) after joint submissions from Microsoft and Netscape, and is now called ECMAScript.

> Note: VBScript is in fact a **safe** subset of Visual Basic for security reasons and cannot access items like disks, system resources, or the operating environment. (It can, however, call COM components that could implement such actions. COM components that are safe can be marked as Safe for Scripting and Safe for Initializing, as we saw in Chapter 6.

While there are third parties supplying alternative scripting languages, most people will use one of the two Microsoft-supplied core options, VBScript or JScript, but which is best? Well, the truth is that there is very little to choose between the capabilities of the two. Both languages can be used by Web authors with minimal programming experience.

At the time of writing, Internet Explorer is the only browser that supports VBScript. Thus, if you are aiming for mass penetration on the Internet, you should probably restrict the client-side scripting to the more commonly supported ECMAScript/JavaScript. If you are developing for an Intranet, where you will have control over the infrastructure and can enforce Internet Explorer as the choice of browser, it would be reasonable to use the more popular VBScript.

With server-side scripting and ASP, the choice of language is less crucial. All script processing is handled on the server, and the output delivered to the browser can be standard platform-independent HTML. In such cases, where the choice of language is unimportant, choose the language for which you have the most investment in staff skills.

The Power of Scripting

The real power of scripting comes with the ability to interact with other objects. This enables accessing object properties, invoking methods, and detecting events, and of course all this happens using COM under the covers. Accessible objects are either:

- Intrinsic (built-in) objects exposed within the script host—often referred to as an **object model**
- External executable software components.

CLIENT-SIDE SCRIPTING

Client-side scripting can be inserted into an HTML page using the <**SCRIPT**> tags pair. To identify the script language, the **LANGUAGE** attribute is used, as shown below.

```
<HTML>
<HEAD>
        <TITLE>Document title
        </TITLE>
        <SCRIPT LANGUAGE="VBSCRIPT">
            Client-side VBS scripting logic
        </SCRIPT>
</HEAD>
<BODY>
</BODY>
</HTML>
```

Prior to scripting, all user interactions had to be handled by communication with the Web server. Script logic now enables client-side processing to occur and can help to avoid some of the time-consuming communication with overburdened servers.

Furthermore, scripting is used to integrate all element objects in a Web page (e.g., tags, images, text, etc.), browser objects (e.g., windows, frames, history, etc.), and any software component that has been installed on the desktop machine (e.g., OLE compliant applications, ActiveX Controls, Java Applets).

SERVER-SIDE SCRIPTING

ASP uses server-side scripting to dynamically create HTML responses. The content generated is typically based on the user's identity, parameters in the HTTP request, and interactions with other objects (e.g., ASP objects, multi-tier client/server business objects, middleware to access databases and legacy systems, BackOffice components, etc.). ASP provides a number of built-in objects and useful components. The built-in objects simplify many of the common server-side tasks, such as handling HTTP request/responses, the user's session, and the Web environment.

Server-side scripting is inserted in an ASP file using either the <SCRIPT> tags pair or <% & %> delimiters. To distinguish client-side scripting from server-side scripting, the latter's **<SCRIPT>** tag should include the **RUNAT="SERVER"** attribute and value. For example:

```
<HTML>
<HEAD>
        <TITLE>Document title
        </TITLE>
        <SCRIPT LANGUAGE="VBSCRIPT" RUNAT="SERVER">
            Server-side VBS scripting logic
        </SCRIPT>
        <SCRIPT LANGUAGE="VBSCRIPT">
            Client-side VBS scripting logic
        </SCRIPT>
</HEAD>
<BODY>
        <% Server-side VBS scripting logic %>
</BODY>
```

Business-Logic Confidentiality

One important security aspect of ASP is that server-side scripting logic is not exposed in the downloaded file. The only information sent over the wire to the client is the generated HTML. This is in contrast with client-side scripting, which can be inspected in its entirety by simply viewing the HTML source code.

This means that if you are concerned about people copying your clever code or seeing your confidential business rules, then you should engage such logic in the Web server. In practice, you will find that both server-side and client-side scripting have specific uses, and that the design of your Web application will require a combination of the two.

ASP Intrinsic Objects

ASP is supplied with six built-in objects that can be used by our server-side scripting. The ASP objects, whose use is fundamental in ASP scripting, are:

- **Server**—provides access to various utility functions
- **Application**—enables the sharing of information across multiple users of an application
- **Session**—enables user context to be carried across multiple HTTP requests (recall from Chapter 6 that HTTP is a context-free protocol)
- **Request**—provides access to information in the HTTP request
- **Response**—provides access to the message being generated to send back in the HTTP response
- **ObjectContext**—provides transaction Web pages and enables a transaction to be committed or aborted.

> For a comprehensive description of the numerous methods, properties, and events exposed by the ASP intrinsic objects, the reader is referred to one of the many books that concentrates on core ASP. For example, *Professional ASP 2.0* by Richard Harrison and others (WROX, ISBN 1-861001-26-6).

These built-in objects are supplemented with other add-in server components that we shall now discuss.

ActiveX Server Components

Using ASP we can create pages dynamically and develop some exciting applications. There is almost no limit to what can be achieved. The process is more like writing an application than creating an HTML page, and ASP pages can soon grow to quite an amazing size with a mixture of text, HTML, and code; in fact, Microsoft likes to call them **Web Applications**.

But let's be realistic here. The code we are using is only interpreted VBScript or JScript. Once we start to create really complex routines, we will see the effects as a slowing down of the server's response while it processes our code. And remember that both VBScript and JScript are limited-functionality languages. They cannot, for example, access files or other applications directly, and so we are soon likely to hit limitations when we start to write serious business applications.

The ideal solution is to minimize the amount of script, develop software components in a high-level language, and integrate them with ASP using COM. It is widely recognized that the most sensible approach is to:

- Use a layered methodology to partition the business and data access logic into software components
- Restrict the ASP logic to:
  - synchronizing the information flow with the software components
  - handling the generation of the presentation logic (which is dynamically deployed onto the desktop for execution).

ASP is often thought of as software "glue" technology—sticking together software components from Microsoft, from third parties, and home-grown ones to form a single integrated solution.

Using Components on the Server

The use of software components with ASP is accomplished by the **CreateObject** method exposed by the ASP intrinsic object called **Server**. Using this, we can create instances of other objects on the server (or another machine), and access their methods and events directly. Fortunately, the use of COM for interobject communication occurs under the covers, and in most cases, the Microsoft development tools insulate the developer from most of these complexities.

> In IIS3 we could create objects using the VB **CreateObject** method. We shall see later that in IIS4 we must call **Server.CreateObject** for the user's security context to be passed through to MTS. As Microsoft puts it, "**Server.CreateObject** is no longer optional, it's the law!"

Suddenly, we are freed from the limitations imposed by the scripting language. If we cannot do it in script, or it is going to take too long to execute, we just use an object written in almost any other language to do the job instead. COM objects, used in this way, are often referred to as **Active Server Components**.

Such components should be installed with Microsoft Transaction Server to provide distributed transaction coordination facilities, build scalable solutions, and provide a security environment. We shall discuss later, in

Chapter 10, the security implications of **Active Server Components** running in the MTS environment.

ASP Session Security

We shall now take a look at the ASP session and the mechanisms used to handle user context across multiple HTTP requests. We shall look at how ASP enables this operation and the security issues that it imposes.

The HTTP protocol is described as a "stateless" protocol because the server that processes the HTTP request does not retain any context information (or state) for use with subsequent requests from the same source. Any reader familiar with building client/server applications will quickly realize that the inability to carry context across multiple requests imposes severe restrictions. There are methods to overcome this restriction, but before ASP came along, building serious Web applications was sometimes a tedious process.

One method used to carry session context across a sequence of HTTP requests is to carry the information in the HTML pages. This is done by storing the information within a dynamically generated HTML form field and using the **Hidden** attribute so that the information is not visible to the user.

For example:

```
<FORM method=post action=process.asp>
    <INPUT type=hidden name=account value=001202123>
<!- context state -->
    <P>Amount <INPUT name=amount size=20> </P>
    <P><INPUT type=submit value=Submit name=submit> </P>
</FORM>
```

An alternative technique to carry the session context across HTTP requests is to store the information in **cookies**. We discussed cookies in detail in Chapter 6. Recapping, a cookie is a small item of information stored in the Web browser and sent to the Web server attached to each HTTP request.

In pre-ASP days, a Web site would carry the session context as cookies, and all such information would be dragged across in every HTTP. If the amount of context was large, then the HTTP requests became bloated and impacted on bandwidth. Another approach was to store the context on disk and use a key to the data as the cookie; since a database key would be small, the size of the HTTP request was barely affected.

ASP builds on this approach but dramatically avoids the programming complexity of the "legacy" cookie-handling mechanism. This is all thanks to **ASP Sessions**.

ASP Sessions

In many traditional applications, a user will log on to the system, perform various activities, and then complete the session by logging off. ASP can provide a similar "session" concept and relate a sequence of HTTP requests over a finite time from the same user.

ASP creates a **Session** object (one of the ASP intrinsic objects that we touched on earlier) whenever an HTTP request is received for an ASP document and no **Session** object is currently associated with the client. Once instantiated, the **Session** object will exist until either:

- The session is aborted via a call to **Session.Abandon**
- No activity from the client is received within a defined time period (the default is 20 minutes, but this can be changed via a call to **Session.Timeout** or a property configured from the Internet Service Manager).

Each **Session** object is stored in memory. Thus care has to be taken on heavily hit sites, because this can become an excessive drain on resources. It is often difficult to get a user leaving a site to access a certain page that includes **Session.Abandon** logic. Users will frequently leave sites by entering the new URL in the browser's address line, and when this happens, the redundant **Session** object hangs around unnecessarily until the timeout occurs. That is why it is important not to set the timeout too high. Alternatively, if it is set too low, irritating timeouts may occur (and the context may be lost) while a user is reading and analyzing a page.

Storing Context

User-context information can be stored in and retrieved from the **Session** object. For example, an ASP script could store information received in the following form:

```
<% Session("username") = Request.Form("username") %>
```

Then, for a later HTTP request, provided that the session object has not been destroyed for one of the above reasons, the ASP script logic can retrieve this information from the **Session** object.

```
<% If Session("username")= "administrator" then

        Response.Redirect "admin.asp"

   End If %>
```

ASP keeps the **Session** object in memory. But if several users are accessing the Web site simultaneously, several **Session** objects will exist. So how does ASP match the appropriate **Session** object to a particular user? Let us investigate . . .

Session Tracking

To identify a **Session** object, ASP allocates each object a unique **session identifier**. The session identifier is stored as a cookie in the Web browser and attached to every HTTP request to the site. The core ASP processing uses the session identifier cookie to associate the user with the appropriate **Session** object and make this object available to the ASP script logic.

An example HTTP response header containing a session identifier cookie is shown below. Note that no expiration time is specified, which means that the cookie will only exist for the lifetime of the browser session. As soon as the user kills the instance of the browser, the cookie will be lost and the session broken—the **Session** object will last until the timeout occurs.

```
Set-Cookie: ASPSESSIONIDQQQQQGAD=GCCLKCBBLABKNDHCPDLOMINB; path= /
```

The name of the cookie used on your machine will be different from the example shown above. The last eight characters used in the session identifier cookie name (after **ASPSESSIONID. . . .**) are randomly generated each time the Web Server machine is booted.

The following simple VB program illustrates the session identifier cookie in use.

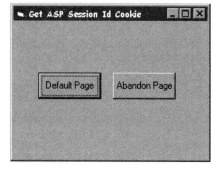

The application contains two buttons, and on selection, they both initiate an HTTP request referencing an ASP file. They both access the same page but pass different parameters tacked onto the end of the URL, i.e., either **mode=normal** or **mode=abandon.**

Mode is the parameter name **normal/abandon** is the parameter value.

The program then displays the HTTP response in two message boxes. The first shows the HTTP Response Header, and the second shows the generated HTML data.

The HTML data returned includes the HTTP Request Headers that were in the original request. This is clarified below:

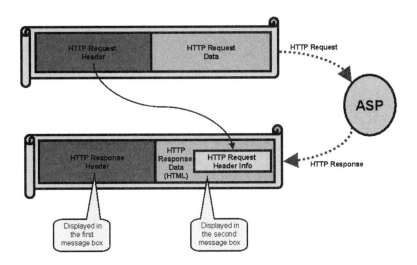

THE CODE

Let us first look at the code that achieves this:

This program is available on the CD-ROM
The URLs of the ASP pages must be updated to match your own environment.

The HTTP protocol is implemented by the Microsoft Internet Transfer Control (**%systemroot%\system32\msinet.ocx**), which can be selected using the Project|Components menu option. This control has been given the identifier **ctrlInternet**. It exposes the **Execute** function that enables an HTTP request to be invoked by specifying two parameters—the URL of the ASP file and the "GET" operation.

The two buttons are given the identifiers **AbandonPage** and **Default-Page**. Once the HTTP request is initiated, the buttons are disabled to prevent an additional request from being invoked while awaiting the response.

The **stillExecuting** property specifies whether the Internet Transfer Control is busy.

```
Option Explicit

Private Sub AbandonPage_Click()
    If Not ctrlInternet.StillExecuting Then
        ctrlInternet.Execute "http://harrison/websec07-a/default.asp?
mode=abandon", "GET"
        AbandonPage.Enabled = False
        DefaultPage.Enabled = False
    End If
End Sub
```

```
Private Sub DefaultPage_Click()
    If Not ctrlInternet.StillExecuting Then
        ctrlInternet.Execute "http://harrison/websec07-a/default.asp?
mode=normal", "GET"
        AbandonPage.Enabled = False
        DefaultPage.Enabled = False
    End If
End Sub
```

The Microsoft Internet Transfer Control fires the event `ctrlInternet_StateChanged` when there is a change in the state of the connection. The state of the connection is passed as an integer value; the value of `icResponseCompleted` (12) means that the request has been completed and all data has been received.

The HTTP response contains two parts—the headers (control information) and the generated HTML data. We can get these using the `GetHeader` and `GetChunk` methods exposed by the Internet Transfer Control. The buttons can then be enabled allowing further requests to be initiated. The `GetChunk` method requires the size of the response to be specified. The pages we are accessing will not exceed the value specified, but we provide some defensive coding by calling `Cancel` to stop any outstanding request and close any connections currently established.

The HTTP response headers and data are displayed using a message box.

```
Private Sub ctrlInternet_StateChanged(ByVal State As Integer)
    Dim vHeader As Variant
    Dim vData As Variant
    On Error GoTo ErrorHandler
```

```
    Select Case State
    Case icResponseCompleted
        vHeader = ctrlInternet.GetHeader()
        vData = ctrlInternet.GetChunk(4096)
        ctrlInternet.Cancel

        MsgBox "Header: " & vHeader
        MsgBox "Data: " & vData
        DefaultPage.Enabled = True
        AbandonPage.Enabled = True

    End Select

    Exit Sub

ErrorHandler:
    MsgBox "Error " & Err.Description

End Sub
```

The ASP file is very simple. It first displays the contents of the HTTP request headers using the **All_HTTP** server variable. This can be accessed using the ASP Request object.

The parameter passed in the request is checked using **Request.Query String("mode")**; if a value of "**abandon**" is passed, then the Session object is deleted using **Session.Abandon**.

```
<%@LANGUAGE="VBSCRIPT" %>
<HTML>
<HEAD>
</HEAD>
<BODY bgColor=wheat>
<CENTER>
<HR>
<H1>Home Page</H1>
<HR>
<h4>Request Headers:</h4>
<%
    =Request.ServerVariables("All_HTTP")
```

(continued)

```
%>
<br><br>
<%

    if Request.QueryString("mode") = "abandon" then
            Session.Abandon
            Response.Write "Session Abandoned"
    end if
%>
</BODY>
</HTML>
```

SESSION HANDLING

We can use our program to see how ASP handles the session identifier cookie.

We shall first hit the Default Page button

We can see in the HTTP Response Headers that an ASP session identifier cookie is returned.

A **Session** object now exists on the server; this is now available for use by the ASP script logic whenever the ASPSESSIONIDGGGGGGAD cookie is attached in any subsequent HTTP request.

The generated HTML data includes the HTTP Request Headers from the original request. At this time the cookie had not yet been created.

> URL =
> http://harrison/websec07-a/default.asp?mode=normal

> Headers:

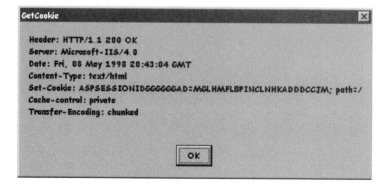

Data:

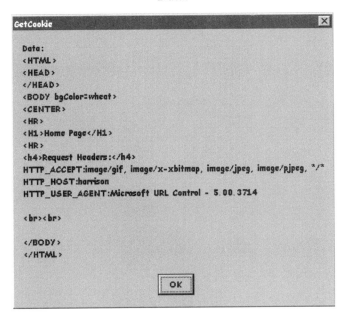

Next we shall hit the Abandon Page button

We can see that there is no cookie information in this HTTP response. However, the Web Browser (or Microsoft Internet Transfer Control) still remembers the earlier cookie information.

We can see from the generated HTML data that the HTTP request contained the session identifier cookie, and this enabled ASP to make the appropriate **Session** object available to the script logic.

Since the mode was abandon, the session was abandoned and the **Session** object deleted.

Headers:

URL = http://harrison/websec07-a/default.asp? mode=abandon

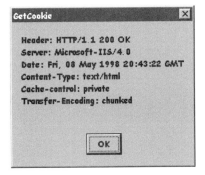

Data:

```
GetCookie                                                    [X]

 Data:
 <HTML>
 <HEAD>
 </HEAD>
 <BODY bgColor=wheat>
 <CENTER>
 <HR>
 <H1>Home Page</H1>
 <HR>
 <h4>Request Headers:</h4>
 HTTP_ACCEPT:image/gif, image/x-xbitmap, image/jpeg, image/pjpeg, */*
 HTTP_HOST:harrison
 HTTP_USER_AGENT:Microsoft URL Control - 5.00.3714
 HTTP_COOKIE:ASPSESSIONIDGGGGGGAD=MGLHMFLBPINCLNHKADDDCCJM

 <br><br>
 Session Abandoned
 </BODY>
 </HTML>

                        [  OK  ]
```

We shall finish by hitting the Default Page button once more.

Although ASP does not currently have a **Session** object allocated, we can see from the HTTP Response Headers that there is no update to the session identifier cookie.

Since no **Session** object existed, ASP will have created a new one (all previous context state will have been lost).

We can see from the generated HTML data that the HTTP request contained the original session identifier cookie. This same value is associated with the new **Session** object.

Headers:

URL =
http://harrison/websec07-a/default.asp?
mode=normal

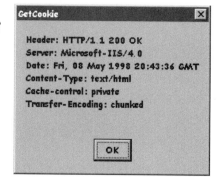

```
GetCookie                              [X]

 Header: HTTP/1.1 200 OK
 Server: Microsoft-IIS/4.0
 Date: Fri, 08 May 1998 20:43:36 GMT
 Content-Type: text/html
 Cache-control: private
 Transfer-Encoding: chunked

                   [  OK  ]
```

Data:

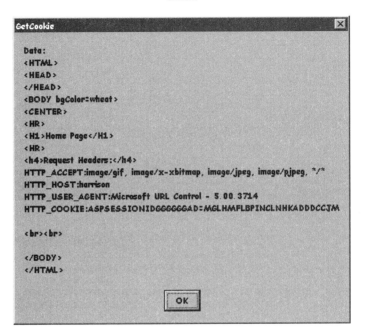

The only time a user will receive a new session identifier cookie is when either the Web browser or the Web server is restarted.

From this discussion we can see that ASP sessions rely on cookies. Support for old Web browsers that do not support cookies can be achieved using an ISAPI filter from Microsoft called a **Cookie Munger**.

This simulates cookies by analyzing and manipulating HTTP Requests and HTTP Responses. Browsers that do not send the ASP Session Identifier are assumed to not support cookies. For these browsers, the following is done:

- The ASP Session Identifier is appended to the end of any local URLs sent to the browser
- The ASP Session Identifier is removed from any requested URLs and a "simulated" ASP Session Identifier cookie is added to the HTTP Request Header.

More information is available at:

http://www.microsoft.com/workshop/server/toolbox/cookie.asp

The processing is very CPU intensive, and the filter should not be used unless required.

Now that we understand how cookie processing works and have seen that it is vital for ASP session handling, let us investigate an issue frequently cited by security experts in regard to this mechanism.

Session Hijacking

One of the major concerns with ASP Sessions is whether an attacker could **hijack a session** by capturing (or guessing) a currently used session identifier cookie. The cookie could then be attached to an HTTP request to invoke ASP logic to use someone else's active **Session** object. This means that the hacker would have avoided any user authentication and have the potential to access the user's information or invoke transactions under the user's identity.

The routine used to generate the session identifier value is a complex algorithm designed to make it difficult to guess a valid value. The session identifiers are 32-bit values that are mixed with random data and encrypted to generate a 16-character cookie string. Both the session identifier's starting value and the encryption key are randomly selected when the Web server is started.

One technique that can be used to provide additional confidence against hijacking is to generate our own more complex cookie string that is greater than 16 characters. This cookie value can be stored in the **Session** object and sent to the user's browser. All subsequent HTTP requests are validated by checking whether this additional cookie is as expected. We shall demonstrate this in Chapter 9.

Another solution is to use Secure Sockets Layer (SSL) encryption, which was discussed in Chapter 5. This prevents a hacker from sniffing the network and analyzing the contents of the HTTP traffic. If SSL is used, it is important to remember that all traffic (including requests for non-HTML files) will attach the session identifier cookie. Thus if we are taking this approach we must use SSL for **all** subsequent requests to the site.

■ Summary

In this chapter we have discussed the fundamentals of ASP, the potent server-based technology that extends IIS to create interactive HTML pages for a public Web site or corporate Intranet application. In addition, we have discussed ASP sessions and addressed the frequent concern that a user's session could be hijacked.

The key points in this chapter are:

- Complex business logic should be implemented in software components that are deployed within Microsoft Transaction Server and use the security features provided by this environment (which we shall address in Chapter 10). ASP scripting should be used as software "glue" and to control the flow of component invocation.
- ASP server-side scripting logic is not exposed in the downloaded file, thus protecting intellectual property.
- ASP Security must be used in conjunction with the core security built into Windows NT and IIS. It should not be used as a replacement.
- VBScript is a safe subset of Visual Basic and cannot access such items as disks, system resources, or the operating environment.
- Session hijacking can be prevented by using additional, stronger identifier cookies and encrypting the network traffic.

We shall now proceed to demonstrate ASP security in action.

ASP Application-Level Security

In the preceding chapter we discussed the fundamentals of using ASP for application-level security and investigated the issues of how ASP handles a user session and identifies the user's session context.

Building our own application-level security enables us to create customized logic to provide further levels of assurance, better defense mechanisms, and custom-made user-tracking facilities while giving the user a convenient, easy-to-use, and personalized system.

In this chapter we shall get our hands dirty with plenty of programming code and study some examples of application-level security using ASP server-side scripting. These will include:

- Enforcing access controls and restricting Web site access to a closed user group (i.e., a defined community of users).

- Forcing users to register their personal details before they are allowed site access and then allowing them to manage this information, so that the burden of this task does not fall on the administrator
- Providing Web access auditing; this could be used for tracking down security breaches, billing, capacity planning, and determining the most popular areas of the site
- Programmatically accessing the information stored in a client's digital certificate
- Providing additional assurances against ASP Sessions being hijacked by someone guessing the ASP Session identifier cookie (as discussed in the previous chapter)

Many of these examples can be taken and used as the basis of your own Web solutions.

> All examples in this chapter can be found on the CD-ROM included with the book.

Since security requirements often provide controls over who can access particular areas of a Web site, we shall start with a look at using ASP script logic to identify the Web user.

ASP User Identification

In Chapter 6, we discussed user privacy and learned that *eating cookies can leave crumbs behind!* Even though many people believe they are accessing a Web site anonymously, the HTTP protocol is in fact providing items of information that can be used to track and profile them.

Using ASP logic, we can inspect such information, located in HTTP Request Headers, to obtain particulars about the user and to drive our programming logic through specific execution routes.

For example, if we detect the IP address (perhaps from the audit file) of a certain individual who is continually using abusive language on a community-based Web site, we could redirect him off to a warning page using the following code.

```
<%
    if Request.ServerVariables("REMOTE_ADDR") = "191.1.2.3" then
        Response.Redirect "warning.asp"
    end if
%>
```

> If the nature of our site is such that we frequently get rude people, the ASP logic could be driven from a text file storing IP addresses. The file could easily be updated, and this would be a better approach than amending the Web page each time.

Server Variables

There are many **ServerVariables** giving information about the browser and IIS that can be used by ASP script logic. Some of the more useful ones for application-level security are listed below:

Variable	Description
ALL_HTTP	HTTP headers sent by the client.
AUTH_PASSWORD	The password entered in the client's authentication dialog (basic authentication)
AUTH_TYPE	The authentication method used.
AUTH_USER	Authenticated user name.
CERT_COOKIE	Unique identifier for client certificate.
CERT_FLAGS	bit0 = 1 if the client certificate is present; bit1 = 1 if the CA is not in the list of trusted CAs.
CERT_ISSUER	Issuer field in the client certificate.
CERT_KEYSIZE	Number of bits in SSL communications key.
CERT_SECRETKEYSIZE	Number of bits in server certificate private key.
CERT_SERIALNUMBER	Serial number field of the client certificate.
CERT_SERVER_ISSUER	Issuer field in the server certificate.
CERT_SERVER_SUBJECT	Subject field in the server certificate.
CERT_SUBJECT	Subject field in the client certificate.
HTTP_<HeaderName>	The value stored in the HTTP header *HeaderName*.
HTTPS	Either ON (if the request came over secure channel) or OFF (non secure channel)
HTTPS_KEYSIZE	Number of bits in SSL communications key.
HTTPS_SECRETKEYSIZE	Number of bits in server certificate private key.
HTTPS_SERVER_ISSUER	Issuer field in the server certificate.
HTTPS_SERVER_SUBJECT	Subject field in the server certificate.
LOCAL_ADDR	IP address on which the request came in (useful for multi-homed machines).
LOGON_USER	Windows NT account that the user was authenticated with.
QUERY_STRING	Query information stored in the string following the question mark (?) in the HTTP request.
REMOTE_ADDR	IP address of the remote machine making the request.
REMOTE_HOST	The name of the remote machine making the request.
REMOTE_USER	Name of user.
SERVER_NAME	The server's host name, DNS alias, or IP address.
SERVER_PORT	The port number to which the request was sent.
SERVER_PORT_SECURE	Either 1 (if the request is received on a secure port) or 0 (non secure)

Let us consider another example where the user helps us by giving a few more clues—his name and a password.

ASP Authentication

In this section we shall see how to use the ASP **Response** object to alter the HTTP Response Headers to deny access to a Web site and challenge the user for his credentials. The user must then enter his user account and password to be allowed access to the site. To keep things simple for now, we shall check the user's credentials against a simple text file that contains valid users.

> We shall meet alternative "real world" examples later in the book when we investigate more sophisticated methods, such as using directory services and relational databases to validate the user.

There are many elementary sites on the Internet that provide a simple log-on mechanism to get past the home page. In such cases, these controls are inadequate, since if a Web surfer knows the URL of a site page, he can navigate to it directly by typing it into the browser's address field.

In our example, we shall use a mechanism that protects every page. If the ASP logic detects that the user has navigated to any Web site page without having first gone through the authentication process, it will redirect the user to another page that forces him to enter his credentials before he can gain access.

This authentication check logic will be needed at the top of every ASP page. However, repeating identical code on each page would be tedious and cause us severe grief if a change in the logic was ever required. Instead, the logic is written in a single file, **checkauth.inc**, and using the **server-side include** statement, the logic is merged into the top of each ASP when the page is invoked.

```
<%@LANGUAGE="VBSCRIPT" %>

<!-- #include file="checkauth.inc" -->

.......... remainder of ASP logic ..........
```

A session variable **authorized** is created and stored in the **Session** object. This can have one of three possible values:

0—not yet authorized

1—authorization in progress

2—authorized

The variable is initialized to a value of **0** in the `Session_OnStart` event in the `global.asa` file. This gets fired the first time a user navigates to one of the site's ASP files.

```
Sub Session_OnStart
    Session("authorized") = 0
End Sub
```

The `checkauth.inc` logic switches on the value of `authorized` to invoke the appropriate logic for the authorization state.

A value of **2** means that the user has been authenticated and the script logic just drops through, enabling the remainder of the ASP file to be processed.

A value of **0** means that the user has not yet been authenticated. The script logic will amend the HTTP Response Header to have an HTTP status code of 401. This tells the browser that user authentication is required. In addition, the header is amended to instruct the browser to proceed with Basic Authentication. At this stage the `authorized` value is updated to 1 so that the ASP logic knows that the next message received will contain the user's credentials and need authentication.

```
case 0
        Session("authorized") = 1
        Response.status = "401"
        Response.Addheader "WWW-Authenticate", "BASIC realm=""This is
a message"""
        Response.end
```

The string "This is a message" is displayed on the browser's dialog that prompts the user for the user account and password.

For a value of **1**, the script logic checks that the user's credentials are valid. This information is collected by the browser's log-on dialog and is encoded using a mechanism called **Base64** (which we shall discuss shortly).

We retrieve this information using the **HTTP_AUTHORIZATION** server variable. This information is always preceded by the text "Basic:" and so the first six characters are ignored (see example below). Furthermore, Base64 can pad the information with the "=" character so that our ASP logic removes any these trailing pad characters.

```
02/7/97    GET/default.asp HTTP/1.0
12:45:13   Accept: image/gif, image/x-xbitmap, image/jpeg, image/pjpeg,
           application/vnd.ms-excel, application/msword, application/
           vnd.ms-powerpoint, */*
           Accept-Language: en
           User-Agent: Mozilla/2.0 (compatible; MSIE 3.0B; Win32)
           Host: 194.1.1.32
           Connection: Keep-Alive
           Authorization: Basic:ZnJlZGR5OnRoZWZyb2c=
           ----------------------------------------------
```

Here is an example of an HTTP trace that shows the authorization string we must parse.

We shall see later that **Basic:ZnJlZGR5OnRoZWZyb2c** is user = freddy and password = thefrog

```
vAuthVal = Request.ServerVariables("HTTP_AUTHORIZATION")
if len(vAuthVal) > 6 then
    vAuthVal = mid(vAuthVal,7)

    while mid(vAuthVal,len(vAuthVal),1) = "=

    vAuthVal = mid(vAuthVal,1,len(vAuthVal)-1)
```

We shall store a list of all valid user credentials (in Base64 format) in an ASCII text file called **auth.txt**. The ASP processing opens this file and then loops through each entry to check if the user's credentials match a valid entry.

If a match is found, then the user's credentials are valid and they are successfully authenticated.

```
Set objFSO = CreateObject("Scripting.FileSystemObject")
Set objAuthFile = objFSO.OpenTextFile("e:\data\auth.txt")

while (not objAuthFile.AtEndOfStream) and (not vAuthorized)
    vFileVal = objAuthFile.ReadLine
    if vAuthVal = vFileVal then
    vAuthorized = true
    end if
wend
```

If the user is authenticated, the authorization state is updated; otherwise the user is forced off and redirected to a page saying "Goodbye". Using the **redirect** method on the **Response** object amends the HTTP Response header and achieves this.

```
if vAuthorized = true then
    Session("authorized") = 2
else
    Response.status = "200"
    Response.redirect "bye.htm"
    Response.end
end if
```

The full source code for the example is as follows:

How it was done—for our eyes only!

In this example, you must enable "Allow Anonymous Authentication"; both Basic Authentication and Windows NT Challenge/Response must be disabled

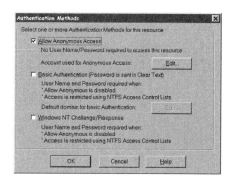

`global.asa`

```
<SCRIPT LANGUAGE="VBScript" RUNAT="Server">
Sub Session_OnStart
    Session("authorized") = 0
End Sub


Sub Application_OnStart
End Sub

</SCRIPT>
```

`default.asp`

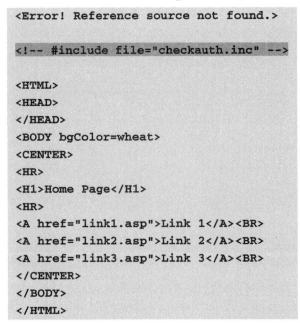

```
<Error! Reference source not found.>

<!-- #include file="checkauth.inc" -->


<HTML>
<HEAD>
</HEAD>
<BODY bgColor=wheat>
<CENTER>
<HR>
<H1>Home Page</H1>
<HR>
<A href="link1.asp">Link 1</A><BR>
<A href="link2.asp">Link 2</A><BR>
<A href="link3.asp">Link 3</A><BR>
</CENTER>
</BODY>
</HTML>
```

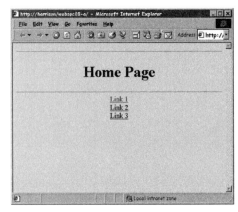

`link1.asp`

Pages `link2.asp` and `link3.asp` are similar, with the titles changed appropriately.

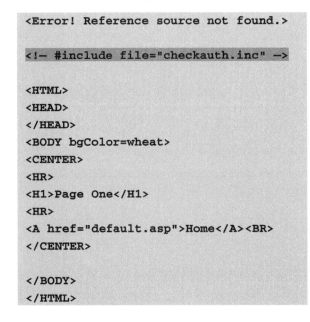

```
<Error! Reference source not found.>

<!— #include file="checkauth.inc" —>


<HTML>
<HEAD>
</HEAD>
<BODY bgColor=wheat>
<CENTER>
<HR>
<H1>Page One</H1>
<HR>
<A href="default.asp">Home</A><BR>
</CENTER>

</BODY>
</HTML>
```

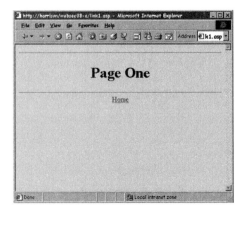

bye.htm

```
<HTML>
<HEAD>
</HEAD>
<BODY bgColor=wheat>
<H1>Goodbye!</H1>
</BODY>
</HTML
```

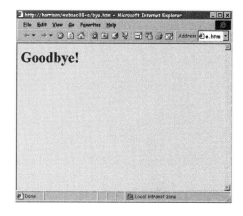

checkauth.inc

```
<%
    select case Session("authorized")

    case 0
        Session("authorized") = 1
        Response.status = "401"
        Response.Addheader "WWW-Authenticate", "BASIC realm=""This is
a message"""
        Response.end

    case 1
        Dim vAuthVal
        Dim vFileVal
        Dim objFSO
        Dim vAuthorized
        Dim objAuthFile

        vAuthorized = false

        vAuthVal = Request.ServerVariables("HTTP_AUTHORIZATION")
        if len(vAuthVal) > 6 then
            vAuthVal = mid(vAuthVal,7)

            while mid(vAuthVal,len(vAuthVal),1) = "="
                vAuthVal = mid(vAuthVal,1,len(vAuthVal)-1)
            wend
```

(continued)

```
        Set objFSO = CreateObject("Scripting.FileSystemObject")
        Set objAuthFile = objFSO.OpenTextFile("e:\data\auth.txt")

        while (not objAuthFile.AtEndOfStream) and (not vAuthorized)
           vFileVal = objAuthFile.ReadLine
           if vAuthVal = vFileVal then
           vAuthorized = true
           end if
        wend
    end if

    If vAuthorized = true then
        Session("authorized") = 2
    else
        Response.status = "200"
        Response.redirect "bye.htm"
        Response.end
    end if
case 2
    ' User has been authenticated...continue
end select
%>
```

Base 64

In the early days on the Internet, e-mail messages were limited to simple text messages containing printable ASCII characters. Because of this simple requirement, many of the standard Internet protocols were designed on the assumption that the character sets could be mapped onto 7 bits. Unfortunately, these protocols are unable to handle the 8-bit characters sets used by many modern-day programs, such as word-processors, spreadsheets, etc.

To avoid the replacement of these Internet protocols, algorithms have been devised for translating files and messages of 8-bit characters into a format represented by fewer bits. This translation process is often called **encoding**; to return a file or message back to its original format is called **decoding**.

There are several encoding schemes in use, the most popular being **uuencode, binhex,** and **Base64.** Whenever an encoded file/message is received, the recipient must know the scheme used so that the appropriate algorithm can be applied to decode the information.

Base64 is the encoding scheme defined by the MIME (Multipurpose Internet Mail Extensions) specification and is considered to be the most robust in passing through heterogeneous networks. This is because the scheme only uses a limited number of characters; these characters are shown below and are known to exist on all systems.

The encoding process involves mapping each sequence of 6 bits into a character from the Base64 character set as given below.

Bit value/encode char	Bit value/encode char	Bit value/encode char	Bit value/encode char
"000000" → "A"	"010000" → "Q"	"100000" → "g"	"110000" → "w"
"000001" → "B"	"010001" → "R"	"100001" → "h"	"110001" → "x"
"000010" → "C"	"010010" → "S"	"100010" → "i"	"110010" → "y"
"000011" → "D"	"010011" → "T"	"100011" → "j"	"110011" → "z"
"000100" → "E"	"010100" → "U"	"100100" → "k"	"110100" → "0"
"000101" → "F"	"010101" → "V"	"100101" → "l"	"110101" → "1"
"000110" → "G"	"010110" → "W"	"100110" → "m"	"110110" → "2"
"000111" → "H"	"010111" → "X"	"100111" → "n"	"110111" → "3"
"001000" → "I"	"011000" → "Y"	"101000" → "o"	"111000" → "4"
"001001" → "J"	"011001" → "Z"	"101001" → "p"	"111001" → "5"
"001010" → "K"	"011010" → "a"	"101010" → "q"	"111010" → "6"
"001011" → "L"	"011011" → "b"	"101011" → "r"	"111011" → "7"
"001100" → "M"	"011100" → "c"	"101100" → "s"	"111100" → "8"
"001101" → "N"	"011101" → "d"	"101101" → "t"	"111101" → "9"
"001110" → "O"	"011110" → "e"	"101110" → "u"	"111110" → "+"
"001111" → "P"	"011111" → "f"	"101111" → "v"	"111111" → "/"

This will all be clarified if we look at an example, so let us consider the message containing the credentials that is collected by the browser log-on dialog and sent to our ASP page for validation. Our imagined user's account name is freddy and his password is thefrog. Basic authentication sends these two items with a ":" character separating them, i.e., "freddy:thefrog".

Considering the ASCII value of each character in turn:

ASCII	Decimal	Binary	ASCII	Decimal	Binary
f	102	01100110	t	116	01110100
r	114	01110010	h	104	01101000
e	101	01100101	e	101	01100101
d	100	01100100	f	102	01100110
d	100	01100100	r	114	01110010
y	121	01111001	o	111	01101111
:	58	00111010	g	103	01100111

So we have a bit sequence of:

"**011001**1001110010011001010110010001**1001000**111100100111010011101000**1101000**0110010101100110011100100110111101100111"

Now considering every six bits we have the following:

6 bits	Base64	6 bits	Base64	6 bits	Base64
011001	Z	111001	5	011001	Z
100111	n	001110	O	110010	y
001001	J	100111	n	011011	b
100101	l	010001	R	110110	2
011001	Z	101000	o	011100	c
000110	G	011001	Z		
010001	R	010110	W		

Note that, as defined by Base64, trailing zero bits are appended to the last character to make it up to 6 bits.

Thus when the user enters for Basic Authentication an account name of freddy and a password of thefrog, the string of characters sent to the Web server is: `"Basic:ZnJlZGR5OnRoZWyb2c"`. There may also be some trailing "=" pad characters.

Authentication File

In our ASP example code, we compared the Base64 encoded authentication string with entries in an authorization file. This file had the credentials of all valid users (again in Base64). An alternative approach would have been to get the ASP script logic to decode the authentication string and compare it against a file with the credentials in readable format, but this would have put a little more work on the server processing.

So how do we get the list of valid credentials in Base64 encoded format into our authentication file? The answer is to set up a file containing a list of valid credentials in the clear and use a simple VB program to generate a Base64 encoded version.

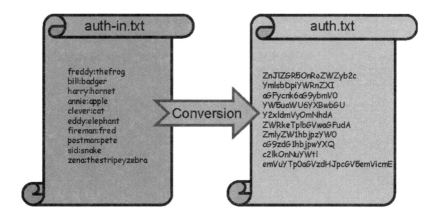

auth-in.txt

```
freddy:thefrog
bill:badger
harry:hornet
annie:apple
clever:cat
eddy:elephant
fireman:fred
postman:pete
sid:snake
zena:thestripeyzebra
```

Conversion

auth.txt

```
ZnJIZGR5OnRoZWZyb2c
YmlsbDpiYWRnZXI
aGFycnk6aG9ybmVO
YW5uaWU6YXBwbGU
Y2xldmVyOmNhdA
ZWRkeTplbGVwaGFudA
ZmlyZW1hbjpzYWO
aG9zdG1hbjpwYXQ
c2lkOnNuYWtl
emVuYTpoaGVzdHJpcGV5emVicmE
```

The user interface is very simple: a single button is displayed which, when clicked, fires the **butGo_click** event and invokes the conversion process. This routine opens the input and output files and then loops, reading each record from the input file, calling the routine **Encode64** to convert it to Base64 format, and then writing the result to the output file.

Encode64 converts a string to Base64 by performing two steps. First each character is converted into a binary digits string by calling **Binary**, and all of the values are concatenated together. Then each set of six binary digits is converted to the equivalent Base64 characters by calling **Base64**, and again the values are concatenated together to form the encoded result.

Base64 switches on the passed 6-bit string parameter to return the appropriate base64 character. If less than six binary digits are passed, then trailing zeros are appended to make it up to a length of six.

Binary converts a decimal number to a binary value by continually dividing by 2 and using the amount remainder as a binary digit. It returns an 8-bit string by adding leading zeros if necessary.

The full code is as follows:

auth.txt Generator Code

butGo_Click

```
Private Sub butGo_Click()
    Dim strIn As String
    Dim strOut As String

    '
    ' Open input and output file                    (continued)
```

```
'
    Open "e:\data\auth-in.txt" For Input As #1
    Open "e:\data\auth.txt" For Output As #2


    '
    ' for each input line, encode it and write it to the
    ' output file - loop until end of file
    '
    Do While Not EOF(1)
        Input #1, strIn
        strOut = Encode64(strIn)
        Print #2, strOut
    Loop

    Close #1
    Close #2


    MsgBox "Conversion completed"

End Sub
```

Encode64

```
Function Encode64(strInput As String) As String
    Dim strBinary As String
    Dim strSix As String
    Dim strE64 As String
    Dim i


    '
    ' Convert string to binary bits
    '
    strBinary = ""
    For i = 1 To Len(strInput)
        strBinary = strBinary & Binary(Asc(Mid(strInput,
i, 1)))
    Next i


    '
    ' Convert each six bit group
    '
    strE64 = ""
```

```
    For i = 1 To Len(strBinary) Step 6
        strSix = Mid(strBinary, i, 6)
        strE64 = strE64 & Base64(strSix)
    Next i

    Encode64 = strE64

End Function
```

Base64

```
Function Base64(strSix As String) As String

    '
    ' Add trailing zero bits if less than 6 bits
    '
    While Len(strSix) < 6
        strSix = strSix & "0"
    Wend

    Select Case strSix
        Case "000000": Base64 = "A"
        Case "000001": Base64 = "B"
        Case "000010": Base64 = "C"
        Case "000011": Base64 = "D"
        Case "000100": Base64 = "E"
        Case "000101": Base64 = "F"
        Case "000110": Base64 = "G"
        Case "000111": Base64 = "H"
        Case "001000": Base64 = "I"
        Case "001001": Base64 = "J"
        Case "001010": Base64 = "K"
        Case "001011": Base64 = "L"
        Case "001100": Base64 = "M"
        Case "001101": Base64 = "N"
        Case "001110": Base64 = "O"
        Case "001111": Base64 = "P"
        Case "010000": Base64 = "Q"
        Case "010001": Base64 = "R"
        Case "010010": Base64 = "S"
        Case "010011": Base64 = "T"
        Case "010100": Base64 = "U"
```

(continued)

```
        Case "010101": Base64 = "V"
        Case "010110": Base64 = "W"
        Case "010111": Base64 = "X"
        Case "011000": Base64 = "Y"
        Case "011001": Base64 = "Z"
        Case "011010": Base64 = "a"
        Case "011011": Base64 = "b"
        Case "011100": Base64 = "c"
        Case "011101": Base64 = "d"
        Case "011110": Base64 = "e"
        Case "011111": Base64 = "f"
        Case "100000": Base64 = "g"
        Case "100001": Base64 = "h"
        Case "100010": Base64 = "i"
        Case "100011": Base64 = "j"
        Case "100100": Base64 = "k"
        Case "100101": Base64 = "l"
        Case "100110": Base64 = "m"
        Case "100111": Base64 = "n"
        Case "101000": Base64 = "o"
        Case "101001": Base64 = "p"
        Case "101010": Base64 = "q"
        Case "101011": Base64 = "r"
        Case "101100": Base64 = "s"
        Case "101101": Base64 = "t"
        Case "101110": Base64 = "u"
        Case "101111": Base64 = "v"
        Case "110000": Base64 = "w"
        Case "110001": Base64 = "x"
        Case "110010": Base64 = "y"
        Case "110011": Base64 = "z"
        Case "110100": Base64 = "0"
        Case "110101": Base64 = "1"
        Case "110110": Base64 = "2"
        Case "110111": Base64 = "3"
        Case "111000": Base64 = "4"
        Case "111001": Base64 = "5"
        Case "111010": Base64 = "6"
        Case "111011": Base64 = "7"
        Case "111100": Base64 = "8"
        Case "111101": Base64 = "9"
        Case "111110": Base64 = "+"
        Case "111111": Base64 = "/"
    End Select

End Function
```

Binary

```
Function Binary(iNumber As Integer) As String

    Dim strRet As String
    Dim iRemainder As Integer
    Dim iNext As Integer

    '
    ' Convert decimal number to binary
    '
    strRet = ""
    While iNumber > 0

        iNext = Int(iNumber/2)
        iRemainder = iNumber - (iNext * 2)
        strRet = Format(iRemainder) & strRet
        iNumber = iNext

    Wend

    '
    ' Add leading zero bits to make up to eight bits
    '
    While Len(strRet) < 8
        strRet = "0" & strRet
    Wend

    Binary = strRet

End Function
```

ASP User Registration

In our next ASP example, we shall demonstrate how to use server-side scripting to force a user to register his personal details, such as name, address, e-mail address, before being allowed access to the pages on a site.

We shall store the information as cookies in the Web browser, but an alternative approach (especially useful for large amounts of information) would be to write the information to a database record and store the record's key as a cookie.

> For high levels of security, the database key (or the cookies representation of it) must be long, complex, and difficult to guess, in order to prevent anyone from impersonating another user. We shall see such a technique later in this chapter where we use Strong Cookies to prevent ASP session hijacking.

Whenever the user accesses the Web site, these cookies are included in the HTTP request and the values can be processed by the ASP logic. If the ASP detects that the cookies are missing, the user is redirected to a screen to enter this information. Until the cookies are created, the user will not be able to proceed to the main site content.

As with the previous example, we want to apply a check at the start of every ASP file. The logic to see if a user has been registered is contained in the server-side include called **checkreg.inc** and included at the start of every ASP file.

```
<%@LANGUAGE="VBSCRIPT" %>


<!-- #include file="checkreg.inc" -->
```

A session variable **registered** is created and stored in the **Session** object. This can have one of two possible values:

0—not yet registered

1—details have been registered

The variable is initialized to a value of **0** in the **Session_OnStart** event in the global.asa file.

```
Sub Session_OnStart
    Session("registered") = 0
End Sub
```

The **checkreg.inc** checks for a cookie collection with the cookie identifier of **UserDetails**. If this is present, then the user has already registered, and the **registered** session variable is amended to a value of **1**.

```
<%
    if Request.Cookies("UserDetails").HasKeys then
        Session("registered") = 1
    end if
```

If the **registered** session variable is **0,** then the user is redirected off to the **register.asp** page to enter his details.

```
    if Session("registered") = 0 then
        Response.redirect "register.asp"
    end if
%>
```

If the **registered** session variable is **1**, the user has registered and the ASP processing can continue. The page is then used to perform two distinct actions:

- Generate the form to collect the details from the user
- Validate the details: if a problem is detected, then go back to previous action; otherwise store information as cookies (and optionally a database) and thank the user for providing the information

> Some ASP developers may have split this logic into three separate ASP files. The choice taken here of locating all related logic into the same ASP file is purely a personal preference.

The route taken through the ASP logic to perform the appropriate action is driven by an ASP variable called **state**. This takes a value of **1** or **2**. When **register.asp** is first invoked, it operates in state **1** and the form is displayed to the user. When the form is submitted, the ASP is driven into state **2** to process the form details; passing the **state** parameter in the URL achieves this.

```
<FORM method="POST" ACTION="register.asp?state=2">
```

The **state** variable is initialized at the start of the ASP script logic by checking a parameter in the URL. If no parameter is passed, a default value of **1** is used.

```
<%
    if not Request.QueryString("state") = "" then
        state = Request.QueryString("state")
    else
        state = 1
    end if
%>
```

When the form is accepted, the logic used to validate the form details is placed in the ASP file before that which is used to display the form. This means that if any validation errors are detected, the script logic can drop through to reprocess the first state; the errors can be displayed and then the form presented for the information to be corrected.

Skeleton of ASP

```
Determine state from any passed parameter

<% if state = 2 then %>
    validate fields
<%      if not vOK then      %>
<%            set state = 1  %>
<%      end if               %>
<% end if

<% if state = 1 then         %>
    display form
<% end if                    %>
```

The full source code for the example is as follows:

How it was done—for our eyes only!

global.asa

```
<SCRIPT LANGUAGE="VBScript" RUNAT="Server">
Sub Session_OnStart
    Session("registered") = 0
End Sub

Sub Application_OnStart
End Sub

</SCRIPT>
```

default.asp

```
<%@LANGUAGE="VBSCRIPT" %>

<!-- #include file="checkreg.inc" -->

<HTML>
<HEAD>
</HEAD>
```

```
<BODY bgColor=aqua>
<CENTER>
<HR>
<H1>Home Page</H1>
<HR>
Welcome
<% = Request.Cookies("UserDetails")("surname") %>
<BR><BR>
<A href="link1.asp">Link 1</A><BR>
<A href="link2.asp">Link 2</A><BR>
<A href="link3.asp">Link 3</A><BR>
<A href="register.asp">Update details</A><BR>
</CENTER>

</BODY>
</HTML>
```

link1.asp

ASP files **link2.asp** and **link3.asp** are similar, with the titles changed appropriately.

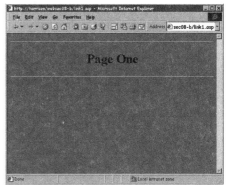

```
<%@LANGUAGE="VBSCRIPT" %>

<!-- #include file="checkreg.inc" -->

<HTML>
<HEAD>
</HEAD>
<BODY BGCOLOR=aqua>
<CENTER>                                    (continued)
```

```
<HR>
<H1>Page One</H1>
<HR>
<A HREF="default.asp">Home</A><BR>
</CENTER>

</BODY>
</HTML>
```

checkreg.inc

```
<%
    if Request.Cookies("UserDetails").HasKeys then
        Session("registered") = 1
    end if

    if Session("registered") = 0 then
        Response.redirect "register.asp"
    end if
%>
```

register.asp

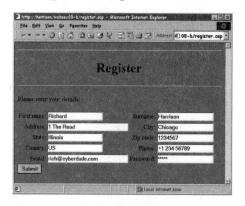
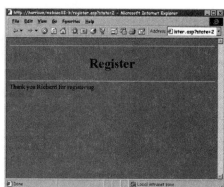

```
<%
    if not Request.QueryString("state") = "" then
        state = Request.QueryString("state")
    else
        state = 1
    end if
%>

<% Response.Buffer = true %>
```

```
<HTML>
<HEAD>
</HEAD>
<BODY BGCOLOR=aqua>
<HR>
<H1 ALIGN="center">Register</h1>
<HR>


<% if state = 2 then %>

<%
    dim vOK
    vOK = true

    REM validate fields...assuming everything is OK

    if vOK then

        REM information could be stored on server using MTS database
component
        REM Set obj = CreateObject( progid )
        REM Call obj.UpdateDetails( userdetails )

        Response.Cookies("UserDetails")("email") = Request.Form
("email")
        Response.Cookies("UserDetails")("password") = Request.Form
("password")
        Response.Cookies("UserDetails")("firstname") = Request.Form
("firstname")
        Response.Cookies("UserDetails")("surname") = Request.Form
("surname")
        Response.Cookies("UserDetails")("address") = Request.Form
("address")
        Response.Cookies("UserDetails")("city") = Request.Form
("city")
        Response.Cookies("UserDetails")("state") = Request.Form
("state")
        Response.Cookies("UserDetails")("zipcode") = Request.Form
("zipcode")
        Response.Cookies("UserDetails")("country") = Request.Form
("country")
```

(continued)

```
        Response.Cookies("UserDetails")("phone") = Request.Form
("phone")
        Response.Cookies("UserDetails").Expires = #December 31,1999#
        Session("registered") = 1

%>


<!- Successful ->
Thank you <% = Request.Form("firstname") %> for registering.<br>
<A HREF="default.asp">Home</A>

<%

    else
        state = 1
%>


<!- Display validation errors ->
<FONT COLOR=red>Validation errors: xxx</FONT><BR>

<%
    end if
%>


<% end if %>


<% if state = 1 then %>

  <P>Please enter your details:</P>
  <FORM method="POST" ACTION="register.asp?state=2">
      <TABLE BORDER="0">
      <TR>
          <TD ALIGN=right>First name:</TD>
          <TD><INPUT type="text" size="20" name="firstname"
            value="<% = Request.Cookies("UserDetails")("firstname")
%>" ></TD>
          <TD ALIGN=right>  Surname:</TD>
          <TD><INPUT type="text" size="20" name="surname"
            value="<% = Request.Cookies("UserDetails")("surname")
%>" ></TD>
```

```
        </TR>
        <TR>
            <TD ALIGN=right>Address:</TD>
            <TD><INPUT type="text" size="30" name="address"
                value="<% = Request.Cookies("UserDetails")("address")
%>" ></TD>
            <TD ALIGN=right>City:</TD>
            <TD><INPUT type="text" size="20" name="city"
                value="<% = Request.Cookies("UserDetails")("city")
%>" ></TD>
        </TR>
        <TR>
            <TD ALIGN=right>State:</TD>
            <TD><INPUT type="text" size="20" name="state"
                value="<% = Request.Cookies("UserDetails")("state")
%>" ></TD>
            <TD ALIGN=right>Zip code:</TD>
            <TD><INPUT type="text" size="20" name="zipcode"
                value="<% = Request.Cookies("UserDetails")("zipcode")
%>" ></TD>
        </TR>
        <TR>
            <TD ALIGN=right>Country:</TD>
            <TD><INPUT type="text" size="20" name="country"
                value="<% = Request.Cookies("UserDetails")("country")
%>" ></TD>
            <TD ALIGN=right>Phone:</TD>
            <TD><INPUT type="text" size="20" name="phone"
                value="<% = Request.Cookies("UserDetails")("phone")
%>" ></TD>
        </TR>
        <TR>
            <TD ALIGN=right>Email:</TD>
            <TD><INPUT type="text" size="30" name="email"
                value="<% = Request.Cookies("UserDetails")("email")
%>" ></TD>
            <TD ALIGN=right>Password:</TD>
            <TD><INPUT type="password" size="20" name="password"
                value="<% = Request.Cookies("UserDetails")("password")
%>" ></TD>
        </TR>
```

(continued)

```
        </TABLE>
    <INPUT type="submit" value="Submit" name="submit">
</form>

<% end if %>

<% Response.Flush %>

</body>
</html>
```

ASP Auditing

Back in Chapter 4, we saw the standard logging facilities provided by IIS4. We shall now see an example of how we can use ASP to generate an audit trail stored in an ASCII text file. This could be used for a number of purposes, including tracking down security breaches, billing, capacity planning, and analyzing which areas of the site are popular.

This example builds on the previous example that enforced registration. All auditing logic is included in the server-side include audit.inc and included in all the ASP files to be audited.

```
<%@LANGUAGE="VBSCRIPT" %>

<!-- #include file="checkreg.inc" -->

<!-- #include file="audit.inc" -->

........ remainder of ASP logic .........
```

Any information available from ASP (in particular the contents of the HTTP Request Header) can be written to the audit trail.

For our example, we are using the user registration information (received as cookies) and information about the browser obtained from the server variables.

```
vLogMsg = Date & " " & Time & ", "
    vLogMsg = vLogMsg & Request.Cookies("UserDetails")
("firstname") & ","
```

```
vLogMag = vLogMsg & Request.ServerVariables("http_referer") & ","
```

A further extension to this example would be to write the audit trail to a filename that includes the date. Logic would have to be included to cut over to the next file when midnight is passed. Having separate files for each day would enable old information to be easily archived.

> Another option would be to use a database; but we won't be discussing such topics until Chapter 11.

The full source code for our example is as follows:

How it was done—for our eyes only!

audit.inc

```
<%
    dim vLogMsg
    dim objFSO
    dim objLogFile


    '
    ' Format audit message
    '
    vLogMsg = Date & " " & Time & ", "
    vLogMsg = vLogMsg & Request.Cookies("UserDetails")("firstname") &
", "
    vLogMsg = vLogMsg & Request.Cookies("UserDetails")("surname") & ",
"
    vLogMsg = vLogMsg & Request.Cookies("UserDetails")("email") & ", "
    vLogMsg = vLogMsg & Request.ServerVariables("script_name") & ", "
    vLogMsg = vLogMsg & Request.ServerVariables("http_referer") & ", "
    vLogMsg = vLogMsg & Request.ServerVariables("http_user_agent")


    '
    ' Open audit file and write message
    '
    Set objFSO = CreateObject("Scripting.FileSystemObject")
    Set objLogFile = objFSO.OpenTextFile("e:\data\audit.log",8)
    Call objLogFile.WriteLine( vLogMsg )

%>
```

EXAMPLE LOG FILE

```
5/13/98 10:30:02 PM, Graham, Taylor, taylor@wfc.com,/websec08-c/
Default.asp, , Mozilla/4.0 (compatible; MSIE 4.01; Windows NT)

5/13/98 10:30:04 PM, Graham, Taylor, taylor@wfc.com,/websec08-c/
link1.asp, http://harrison/websec08-c/, Mozilla/4.0 (compatible;
MSIE 4.01; Windows NT)

5/13/98 10:30:06 PM, Graham, Taylor, taylor@wfc.com,/websec08-c/
default.asp, http://harrison/websec08-c/link1.asp, Mozilla/4.0
(compatible; MSIE 4.01; Windows NT)

5/13/98 10:30:07 PM, Graham, Taylor, taylor@wfc.com,/websec08-c/
link2.asp, http://harrison/websec08-c/default.asp, Mozilla/4.0
(compatible; MSIE 4.01; Windows NT)

5/13/98 10:30:08 PM, Graham, Taylor, taylor@wfc.com,/websec08-c/
default.asp, http://harrison/websec08-c/link2.asp, Mozilla/4.0
(compatible; MSIE 4.01; Windows NT)

5/13/98 10:30:09 PM, Graham, Taylor, taylor@wfc.com,/websec08-c/
link3.asp, http://harrison/websec08-c/default.asp, Mozilla/4.0
(compatible; MSIE 4.01; Windows NT)

5/13/98 10:30:10 PM, Graham, Taylor, taylor@wfc.com,/websec08-c/
default.asp, http://harrison/websec08-c/link3.asp, Mozilla/4.0
(compatible; MSIE 4.01; Windows NT)

5/13/98 10:30:19 PM, Graham, Taylor, taylor@wfc.com,/websec08-c/
default.asp, http://harrison/websec08-c/register.asp?state=2,
Mozilla/4.0 (compatible; MSIE 4.01; Windows NT)
```

ASP Client Certificate Processing

In our next example we shall investigate how to use ASP logic to access the information stored in a user's digital certificate. We discussed the use of certificates and related topics in Chapter 5 when we looked at Secure Channels.

Our example will store the user's personal information on the server and apply the user's e-mail address, stored in the digital certificate, to uniquely identify the user's details. The user's details will be stored in an ASCII text file. One file will exist for each user.

The name of the file will be the user's e-mail address with the characters ".txt" appended. So the details for a user with an e-mail address of **bill@bill.com** would be stored in the file named **bill@bill.com.txt**.

> Again, a more realistic approach would be to store the information in a database and use the e-mail address as the key to the record. But we don't want to get bogged down in database issues ... that fun comes later!

The information stored in the client certificate is accessible using the **ClientCertificate** collection in the **Request** object:

i.e., Request.ClientCertificate(*Key[SubField]*)

where *Key[SubField]* is the name of the certification field to retrieve.
Values for *Key* are:

Value	Meaning
Certificate	Entire certificate content.
Flags	Additional client certificate information (use include file **\inetpub\ aspsamp\samples\cervbs.inc**)
	- **ceCertPresent**—client certificate is present.
	- **ceUnrecognizedIssuer**—last certificate in the chain is from an unknown issuer.
Issuer	Information about certificate Issuer. Can be used in combination with *SubField*
SerialNumber	Serial number of certificate.
Subject	Information about certificate Subject. Can be used in combination with *SubField*
ValidFrom	Date when certificate becomes valid.
ValidUntil	Date when certificate expires

Values for *SubField* are:

Value	Meaning
C	Country of origin
CN	Common name
GN	Given name
I	Initials
L	Locality
O	Organization name
OU	Organization unit
S	State/province
T	Title of person or organization

As examples:

- `Request.ClientCertificate("SUBJECTCN")`—returns the user's (common) name from the certificate
- `Request.ClientCertificate("SUBJECTEMAIL")`—accesses the user's e-mail address from the certificate

In order to enable the exchange of certificates, the Web site must be enabled for SSL. The user must navigate to the site using a protocol of `https://` rather than the usual `http://`.

> Of course, the `https://` prefix will normally be included in the hyperlink and need not be specified by the user.

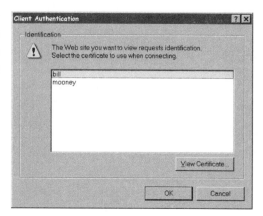

At this stage, the list of installed client certificates is displayed and the user must select the one that is to be used and transmitted to the Web server.

The default page of our example provides a menu to access the following pages:

- `certificate.asp`, which dumps out the complete contents of the user's certificate
- `profile.asp`, which displays the user's personal information and allows the user to amend and update the details.

The code in `certificate.asp` is used to iterate through the `ClientCertificate` collection and output both the key and the contents to the generated page.

```
<%
    for each key in Request.ClientCertificate
        Response.Write (key & "=" & _
        Request.ClientCertificate(key) & <br>")
    next
%>
```

The **profile.asp** page operates in two modes:

- Display the data
- Update and redisplay the data

The second of these is achieved by passing a **mode** parameter in the URL.

profile.asp?mode=update

At the top of the ASP file, a test is made to see which mode the script is operating in.

```
if Request.QueryString("mode") = "update" then
      Call WriteData()
else
      Call ReadData()
end if
```

Depending on the mode, a function is called to either write to or read from the text file containing the profile. The information is also stored in the **Session** object. With either mode, the script logic drops through to an HTML form to display the data and allows further amendments to be made.

The information stored in the ASCII file is written using one line per item. The approach used relies on the **ReadData** function operating on the items in the same order as the **WriteData** function.

The source code for the example is as follows:

How it was done—for our eyes only!

In this example, you must enable "Required Secure Channel" and "Require Client Certificates" on IIS using the Internet Service Manager

default.asp

```
<%@LANGUAGE="VBSCRIPT" %>
<HTML>
<HEAD>
<% Session("name") = Request.ClientCertificate("SUBJECTCN") %>
<% Session("email") = Request.ClientCertificate("SUBJECTEMAIL") %>
</HEAD>
<BODY bgColor=pink>
<CENTER>
<HR>
<H1>Home Page</H1>Welcome
<% =Session("Name") %>
<HR>
<BR>
<A href="profile.asp">Profile
Details</A><BR>
<A href="certificate.asp">Certificate Details</A><BR>

</CENTER>
</BODY>
</HTML>
```

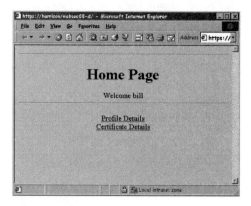

certificate.asp

```
<%@LANGUAGE="VBSCRIPT" %>
<HTML>
<HEAD>
```

```
</HEAD>
<BODY bgColor=pink>
<CENTER>
<HR>
<H1>Certificate Details</H1>
<% =session("name") %>
<HR>
<H4>The contents of your certificate are:</H4>
<%
    for each key in Request.ClientCertificate
        Response.Write (key & "=" & _
        Request.ClientCertificate(key) & <br>")
    next
%>
</CENTER>
<HR>
<A href="default.asp">Back</A> </CENTER>
</BODY>
</HTML>
```

profile.asp

```
<%@LANGUAGE="VBSCRIPT" %>
<HTML>
<HEAD>
<%

        Dim vFileName
        Dim objFSO
        Dim objProfile

        vFileName = "e:\data\" & Session("Email") & ".txt"
        Set objFSO = CreateObject("Scripting.FileSystemObject")

        if Request.QueryString("mode") = "update" then
             Call WriteData()
        else
             Call ReadData()
        end if

        Set objFSO = nothing
%>

<%
sub WriteData()
        Set objProfile = objFSO.CreateTextFile(vFileName) ' Overwrite
mode
        Session("firstname") = Request.Form("firstname")
        Session("surname") = Request.Form("surname")
        Session("address") = Request.Form("address")
```

```
        Session("phone") = Request.Form("phone")
        Session("timestamp") = Time() & ", " &
FormatDateTime(Date(),1) 'Long date

        objProfile.WriteLine Session("firstname")
        objProfile.WriteLine Session("surname")
        objProfile.WriteLine Session("address")
        objProfile.WriteLine Session("phone")
        objProfile.WriteLine Session("timestamp")

        Set objProfile = nothing
end sub
%>


<%
sub ReadData()
        Set objProfile = objFSO.OpenTextFile(vFileName) ' Reading Mode

        Session("firstname") = objProfile.ReadLine
        Session("surname") = objProfile.ReadLine
        Session("address") = objProfile.ReadLine
        Session("phone") = objProfile.ReadLine
        Session("timestamp") = objProfile.ReadLine

        Set objProfile = nothing

end sub
%>



</HEAD>
<BODY bgColor=pink>
<CENTER>
<HR>
<H1>Profile</H1>
<% =session("name") %>
<HR>
<br>
<FORM method=post action="profile.asp?mode=update" id=form1 name=form1>
<TABLE>
<TR>
<TD>First name:</TD>
```

```
<TD><INPUT id=firstname name=firstname maxlength=20 size=20
          value="<% =Session("firstname") %>"></TD>
</TR>
<TR>
<TD>Surname:</TD>
<TD><INPUT id=surname name=surname maxlength=20 size=20
          value="<% =Session("surname") %>"></TD>
</TR>
<TR>
<TD>Address:</TD>
<TD><INPUT id=address name=address maxlength=60 size=60
          value="<% =Session("address") %>"></TD>
</TR>
<TR>
<TD>Phone:</TD>
<TD><INPUT id=phone name=phone maxlength=20 size=20
          value="<% =Session("phone") %>"></TD>
</TR>
<TR>
<TD>Common Name: </TD>
<TD><% = Session("name") %></TD>
</TR>
<TR>
<TD>Email:</TD>
<TD><% = Session("email") %></TD>
</TR>
<TR>
<TR>
<TD>Last update:</TD>
<TD><% = Session("timestamp") %></TD>
</TR>
<TR>
<TD></TD>
<TD><INPUT type=submit value=Submit id=submit name=submit></TD>
</TR>
</TABLE>

</FORM>
</CENTER>
<HR>
<A href="default.asp">Back</A> </CENTER>

</BODY>
</HTML>
```

EXAMPLE PROFILE—*bill@bill.com.txt*

```
Billy
Bones
VR Stadium, Wonderland, Herts
+44 19232 454545
11:25:01 PM, Wednesday, May 13, 1998
```

Protection Against an ASP Session Hijacker

In the previous chapter we saw that ASP uses a 32-bit session identifier that is then encrypted to generate a 16-character Session Identifier cookie. It was also mentioned that to provide further assurances against someone guessing the session identifier of an active session, we could implement our own stronger (i.e., longer) cookie. In this section we shall illustrate this.

The logic to handle this *Strong Cookie* is implemented in the server-side include called **checkid.inc**. This is included at the start of each ASP file. The *Strong Cookie* is stored in the **checkid** variable within the **Session** object and in the browser's cookie collection with the key **("userdetails")** **("checkid")**. When an ASP HTTP request is received, the **checkid** session variable is checked to see whether a *Strong Cookie* has been stored.

```
<%
if Session("checkid") = "" then
```

If the *Strong Cookie* has not been created, we generate one. In this example, we have chosen to generate a character string consisting of thirty-six capital letters. You can use any algorithm you like, but a browser user who inspects the cookie should not be able to guess the logic that has been chosen; otherwise he will have a headstart in attempting to guess and hijack an active ASP session. In our case, even if our algorithm was known, the chance of someone guessing our *Strong Cookie* is unlikely.

Random numbers can be generated using **randomize** and **rnd**. The generator is not really random but instead uses a long sequence of numbers that are calculated mathematically. However, the long length of the sequence means that it is usually more than adequate for most needs.

Randomize, when called without any parameters, initializes the random number generator with a **seed** value taken from the system clock which in effect starts the sequence of numbers at an unpredictable position.

Rnd, when called with a positive parameter, gets the next random number in the sequence.

Choosing thirty-six characters in the ASCII range of 65 to 90 generates the *Strong Cookie*.

```
randomize
checkid = ""
for i = 1 to 36
    checkid = checkid + chr(65 + int(rnd(2)*26))
next
```

The cookie is then stored in the **Session** object and added to the HTTP Response headers to send to the browser.

```
Session("checkid") = checkid
Response.Cookies("userdetails")("checkid") =
Session("checkid")
```

If, when ASP receives an HTTP request, the **checkid** session variable does exist, the value is compared to the *Strong Cookie* received in the HTTP Request. If there is a mismatch, then a security violation is assumed, and from then onward the users will only get a "Goodbye" screen displayed.

```
else
    if not Session("checkid") = Request.Cookies
("userdetails")("checkid") then
        Response.Redirect "bye.htm"
    end if
end if
%>
```

We have illustrated the security violation by including an ASP page, called **link3.asp**, which when called overwrites the *Strong Cookie* with an invalid value, thus causing all further accesses to be rejected.

The full source code for this example is as follows:

How it was done—for our eyes only!

default.asp

```
<%@LANGUAGE="VBSCRIPT" %>
```

```
<!-- #include file="checkid.inc" -->
```

```
<HTML>
<HEAD>
</HEAD>
<BODY bgColor=silver>
<CENTER>
<HR>
<H1>Home Page</H1>
<!-- #include file="debug.inc" -->
<HR>
<A href="link1.asp">Link 1</A><BR>
<A href="link2.asp">Link 2</A><BR>
<A href="link3.asp">Corrupt the ID
cookie</A><BR>
</CENTER>
</BODY>
</HTML>
```

link1.asp

Page **link2.asp** is similar, with the title changed appropriately.

```
<%@LANGUAGE="VBSCRIPT" %>

<!-- #include file="checkid.inc" -->

<HTML>
<HEAD>
</HEAD>
<BODY bgColor=silver>
<CENTER>
<HR>
<H1>Page One</H1>
<!-- #include file="debug.inc" -->
<HR>
<A href="default.asp">Home</A><BR>
</CENTER>
</BODY>
</HTML>
```

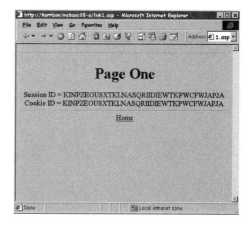

link3.asp

```
<%@LANGUAGE="VBSCRIPT" %>

<!-- #include file="checkid.inc" -->

<% Response.Cookies("userdetails")
("checkid") = "junk" %>
<HTML>
<HEAD>
</HEAD>
<BODY bgColor=silver>
<CENTER>
<HR>
<H1>Cookie Corrupted</H1>
<!-- #include file="debug.inc" -->
<HR>
<A href="default.asp">Home</A><BR>
</CENTER>
</BODY>
</HTML>
```

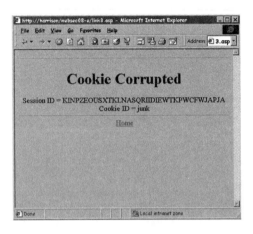

bye.htm

```
<HTML>
<HEAD>
</HEAD>
<BODY bgColor=silver>
<H1>Goodbye!</H1>
</BODY>
</HTML>
```

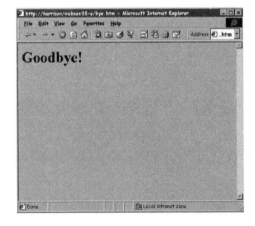

checkid.inc

```
<%
  if Session("checkid") = "" then
    randomize
    checkid = ""
```

```
    for i = 1 to 36
        checkid = checkid + chr(65 + int(rnd(2)*26))
    next
    Session("checkid") = checkid
    Response.Cookies("userdetails")("checkid") = Session("checkid")
  else
    if not Session("checkid") =
Request.Cookies("userdetails")("checkid") then
        Response.Redirect "bye.htm"
    end if
  end if
%>
```

```
            debug.inc
```

```
Session ID = <% = Session("checkid") %> <br>
Cookie ID = <% = Request.Cookies("userdetails")("checkid") %> <br>
```

■ Summary

In this chapter we have seen some examples of ASP Security in action and provided code that can be taken and tweaked as required to form the basis of your Web applications. Some of the examples may have benefited from the use of database, but the purpose of this chapter was to focus on the potential we can leverage from ASP to apply application-level security.

By using ASP script logic we can build upon the core security facilities provided by the core products. Furthermore, customized logic can be written to provide additional levels of protection and specific user-tracking facilities while giving the user a convenient, easy-to-use, and personalized system.

In this chapter we have demonstrated how to use ASP logic to:

- Force users to provide their credentials (for authentication/user tracking/marketing purposes) and use this information to determine whether site access should be either granted or denied.

- Direct users through a Web site via a specific route of pages (e.g., ensure that a user goes through a log-on screen); with standard HTML pages a user could navigate directly to any Web page by keying the URL in the browser's address field.

- Generate audit trails using the information present in the HTTP Request Headers, cookies, Session objects, and so on.

- Access the information stored in a client's digital certificate; this information can be used to provide an alternative authentication mechanism to providing username/password.

- Generate *Strong Cookies* to help protect against any attempt to hijack an ASP session.

The power provided by ASP means that it is a fundamental component in Microsoft Web solutions, and we will encounter its use throughout the remainder of the book. The next chapter is no exception, for in it we use a combination of ASP and components provided by Microsoft Certificate Server to implement a public key infrastructure to manage, generate, and deploy digital certificates.

Creating Our Own Public Key Infrastructure with Microsoft Certificate Server

In this chapter we shall investigate how to deploy a Web security infrastructure based on public keys and digital certificates. To assist us with this task, we shall call on the services offered us by Microsoft Certificate Server. This is an optional component supplied with the Windows NT 4.0 Option Pack.

The application of digital certificates is becoming an increasingly useful mechanism for user authentication and nonrepudiation within a variety of Internet/Intranet applications, including electronic commerce, financial services, and confidential messaging. In Chapter 5 we saw how to use such technology to implement secured channels using digital certificates issued by a trusted third party, such as Verisign.

With Microsoft Certificate Server we can become that trusted third party (i.e., a Certificate Authority) and manage the generation and distribution of digital certificates for our own communities of users, such as our customer base (Internet), business partners (Extranets) and employees (Intranets).

Certificate Server conforms to the industry standards for digital certificates that we met in Chapter 5. In particular, it issues certificates that conform to the standard X.509 specifications. Certificate requests are received in PKCS #10 formats, and signed certificates are issued using PKCS #7 signature blocks. In addition, Certificate Server provides a robust and secure framework for the management of certificate information. It can seamlessly integrate with other components in Windows NT and BackOffice.

In this chapter we shall:

- Investigate how to create and deploy a public key infrastructure that enables us to achieve high levels of security using strong authentication and encryption technologies.
- Look at the internal architecture of Certificate Server and see how to extend the standard product to handle nonstandard requirements
- Discuss **public key infrastructure** (PKI) issues such as:
  - Certificate hierarchy
  - Certificate enrollment
  - Certificate revocation
- Develop a "secured" example site that has several advantages over the standard certificate enrollment facilities provided by the base product.

To start, we shall discuss the installation of Certificate Server and address the various issues that arise during the setup process. So let's get started.

Getting Started

Certificate Server is installed from the Windows NT 4.0 Option Pack setup program by enabling the checkbox in the list of available components. At the appropriate stage in the installation process, the Certificate Server Configuration Wizard walks us through the various configuration options.

The first important issue to consider is whether our CA should be a Root CA or not. To understand what this means, we must understand **Certificate Hierarchy**.

Certificate Hierarchy

While our close partners and employees would certainly trust certificates issued by our CA, it is most likely that the large and global Internet population would never have heard of our CA and so could not have the same level of confidence in it.

It is possible to have multilevel "trees of trust" where one CA may control the issuing of certificates on behalf of another CA. A user considering the integrity of a certificate will consider the trustworthiness of each CA up the certificate chain until he reaches a CA that he trusts.

Ultimately, at the top of the tree, there must be a CA that no one can vouch for. Certificates issued by such a CA are self-signed, and it is known as the **Root CA**. We saw in Chapter 5 that the well-known, trusted Root CAs, such as Verisign, AT&T, Thawte, etc., are installed by default into Microsoft cryptographic software layers for use by products like IE and IIS.

If we configure Microsoft Certificate Server so that we are a Root CA, then we will be at the top of the certificate trust hierarchy. Our certificates will be self-signed because there is no one higher to perform this task.

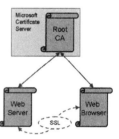

A secured channel could be established between a Web browser and a Web server using certificates generated by our CA.

Alternatively, we can be configured as a Non-Root authority, meaning that a trusted CA has signed our certificate. Typically but not necessarily, this trusted CA will be a Root CA.

Consider the example shown in the diagram. Secured channels can be established using pairs of certificates from anywhere in the certificate hierarchy. Additional controls, such as examining the contents of the certificate, can then be applied to achieve further access restrictions.

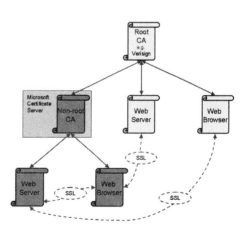

A CA can use Certificate Server to manage its certificates and generate the following different types of certificates:

- CA certificate—used to validate certificates issued by the CA
- Server certificate—used to authenticate a Web server
- Client certificate—used to authenticate a user (Web browser or e-mail)

Installing Certificate Server

Once we have decided whether our Certificate Authority is a Root CA or a Non-Root CA, we can proceed with the installation.

At the first screen we have to specify the physical location where various items will be stored; these are:

- The Shared Folder—a public area used to install the CA certificates
- The Database Location—where the database storing the certificates is located
- The Log Location—where the transaction log is located

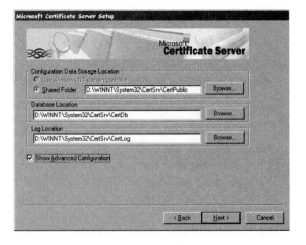

If the Show Advanced Configuration checkbox is selected, the following configuration dialog is displayed.

The first part of the screen is really designed for Microsoft's future use, when the user will be able to select from multiple cryptographic services. With the current implementation, the only option available is the Microsoft

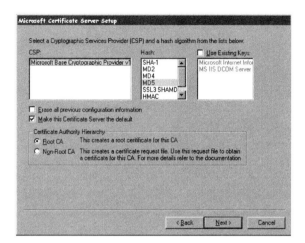

Base Cryptographic Provider. This supports several hashing algorithms; the selection defaults to MD5.

The Use Existing Keys option is intended for use when installing MS Certificate Server or using keys generated by another application. On initial installation it can be left blank. Similarly, the Erase all previous configuration information allows the existing configuration to be kept.

The Make this Certificate Server the default flags this as the Certificate Server instance to be used.

The last option allows us to elect to be either a Root CA or a Non-Root CA. For the example discussed in this chapter we shall be configured as a Root CA.

(If we selected Non-Root CA, then a certificate request file is generated for sending to the trusted CA. The returned signed CA certificate can then be installed using a utility called **CertHier.EXE**).

> The version of Certificate Server available at the time of writing did not support **Non-Root** Certificate Authority hierarchies. This was due to a limitation in the Secure Channels software.

Finally, the Wizard requests various items of information that identify our CA.

The items and our example are shown in the screen dump.

The last item, CA Description, is for internal use only and not stored in any certificate.

Once the Wizard has captured this information, the installation is invoked and the processing includes the following:

If the CA is a Root CA, then the process:

• Generates a public/private key pair and a self-signed root (site) certificate for this CA

Otherwise, the CA is a Non-Root CA and it

• Generates a certificate request file to submit to a trusted CA

Then, for both a Root CA and a Non-Root CA, the installation continues to:

• Add the Certificate Authority service to the list of system services

For testing purposes, we can also start the Certificate Authority service from a command line prompt, using

   certsrv –z

This generates various diagnostic messages that can be useful for troubleshooting problems.

- A database is created to store and manage the information about certificates issued by the CA

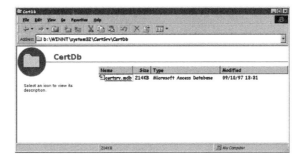

- An ODBC System Data source is set up to point to this database

- The Certificate Server's certificates are written to the Shared Folder
- Hyperlink is added to a Web page to allow users to access and install the CA certificate.

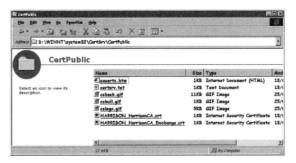

Name of machine = HARRISON
Name of CA = HarrisonCA

`HARRISON_HarrisonCA.crt` is the Certificate Server's signature certificate.

`HARRISON_HarrisonCA_Exchange.crt` is the Certificate Server's key exchange certificate; this is used for sending encrypted information to the CA (not currently used).

- Web-based administration and enrollment tools are installed in the `%systemroot%\system32\CertSrv` directory and the subdirectories `CertAdm`, `CertControl`, `CertEnroll`, and `CertQue`.

- A virtual root called `certsrv` is set up so that the pages can be accessed using

http://harrison/certsrv

harrison is my machine name; amend this to match your own environment

Once the installation has completed, if our CA is to be a Root CA, the following dialog will be displayed.

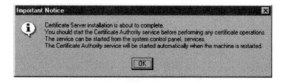

Alternatively, if our CA is set to be a Non-Root CA, then we get this dialog confirming the above explanation regarding the need to obtain a signed CA certificate

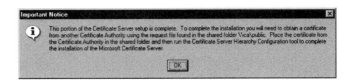

Once the Certificate Authority has been started, the installation of Certificate Server is complete and we are ready to be a Certificate Authority.

The first thing we need to do is generate a server certificate for our Web server.

Server Certificate Enrollment

In Chapter 5, we saw how to configure and use digital certificates in IIS. In that earlier case, we generated a Certificate Request file and sent it to the Entrust CA for signature.

This time, we want to have our certificate request signed by our own Harrison CA. This can be done in the same manner as when we sent the certificate request to Entrust. Certificate Server has a facility (which we shall meet shortly) to receive and process certificate request files.

However, there is an alternative and more automated mechanism that we can use, and we shall address this now.

Automated Enrollment

Recapping from our previous discussions, the configuration of certificates with IIS is handled by the Key Manager utility, which can be found by selecting the key manager tool button within the Internet Service Manager (MMC).

To create a new public/private key pair, click on the Web service and then select the Create New Key option from the Key menu. This invokes the Create New Key wizard.

The first screen allows us to either create the certificate request file (as we did when we used Entrust) or send the certificate request directly to Certificate Server.

In order to automate the process, we shall choose the second option.

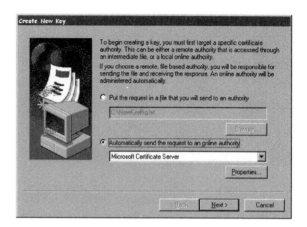

The **Create New Key** wizard steps through several screens to capture information about the organization that owns the Web server. Refer back to Chapter 6 to see the screens that are involved.

Because the Key Manager is communicating with Certificate Server direct, the generated key certificate is automatically installed into IIS and we can finally complete the process by selecting the **Commit Changes Now** menu option.

We now have a Server Certificate installed that has been signed by the **Harrison CA.**

Web Enrollment

While it is more convenient to have the Key Manager and Certificate Server communicating directly, this approach is not suitable when we want to generate certificates for remote machines (perhaps not even on Microsoft platforms).

Certificate Server has a facility for receiving and processing server certificate requests via a Web page. This facility is accessed from the enrollment tools located at:

http:/harrison/certsrv

The certificate request is pasted into the Web page and then submitted for processing.

The generated key certificate can then be downloaded and installed using the Key Manager, as discussed in Chapter 5.

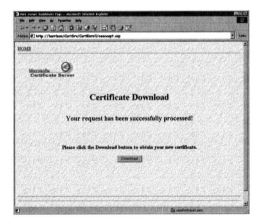

Certificate Authority Certificate List

There is one more thing to be done before proceeding, and its omission is a common problem that stumps many when trying to set up secured channels. IIS must be aware of the Root CA so that it can authenticate users who establish SSL sessions using client certificates issued by this CA.

In our case, the Root CA certificate is called **HARRISON_HarrisonCA. crt** and is located in the Certificate Server public folder.

If we are working on the same machine as this folder, we can access this file directly. Alternatively, we can access the file remotely via the following URL:

http://harrison/certsrv/certenroll/cacerts.htm

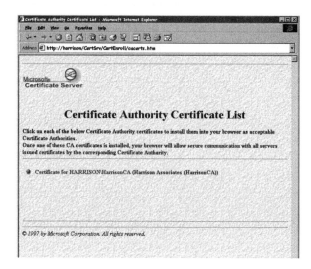

By double-clicking on the file or selecting the hyperlink, we invoke the New Site Certificate utility and can accept the certificate by selecting the OK button.

This is now stored in the systems Certificate Store. To make this known to IIS, we use a utility called **IISCA** that is invoked from command window. IISCA is located in the **%systemroot%\system32\ inetsrv** directory.

The Web Service must now be restarted.

Client Certificate Enrollment

We can now start to consider the client side of the equation.

Certificate Server contains a Web page for obtaining a client certificate. Support is provided for both Internet Explorer (v3.0 on) and Netscape Navigator (v3.0 on).

This facility is accessed from the enrollment tools located at:

http://harrison/certsrv

The browser type is automatically detected, and the user is redirected to a page that supports it.

We can then enter our personal information and submit the request for processing.

If the request is successfully processed and a certificate is issued, the certificate download page will be displayed.

On clicking the Download button, the certificate will be installed. Later in this chapter we shall discuss what is actually going on behind the scenes when the certificate is downloaded.

The certificate can be inspected in the Personal Certificates located in the Content tab of Internet Options.

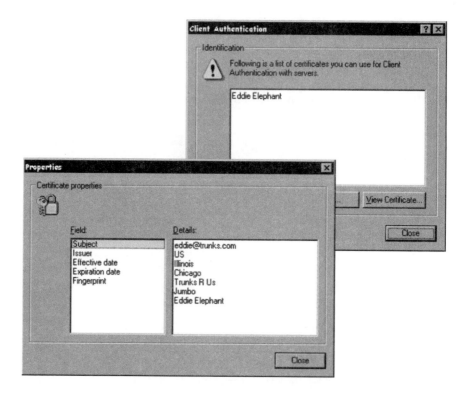

In order to establish a secure channel with our Web server, the client must also install the Root CA certificate (i.e., for Harrison CA) so that it can decipher the server certificate. This is done using the Certificate Authority Certificate List Web page, as discussed earlier in this chapter.

> **Both IE and IIS must have the Root CA (Harrison CA) certificate installed for them to successfully set up a secure channel between themselves.**

Now that we have seen how Certificate Server is installed and used for the deployment of certificates, let us drill down and investigate the product's architecture and components.

Certificate Server Architecture

Microsoft Certificate Server runs as a series of processes, as shown in the following diagram.

The key components of Certificate Server are:

- Server Engine
- Entry Module
- Exit Module
- Policy Module
- Admin Tools

The purpose of the different components will become clear through the remainder of the chapter. Keep referring to this diagram to understand where the different items fit in the overall scheme.

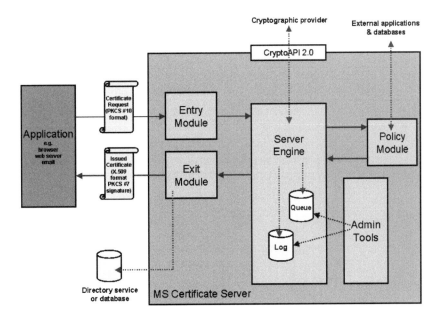

As we would naturally expect, these modules communicate with each other using COM, and the interfaces are fully published in the Microsoft Certificate Server documentation. This enables Certificate Server to be easily extended to support nonstandard requirements and provide seamless integration with existing components and applications.

We shall now discuss how a certificate request is processed, and we will see the purpose of each of the Certificate Server components.

Certificate Request Processing

Microsoft Certificate Server is designed to conform to industry standards and can process certificate requests that originate from many different types of applications, e.g., Web servers, Web browsers, e-mail clients ... in fact anything that needs a digital certificate.

The certificate request (in PKCS #10 format; see Chapter 5) is initially received via the **Entry Module**. This is responsible for understanding the specific protocols between the Application and Certificate Server. This approach provides great flexibility, because different modules can be provided to support various transport mechanisms. Entry Modules can be developed to handle nonstandard requirements that are not supported by the Microsoft-supplied implementations.

The Entry Module passes a certificate request to the **Server Engine**. The request is first stored in the queue and then passed on to the **Policy Module**. The Policy Module interrogates the certificate request and applies business rules to determine whether the request should be accepted, denied, or left pending awaiting further investigation. If necessary, the Policy Module can communicate with other applications or databases to determine the outcome of the request. For example, we might want to check in a customer database to find the status of the applicant's account.

If the Policy Module is to grant the certificate request, it can specify the exact contents of the certificate. This will usually be based on the information in the request but can be massaged as required. The Policy Module can also write additional attributes called **certificate extensions** to the published certificate.

The default Microsoft-supplied Policy Module will accept all certificate requests, although the Web enrollment page can be secured so that only a predefined set of users in the Windows NT Security database can actually initiate the request. We shall see below how to develop a customized Policy Module that supports our own business requirements. Customized Policy Modules can also be written to generate certificates in formats other than the X.509 standard.

Once the Policy Module has made a decision on the status of the certificate request, it passes the appropriate information back to the Server Engine. This updates the status of the queue and logs the completed transaction. If the certificate request has been granted, the Server Engine generates the certificate and digitally signs it.

The issued certificate (in X.509 format with PKCS #7 signature; see Chapter 5) is then passed on to the **Exit Module,** which is responsible for delivering the certificate to the client and/or storing it in a certificate repository. The Exit Module (like the Entry Module) is responsible for handling the transport and protocol specifics, and a customized Exit Module can be created for nonstandard requirements.

Certificate Enrollment Control

As part of Certificate Server, Microsoft has provided a COM control called the **Certificate Enrollment Control** (CEC) that simplifies the processing required to communicate with the Entry Module and the Exit Module. It can be embedded in a Web page or in a Windows application written in any language that supports COM (e.g., VB, VC++, VJ++, etc.).

The following diagram illustrates how the CEC functions within Internet Explorer:

- The Web page (HTML and script logic) capturing the user's credentials, using the CEC to format the information (PKCS #10 format), and then passing it to the Certificate Server Entry Module (dashed line)

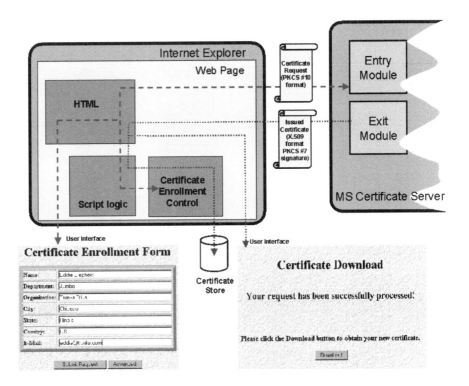

- The Certificate Server Exit Module generating a Web page containing the certificate (X.509 format PKCS #7 signature): when the user selects the Download button, the Web page (HTML and script logic) passes the certificate to the CEC to store it in the local certificate store (dotted line).

Let us now consider this in a little more depth.

A certificate can be requested using the Certificate Enrollment Form. This enables the user to enter his Name, Department, Organization, City, State, Country, and E-mail Address, and submit the information to request a certificate.

Since the CEC is a nonvisual control, the fact that it is present within the Web page is transparent to the user. When the user hits the Submit button, the script logic in the page takes the information entered by the user and passes it on to the CEC. The CEC then formats the certificate request and returns it (in PKCS #10 format) to the script logic. The script logic then inserts the formatted certificate request into a hidden field within an HTML form and finally submits the form to the Certificate Server using HTTP.

The response received is a Web page informing the user whether the certificate requested was accepted or denied. If the certificate request was accepted, the Web page will contain the signed certificate (in PCKS #7 format). If you select the View|Source menu option, you will see the certificate, although it will be a meaningless string of characters. The certificate is installed using the Download button (strictly speaking this should really be tagged as Install, since the certificate is in the page and already downloaded). Script logic attached to the button takes the certificates and passes it through the CEC. The CEC then stores the certificate in the certificate store.

We shall further discuss the use of the CEC when we see an example later in this chapter.

Certificate Server Admin Tools

Certificate Server provides Web-based facilities for managing and inspecting the Certificate Log File and Certificate Queue. These are accessed from the enrollment tools located at:

http://harrison/certsrv

Replace **harrison** with the name of your machine.

Certificate Administration Log Utility

On selecting the Certificate Administration Log Utility, we access a Web page showing one line for each entry in the server log.

Pages show a maximum of 25 entries. Buttons are provided to navigate between different pages.

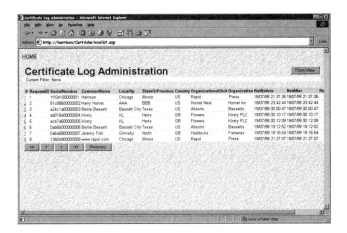

Clicking a hyperlink on the entry number in the first column produces a Form View for the selected entry.

The Form View shows the information for a single log entry.

Buttons are provided to navigate through the log entries. A filter button is provided in which filter criteria can be specified, e.g., only show certificates for the US.

Note also that there is a button that we can use to Revoke the certificate. We shall investigate this below.

Certificate Administration Queue Utility

The Queue facility is similar to the Log utility but is used by the Certificate Server administrator to track the status of each certificate operation. In particular it shows the certificate disposition, e.g., issued, denied, or pending further investigation.

On selecting the Certificate Administration Queue Utility, we access a Web page showing one line for each entry in the server queue.

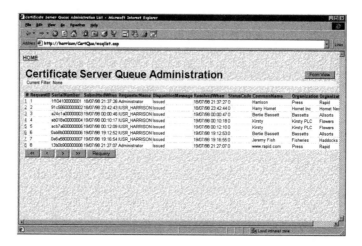

As before, a Form View can be selected by clicking the hyperlink on the entry number in the first column.

The Form View shows the information for a single queue entry.

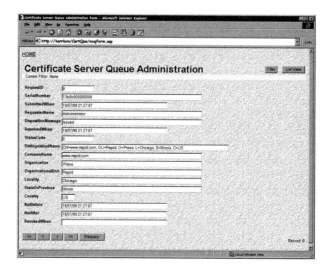

Revoking Certificates

Once we have issued certificates to our community of users, they will be able to access our system using secured channels until the expiration date in the certificate is reached. But what do we do if we wish to prevent a user from accessing our system before the expiration date (e.g., a staff member who leaves our employment after receiving a certificate). The solution is to **revoke** the certificate so that the system no longer accepts it as valid and any attempt to establish a connection breaks down.

It is the responsibility of a CA to maintain and publish a file called the **Certificate Revocation List** (CRL) which contains a list of all certificates that have been revoked.

When the process validates a certificate by checking that it has the correct digital signature for the CA that issued the certificate, it can also check that the certificate is not on the CA's published CRL. For example, a Web server can check that a user's client certificate has not been revoked by an examination of the CRL.

Revoking Certificates with Certificate Server

The Certificate Server administrator can revoke a selected certificate at any time using the Revoke button on the Form View of the Certificate Administration Log Utility. This action will flag the certificate in the Certificate Log as pending revocation.

We can generate a CRL and publish it to the default location using the Start|Programs| Windows NT 4.0 Option Pack|Microsoft Certificate Server|Generate New Certificate Revocation List menu option.

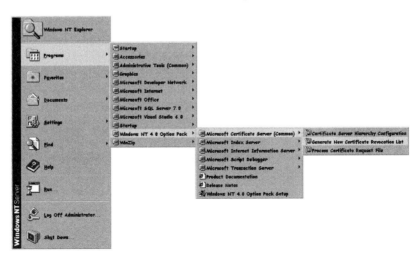

Alternatively, we can publish the CRL by invoking the following instruction from a command prompt:

certutil –crl –

In our case the CRL is called **HarrisonCA.CRL** and will appear in the default directory (i.e., the file name takes on the name of the CA).

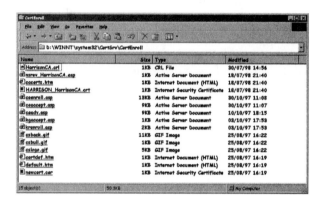

We can inspect the CRL and see the serial numbers of the certificates that have been revoked using the following instruction from a command prompt:

certmgr -crl -v HarrisonCA.crl

```
==============CRL # 1 ==========

Issuer::
 [0,0] 2.5.4.6 (C) ValueType: 4
  55 53                            'US'
 [1,0] 2.5.4.8 (S) ValueType: 4
  49 6C 6C 69 6E 6F 69 73          'Illinois'
 [2,0] 2.5.4.7 (L) ValueType: 4
  43 68 69 63 61 67 6F             'Chicago'
 [3,0] 2.5.4.10 (O) ValueType: 4
  48 61 72 72 69 73 6F 6E 20 41 73 73 6F 63 69 61  'Harrison Associa'
  74 65 73 20 49 6E 63            'tes Inc'
 [4,0] 2.5.4.11 (OU) ValueType: 4
  52 69 63 68                      'Rich'
 [5,0] 2.5.4.3 (CN) ValueType: 4
  48 61 72 72 69 73 6F 6E 43 41    'HarrisonCA'
ThisUpdate::
 Wed Sep 30 21:24:49 1998
NextUpdate::
 Thu Oct 01 22:34:49 1998
```

```
SHA1 Thumbprint::
   91D8C6A4 916280C3 ADFB4DCC 4838B634 30A076FF
MD5 Thumbprint::
   45D19A0C 2E884792 998378EA 07766E40
Version:: 1
SignatureAlgorithm:: 1.2.840.113549.1.1.4
SignatureAlgorithm.Parameters::
   05 00                              '.'
----- Entries -----
  [0] SerialNumber:: AB 01 8E 00 00 00 04
  [0] RevocationDate:: Thu Jul 23 00:20:37 1998
  [0] Extensions:: NONE
  [1] SerialNumber:: AC B7 A6 00 00 00 05
  [1] RevocationDate:: Wed Jul 22 23:56:38 1998
  [1] Extensions:: NONE
  ...
snipped
  ...
  [9] SerialNumber:: 02 EB 02 00 00 00 5B
  [9] RevocationDate:: Mon Jul 27 14:22:57 1998
  [9] Extensions:: NONE

CertMgr Succeeded
```

Getting IIS to Check Revoked Certificates

We can configure IIS to reject all certificates that have been revoked and are present in the **Certificate Revocation List** (CRL). This option cannot be configured via the Internet Service Manager (MMC), and instead the following registry setting must be set:

**[HKEY_LOCAL_MACHINE\SYSTEM\CurrentControlSet\Services\
    InetInfo\Parameters]
"CheckCertRevocation"=dword:00000001**

> Note: the current implementation of IIS will not immediately detect when a new CRL is generated (even if the machine is rebooted), and it can take up to 24 hours before IIS will update its cached copy of the CRL. Microsoft says that future versions of Certificate Server will provide facilities to schedule the automated generation of CRLs, and IIS will provide greater control over accepting CRLs, including the ability to enable their immediate use.

When a user attempts to establish a secured channel using a revoked certificate, the connection will fail a 403.7 Forbidden error.

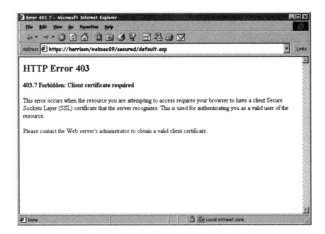

The "Extranet" Application

We shall now demonstrate a Web site that uses the software technology discussed in this chapter to implement an Extranet—i.e., a Web site that implements access controls restricting access to staff members of partner organizations. Furthermore, the use of secured channels will ensure that all information transported over the network is encrypted and cannot be unknowingly tampered with.

> The code for this example can be found on the CD-ROM included with this book.

Application Strategy

Users of our Extranet will only be able to access the secured area of the site if they have a valid certificate issued by our own CA. In addition, facilities will be provided for visitors to provide specific information and request a certificate.

With the standard Certificate Enrollment facilities provided by Microsoft, an issued certificate is immediately issued in a dynamically generated Web page that is returned to the user. In our example we shall expand on the base solution provided by Microsoft and apply additional strong levels of verification by:

- Implementing a policy module to analyze the information about the user supplied in the certificate request
- Having confidence in the origination of the request by sending the issued certificate back by e-mail, thus validating the e-mail address submitted

The site is designed such that the Web contents and application logic are partitioned around two distinct subdirectories:

- The Unrestricted area—the home directory (or virtual directory) containing the files that can be accessed by anyone
- The Extranet area—the subdirectory called "**secured**" containing the files that combine to form the private area of the site.

The Web site is secured to allow anonymous access to all areas except the "**secured**" virtual root; this is configured to enforce a secured channel to be established.

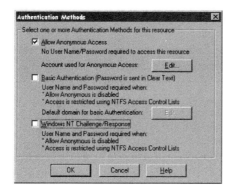 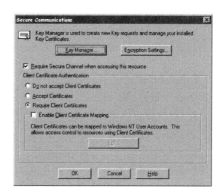

Application Architecture

The directories and the ASP logic implemented are as follows:
The Anonymous area:

- **default.asp**—handles the main screen/menu options
- **certreq.asp**—handles the capture of user details and the certificate request submission
- **certissue.asp**—handles the issuing of a certificate and generation of an HTML page containing the certificate plus installation logic; this is e-mailed to the user
- **cacerts.asp**—handles the installation of the CA certificate
- **unsuitable.asp**—handles users with unsupported browsers

HARRISON_HarrisonCA.crt is the Certificate Server's signature certificate. The other files are project information used by Visual Interdev.

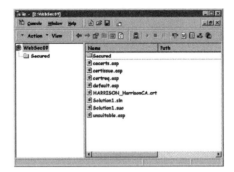

The Extranet area:

• default.asp—handles the main screen/menu options

In a "real world" site, this directory is where we would place our confidential Web content.

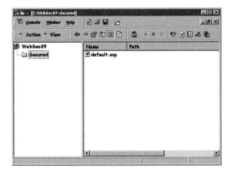

Policy Module

For our example we will only accept requests from the following organizations: Partner1, Partner2, and Partner3. This policy has been kept simple so that we can focus on the approach rather than the actual implementation. It would be easy to amend the example to validate the information in the certificate request against an external file or database that could easily be updated without needing to touch any code.

A Policy Module is implemented by developing a COM object with a ProgId of **CertificateAuthority.Policy**. We shall implement our policy using VB in a file called **certpolicy.dll**.

Certificate Server is installed to use the default Policy Module (implemented in a file called **certpdef.dll**). To install our new Policy Module we must:

- First unregister the default Policy Module using regsvr32 /u
- Then register the new Policy Module using regsvr32

Application Logic

Let us now look at the main points of interest in the application. We can consider this in four distinct stages:

- The Web browser captures the user's details and initiates a certificate request
- The Web server (ASP) receives the certificate request and interfaces with Certificate Server to obtain a certificate
- The certificate details and installation logic are e-mailed to the browser; all of this information is located within a single "Install Certificate" HTML file
- The user loads the HTML file into a Web browser and installs the certificate

We shall now consider each of these in turn.

Requesting a Certificate

The Certificate Enrollment page is implemented by **certreq.asp**. Our example has been designed and implemented for users with Internet Explorer version 3.02 or later. Note that Certificate Server can handle certificate requests and subsequent certificate installation using later versions of Netscape Navigator. For the sake of clarity, our example does not address this. This approach is quite acceptable for Extranet/Intranet systems where we can dictate exactly what software users must have. This is not true for the Internet, where users have a wide variety of systems and software.

When the user first requests this ASP page, the browser type is checked using the standard Browser type control supplied with ASP/IIS. Users with nonsupported browsers are redirected to a page informing them of this.

```
Set BrowserCap = Server.CreateObject("MSWC.BrowserType")

BrowserType = UCase(BrowserCap.browser)
BrowserVersion = BrowserCap.version

If BrowserType <> "IE" Or BrowserVersion < 3.02 Then
    Response.Redirect "unsuitable.asp"
End if
```

The Web page contains two HTML forms with identifiers **ReqForm** and **ReqData**. The **ReqData** form has three hidden fields and a submit button. This is used to submit the certificate request to the server. The **ReqForm** form contains the fields that are used to accept information from the user. To clarify this, refer to the diagram at the end of this section.

The Web page also contains the CEC (as discussed above) with an identifier called **IControl**. This is used to simplify getting the information into PKCS formats. A **codebase** attribute is specified. If the user does not have the CEC or the version indicates that the installed copy is out of date, the Control is downloaded and installed (the security levels in IE must be set to allow this; see Chapter 6).

```
<OBJECT
  classid="clsid:43F8F289-7A20-11D0-8F06-00C04FC295E1"
    codebase="/CertEnroll/xenroll.cab#Version=5,102,1680,
101"
  id=IControl >
</OBJECT>
```

Script logic (a function called **RequestCertificate**) gets invoked when the user hits the Submit button.

```
<INPUT TYPE="Submit" NAME="Request" value="Request
certificate"
        onClick="RequestCertificate()">
```

```
<SCRIPT LANGUAGE="JAVASCRIPT">
        function RequestCertificate() {
```

This function first gets the user information from the **ReqForm** and creates a string called the **Distinguished Name** (DN) which follows the X500 naming convention. We shall discuss DNs in chapter 12 when we investigate Directory Services.

```
CommonName = document.ReqForm.CommonName.value;
OrgUnit = document.ReqForm.OrgUnit.value;
Org = document.ReqForm.Org.value;
Locality = document.ReqForm.Locality.value;
State = document.ReqForm.State.value;
Country = document.ReqForm.Country.value;
Email= document.ReqForm.Email.value;;
```

```
DN = "";
DN = DN + "C=" + Country + ";";
DN = DN + "S=" + State + ";";
DN = DN + "L=" + Locality + ";";
DN = DN + "O=" + Org + ";";
DN = DN + "OU=" + OrgUnit + ";";
DN = DN + "CN=" + CommonName + ";";
DN = DN + "Email=" + Email + ";";
```

Next we must specify the type of key to be generated. For the Microsoft Base Cryptographic Provider, we set this to 1 to specify that we require an exchange key.

```
IControl.KeySpec = 1;
```

The next item of code uses a unique number called an **Object Identifier** (OID). This magic number describes the purpose of the certificate being requested; i.e., client authentication.

> Microsoft's support for cryptography is provided by the CryptoAPI, which has been designed so that other vendors can easily extend the base offerings. Such extensions are identified using unique object identifiers (OID). When the CryptoAPI is called passing an OID, the CryptoAPI maps the call onto a developer-supplied DLL to invoke the appropriate functionality.
>
> OIDs from Microsoft that we might encounter include the encoding certificates for code signing, network authentication, client authentication, and e-mail.

The OID value is both used by the CEC and passed through via the ReqData form to the ASP logic that processes the certificate request. The generated certificate request in PCKS #10 format is assigned to the variable **szPKCS10**

```
document.ReqData.CertUsage.value = "1.3.6.1.5.5.7.3.2";
szPKCS10 = IControl.CreatePKCS10(DN, document.ReqData.CertUsage.value);
```

The certificate request and the e-mail address are also added to the hidden fields in the ReqData form, and the form is then submitted. The information that has been populated in the ReqData form is passed on to a Certificate Server Entry Module (an ASP called **certissue.asp**) to process the certificate request.

```
document.ReqData.CertRequest.value = szPKCS10;
document.ReqData.CertEmail.value = Email;
```

```
if (szPKCS10.length > 10)
        document.ReqData.submit();
    else {
        Msg = "The data you have entered appears to be
invalid.";
        alert(Msg);
        window.navigate ("default.htm")
        }
    }
</SCRIPT>
```

This processing is clarified in the diagram below:

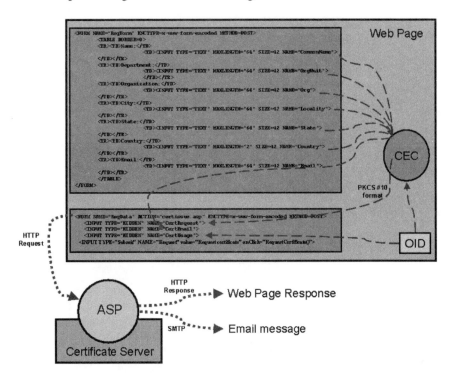

324

Handling a Certificate Request

Before handling the user interface part of the Web page, the `certissue.asp` logic first attempts to generate the signed certificate. We shall now investigate how it does this.

Certificate Server exposes a large number of COM interfaces to access its standard functionality and to extend the basic offerings. We shall use two of these interfaces to handle the request:

- The `ICertRequest` interface is used to pass the certificate request on to the Server Engine for processing
- The `ICertConfig` interface is used to obtain configuration information about the Certificate Servers

```
Set ICertRequest = Server.CreateObject("CertificateAuthority.Request")
Set ICertConfig   = Server.CreateObject("CertificateAuthority.Config")
```

Three variables are initialized:

- `ConfigString` is set to the default configuration string for the certificate server
- `PKCS10` is set to the certificate request (in PKCS #10 format) that is passed from the **ReqData** that we met previously
- `Email` is set to the user's e-mail address; this was entered by the user and is passed from the **ReqData** form

```
ConfigString = ICertConfig.GetConfig(0)
PKCS10 = Request.Form("CertRequest")
Email = Request.Form("CertEmail")
```

The certificate request can now be submitted to the Server Engine using the `Submit` method on the `ICertRequest` interface. The first parameter is a set of flags that indicates the format of the certificate request. In our case, the value of `257` indicates that it is a PKCS #10 certificate request. The returned value is the status of the request, e.g., failed, denied, issued, pending—a value of 3 indicates that the certificate was granted.

```
DispositionCode = ICertRequest.Submit(257, PKCS10, "", ConfigString)
```

The `GetCertificate` method on the `ICertRequest` interface returns the issued certificate (plus the chain of certificates up to the Root CA) formatted as a PKCS #7 string.

```
LastStatus = ICertRequest.GetLastStatus()
Certificate = ICertRequest.GetCertificate(257)
```

The subsequent processing only occurs if a certificate was issued (i.e., **DispositionCode = 3**).

First a sequence of script code is generated which assigns the certificate information to a variable called **szPKCS7**. This script will be used in the HTML that installs the certificate into the client's certificate store.

Next an HTML file is dynamically generated. Most of it is fixed, once and for all, but the script logic that assigns the certificate to the **szPKCS7** variable is inserted. The HTML is written to a temporary file, but care is required because several certificate requests may be occurring concurrently. The solution is to use a filename based upon the e-mail address of the user. The HTML file is written using **FileSystemObject**. This is a standard object supplied with ASP that provides access to a computer's file system.

```
vFileName = "e:\certs\" & Email & ".htm"
Set objFSO = CreateObject("Scripting.FileSystemObject")
Set objAtt = objFSO.CreateTextFile(vFileName) ' Overwrite mode
```

The HTML is then written to this file using a series of **objAtt.Write-Line** statements.

Finally, an e-mail is sent to the user with the HTML certificate installation file attached to the message.

E-mail and Collaboration Data Objects

E-mail is sent to the applicant using the SMTP service installed as part of IIS or Microsoft Exchange Server 5.5. We can interface ASP to either service using a Microsoft component called **Collaboration Data Objects for NT Server** (CDONTS) which is designed for the easy transmission of electronic mail.

To send an e-mail message we first create the CDO **NewMail** object. This provides the simplest method for sending an e-mail message, and we can complete the operation in just a few lines of code.

```
Dim objNewMail

Set objNewMail = CreateObject("CDONTS.NewMail")
```

It is easy to attach files to messages using the **AttachFile** method on the **NewMail** object. We use this method to attach the HTML file containing the issued certificate plus script logic to install the certificate. The first parameter is the name of the file, the second parameter is the caption shown on the attachment in the message.

```
Call objNewMail.AttachFile(vFileName,"installcert.htm")
```

Finally we use the **Send** method, again in the **NewMail** object, to transmit the message.

```
Call objNewMail.Send("Harrison Certificate Server", Email, _
     "Your client certificate", "Click on the HTML attachment to
install", 0)

Set objNewMail = Nothing
```

Note that there is no log-on authentication with this call, and it is up to us (in the first parameter) to specify who the message is from. Specifying an empty string would send anonymous mail. It would also be easy to use a false e-mail address and impersonate someone else.

As the sending of confidential information by e-mail becomes an ever more common practice, it is increasingly vital to have the confidence that:

- Messages cannot be intercepted and read by anyone other than the intended recipient
- Messages cannot be forged and the sender impersonated

The latest generation of e-mail clients, such as Outlook 98 and Outlook Express, now support the S/MIME specification for secure electronic mail. This uses the public/private cryptography techniques that we met earlier to encrypt the message content, guarantee the source of the message, and ensure that it has not been tampered with.

Installing the Certificate

Once the user receives the e-mail message, he can double-click on the attachment to invoke the browser containing the **Install Certificate** HTML page.

The HTML page includes the CEC with the identifier **IControl**. As before, this is used to help in handling information in PKCS formats.

```
<OBJECT classid="clsid:43F8F289-7A20-11D0-8F06-00C04FC295E1"
       id=IControl >
</OBJECT>
```

The page contains an item of text plus a button. The text informs the user to click on the button to install the certificate. When the user clicks on the **Install** button, the script function `InstallCert()` gets invoked.

```
<INPUT TYPE=BUTTON VALUE="Install" NAME="butInstall"
      OnClick="InstallCert()">
```

At the top of this function is the certificate plus the chain of certificates up to the Root CA assigned to the variable `szPKCS7`. This information is quite lengthy and spreads over more than 30 lines.

```
szPKCS7 = szPKCS7 & "MIIF4wYJKoZIhvcNAQcCoIIF1DCCBdACAQExADALBgkqhkiG
9w0BBwGgggW4MIIC"
szPKCS7 = szPKCS7 & "EzCCAb2gAwIBAgIQpDdPSxAAq5IR0h5+meUwhDANBgkqhkiG
9w0BAQQFADBsMQsw"
... ... ... etc ... ... ...
szPKCS7 = szPKCS7 & "BQADQQA1HYn9YyOiUMh/OY1/dbjH8Aug26XUFBE1Smg3zg2rp
B/Mxgo9eWhxKKe9"
szPKCS7 = szPKCS7 & "YDLEjQT8vVSdZzJJRLFGgQi67iZSMQA="
```

To store the certificate in the user's certificate store, we use the CEC and invoke the `acceptPKCS7` method. This takes a single parameter containing the issued chain of certificates.

If a Root CA certificate is found in the certificate chain that is not already stored in the user's certificate store, the user is given a warning to either accept or reject it.

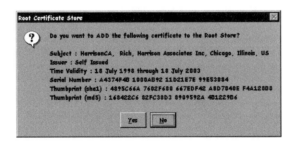

Any error calling `acceptPKCS7` method will throw a VB error which is picked up by checking the **err** object. If the certificate is accepted, we get the following dialog.

```
IControl.AcceptPKCS7(szPKCS7)
If err.Number = 0 Then
    Message = "Your new certificate has been successfully installed."
    Result = MsgBox (Message,0,"Install certificate")
Else
    Message = "Unable to install the certificate:" & vbcrlf & vbcrlf
    Message = Message & "Error: " & Hex(err)
    Result = MsgBox (Message,48,"Install certificate")
End If
```

Finally, a new, simple Web page is dynamically written to the browser to provide a hyperlink back to the online Web site.

```
Document.Write "<HTML><HEAD></HEAD><BODY BGCOLOR=lavender>"
REM replace with links to site
Document.Write "<A HREF=""http://harrison/Websec09"">Continue</A>"
Document.Write "</BODY></HEAD><HTML>"
```

Applying the Certificate Issuing Policy

When the certificate request is submitted to the Server Engine for processing, the Policy Module is called to analyze the information in the request and determine whether the certificate should be issued, denied, or left pending for further investigation.

The Policy Module is implemented by developing a COM object with a ProgId of CertificateAuthority.Policy. The main work of this object is handled by the **VerifyRequest** method. The parameters are:

```
Public Function VerifyRequest( _
    strConfig As String, _          ' configuration string
    Context As Long, _              ' identifies the request
    bNewRequest As Long, _          ' True = new request, False = admin
                                      check
    Flags As Long) _                ' not used
    As Long                         ' returns disposition of request
```

We use the **CCrtServerPolicy** object to extract the information in the certificate request. We first create this object and then pass through the certificate request context.

To use this object we must ensure that a reference is enabled to the "Certif 1.0 Type Library."

Note that we have also enabled a reference to "Microsoft CDO for NTS 1.2 Library." We shall be using CDO for e-mail again soon.

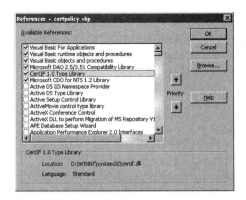

```
Set objCertServer = New CCertServerPolicy
objCertServer.SetContext Context
```

Now we can use the `GetRequestProperty` method to return a named property from the certificate request. The first parameter is the name of the property to retrieve; the second parameter is the property type. Constants for the property names and property types are stored in the file **constants.bas**. Using this method we retrieve various items from the certificate request and assign them to local variables.

```
vNameText = objCertServer.GetRequestProperty( _
        wszPROPSUBJECTDOT & wszPROPCOMMONNAME, PROPTYPE_STRING)
    vOrganization = objCertServer.GetCertificateProperty( _
        wszPROPSUBJECTDOT & wszPROPORGANIZATION, PROPTYPE_STRING)
… … … and so on for all other user information.
```

Having retrieved the contents of the certificate requests, we can then apply our business logic. In our case we are just checking that **organization** is one of three possible fixed values. When this condition is satisfied, the function is set to return the constant **VR_INSTANT_OK** (declared in constants.bas) to indicate that the certificate request should be granted.

```
If vOrganization = "Partner1" Or _
    vOrganization = "Partner2" Or _
    vOrganization = "Partner3" Then


    VerifyRequest = VR_INSTANT_OK
```

If it is determined that the certificate request does not match the exact criteria required, we send an e-mail explaining why. The function is set to return the constant **VR_INSTANT_BAD** to deny the request.

```
Else
    Set objMail = CreateObject("CDONTS.Newmail")
    Call objMail.Send("manager@hornet.net", vE-mail, _
            "Application for certificate", _
            "Access to our secured area is restricted to our partners
only" & _
            " ... please telephone +44 1234 1234321 for more
information")

    VerifyRequest = VR_INSTANT_BAD

End If
```

How it was done—for our eyes only!

The application code for the Extranet Site, in its entirety, is as follows:

Web Site Code

default.asp

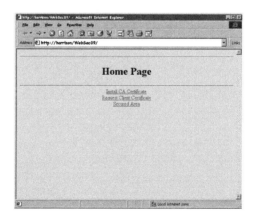

```
<%@LANGUAGE="VBSCRIPT" %>

<HTML>
<HEAD>
```

(continued)

```
</HEAD>
<BODY bgColor=lavender>
<CENTER>
<HR>
<H1>Home Page</H1>
<HR>
<A href="cacerts.asp">Install CA Certificate</A><BR>
<A href="certreq.asp">Request Client Certificate</A><BR>
<A href="https://harrison:443/websec09/secured/default.asp">Secured
Area</A><BR>
</CENTER>
</BODY>
</HTML>
```

certreq.asp

```
<%@ Language=VBScript %>

<%

        Option Explicit

        Response.Expires = 0

        Dim BrowserType, BrowserVersion, BrowserCap

        Set BrowserCap = Server.CreateObject("MSWC.BrowserType")
```

```
        BrowserType = UCase(BrowserCap.browser)
        BrowserVersion = BrowserCap.version

        If BrowserType <> "IE" Or BrowserVersion < 3.02 Then
        Response.Redirect "unsuitable.asp"
        End if

%>

<HTML>
<HEAD>
<TITLE>Certificate Server Enrollment Form</TITLE>

<SCRIPT LANGUAGE="JAVASCRIPT">
        function geterror(message, url, value) {
            alert(msg);
            return false;
        }
</SCRIPT>

<SCRIPT LANGUAGE="JAVASCRIPT">
        function RequestCertificate() {

            CommonName = document.ReqForm.CommonName.value;
            OrgUnit = document.ReqForm.OrgUnit.value;
            Org = document.ReqForm.Org.value;
            Locality = document.ReqForm.Locality.value;
            State = document.ReqForm.State.value;
            Country = document.ReqForm.Country.value;
            Email= document.ReqForm.Email.value;

            szPKCS10 = "";

            DN = "";
            DN = DN + "C=" + Country + ";";
            DN = DN + "S=" + State + ";";
            DN = DN + "L=" + Locality + ";";
            DN = DN + "O=" + Org + ";";
            DN = DN + "OU=" + OrgUnit + ";";
            DN = DN + "CN=" + CommonName + ";";
            DN = DN + "Email=" + Email + ";";
```

(continued)

```
                onerror=geterror;

                IControl.KeySpec = 1;
                document.ReqData.CertUsage.value = "1.3.6.1.5.5.7.3.2";

                szPKCS10 = IControl.CreatePKCS10(DN, document.ReqData.
        CertUsage.value);
                document.ReqData.CertRequest.value = szPKCS10;

                document.ReqData.CertEmail.value = Email;

                if (szPKCS10.length > 10)
                        document.ReqData.submit();
                else {
                        Msg = "The data you have entered appears to be
        invalid.";
                        alert(Msg);
                        window.navigate ("default.htm")
                        }
                }
</SCRIPT>

<OBJECT
  classid="clsid:43F8F289-7A20-11D0-8F06-00C04FC295E1"
    codebase="/CertEnroll/xenroll.cab#Version=5,102,1680,101"
  id=IControl >
</OBJECT>

</HEAD>

<BODY bgColor=lavender>
<CENTER>
<HR>
<H1>Certificate Enrollment Form</H1>
<HR>

<FORM NAME="ReqForm" ENCTYPE=x-www-form-encoded METHOD=POST>

        <TABLE BORDER=0>
        <TR><TD>Name:</TD>
                <TD><INPUT TYPE="TEXT" MAXLENGTH="64" SIZE=42
NAME="CommonName">
```

```
            </TD></TR>
         <TR><TD>Department:</TD>
               <TD><INPUT TYPE="TEXT" MAXLENGTH="64" SIZE=42
NAME="OrgUnit">
         </TD></TR>
         <TR><TD>Organization:</TD>
               <TD><INPUT TYPE="TEXT" MAXLENGTH="64" SIZE=42
NAME="Org">
         </TD></TR>
         <TR><TD>City:</TD>
               <TD><INPUT TYPE="TEXT" MAXLENGTH="64" SIZE=42
NAME="Locality">
         </TD></TR>
         <TR><TD>State:</TD>
               <TD><INPUT TYPE="TEXT" MAXLENGTH="64" SIZE=42
NAME="State">
         </TD></TR>
         <TR><TD>Country:</TD>
               <TD><INPUT TYPE="TEXT" MAXLENGTH="2" SIZE=42
NAME="Country">
         </TD></TR>
         <TR><TD>Email:</TD>
               <TD><INPUT TYPE="TEXT" MAXLENGTH="64" SIZE=42
NAME="Email">
         </TD></TR>
         </TABLE>
</FORM>

<FORM NAME="ReqData" ACTION="certissue.asp" ENCTYPE=x-www-form-encoded
METHOD=POST>
   <INPUT TYPE="HIDDEN" NAME="CertRequest">
   <INPUT TYPE="HIDDEN" NAME="CertEmail">
   <INPUT TYPE="HIDDEN" NAME="CertUsage">
   <INPUT TYPE="Submit" NAME="Request" value="Request certificate"
onClick="RequestCertificate()">
</FORM>

</CENTER>
<HR>
<A href="default.asp">Home</A><BR>
</BODY>
</HTML>
```

`certissue.asp`

```
<%@ Language=VBScript %>

<% Option Explicit %>

<% Response.Expires = 0 %>

<HTML>
<HEAD>
<TITLE>Certificate Issue</TITLE>

<%
        '
        'Process the Certificate Request
        '

        On Error Resume Next

        Dim Certificate, DispositionCode, LastStatus,ConfigString,
PKCS10, Email

        Dim ICertRequest, ICertConfig

        Set ICertRequest =
Server.CreateObject("CertificateAuthority.Request")
        Set ICertConfig   =
Server.CreateObject("CertificateAuthority.Config")
```

```
ConfigString = ICertConfig.GetConfig(0)
PKCS10 = Request.Form("CertRequest")
Email = Request.Form("CertEmail")

DispositionCode = ICertRequest.Submit(257, PKCS10, "",
ConfigString)
LastStatus = ICertRequest.GetLastStatus()
Certificate = ICertRequest.GetCertificate(257)

if DispositionCode = 3 then
        '
        ' Format the Certificate
        '
        Dim FormatedCert, qc, CharsLeft, OutP, BeginLine

        FormatedCert = ""
        qc = chr(34)
        CharsLeft = True
        OutP = 1

        While(CharsLeft)
                BeginLine = OutP
                OutP = InStr(OutP, Certificate, vbNewLine)

                If (OutP > 0) Then
                        FormatedCert = FormatedCert & "szPKCS7 =
szPKCS7 & " & qc & _
                        Mid(Certificate, BeginLine, OutP-BeginLine)
& qc

                        If (OutP >= (len(Certificate) -
len(vbNewLine))) Then
                                CharsLeft = False
                        End If

                Else
                        CharsLeft = False
                End If
                FormatedCert = FormatedCert & vbNewLine
                OutP = OutP + len(vbNewLine)
        Wend
```

(continued)

```vbscript
          '
          ' Open file for HTML mail attachment - this will contain
          ' the certificate plus script logic to install it
          '
          Dim vFileName, objFSO, objAtt

          vFileName = "e:\certs\" & Email & ".htm"
          Set objFSO = CreateObject("Scripting.FileSystemObject")
          Set objAtt = objFSO.CreateTextFile(vFileName) '
Overwrite mode

          objAtt.WriteLine "<HTML><HEAD>"
          objAtt.WriteLine "<TITLE>Install certificate</TITLE>"
          objAtt.WriteLine "<OBJECT classid=""clsid:43F8F289-7A20-
                            11D0-8F06-00C04FC295E1"" "
          objAtt.WriteLine "   id=IControl > "
          objAtt.WriteLine "</OBJECT> "
          objAtt.WriteLine "<SCRIPT LANGUAGE=""VBSCRIPT""> "
          objAtt.WriteLine "Sub InstallCert() "
          objAtt.WriteLine "   Dim Result, Message "
          objAtt.WriteLine "   On Error Resume Next "
          objAtt.WriteLine "   szPKCS7 = """" "

          objAtt.WriteLine  FormatedCert ' This is the generated
certificate

          objAtt.WriteLine "   IControl.AcceptPKCS7(szPKCS7) "
          objAtt.WriteLine "   If err.Number = 0 Then "
          objAtt.WriteLine "      Message = ""Your new certificate
                            has been successfully
                            installed."" "
          objAtt.WriteLine "      Result = MsgBox (Message,0,
                            ""Install certificate"") "
          objAtt.WriteLine "   Else "
          objAtt.WriteLine "      Message = ""Unable to install
                            the certificate:"" & vbcrlf &
                            vbcrlf "
          objAtt.WriteLine "      Message = Message & ""Error: ""
                            & Hex(err) "
          objAtt.WriteLine "      Result = MsgBox (Message,48,
                            ""Install certificate"") "
          objAtt.WriteLine "   End If"
          objAtt.WriteLine "   Document.Write ""<HTML><HEAD>
                            </HEAD><BODY BGCOLOR=lavender>"" "
          objAtt.WriteLine "   REM replace with links to site "
```

```
            objAtt.WriteLine  "     Document.Write ""<A HREF=
                              """"http://harrison/websec09"""">
                              Continue</A>"" "
            objAtt.WriteLine  "     Document.Write ""</BODY>
                              </HEAD><HTML>"" "
            objAtt.WriteLine  "End Sub"
            objAtt.WriteLine  "</SCRIPT>"
            objAtt.WriteLine  "</HEAD>"
            objAtt.WriteLine  "<BODY BGCOLOR=lavender> "
            objAtt.WriteLine  "<CENTER><HR><H1>Install Certificate
                              </H1><HR>"
            objAtt.WriteLine  "<P>Click below to install your
                              certificate."
            objAtt.WriteLine  "<FORM>"
            objAtt.WriteLine  "<INPUT TYPE=BUTTON VALUE=""Install""
                              NAME=""butInstall"" "
            objAtt.WriteLine  "        OnClick=""InstallCert()"">"
            objAtt.WriteLine  "</FORM>"
            objAtt.WriteLine  "</CENTER><HR></BODY></HTML>"

        Set objAtt = nothing
        '
        ' And finally, lets e-mail the generated HTML Web page
containing
        ' the client certificate to the user
        '
        Dim objNewMail

        Set objNewMail = CreateObject("CDONTS.NewMail")
        Call objNewMail.AttachFile(vFileName,"installcert.htm")
        Call objNewMail.Send("Harrison Certificate Server",
Email, _
                "Your client certificate", "Click on the HTML
attachment to install", 0)

        Set objNewMail = Nothing
    End If
%>

<BODY BGCOLOR="lavender">
<CENTER>
```

(continued)

```
<HR>
<H1>Certificate Issue</H1>
<HR>

<% If DispositionCode = 3 Then %>

        <P>Your certificate request has been successfully processed
and
        is being sent by email to
        <B><% = Email %></B><BR><BR>

<% Else %>

        <P>Certificate Server is unable to process your request.
        <P> DispositionCode = <% =DispositionCode %>
        <P>Last Status Error Code = <%=HEX(LastStatus)%>
        <P>Please call your account representative

<% End If %>

</CENTER>
<HR>
<A href="default.asp">Home</A><BR>
</BODY>
</HTML>
```

EXAMPLE E-MAIL MESSAGE CONTAINING A CERTIFICATE

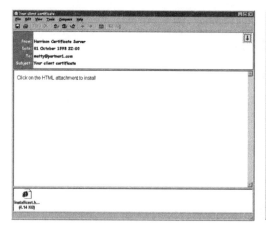
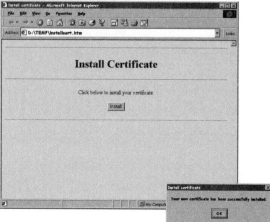

```
<HTML><HEAD>
<TITLE>Install certificate</TITLE>
<OBJECT classid="clsid:43F8F289-7A20-11D0-8F06-00C04FC295E1"
        id=IControl >
</OBJECT>
<SCRIPT LANGUAGE="VBSCRIPT">
Sub InstallCert()
   Dim Result, Message
   On Error Resume Next
szPKCS7 = ""
szPKCS7 = szPKCS7 & "MIIF4wYJKoZIhvcNAQcCoIIF1DCCBdACAQExADALBgkqhkiG
9w0BBwGgggW4MIIC"
szPKCS7 = szPKCS7 & "EzCCAb2gAwIBAgIQpDdPSxAAq5IR0h5+meUwhDANBgkqhkiG
9w0BAQQFADBsMQsw"
szPKCS7 = szPKCS7 & "CQYDVQQGEwJVUzERMA8GA1UECBMISWxsaW5vaXMxEDAOBg
NVBAcTB0NoaWNhZ28x"
szPKCS7 = szPKCS7 & "EzARBgNVBAoTCldyb3ggUHJlc3MxDjAMBgNVBAsTBVJhcG
lkMRMwEQYDVQQDEwpI"
szPKCS7 = szPKCS7 & "YXJyaXNvbkNBMB4XDTk4MDcxODIwNDAwM1oXDTAzMDcxOD
IwNDAwM1owbDELMAkG"
szPKCS7 = szPKCS7 & "A1UEBhMCVVMxETAPBgNVBAgTCElsbGlub2lzMRAwDgYDVQ
QHEwdDaGljYWdvMRMw"
szPKCS7 = szPKCS7 & "EQYDVQQKEwpXcm94IFByZXNzMQ4wDAYDVQQLEwVSYXBpZD
ETMBEGA1UEAxMKSGFy"
szPKCS7 = szPKCS7 & "cmlzb25DQTBbMA0GCSqGSIb3DQEBAQUAA0oAMEcCQGoCd3
PovC9HpVLdWkEvpKWk"
szPKCS7 = szPKCS7 & "ci+Pzt4iYjsHmQOLqzVg8u+YAc95G0jDKcxYf6RFMdY53T
NkUhfhIKHeIqUkQGMC"
szPKCS7 = szPKCS7 & "AwEAAaM8MDowCwYDVR0PBAQDAgHEMAwGA1UdEwQFMAMBAf
8wHQYDVR0OBBYEFIUZ"
szPKCS7 = szPKCS7 & "LWaK58/Au8i5Xm6M+0Xa7goZMA0GCSqGSIb3DQEBBAUAA0
EAVBnjgAHdbyNuaJg9"
szPKCS7 = szPKCS7 & "PsAgbVX6y9Tn/MntTJowoQHwUxu7QreNhGI5pviroj09cA
Y2wCpUJ3YAxIJRtb0y"
szPKCS7 = szPKCS7 & "8yejljCCA50wggNHoAMCAQICBz4ntQAAAGMwDQYJKoZIhvc
NAQEEBQAwbDELMAkG"
szPKCS7 = szPKCS7 & "A1UEBhMCVVMxETAPBgNVBAgTCElsbGlub2lzMRAwDgYDVQ
QHEwdDaGljYWdvMRMw"
szPKCS7 = szPKCS7 & "EQYDVQQKEwpXcm94IFByZXNzMQ4wDAYDVQQLEwVSYXBpZD
ETMBEGA1UEAxMKSGFy"
szPKCS7 = szPKCS7 & "cmlzb25DQTAeFw05ODA3MzEyMDIzMzBaFw05OTA3MzEyMD
IzMzBaMIGHMRwwGgYJ"
```

(continued)

```
szPKCS7 = szPKCS7 & "KoZIhvcNAQkBFgltYXR0QHByLmNvLnVrMQswCQYDVQQGEw
JHQjEOMAwGA1UECBMF"
szPKCS7 = szPKCS7 & "SGVydHMxCzAJBgNVBAcTAktMMRMwEQYDVQQKEwpQZXQgUm
VzY3V1MQ0wCwYDVQQL"
szPKCS7 = szPKCS7 & "EwRDYXR6MRkwFwYDVQQDExBNYXR0aGV3IEhhcnJpc29uM
FwwDQYJKoZIhvcNAQEB"
szPKCS7 = szPKCS7 & "BQADSwAwSAJBALvgOwxWJeP4o8NEpLIJ4tBOrDCOKH6JOx
OKlqTtQT427c8saO0R"
szPKCS7 = szPKCS7 & "uAIZk42HajOmwghvifdi1uNg8oqWcYIqSAUCAwEAAaOCAb
AwggGsMAsGA1UdDwQE"
szPKCS7 = szPKCS7 & "AwIAODATBgNVHSUEDDAKBggrBgEFBQcDAjCBpQYDVR0jBI
GdMIGagBSFGS1miufP"
szPKCS7 = szPKCS7 & "wLvIuV5ujPtF2u4KGaFwpG4wbDELMAkGA1UEBhMCVVMxET
APBgNVBAgTCElsbGlu"
szPKCS7 = szPKCS7 & "b21zMRAwDgYDVQQHEwdDaGljYWdvMRMwEQYDVQQKEwpXcm
94IFByZXNzMQ4wDAYD"
szPKCS7 = szPKCS7 & "VQQLEwVSYXBpZDETMBEGA1UEAxMKSGFycmlzb25DQYIQpDd
PSxAAq5IR0h5+meUw"
szPKCS7 = szPKCS7 & "hDB9BgNVHR8EdjB0MDegNaAzhjFodHRwOi8vSEFSUklTTT04
vQ2VydFNydi9DZXJ0"
szPKCS7 = szPKCS7 & "RW5yb2xsL0hhcnJpc29uQ0EuY3JsMDmgN6A1hjNmaWxlOi8
vXFxIQVJSSVNPT1xD"
szPKCS7 = szPKCS7 & "ZXJ0U3J2XENlcnRFbnJvbGxcSGFycmlzb25DQS5jcmwwCQY
DVR0TBAIwADBWBggr"
szPKCS7 = szPKCS7 & "BgEFBQcBAQRKMEgwRgYIKwYBBQUHMAKGOmh0dHA6Ly9IQVJ
SSVNPTi9DZXJ0U3J2"
szPKCS7 = szPKCS7 & "L0NlcnRFbnJvbGwvSEFSUklTT05fSGFycmlzb25DQS5jcnQ
wDQYJKoZIhvcNAQEE"
szPKCS7 = szPKCS7 & "BQADQQAlHYn9YyOiUMh/OY1/dbjH8Aug26XUFBElSmg3zg2
rpB/Mxgo9eWhxKKe9"
szPKCS7 = szPKCS7 & "YDLEjQT8vVSdZzJJRLFGgQi67iZSMQA="
```

```
    IControl.AcceptPKCS7(szPKCS7)
    If err.Number = 0 Then
        Message = "Your new certificate has been successfully
installed."
        Result = MsgBox (Message,0,"Install certificate")
    Else
        Message = "Unable to install the certificate:" & vbcrlf & vbcrlf
        Message = Message & "Error: " & Hex(err)
        Result = MsgBox (Message,48,"Install certificate")
```

```
    End If
    Document.Write "<HTML><HEAD></HEAD><BODY BGCOLOR=lavender>"
    REM replace with links to site
    Document.Write "<A HREF=""http://harrison/websec09"">Continue</A>"
    Document.Write "</BODY></HEAD><HTML>"
End Sub
</SCRIPT>
</HEAD>
<BODY BGCOLOR=lavender>
<CENTER><HR><H1>Install Certificate</H1><HR>
<P>Click below to install your certificate.
<FORM>
<INPUT TYPE=BUTTON VALUE="Install" NAME="butInstall"
        OnClick="InstallCert()">
</FORM>
</CENTER><HR></BODY></HTML>
```

`cacerts.asp`

```
<%@ Language=VBScript %>
<HTML>
<HEAD>
<TITLE>Certificate Authority Certificate List</TITLE>
</HEAD>
<BODY bgColor=lavender>
<HR>
<CENTER>
```

(continued)

```
<H1>Certificate Authority Certificate</H1>
<H1>
<HR></H1>
<P>
Click on the Certificate Authority certificate below to
install it into your browser.
<P>
Once the CA certificate is installed, your browser will
allow secure communication with all servers issued certificates by
this Certificate Authority.
<UL>
<LI><A HREF="HARRISON_HarrisonCA.crt">Certificate for
HARRISON\HarrisonCA
</A> (Harrison Associates (HarrisonCA))
 </LI>
</UL>
<P>
</CENTER>
<HR>
<A href="default.asp">Home</A><BR>
</BODY>
</HTML>
```

unsuitable.asp

```
<%@ Language=VBScript %>
<HTML>
<HEAD>
<META NAME="GENERATOR" Content="Microsoft Visual Studio 6.0">
```

```
</HEAD>
<BODY bgColor=lavender>
<CENTER>
<HR>
<H1>Certificate Enrollment Form</H1>
<HR>

<P>Your browser does not appear to meet the requirements for
Certificate Enrollment.<BR>
Please upgrade your browser to latest version of Microsoft Internet
Explorer.<BR><BR>

<HR>
<A href="default.asp">Home</A><BR>
</BODY>
</HTML>
```

secured/default.asp

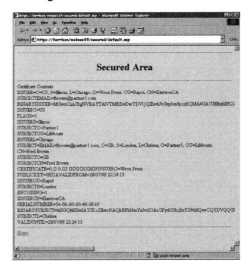

```
<%@LANGUAGE="VBSCRIPT" %>

<HTML>
<HEAD>
</HEAD>
<BODY bgColor=lavender>
<CENTER>
```

(continued)

```
<HR>
<H1>Secured Area</H1>
<HR>
</CENTER>
Certificate Contents<BR>
<%
    For Each key In Request.ClientCertificate
        Response.Write (key & "=" & _
        Request.ClientCertificate(key) & "<br>")
    Next
%>
<HR>
<A href="http://harrison/websec09/default.asp">Home</A><BR>
</BODY>
</HTML>
```

Policy Module Code

policy.cls (ProgId = CertificateAuthority.Policy)

ClassName = "Policy"
Instancing = "MultiUse"

```
Option Explicit

Public Function Initialize( _
    strConfig As String)
End Function

Public Function ShutDown()
End Function

Public Function GetDescription() As String
    GetDescription = "HarrisonCA Certificate Policy Module"
End Function

Public Function VerifyRequest( _
    strConfig As String, _
    Context As Long, _
```

```
bNewRequest As Long, _
Flags As Long) As Long

Dim objCertServer As CCertServerPolicy
Dim objMail As NewMail
Dim vNotBefore As Variant
Dim vNotAfter As Variant
Dim vCertVersion As Variant
Dim vCertType As Variant
Dim vNameText As Variant
Dim vOrganization As Variant
Dim vOrganizationUnit As Variant
Dim vLocality As Variant
Dim vState As Variant
Dim vCountry As Variant
Dim vEmail As Variant


On Error Resume Next

Set objCertServer = New CCertServerPolicy
objCertServer.SetContext Context

'
'Collect user information from the request:
'
vNameText = objCertServer.GetRequestProperty( _
        wszPROPSUBJECTDOT & wszPROPCOMMONNAME, PROPTYPE_STRING)
vOrganization = objCertServer.GetCertificateProperty( _
        wszPROPSUBJECTDOT & wszPROPORGANIZATION, PROPTYPE_STRING)
vOrganizationUnit = objCertServer.GetCertificateProperty( _
        wszPROPSUBJECTDOT & wszPROPORGUNIT, PROPTYPE_STRING)
vLocality = objCertServer.GetCertificateProperty( _
        wszPROPSUBJECTDOT & wszPROPLOCALITY, PROPTYPE_STRING)
vState = objCertServer.GetCertificateProperty( _
        wszPROPSUBJECTDOT & wszPROPSTATE, PROPTYPE_STRING)
vCountry = objCertServer.GetCertificateProperty( _
        wszPROPSUBJECTDOT & wszPROPCOUNTRY, PROPTYPE_STRING)
vEmail = objCertServer.GetCertificateProperty( _
        wszPROPSUBJECTDOT & wszPROPEMAIL, PROPTYPE_STRING)
vNotBefore = objCertServer.GetCertificateProperty( _
```

(continued)

```
            wszPROPCERTIFICATENOTBEFOREDATE, PROPTYPE_DATE)
    vNotAfter = objCertServer.GetCertificateProperty( _
            wszPROPCERTIFICATENOTAFTERDATE, PROPTYPE_DATE)


    '
    ' Implement Business Rules
    '

    If vOrganization = "Partner1" Or _
        vOrganization = "Partner2" Or _
        vOrganization = "Partner3" Then


        VerifyRequest = VR_INSTANT_OK


    Else


        Set objMail = CreateObject("CDONTS.Newmail")
        Call objMail.Send("manager@hornet.net", vEmail, _
                "Application for certificate", _
                "Access to our secured area is restricted to our
partners only" & _
                " ... please telephone +44 1234 1234321 for more
information")


        VerifyRequest = VR_INSTANT_BAD


    End If



    Set objCertServer = Nothing


End Function
```

        entry.bas

```
Sub Main()
End Sub
```

        constants.bas

```
Public Const VR_PENDING As Long = 0
Public Const VR_INSTANT_OK As Long = 1
Public Const VR_INSTANT_BAD As Long = 2
```

```
Public Const wszPROPDISTINGUISHEDNAME As String = "DistinguishedName"
Public Const wszPROPRAWNAME As String = "RawName"
Public Const wszPROPNAMETYPE As String = "NameType"
Public Const wszPROPCOUNTRY As String = "Country"
Public Const wszPROPORGANIZATION As String = "Organization"
Public Const wszPROPORGUNIT As String = "OrgUnit"
Public Const wszPROPCOMMONNAME As String = "CommonName"
Public Const wszPROPLOCALITY As String = "Locality"
Public Const wszPROPSTATE As String = "State"
Public Const wszPROPTITLE As String = "Title"
Public Const wszPROPGIVENNAME As String = "GivenName"
Public Const wszPROPINITIALS As String = "Initials"
Public Const wszPROPSURNAME As String = "SurName"
Public Const wszPROPDOMAINCOMPONENT As String = "DomainComponent"
Public Const wszPROPEMAIL As String = "EMail"
Public Const wszPROPSUBJECTDOT As String = "Subject."
Public Const wszPROPISSUERDOT As String = "Issuer."
Public Const wszPROPCERTIFICATEREQUESTID As String = "RequestID"
Public Const wszPROPRAWCERTIFICATE As String = "RawCertificate"
Public Const wszPROPCERTIFICATETYPE As String = "CertificateType"
Public Const wszPROPCERTIFICATESERIALNUMBER As String = "SerialNumber"
Public Const wszPROPCERTIFICATEISSUERNAMEID As String = "IssuerNameID"
Public Const wszPROPCERTIFICATESUBJECTNAMEID As String =
"SubjectNameID"
Public Const wszPROPCERTIFICATENOTBEFOREDATE As String = "NotBefore"
Public Const wszPROPCERTIFICATENOTAFTERDATE As String = "NotAfter"

Public Const PROPTYPE_LONG As Long = &H1
Public Const PROPTYPE_DATE As Long = &H2
Public Const PROPTYPE_BINARY As Long = &H3
Public Const PROPTYPE_STRING As Long = &H4
Public Const PROPTYPE_ANSI As Long = &H5
Public Const PROPTYPE_MASK As Long = &HFF
```

■ Summary

In this chapter we have shown how to use Microsoft Certificate Server to set up an infrastructure, based on public-key cryptography using digital certificates, that enables us to have a high level of confidence that we are doing secured electronic business with our business partners.

The key points in this chapter are:

- Microsoft Certificate Server is a standards-based, highly customizable product for managing the issuing, revocation, and renewal of digital certificates.

- It provides facilities to receive certificate requests (in PKCS #10 format) and verify the information in the request. Optionally, it can issue a X.509 certificate (or chain of certificates) in a PKCS #7 format.

- It can provide seamless integration with other components and external systems; its open architecture means that it can be readily extended to handle nonstandard requirements.

While it is possible to set up a similar infrastructure using well-known trusted third parties, implementing our own CA using Microsoft Certificate Server reduces our costs and gives us greater control over certification policies.

Component Security with MTS

In Chapter 7, we mentioned that the ideal approach for building Web applications is to minimize the amount of script, develop software components in a high-level language, and integrate them with ASP using COM. We shall now move on to discuss how to integrate ASP with such software components as are installed in the **Microsoft Transaction Server** (MTS) environment.

Naturally, we shall be concentrating on the security implications of MTS. IIS has been built as an MTS application, and this tight integration enables ASP- and COM-compliant software components to combine and deliver reliable business-critical Web applications.

Because of the demand for dynamic content, Web computing has become a flexible and scalable implementation of multi-tier computing. MTS is designed to reduce the time and complexity of the development of multi-tier applications by supplying much of the infrastructure to provide a robust, scalable, high-performance, and distributed architecture.

In this chapter we shall see:

- The major features of the MTS environment and how it offers support for security
- The architecture of IIS4, which is built as an MTS application, and how this enables scalable, high-performance, robust Web solutions
- The administration of MTS using a friendly GUI interface
- How MTS security can be applied by either configuration or within the programming logic
- How we can provide access controls down to the COM-interface level of a software component
- How to control who has access to MTS Administration facilities.

> **The chapter will assume an understanding of basic concepts of ActiveX and COM. An overview of these technologies is included in Appendix A.**

We shall begin with a *brief* overview of the features of MTS and the benefits it offers.

MTS Fundamentals

The aim of MTS is to provide a complete infrastructure that extends COM and acts as an **object broker**. An object broker acts as a middle layer, assisting in the interoperability between client applications and software components that expose functionality on which the clients may call.

By using MTS, a developer is insulated from many of the complexities that are encountered when developing multi-tier computing architectures. It automatically manages all threading issues, object repooling, sharing of resources, and handling of transaction context across objects.

Furthermore, MTS provides a simple yet powerful security framework for controlling who has access to the functionality within a software component. We can restrict user access to particular objects or particular interfaces exposed by the object.

This all means that a developer only needs to concentrate on developing the "business logic" as the underlying plumbing, and the infrastructure is handled for him.

MTS Explorer

The User Interface for MTS administration is the **MTS Explorer**. This is a snap-in to the Microsoft Management Console (MMC), which we met in Chapter 4. The MTS Explorer enables the administrator to:

- Install and configure MTS (COM) components
- Control deployment and distribution of components to multiple systems
- Monitor the state of running objects and transactions

The following screenshots show the MTS Explorer. The first shows an installed component and the set of interfaces it exposes. The second shows transaction statistics.

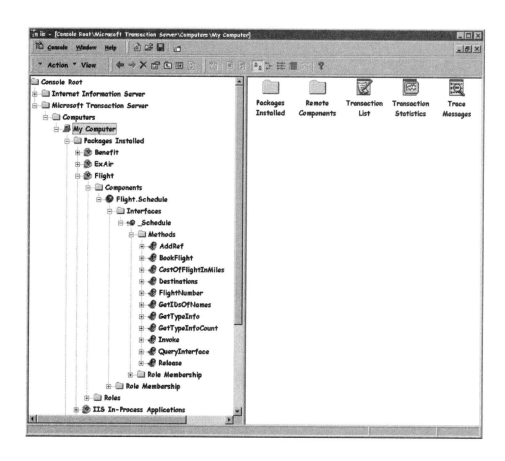

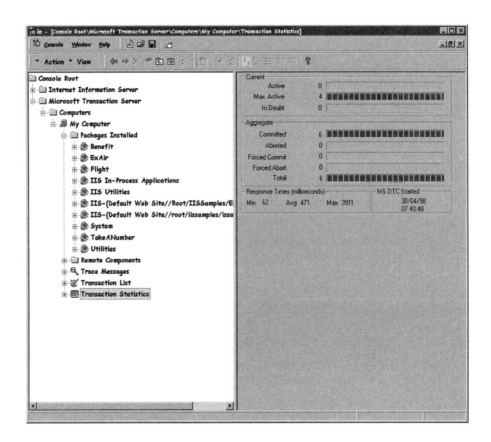

Packages

An MTS component is an in-process (i.e., a DLL) ActiveX/COM software component. Several components needed for a single application can be grouped together to form a **package**. An overview of ActiveX and DCOM is given in Appendix A.

The MTS Explorer provides export facilities which:

- Enable packages to be easily transferred to another MTS installation
- Generate a client installation program to install the type libraries and proxy stubs enabling the remote client system to communicate with the MTS components

Execution Environment

Once a software component has been registered with MTS, the **execution environment** will handle any request from a client application to create an instance of the component. The environment wraps the component to provide a multiple thread of execution, context information, transaction capabilities, and resource sharing.

The client proxy communicates with an MTS stub, so that MTS intercepts the call and eventually invokes the logic in the installed component.

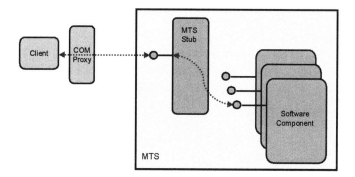

The MTS execution environment can be resident in the same process as the client-calling object or can be loaded into an external surrogate process provided by the MTS installation (**MTX.EXE**). Locating it in the same process as the client means that if the component misbehaves and causes a process crash, it will kill the client. However, it will perform much faster than using a separate process.

MTS maintains the standard COM principle of location transparency. That is, the client can access a component without knowing where it is physically located; COM locates the component using information stored in the Windows Registry.

Distributed Transaction Coordination

Developing code to handle transactions is difficult, and the complexity of the task grows as the number of transactions increases and becomes distributed over multiple platforms. By writing an application as a series of COM-compliant software components and installing them in the MTS environment, the need to develop one's own transaction processing is eliminated

When MTS is installed, a service called the **Distributed Transaction Coordinator** (DTC) is also installed and configured to start up when the system is booted. Whereas COM provides the inter-object communication infrastructure, DTC is responsible for managing transactions across networks. DTC interoperates with the database's **resource manager**. This is the part of the database responsible for ensuring the integrity of the database.

DTC monitors transactions for any failure. If a problem occurs, it will automatically handle the database rollback. With a single component operating on a single database, this would be a simple task to handle. MTS and DTC come into their own when operating with a multi-tier client-server application that spans multiple distributed databases.

Performance and Scalability

MTS provides **"just in time" activation** and **"as soon as possible" deactivation** to improve performance and scalability. With standard COM, an object is released either when the client deletes the object or when the client processing is terminated. With MTS, however, clients can hold on to references to objects, but the objects become "deactivated" for the period when their services are not required. When a client needs the services of an object, MTS will try to assign one from its pool of deactivated objects (if available) before resorting to the instantiation of a new object (if none is available). This increases performance and scalability because:

- A few objects can be shared over many clients, thus reducing the demand on system resources
- Objects can be initialized and waiting "ready to go"; this enables them to react to a request immediately on demand

Establishing database connections is a notoriously expensive operation and in large systems can result in unacceptable performance levels. Another advantage of MTS is that it provides **resource dispensers** to recycle valuable system resources in a similar fashion to the way it recycles objects.

For example, an ODBC resource dispenser is available which recycles database connections. When an ODBC database connection is no longer required, MTS just deactivates the connection rather than close it. When a component requires an ODBC database connection, MTS will first try to assign a connection from its pool of deactivated connections. A new ODBC database connection is only established if the pool of available connections is empty.

MTS and ASP

In Chapter 7, we saw that ASP script logic can interface with COM-compliant software components, including those that are installed in MTS. We also discussed the advantages of using a high-level language like VB over ASP, and why it is advisable to put most of the Web application logic into the components rather than into the ASP script.

For ASP to call on the services of a COM component, it must first instantiate it and obtain a reference to it. This is done by using the **Create-Object** method that is exposed by an ASP intrinsic object called **Server**. The **CreateObject** method call requires a parameter called the **ProgId** (programmatic identifier). This is a text string that uniquely identifies every component installed on the system.

For example:

```
Dim objDetails
Set objDetails = Server.CreateObject("UserDetails.Update")
```

Once the software component has been successfully instantiated, then methods that it exposes can be invoked.

For example:

```
Call ObjDetails.StoreEmailAddress( Request.Form("email"),        _
                                   Request.Form("firstname"), _
                                   Request.Form("surname") )
```

> **Important:** VBScript also includes the **CreateObject** functionality as part of its base language and can be used to create MTS objects. With IIS3 we could save typing and just use **CreateObject**. However, when using MTS objects with IIS4 and ASP, we *must* call the ASP intrinsic object and use the full **Server.CreateObject**. This is so that ASP passes the appropriate user-context information on to MTS so that the role-based security (to be discussed below) works.

Reliability with Bulletproof Web Applications

One of the biggest improvements that IIS4 offers over its predecessors is **crash protection.** This is achieved by enabling Web applications to be configured to run "**out-of-process**" in their own process space—this is called **process isolation**.

Should an application crash because of a misbehaving software component, it will automatically be restarted upon the next request. Furthermore, this prevents a single Web application from crashing or freezing up the main IIS Server process, which would stop all Web activity.

Web Applications

A **Web application** is created by flagging a directory to be the **application start point**. This will contain a collection of HTML pages, server extensions (such as ASP and ISAPI), and ActiveX server components. We shall see that executable logic for a Web application is implemented as an MTS package.

APPLICATION NAMESPACE

The **Application Namespace** (or scope) will then include all items within the directory and the subdirectories below, with the exception of those included in another Web application. The following diagram clarifies this:

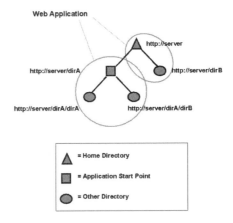

CREATING A WEB APPLICATION

We can use MMC to create the Web application. This is done by selecting the directory start point, right-clicking, and choosing the Properties menu option. This invokes the properties dialog, which consists of several property sheets. Depending on the type of directory, select one of the following tabs: Home Directory, Virtual Directory, or Directory. Finally, to create the application, select the Create button in the Application Settings frame.

The following screenshot shows the different icons that appear in the explorer pane of Internet Service Manager (MMC). The "blue box" icon indicates an application start point.

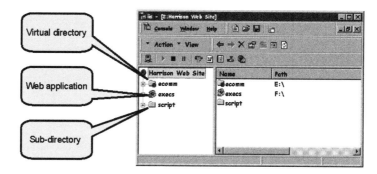
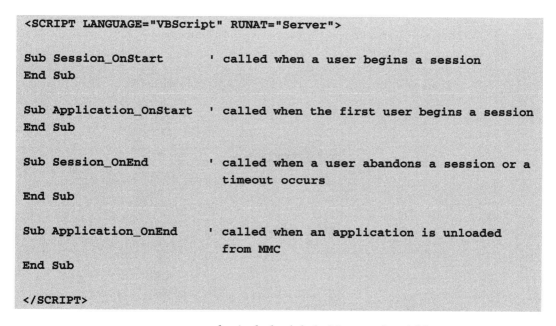

Once a Web application has been created, the following events located in the `global.asa` file, which is resident at the directory start point, will be fired:

```vbscript
<SCRIPT LANGUAGE="VBScript" RUNAT="Server">

Sub Session_OnStart        ' called when a user begins a session
End Sub


Sub Application_OnStart   ' called when the first user begins a session
End Sub


Sub Session_OnEnd          ' called when a user abandons a session or a
                             timeout occurs
End Sub


Sub Application_OnEnd      ' called when an application is unloaded
                             from MMC
End Sub

</SCRIPT>
```

`global.asa` may also include global objects and variables.

APPLICATION PROCESS ISOLATION

Once an application has been created, we can optionally specify that the application must run in a separate memory space (out-of-process) to provide the crash protection already discussed.

This is done by selecting the Run in separate memory space checkbox, located in the Application Settings frame on the Directories properties sheet.

The Web Application Manager

The goal of process isolation is achieved thanks to a subsystem called the **Web Application Manager** (WAM). A WAM can optionally be run in its own memory space and is then separated from the main Web server. Each application namespace has its own WAM and is responsible for loading the ISAPI Extensions (and thus any ASP logic) used by the application.

> We discussed ISAPI briefly in Chapter 7.

A WAM is an in-process COM object that is shipped as the file **WAM.DLL**. The Web Server executable **INETINFO.EXE** normally hosts the WAMs. However, the WAMs responsible for applications that are process-isolated are hosted in a surrogate process created by the executable **MTX.EXE**. Note that only one instance of the WAM object is created per Web application.

Each instance of a WAM is registered with Transaction Server. We can see this in the following MMC screen dump, which shows our Harrison Web Site configured for process isolation, residing in the IIS-{Harrison Web Site//Root} package within the MTS configuration. All WAMs that are not process-isolated are configured in the default IIS In-Process Applications package.

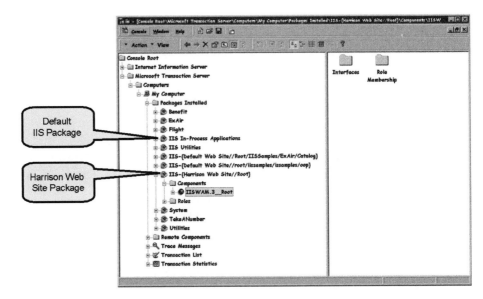

> Playing around with the WAM package configurations in the MTS snap-in is very, very dangerous!! Look, but don't touch!

HANDLING AN HTTP REQUEST FOR A SERVER EXTENSION

When IIS receives an HTTP request for a static file, such as an HTML file or a graphics file, the Web Service retrieves the file and generates the HTTP response containing the file contents. Otherwise the request must be for a server extension. If the HTTP request is for a CGI extension, the appropriate executable is invoked and is responsible for dynamically generating the HTTP response.

Alternatively, if the HTTP request requires the use of an ISAPI extension, IIS determines from the URL the associated application namespace and checks to see if the WAM for that application has already been created. If the WAM does not exist, it is created. It is also the responsibility of MTS to ensure that the WAM is created in the correct process; that is, either in **INETINFO.EXE** (if in-process) or in a newly created **MTX.EXE** (if process-isolated). Once started, the WAM processes the HTTP request, and this involves loading the ISAPI extension.

A WAM and its ISAPI extensions remain loaded after being used and are then ready for subsequent HTTP requests for server extensions within that application. Should an ISAPI extension or another in-process loaded COM component misbehave in the **MTX.EXE** process and cause it to crash, the next request for that application will cause a new instance of the WAM to be created. However, if any logic within the **INETINFO.EXE** crashes, the Web Server is lost for good and has to be manually restarted.

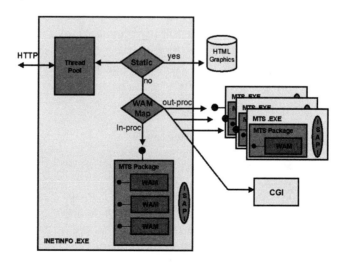

UNLOADING ISOLATED APPLICATIONS

It is possible to unload the WAM using the Unload button located in the Application Settings frame on the Directories properties sheet. This enables us to update the ISAPI extensions and in-process COM components without stopping the whole Web server.

CONSIDERATIONS FOR ISOLATED APPLICATIONS

Applications running within a WAM located in the main Web server will be invoked slightly faster than those that are resident in an isolated process. This is mainly due to the extra time taken for the interprocess communication. There is also a delay for the first application request while the isolated process is instantiated. Note that this is a onetime cost, unlike CGI, which creates a process on every request. Once created, isolated ISAPI server extensions run much faster than CGI server extensions.

Another consideration is that using isolated processes will require additional memory.

We need to take care when migrating ISAPI applications from IIS3 to IIS4, because it is now possible to have multiple copies of the same ISAPI DLL loaded in more than one process. For example, care has to be taken that the ISAPI extension does not permanently lock any resource; otherwise the other instances will never be able to gain access.

MTS Package Security

We shall now take a look at the issues of MTS Package security. Remember from the discussion above that a package is a collection of COM components that combine to form an application.

We shall start by discussing the user security context, called the **Package Identity**, under which the package executes. We shall then take a look at two types of security that can be applied:

- Declarative Security
- Programmatic Security.

Package Identity

When we discussed Windows NT Security in Chapter 2, we saw that when a Windows NT system resource is accessed, the permissions are checked to determine whether the accessor should be granted or denied access. MTS security expands on this, introducing the concept of package identity, whereby a package can be configured to run as a "virtual user." MTS will insulate the client users from the system resource.

The MTS administrator can assign a single user account to a package and configure the system resource to grant appropriate access privileges to the package's user account. An MTS component within the package runs with the security context of the assigned user account and thus gets access to the resource.

The package identity is requested when the MTS administrator creates a new package. Alternatively, it can be set via the Identity property sheet.

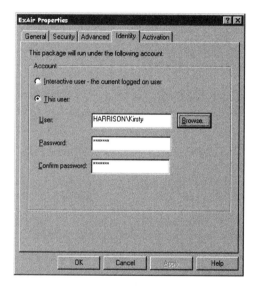

From the screen dump you can see that it is still possible for the package to be configured to run in the user context of the client user. However, the package identity security model is often viewed as offering a simpler implementation of security . . . as will be demonstrated in the next chapter when we consider database access.

Declarative Security

Declarative security is where the MTS administrator uses the MTS Explorer to control access to packages, components, and interfaces. This is done after the software components have been built and is a procedure undertaken as part of the system deployment.

For example, consider the following:

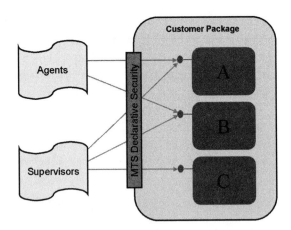

A group of users called **Agents** are granted access to components A and B in the **Customer** package but cannot access component C. A group of users called **Supervisors** are granted access to all components.

This shows applying the restrictions at the component level. It is possible to apply a finer grain of control and restrict access at the COM interface level. For example, we could organize the functionality in the above C component so that any read-only functionality is exposed in a different interface to the remainder. The users who are **Agents** could then be granted access to the read-only functionality.

Remember to refer to the explanation of COM in Appendix A if you are unsure what a COM Interface is.

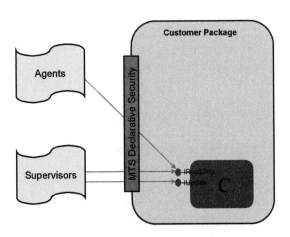

The diagram shows the component called C exposing two interfaces, IReadOnly and IUpdate. All public methods that can be called will be associated to one interface or the other.

The Agents are granted access to the methods in the IReadOnly interface but cannot access the methods in the IUpdate interface. The Supervisors are granted access to all methods.

Declarative security is only applied when the caller is from outside the package. In this case the user context under which the caller is executing is obtained and the access permissions is determined. MTS trusts all calls from within a package and no additional security checks are made.

Programmatic Security

Programmatic security is where the executable program logic behaves according to the user who is accessing the component. Depending on the user identified, the logic within the implementation of the software components will take appropriate actions.

As an example, consider again our Agents and Supervisors, and a Loans Authorization component that exposes a method called ApproveLoan.

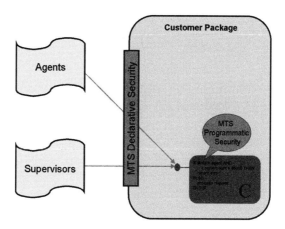

Business rules might dictate that Agents can only authorize loans up to $5,000, whereas Supervisors can authorize loans up to $30,000. The ApproveLoan implementation could determine the type of user and apply the appropriate validation.

We shall see in the next chapter how Programmatic Security is implemented using the IsCallerInRole method of the MTS Context Object.

Roles

Both Declarative Security and Programmatic Security are implemented with a concept called **roles**. A role is a collection of Windows NT user accounts and user groups. These operate in a similar manner to a user group in that they reduce the administrative burden as users come and go. However, unlike user groups, a role is only applicable to the packages in which it is defined.

An MTS administrator uses the MTS Explorer to:

- Create roles
- Add user accounts/groups to a role
- Delete user accounts/groups from a role
- Grant access permissions to a package/component/interface for a particular role

A developer can use procedural logic to ascertain the caller's role and perform appropriate business logic.

> If you call an MTS component from an out-of-process ASP Web application using the VBScript `CreateObject` command, the user context passed to MTS will be whatever context the out-of-process applications is running as (by default this is **IWAM_sysname**) and Role Security will fail.
> Always call MTS components using `Server.CreateObject`.

MTS Security Administration

In this next section, we shall investigate how an Administrator configures the MTS environment to apply the various security measures we have discussed. Not surprisingly, such tasks are done using the MTS Explorer.

We shall see how to:

- Create a package
- Configure roles
- Configure authentication

Creating a Package

Before we can add our COM components to the MTS environment, we must create the package in which the components are to reside.

PACKAGE WIZARD

A package is created using the Package Wizard. This is invoked by right-clicking on "Packages installed" and selecting the New|Package menu option.

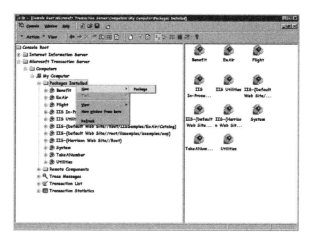

The wizard then follows one of two routes:

1. Installation of a pre-built package by specifying a .PAK file
2. Creation of a new empty package by specifying the name

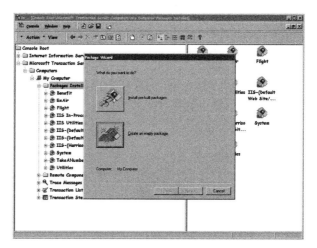

The subsequent screen dumps show a package called **Harrison** being created.

Now that the package has been created, we can add the components.

COMPONENT WIZARD

A component is inserted into an existing package using the Component Wizard. This is invoked by right-clicking on the package name and selecting the New|Component menu option.

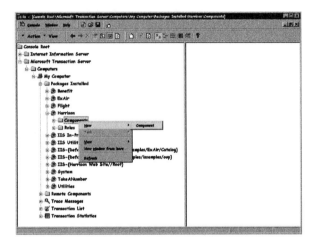

The wizard then follows one of two routes:

1. It installs a new component by specifying a DLL and optionally a Type Library (if interface information is not resident in DLL)
2. It imports a component that is already registered on the machine (not necessarily in MTS)

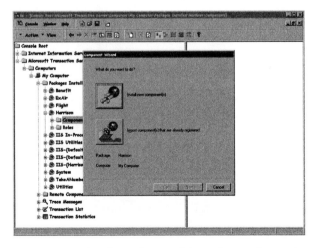

Once a component has been inserted into the package, the exposed interfaces can be inspected.

Role Management

At this stage we can see that there are a number of Roles/Roles Membership folders in the hierarchy. By clicking on these folders we will see roles that are configured. For a new component the panes will be empty, indicating that by default no roles are configured.

CREATING A ROLE

We can create a new role for a package by right-clicking on the Roles folder and selecting the New|Role menu option.

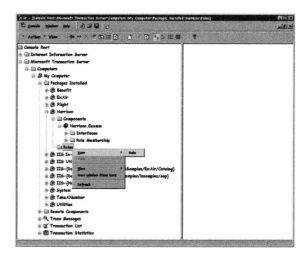

A dialog is then displayed allowing the role name to be specified.

A role name can be of any length and can include spaces. The edit field actually allows certain punctuation characters to be entered and then rejects them when the OK button is entered.

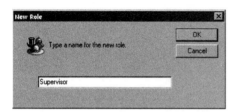 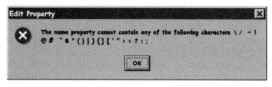

The GUID can be inspected, if we right-click on the role that we have inserted and select the Properties menu option.

Under the covers, each role name is assigned a globally unique identifier (GUID). Since a GUID is unique, it is possible to insert the same role name more than once in the same package. However, apart from causing a management nightmare, this would make programmatic security unreliable, since it is the role's text name that is used in the programmatic logic.

It is, however, safe to use the same role names in more than one package.

ASSIGNING USERS TO ROLES

Once a role has been created, Windows NT users and user groups can then be assigned to the role.

If we open the Roles folder, we find a node for each inserted role. Drilling down further we find for each role a folder called Users.

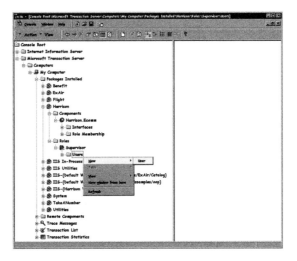

We assign users to a role by right-clicking on the Users folder and selecting the New|User menu option.

A standard Windows NT User Selection dialog is then displayed, allowing required users and user groups to be selected.

The selected users and user groups are then inserted into the explorer hierarchy under the assigned role.

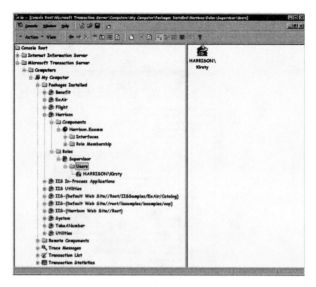

One technique to minimize administration is to create a single Windows NT user group for each role and assign this group to the role using MTS Explorer. Once this has been done, all subsequent administration of user accounts can be done using the Windows NT User Manager alone.

ASSIGNING ROLES TO COMPONENTS AND INTERFACES

Now that our roles have been created, we can implement Declarative Security and define which roles have access to a component or a particular interface exposed by a component.

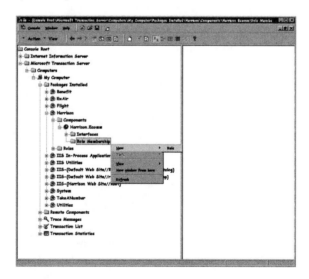

Role Membership folders are located in the explorer hierarchy for both components and for each of their interfaces.

We enable access to a component or interface by adding a role to the Role Membership folder. This is done by right-clicking on the **Role Member-ship** folder and selecting the New|Role menu option.

A dialog is then displayed showing that all roles have been created for the package. The required role(s) can then be selected.

Subsequently, the roles that are granted access to the component or interface are shown in the item's **Role Membership** folder.

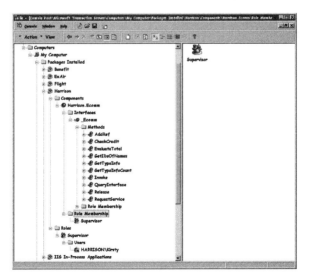

Authentication Controls

We shall now discuss the final tasks that are required to configure MTS in order to apply the security measures we have discussed so far:

- Enabling MTS authorization checking.
- Enabling DCOM security.

ENABLING AUTHORIZATION CHECKING

To enable MTS security we must turn on the authorization checking and set the authentication level.

Authorization checking is enabled at the package level using the Security tab on the package property sheet. When a component is added, by default the authorization checking is disabled.

Various authorization levels can be set, and they are listed below in an order that reflects the level of assurance provided. The more complex (and thus more secure) mechanisms provide higher levels of assurance but are, unfortunately, CPU-intensive. For most requirements, using the default Packet, is recommended, because it provides a compromise between security and CPU usage.

The authorization levels available are:

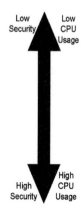

- **None**—no checking on the caller is made
- **Connect**—the caller's identity is checked once—on the first call to the package
- **Call**—the caller's identity is checked on every call to the package
- **Packet**—as Call plus the caller's identity is sent encrypted to prevent impersonation
- **Packet integrity**—as Packet plus the network packets are checked for tampering
- **Packet privacy**—as Packet integrity plus network packets are encrypted

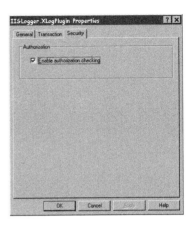

Once authorization checking has been enabled at a package level, by default the security checking will be applied to all components in the package.

Authorization checking for each component can be selectively enabled/disabled by means of the Security tab on the component property sheet.

ENABLING DCOM SECURITY

DCOM must be enabled for each machine containing an MTS installation that IIS communicates with. This is done by running the **DCOMCNFG.EXE** configuration utility from the Start|Run dialog.

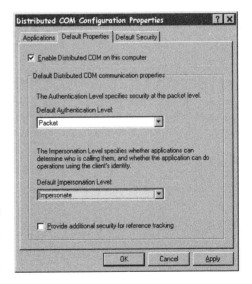

There are three things that must be set on the Default Properties tab.

First, the Enable Distributed COM on this computer checkbox must be enabled.

Next, the Default Authentication Level must be set to a level equal to or greater than the level set for the packages in MTS.

Finally, the Default Impersonation Level must be set to Identify. This allows MTS to run components under the security context of the client. Values other than this will cause MTS to fail (more information on this is available on the Microsoft Knowledge Base Article ID: Q180119).

MTS Administration Permissions

By default, anyone logging on to a machine with an MTS installation can modify the configuration settings that we have discussed in this chapter.

Since an MTS administrator yields considerable control over a system, it is important to be able to apply restrictions on who has such power.

When MTS is installed, a package called System is included in the environment, and it controls who has access to the MTS administration facilities. The package contains the two r entries:

- Administrator—this role has full access to MTS administration functions

- Reader—this role only has read access to MTS administration information; items cannot be created, modified, or deleted

To enable MTS Administration security, we must first add user accounts to the above roles.

One approach would be to create two Windows NT user groups called MTS Administrators and MTS Readers, and assign these to the roles. This would mean that all subsequent user administration could be done via the Windows NT User Manager.

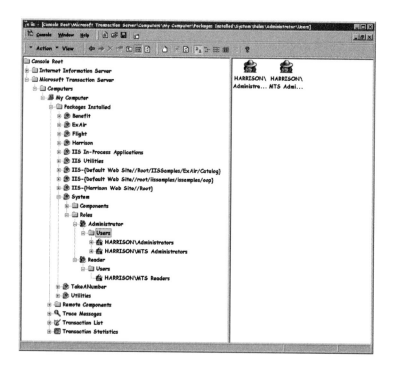

Next we must assign a Package Identity to the system package. The user account used must have administrative permissions for the local machine. A warning is given if an unsuitable user account is specified.

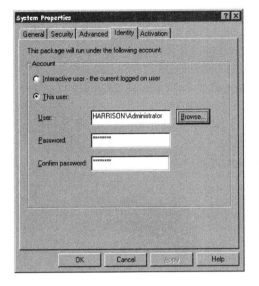

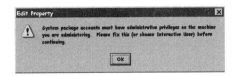

Take care: if you assign the Package Identity before adding the users to the package roles, the MTS Administration facility becomes inoperative. No users will exist that have permission to configure MTS. The only solution is to reinstall MTS!

Finally, the MTS processes must be restarted by right-clicking on the My Computer icon and selecting the Shutdown Server Processes menu option. The MTS Administration facilities will then be operating under the new security context.

■ Summary

In this chapter we have seen how MTS implements security for software components and looked at the procedures involved in administering the MTS environment.

In addition, we have taken an in-depth look at the architecture of IIS4. Because it has been built as an MTS application, IIS4 can provide us with a foundation for building Web solutions that are scalable, high-performance, and robust.

The key points in this chapter are:

• MTS provides a complete infrastructure for building multi-tier applications and insulates the application developer from addressing infrastructure issues such as multi-threading, object repooling, sharing of resources, and handling of transaction context across objects.

• MTS offers facilities for applying access controls to components resident in the environment. The methods are:

- Programmatic—access controls are built into the programming logic
- Declarative—access controls are applied using the MTS configuration facilities

- A Package is a set of components grouped together for a single application. Security checks are only applied to calls from outside the package. All calls from within the package are trusted.

- A package can contain a number of roles which are an abstraction of Windows NT users and user accounts. Access to components and interfaces can be restricted to members of specific role(s).

- The configuration of the roles in the System package dictates which users have access to the MTS administration facilities.

In the next chapter we shall take a look at how to use MTS Security for Web solutions and focus on using MTS to securely access a database.

Web Database Security with MTS/ASP

With Internet technology being increasingly used for business-critical systems, the integration of database and Web technology has been fundamental for its rapid growth. With this importance, many readers may have expected a Web Security book to contain several chapters dedicated to database topics. Fortunately, as we shall see, MTS makes the implementation of database security simple, enabling us to demonstrate the subject in a single chapter.

So in this chapter we shall demonstrate MTS Security (programmatic and declarative) in order to:

- Limit database access functionality to suitable levels that are appropriate for a particular user

- Format the presentation layers in an appropriate manner for a particular user

We shall also see the Personal Information feature of IE4 in action. This is a mechanism whereby a user can once and for all set up a range of personal information items that he is prepared to expose to any site he visits. But as we shall see, whenever a particular Web site attempts to access this information, the user has ultimate control over whether the information is actually released.

> The code for the examples in this chapter can be found on the **CD-ROM** included with this book.

The "Guest Book" Application

For this chapter we shall study a Guest Book application to highlight various database security issues. The application implementation demonstrates how to use MTS to apply a simple security strategy that enforces strong protection of our database.

The application allows two types of visitors:

- A Web site user (anonymous) who may:
  - record various personal details plus any comments or feedback
  - view the comments left by previous visitors (but not any of the personal details)
- A Web site manager (authenticated) who may:
  - view all details left by visitors (with a hyperlink to the e-mail address allowing a quick message of thanks to be returned)
  - delete any entries which contain offensive remarks

The database access components utilize the Microsoft **ActiveX Data Objects** (ADO). This is a high-performance, low-overhead mechanism to access any data store that provides an OLE DB interface. The Guest Book application was built using Microsoft **SQL Server 7.0**, but the use of ADO means that you should be able to easily use alternative databases.

> The intricacies of ADO are a large and complex topic that is outside the area of security. Any reader requiring detailed information on the subject is referred to:
>   http://www.microsoft.com/data/

Database Security Strategy

The MTS database security strategy used is as follows:

- The database is configured such that only one SQL Server user account exists and has the privilege to directly access the database. Preventing user accounts from having direct access to the database eliminates any risk of a user accessing the database with a database query/manipulation tool and hacking the contents. Furthermore, using a single database access account avoids the headache of continually managing the database. With a large user base, accounts must be frequently added or deleted, and this becomes a major headache for any database administrator.

- All Web access to the database functionality must be done via MTS components. This enables us to apply appropriate MTS Role security restrictions to the various components and interfaces. Standard users are mapped onto the above account that is allowed to access the database.

The MTS database approach also means that a separate database connection is not required for each user. Instead many users sessions are funneled into a single connection, and this makes considerable savings to the precious resources on the database server. (For example, a thousand users simultaneously accessing an SQL Server system directly would normally require a 37M [$1000 \times 37K$] overhead of memory.)

Component Architecture

The approach taken in this example is to minimize the amount of ASP script and partition the database logic into software components developed with Visual Basic and hosted within MTS. The ASP logic is used to synchronize the information flow and handle the generation of the presentation logic.

The ASP logic is deployed in the following files:

- **default.asp**—handles the main menu
- **guestinsert.asp**—handles a user adding an entry to the Guest Book database
- **guestdelete.asp**—handles a manager deleting an entry from the Guest Book database
- **guestread.asp**—handles a user reading the comments in the Guest Book database

- **authguestread.asp**—handles a manager reading the entries in the Guest Book database

- **guestread.inc**—this is the server-side include that contains the main logic used by **guestread.asp** and **authguestread.asp**

There is one VB component called GuestBook. The interfaces and their methods that are exposed by this component are as follows:

- **IAnonymous**—functionality for use by all site visitors:
  - **InsertComment**—allows a new entry to be added to the Guest Book database
  - **ReadComments**—allows entries to be read from the Guest Book database; we shall use MTS programmatic Security to determine what information a particular user is allowed to see
  - **NewCollection**—utility function that creates a VB collection object and returns a reference to it

- **IManagement**—functionality for use by the Web site manager only:

  - **DeleteComment**—allows an existing entry to be deleted from the Guest Book database

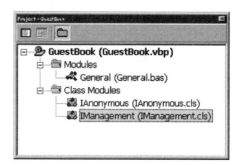

The interaction between the ASP files and MTS components is depicted below:

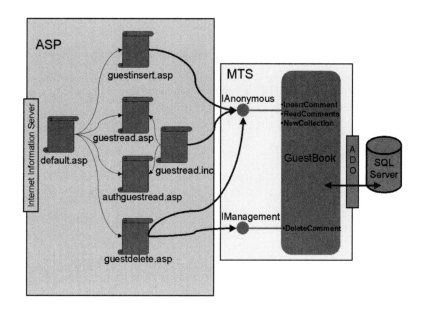

Security Configuration

This section describes the security configuration required by the Guest Book application.

WINDOWS NT SECURITY

IIS distinguishes a Web site manager from a standard user by forcing them to be authorized.

Authentication is invoked when the user first navigates to the file authguestread.asp. This file has NT Security permissions applied such that the normal anonymous Internet user's password (**IUSR_sys-name**) is not granted read access.

Remember, as soon as IIS detects that the

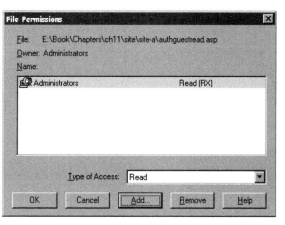

anonymous user does not have access to the resource requested, it informs the Web browser to supply the user's credentials. Refer back to Chapter 4, if necessary, to recap on the processing that occurs to achieve this.

All other ASP files are secured to allow anonymous access.

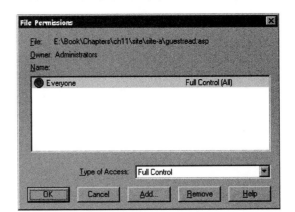

MTS DECLARATIVE SECURITY

As we shall see, the Guest Book application uses both MTS programmatic and declarative security. The latter is implemented by creating two MTS Roles: Anonymous and Manager.

The user group Everyone is assigned to the Anonymous role, while the local Administrators group is assigned to the Manager role.

Access to the **IAnonymous** interface is given to both roles.

Access to the **IManagement** interface is restricted to the Manager role.

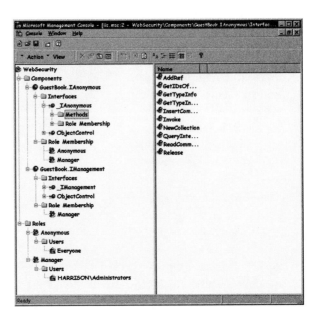

Enable authorization checking must be enabled for the package's properties so that the Role functionality can operate.

IIS AUTHENTICATION METHODS

IIS must be configured to enable user authentication. For example, it doesn't matter which type of authentication we enable, but we saw in Chapter 4 the security advantages that Windows NT Challenge/Response has over Basic Authentication.

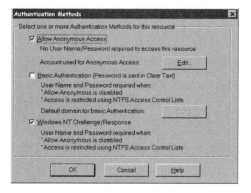

Application Logic

Let us now look at the main points of interest in the application. First we shall look at the common issues that are applicable throughout the Guest Book application, and then we shall drill into each function in turn.

Common Processing Issues

PROJECT REFERENCES

When creating the VB software component, we must add a reference to the following items in our project:

- Microsoft Transaction Server Type Library
- Microsoft ActiveX Data Objects 2.0 Library
- Microsoft ActiveX Data Objects Recordset 2.0 Library

This is done from the Project|References menu option.

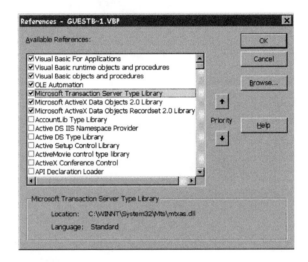

PARAMETER PASSING

All parameters that are passed between ASP and the software components are grouped together into a VB collection and passed as single parameter.

The use of a collection in this manner has several advantages:

- It is easy to modify the data that is being passed around without changing the interface definition
- The code is easier on the eye by avoiding a huge list of function parameters
- A method can return several values in a collection

ASP does not provide a standard mechanism to create a VB collection. Because of this, a method called **NewCollection** is implemented in the **IAnonymous** interface and can be called from ASP to create a reference to a new collection ready for parameter passing.

For example:

```
Set objAGuestBook =
Server.CreateObject("GuestBook.IAnonymous")
Set objData = objAGuestBook.NewCollection
```

Once the collection is created, we can add various items to it before invoking the target method. For example:

```
objData.Add vCommentId,"commentid"
Set objResponse = objMGuestBook.DeleteComment(objData)
```

ERROR HANDLING

All component methods in our Guest Book application return a collection, and it always includes an item called **error**. If **error** is set to **false**, then no error has occurred. If **error** is set to **true**, then another item called **errorinfo** will exist and contain a detailed explanation of the problem that occurred in the component. All calls to a component will first check for any error and, if necessary, display the problem.

For example:

```
Set objResponse = objMGuestBook.DeleteComment(objData)
if objResponse("error") then
    Response.Write "<FONT color=red>" & _
          objResponse("errorinfo") & _
          "</FONT><BR>"
else
   ' everything is OK
```

All errors are also written to an ASCII file that is called **trace.txt**. In a production environment this would ideally be written to the Windows NT Event Log.

MTS PLUMBING

We shall now look at the standard MTS plumbing code that is present in all of our VB components.

At the top of each component we state that the component supports the standard MTS interface **ObjectControl**. This means that our component will implement all of the methods defined by this interface.

```
Implements ObjectControl
```

MTS assigns a Context Object to the instance of our object. This contains information about the object's execution environment within MTS. A reference to this object is stored in a private variable called **objMTSContext**.

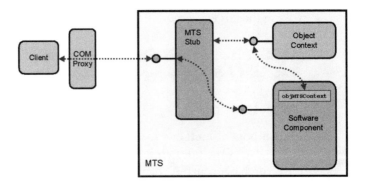

```
Private objMTSContext As ObjectContext
```

There are three methods in the **ObjectControl** interface. The first is **CanBePooled**. This expects a Boolean value to be returned and indicates whether the object can be **recycled**. A recycled object is not destroyed after use. Instead it is placed in a pool, and is ready on hot standby for future use. (Note that the current version of MTS does not actually implement the pooling of objects. However, the MTS object model has been published to cater for this future addition to the product.)

```
Private Function ObjectControl_CanBePooled() As Boolean
    ObjectControl_CanBePooled = True
End Function
```

The two other methods are **Deactivate** and **Activate**.

The **Activate** method is called when the object is "activated." This is when MTS makes the object ready for use by a client process. It is in this function that we grab a reference to the MTS Context Object by calling the global function **GetObjectContext** (accessible because we specified the Microsoft Transaction Server Type Library in the Project References).

```
Private Sub ObjectControl_Activate()
    On Error GoTo ActivateErr

    Set objMTSContext = GetObjectContext()

    Exit Sub

ActivateErr:
    Call RaiseError("ObjectControl_Activate")
End Sub
```

The **Deactivate** method is called when the current instance of the object is no longer required and should be used to clean up any items that may have been created. We also deleted any database references.

```
Private Sub ObjectControl_Deactivate()
    Set objMTSContext = Nothing
    Set oDb = Nothing
End Sub
```

Main Menu

The ASP pages in the Guest Book application follow a similar style to the previous examples seen in this book. The default page (default.asp) is used as the main menu and allows us to access the different items of functionality:

- Adding an entry to the Guest Book
- Reading the comments in the Guest Book
- Forcing User Authentication and, if the user is a manager, Reading all information in the Guest Book

Adding a Comment

Adding an entry to the Guest Book is implemented using the ASP file **guestinsert.asp** and the VB **InsertComment** component.

guestinsert.asp handles the task in two distinct stages. A parameter called **state** is passed in the URL to indicate the stage that the script processing is currently at. At the top of the ASP file, the **state** variable is determined.

```
<%
   If Not Request.QueryString("state") = "" Then
      state = Request.QueryString("state")
   Else
      state = 1
   End If
%>
```

When **state** is **1**, the ASP generates the HTML form enabling the user to enter its details. When the form is submitted, the same ASP page is invoked, passing in the URL a **state** parameter with a value of 2.

When **state** is **2**, the entered form is first validated. If all conditions are satisfied, the VB component is created, a parameter collection is created, and the **InsertComment** function is invoked.

```
Set objGuestBook = Server.CreateObject("GuestBook.IAnonymous")

Set objData = objGuestBook.NewCollection
objData.Add Request.Form("fullname"),"fullname"
objData.Add Request.Form("email"),"email"
objData.Add Request.Form("company"),"company"
objData.Add Request.Form("city"),"city"
objData.Add Request.Form("country"),"country"
objData.Add Request.Form("comment"),"comment"

Set objResponse = objGuestBook.InsertComment(objData)
```

If any errors occur, the **state** variable is amended to **1** and the logic drops through to redisplay the form. Any values previously entered are redisplayed.

The VB component uses an ADO Recordset object to create a new empty database record. This is then populated with the information passed in the collection parameter and finally updated.

This example also illustrates the Personal Information feature of IE4 and how a Web site can use this to retrieve details about the visitor.

PROFILE ASSISTANT

The Profile Assistant feature of IE4 enables a user to specify a number of personal information items that he is willing to provide to Web sites he might visit. This avoids the user having to rekey such information at each new site.

The facility is available from the Internet Options|Content menu option and selecting the Edit Profile button in the Personal Information section.

In a series of tabbed dialog sheets, the user can specify a heap of information about himself and his company.

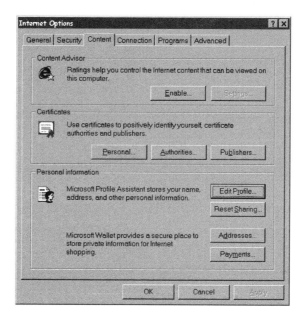

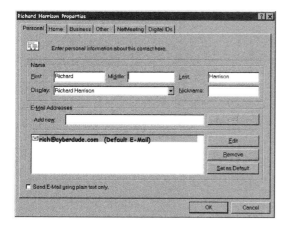

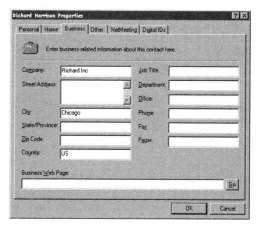

In our application, we use client-side script logic to determine the type of Web browser the user is using. If it is IE4/IE5, then we additionally display a "Use my Profile Information" button on the form. To achieve portability across a maximum number of browsers, this script logic is written in JavaScript.

```
<SCRIPT language=JSCRIPT>
<!--
        var ua = navigator.userAgent;
        if ((ua.indexOf("MSIE") != -1) & ((ua.indexOf("4.") != -1) |
            (ua.indexOf("5.") != -1)))
        document.write('<INPUT TYPE="BUTTON" '
                + 'VALUE="Use my Profile Information" '
                + 'onclick="getProfile()">'
                + '<BR><BR>');
-->
</SCRIPT>
```

If a user clicks on this button, the `getProfile()` function is invoked. This is used to retrieve the information from the user's profile and populate the HTML form.

```
<SCRIPT LANGUAGE="JSCRIPT">
  <!-
  function getProfile()
    {
    var blnOK;
```

The information is accessed using an object called `userProfile` that is available within the browser hierarchy. This provides a series of methods that allow our script to read the user's personal information.

```
pr = navigator.userProfile;
```

The scripting must first set up a series of "read requests" to specify which items are required to be read from the user's profile. This is done by calling `addReadRequest` and passing a parameter that references the required item.

```
pr.clearRequest();
blnOK = pr.addReadRequest("Vcard.FirstName");
blnOK = pr.addReadRequest("Vcard.LastName");
```

```
blnOK = pr.addReadRequest("Vcard.Company");
blnOK = pr.addReadRequest("Vcard.Business.City");
blnOK = pr.addReadRequest("Vcard.Business.Country");
blnOK = pr.addReadRequest("Vcard.Email");
```

Note that all of the parameter names begin with **Vcard**. This is a specification for an electronic business card. The full list of possible parameters is as follows:

`Vcard.DisplayName`	`Vcard.Business.StreetAddress`
`Vcard.FirstName`	`Vcard.Business.City`
`Vcard.MiddleName`	`Vcard.Business.State`
`Vcard.LastName`	`Vcard.Business.ZipCode`
`Vcard.Email`	`Vcard.Business.Country`
`Vcard.Cellular`	`Vcard.Business.Phone`
`Vcard.Gender`	`Vcard.Business.Fax`
`Vcard.JobTitle`	`Vcard.Home.StreetAddress`
`Vcard.Pager`	`Vcard.Home.City`
`Vcard.Notes`	`Vcard.Home.State`
`Vcard.Homepage`	`Vcard.Home.ZipCode`
`Vcard.Company`	`Vcard.Home.Country`
`Vcard.Department`	`Vcard.Home.Phone`
`Vcard.Office`	`Vcard.Home.Fax`
`Vcard.Business.URL`	

The reading of the information is then invoked by calling the method **doReadRequest**. The first parameter is to inform the user what the site intends to do with the user's personal details. The second parameter is the *friendly name* of the organization requesting the information.

```
pr.doReadRequest(3, "Harrison Associates");
```

In our example, the parameter value of **3** means "Used to customize the content and design of the site." A full list of values is given below:

Usage Code	Meaning
0	Used for system administration.
1	Used for research and/or product development.
2	Used for completion and support of current transaction.
3	Used to customize the content and design of a site.

(continued)

Usage Code	Meaning
4	Used to improve the content of site including advertisements.
5	Used for notifying visitors about updates to the site.
6	Used for contacting visitors for marketing of services or products.
7	Used for linking other collected information.
8	Used by site for other purposes.
9	Disclosed to others for customization or improvement of the content and design of the site.
10	Disclosed to others, who may contact you, for marketing of services and/or products.
11	Disclosed to others, who may contact you, for marketing of services and/or products, but you will have the opportunity to ask a site not to do this.
12	Disclosed to others for any other purpose.

When the method **doReadRequest** is called, a dialog is displayed telling the user what items have been requested and what the information will be used for.

This provides the user with an opportunity to reject the request for his information.

The user is also warned if the information is going to be sent over an unsecured channel, because in such cases, although this is unlikely, it could be intercepted and examined by a third party.

In our example, we only have a single field in the HTML form for the visitor's name. Thus we concatenate the First Name and Last Name fields retrieved.

```
nv = pr.getAttribute("Vcard.FirstName");
if (nv != null) nv = nv + " "
else nv = "";
lv = pr.getAttribute("Vcard.LastName");
if (lv != null) nv = nv + lv;
```

Finally the HTML form is populated with the profile information.

```
    fm = document.forms(0);
    fm("fullname").value = nv;
    fm("email").value = pr.getAttribute("Vcard.Email")
    fm("company").value = pr.getAttribute("Vcard.Company");
    fm("city").value = pr.getAttribute("Vcard.Business.City");
    fm("country").value = pr.getAttribute("Vcard.Business.Country");
    }
    -->
</SCRIPT>
```

Reading the Comments

One of the statements displayed on the Web page for adding a comment is that the personal information left by a visitor will not be disclosed to others. Thus our functionality to display the comments must operate in two modes:

- For the general public (i.e., users in the Anonymous role) only the comments will be displayed; this mode is accessed using the ASP file called **guestread.asp**
- For Web site managers (i.e., users in the Manager role) all user information will be displayed; this mode is accessed using the ASP file called **authguestread.asp**

The functionality for the two modes is very similar, and we need an approach that does not duplicate either ASP or VB code. The main ASP logic is contained in a single-server side include file called **guestread.inc**, and this is included by the two main ASP files mentioned above. In addition, the information is retrieved from the database using a single software component. This uses MTS programmatic security to ensure that the returned database information is restricted to just what is appropriate to the client user.

We mentioned earlier that **authguestread.asp** has NT permissions applied such that an anonymous user does not have access. When a user navigates to this ASP file, NT security is enforced and the user is authenticated. Only those with suitable access permissions will be allowed to proceed. From then on, the ASP session will run under the security context of the authenticated user.

The **ReadComments** method in the software component handles the retrieval of the database information. The parameter collection includes two items, **lMaxItems** and **lStartId**, which are passed from ASP. **lMaxItems** specifies how many records are returned at a time. **lStartId** is the key to the comments table from which the **read** operation should start. The information is read using ADO recordsets.

```
Let vSQL = "SELECT Comments.* " & _
    "FROM Comments " & _
    "WHERE Comments.CommentId <= " & lStartId & _
    "ORDER BY Comments.CommentId DESC;"

Set oRs = objMTSContext.CreateInstance("ADODB.Recordset")
oRs.MaxRecords = lMaxItems
oRs.Open vSQL, vDbConn, , , adCmdText
```

MTS PROGRAMMATIC SECURITY

Recapping from the previous chapter, MTS programmatic security is where the programming logic can determine if the user's security context resides within a particular MTS role. This is achieved using the **IsCallerInRole** method of the MTS Context Object.

```
vRole = "Anonymous User"
```

```
If objMTSContext.IsSecurityEnabled And _
    objMTSContext.IsCallerInRole("Manager") Then
        vRole = "Manager"
End If
```

Once the role is ascertained, the logic can switch on this value to invoke appropriate code for the user. We use this to determine which information should be passed from the record set back to the ASP page; i.e., if it is a Manager we return all database information, otherwise we just return the comments.

In addition, the Role is added to the collection that is returned to the ASP logic. ASP can then generate appropriate HTML for the type of user. If it is a Manager, we want to display all database information and include a Delete button for the manager to remove unsavory comments. For other users, HTML will only display the comments.

A STRANGE OCCURRENCE

There was one *strange* occurrence found during the creation of this example when running under the security context of a Manager (after authentication). If we then accessed the guestread.asp file and hit the IE4 Refresh button several times in rapid succession, the browser would unpredictably sometimes switch to running under the context of an anonymous user. This was clearly seen by displaying the **AUTH_USER** server variable at the top of the ASP script. It would start showing the NT user account and then subsequently switch to blank. From then on, the script processing would only display the comments.

```
Response.Write "<CENTER>User: " & Request.ServerVariables("AUTH_USER")
& _
            "<BR>Role: " & vRole & "<BR><BR></CENTER>"
```

The workaround (in **guestread.asp**) was to redirect the user to the authenticated ASP page (**authguestread.asp**) whenever the loss of security context was detected. This activity is transparent to the user, who just continues to see the complete list of user details/comments.

```
<%
    If Session("authorized") = 1 And
Request.ServerVariables("AUTH_USER") = "" Then
        Response.Redirect "authguestread.asp"
    End If
%>
```

Deleting a Comment

A comment should only be able to be deleted by a **Manager**. As we have just discussed, this is implemented using MTS programmatic security and only displaying the Delete button for this type of user. The Delete button is used to submit an HTML form that invokes **guestdelete.asp** to handle the record deletion.

This ASP file then passes control on to a software component that exposes the **DeleteComment** method to action the request.

MTS DECLARATIVE SECURITY

But what is stopping an anonymous Web user from navigating to the **guestdelete.asp** ASP file directly by keying the URL into the address line of the browser? We could prevent this by applying NT permissions to the ASP file or using MTS programmatic security. However, our example demonstrates an alternative approach, using MTS declarative security.

First, the delete functionality is encapsulated behind a COM Interface different from the other functions (**DeleteComment** is resident in the object called **GuestBook.IManagement**). Then, using the MTS Explorer, the Role Membership is defined such that only Managers can access this component. This was discussed earlier in the chapter.

Any attempt by an unauthorized user to access the **DeleteComment** method will cause an exception with a VB error 70 (Permission denied: "DeleteComment") to occur. A failure code is then returned to the user.

How it was done—for our eyes only!

The application code for the Guest Book example, in its entirety, is as follows:

Web Site Code

global.asa

```
<SCRIPT LANGUAGE="VBScript" RUNAT="Server">
Sub Session_OnStart
   Session("authorized") = 0
End Sub


Sub Application_OnStart
End Sub


</SCRIPT>
```

default.asp

```
<%@LANGUAGE="VBSCRIPT" %>


<HTML>
<HEAD>
<TITLE>Guest Book Security Demo</TITLE>
</HEAD>
<BODY bgColor=wheat>
<CENTER>
<HR>
<H1>Home Page</H1>
<HR>
<img src=fish.gif><br><br>
<A href="guestinsert.asp">Write an Entry</A><BR>
<A href="guestread.asp">Read the Entries</A><BR>
<A href="authguestread.asp">Read the Entries (Forced
Authentication)</A><BR>
</CENTER>
</BODY>
</HTML>
```

guestinsert.asp

```
<%@LANGUAGE="VBSCRIPT" %>
<% Option Explicit %>


<% Dim state %>
```

(continued)

```
<%
    If Not Request.QueryString("state") = "" Then
        state = Request.QueryString("state")
    Else
        state = 1
    End If
%>


<HTML>
<TITLE>Guest Book Security Demo</TITLE>
<HEAD>
</HEAD>
<BODY bgColor=wheat>
<CENTER>
<HR>
<H1>Write to the Guest Book</H1>
<HR>
</CENTER>
```

```asp
<% If state = 2 Then %>
<%
        ' do field validation
        If Request.Form("comment") = "" Then
                Response.Write "<FONT color=red>" & _
                        "<P>Comment field is mandatory</P>" & _
                        "</FONT>"
                state = 1

        End If

        If Not state = 1 Then
                ' field validation OK
                Dim objGuestBook
                Dim objData
                Dim objResponse

                Set objGuestBook =
                Server.CreateObject("GuestBook.IAnonymous")

                Set objData = objGuestBook.NewCollection
                objData.Add Request.Form("fullname"),"fullname"
                objData.Add Request.Form("email"),"email"
                objData.Add Request.Form("company"),"company"
                objData.Add Request.Form("city"),"city"
                objData.Add Request.Form("country"),"country"
                objData.Add Request.Form("comment"),"comment"

                Set objResponse = objGuestBook.InsertComment(objData)
                If objResponse("error") Then
                        Response.Write "<FONT color=red>" & _
                                objResponse("errorinfo") & _
                                "</FONT><BR>"
                        state = 1
                Else
                        Response.Write "<P>Guest Book updated - " & _
                                        "thank you for your feedback.</P>"
                End If

        End If
%>
```

(continued)

```
<% End If %>

<% If state = 1 Then %>
<CENTER>
<FORM method=post action=guestinsert.asp?state=2 id=form1 name=form1>
        <TABLE border=0 cellPadding=1 cellSpacing=1 width=90%>
    <TR>
        <TD align=right vAlign=top >Name:</TD>
        <TD><INPUT id=fullname name=fullname size=40
            value="<% = Request.form("fullname") %>"
            ></TD></TR>
    <TR>
        <TD align=right vAlign=top>Email:</TD>
        <TD><INPUT id=email name=email size=40
            value="<% = Request.form("email") %>"
            ></TD></TR>
    <TR>
        <TD align=right vAlign=top>Company:</TD>
        <TD><INPUT id=company name=company size=30
            value="<% = Request.form("company") %>"
            ></TD></TR>
    <TR>
        <TD align=right vAlign=top>City:</TD>
        <TD><INPUT id=city name=city size=20
            value="<% = Request.form("city") %>"
            ></TD></TR>
    <TR>
        <TD align=right vAlign=top>Country:</TD>
        <TD><INPUT id=country name=country size=15
            value="<% = Request.form("country") %>"
            ></TD></TR>
    <TR>
        <TD align=right vAlign=top>Comments:</TD>
        <TD><TEXTAREA id=comment name=comment
            cols=50 rows=10><% = Request.form("comment")
%></TEXTAREA>
            </TD></TR>
    <TR>
        <TD> 
        <TD>
```

```
<SCRIPT language=JSCRIPT>
<!--
          var ua = navigator.userAgent;
          if ((ua.indexOf("MSIE") != -1) & ((ua.indexOf("4.") != -1) |

      (ua.indexOf("5.") != -1)))
          document.write('<INPUT TYPE="BUTTON" '
                     + 'VALUE="Use my Profile Information" '
                     + 'onclick="getProfile()">'
                     + '<BR><BR>');
-->
</SCRIPT>
        <INPUT id=butsubmit name=butsubmit
                                 type=submit value="Submit "></TD></TR>
        </TABLE>
</FORM>
</CENTER>

<% End If %>

<HR>
The personal information you provide will <B>not</B>
be disclosed to other organizations.<BR>
Your comments will be made available to other visitors.<BR>
<A href="default.asp">Home</A><BR></P>

</BODY>

<SCRIPT LANGUAGE="JSCRIPT">
  <!-
  function getProfile()
   {
   var blnOK;
   pr = navigator.userProfile;
   pr.clearRequest();
   blnOK = pr.addReadRequest("Vcard.FirstName");
   blnOK = pr.addReadRequest("Vcard.LastName");
   blnOK = pr.addReadRequest("Vcard.Company");
   blnOK = pr.addReadRequest("Vcard.Business.City");
   blnOK = pr.addReadRequest("Vcard.Business.Country");
```

(continued)

```
    blnOK = pr.addReadRequest("Vcard.Email");
    pr.doReadRequest(3, "Harrison Associates");

    nv = pr.getAttribute("Vcard.FirstName");
    if (nv != null) nv = nv + " "
    else nv = "";
    lv = pr.getAttribute("Vcard.LastName");
    if (lv != null) nv = nv + lv;

    fm = document.forms(0);
    fm("fullname").value = nv;
    fm("email").value = pr.getAttribute("Vcard.Email")
    fm("company").value = pr.getAttribute("Vcard.Company");
    fm("city").value = pr.getAttribute("Vcard.Business.City");
    fm("country").value = pr.getAttribute("Vcard.Business.Country");
    }
    -->
</SCRIPT>

</HTML>
```

`guestread.asp`

```
<%@LANGUAGE="VBSCRIPT" %>

<% Option explicit %>

<%
    If Session("authorized") = 1 And
Request.ServerVariables("AUTH_USER") = "" Then
        Response.Redirect "authguestread.asp"
    End If
%>

<!-- #include file="guestread.inc" -->
```

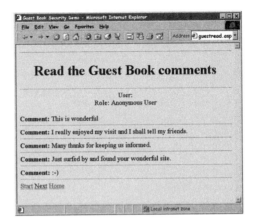

`authguestread.asp`

```
<%@LANGUAGE="VBSCRIPT" %>


<% Option explicit %>


<% Session("authorized") = 1 %>


<!-- #include file="guestread.inc" -->
```

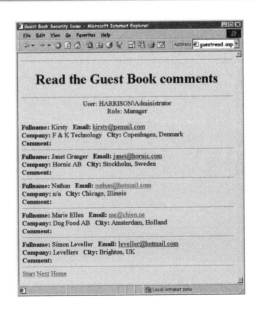

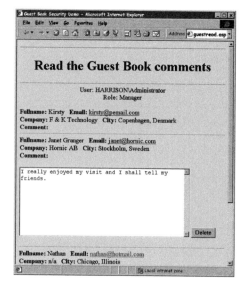

Uses dynamic HTML. Click on details for the comment field to be displayed/hidden.

Click on e-mail address for e-mail form to be instantiated

guestread.inc

```
<% Dim vStartId %>

<%
    If not Request.QueryString("startid") = "" then
        vStartId = Request.QueryString("startid")
    Else
        vStartId = 999999999
    End If
%>
<HTML>
<HEAD>
<TITLE>Guest Book Security Demo</TITLE>

<SCRIPT LANGUAGE=javascript>
function comment_click(obj)
{
    if (obj.style.display == "none")
        obj.style.display = ""
    else
        obj.style.display = "none";

}
</SCRIPT>
```

```
</HEAD>
<BODY bgColor=wheat>
<CENTER>
<HR>
<H1>Read the Guest Book comments</H1>
<HR>
</CENTER>
<%
    Dim objGuestBook
    Dim objData
    Dim objResponse
    Dim objItems
    Dim objItem
    Dim vRole

    Set objGuestBook = Server.CreateObject("GuestBook.IAnonymous")

    Set objData = objGuestBook.NewCollection

    objData.Add vStartId,"startid"
    objData.Add 5,"maxitems"

    Set objResponse = objGuestBook.ReadComments(objData)
    If objResponse("error") Then
        Response.Write "<FONT color=red>" & _
                    objResponse("errorinfo") & _
                    "</FONT><BR>"
    Else
        Set objItems = objResponse("items")
        vRole = objResponse("role")

        Response.Write "<CENTER>User: " & Request.ServerVariables
("AUTH_USER") & _
                    "<BR>Role: " & vRole & "<BR><BR></CENTER>"

        If objItems.count = 0 then
                Response.Write "<FONT color=red>" & _
                        "*** End of List ***" & _
                        "</FONT><BR>"
                vStartId = 0
        Else
```

(continued)

```
            For Each objItem in objItems
                If vRole = "Manager" Then
                    Response.Write "<SPAN LANGUAGE=javascript " & _
                                "style=""cursor: hand;""" & _
                                "onclick=""return comment_click(span"
 & _
                                objItem("commentid") & _
                                " )"" >"
                    Response.Write "<B>Fullname:</B> " & _
                                ObjItem("fullname") & "  
 "
                    Response.Write "<B>Email:</B> " & _
                                "<A HREF=mailto:" & objItem("email")
& ">" & _
                                objItem("email") & "</A><BR>"
                    Response.Write "<B>Company:</B> " & _
                                ObjItem("company") &
"   "
                    Response.Write "<B>City:</B> " & _
                                ObjItem("city") & ", " & _
                                ObjItem("country") & "<BR>"
                    Response.Write "<B>Comment:</B></SPAN> "
                    Response.Write "<SPAN id=span" &_
                                ObjItem("commentid") & _
                                " STYLE=""display:none"" >"

                    Response.Write "<FORM method=POST
action=guestDelete.asp>"
                    Response.Write "<TEXTAREA id=comment name=comment "
& _
                                "cols=50 rows=10>" & _
                                objItem("comment") & _
                                "</TEXTAREA> "
                    Response.Write "<INPUT type=hidden value=" & _
                                ObjItem("commentid") & _
                                " id=commentid name=commentid>"
                    Response.Write "<INPUT type=submit value=Delete "
& _
                                "id=butDelete name=butDelete></FORM>
</SPAN>"
```

```
            Else
                Response.Write "<B>Comment:</B> " & objItem
("comment")

            End If

            Response.Write "<HR>"

            vStartId = CLng(objItem("commentid"))
        Next

        vStartId = vStartId - 1

    End If
  End If

%>

<A href="guestread.asp">Start</A>
<A href="guestread.asp?startid=<% = vStartId %>">Next</A>
<A href="default.asp">Home</A>
</CENTER>

</BODY>
</HTML>
```

guestdelete.asp

```
<%@LANGUAGE="VBSCRIPT" %>
<% Option Explicit %>

<HTML>
<TITLE>Guest Book Security Demo</TITLE>
<HEAD>
</HEAD>
<BODY bgColor=wheat>
<CENTER>
<HR>
<H1>Delete Guest Book entry</H1>
<HR>
```

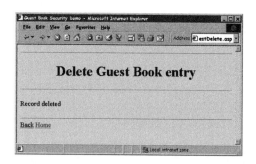

```
</CENTER>
<%
    Dim objAGuestBook
    Dim objMGuestBook
    Dim objData
    Dim objResponse
    Dim vCommentId

    vCommentId = Request.Form("commentid")

    Set objAGuestBook = Server.CreateObject("GuestBook.IAnonymous")
    Set objMGuestBook = Server.CreateObject("GuestBook.IManagement")

    Set objData = objAGuestBook.NewCollection
    objData.Add vCommentId,"commentid"

    Set objResponse = objMGuestBook.DeleteComment(objData)
    if objResponse("error") then
        Response.Write "<FONT color=red>" & _
                objResponse("errorinfo") & _
            "</FONT><BR>"
    else
        Response.Write "<P>Record deleted</P>"
    end if

%>
<HR>
<A href="authguestread.asp?startid=<% = vCommentId %>">Back</A>
<A href="default.asp">Home</A>

</BODY>
</HTML>
```

VB Software Component Code

IANONYMOUS—`IAnonymous.cls`

```
Option Base 0
Option Explicit
Implements ObjectControl

Private oRs As ADODB.Recordset

Private objMTSContext As ObjectContext


Private Function ObjectControl_CanBePooled() As Boolean
    ObjectControl_CanBePooled = True
End Function


Private Sub ObjectControl_Deactivate()
    Set objMTSContext = Nothing
    Set oRs = Nothing
End Sub


Private Sub ObjectControl_Activate()
    On Error GoTo ActivateErr

    Set objMTSContext = GetObjectContext()

    Exit Sub

ActivateErr:
    Call RaiseError("ObjectControl_Activate")

End Sub


Public Function InsertComment(ByVal vGuestBookData As Variant) As
Variant
    On Error GoTo InsertCommentErr

    Dim vResponse As New Collection

    Set oRs = objMTSContext.CreateInstance("ADODB.Recordset")

    oRs.Open "comments", vDbConn, adOpenKeyset, adLockPessimistic,
adCmdTable
```

```
    oRs.AddNew

    oRs.Fields("fullname") = Trim(vGuestBookData("fullname"))
    oRs.Fields("email") = Trim(LCase(vGuestBookData("email")))
    oRs.Fields("company") = Trim(vGuestBookData("company"))
    oRs.Fields("city") = Trim(vGuestBookData("city"))
    oRs.Fields("country") = Trim(vGuestBookData("country"))
    oRs.Fields("comment") = Trim(vGuestBookData("comment"))
    oRs.Fields("timedate") = Time + Date
    oRs.Update

    vResponse.Add False, Key:="error"

    oRs.Close

    objMTSContext.SetComplete
    Set InsertComment = vResponse

    Exit Function

InsertCommentErr:
    objMTSContext.SetAbort
    Set InsertComment = RaiseError("InsertComment")

End Function
```

```
Public Function ReadComments(ByVal vGuestBookData As Variant) As
Variant
    On Error GoTo ReadCommentsErr

    Dim vResponse As New Collection
    Dim vItems As New Collection
    Dim vRole As String
    Dim vSQL As Variant
    Dim lMaxItems As Long
    Dim lStartId As Long

    vRole = "Anonymous User"
    lMaxItems = vGuestBookData("maxitems")
    lStartId = vGuestBookData("startid")
```

```
    Let vSQL = "SELECT Comments.* " & _
        "FROM Comments " & _
        "WHERE Comments.CommentId <= " & lStartId & _
        "ORDER BY Comments.CommentId DESC;"

    Set oRs = objMTSContext.CreateInstance("ADODB.Recordset")
    oRs.MaxRecords = lMaxItems
    oRs.Open vSQL, vDbConn, , , adCmdText

    Rem useful for debugging
    Rem Trace (objMTSContext.Security.GetOriginalCallerName)

    While Not oRs.EOF
        Dim CommentItem As New Collection

        CommentItem.Add CStr(oRs.Fields("commentid")), Key:=
"commentid"
        CommentItem.Add CStr(oRs.Fields("comment")), Key:="comment"


        If objMTSContext.IsSecurityEnabled And _
            objMTSContext.IsCallerInRole("Manager") Then
                vRole = "Manager"
        End If

        If vRole = "Manager" Then
            CommentItem.Add Trim(CStr(oRs.Fields("fullname"))), Key:=
"fullname"
            CommentItem.Add Trim(CStr(oRs.Fields("company"))), Key:=
"company"
            CommentItem.Add Trim(CStr(oRs.Fields("email"))), Key:=
"email"
            CommentItem.Add Trim(CStr(oRs.Fields("city"))), Key:=
"city"
            CommentItem.Add Trim(CStr(oRs.Fields("country"))), Key:=
"country"
        End If


    vItems.Add CommentItem
```

```
            Set CommentItem = Nothing
            oRs.MoveNext
      Wend

      oRs.Close

      vResponse.Add False, Key:="error"
      vResponse.Add vItems, Key:="items"
      vResponse.Add vRole, Key:="role"

      objMTSContext.SetComplete
      Set ReadComments = vResponse

      Exit Function


ReadCommentsErr:
      objMTSContext.SetAbort
      Set ReadComments = RaiseError("ReadComments")

End Function
```

```
Public Function NewCollection() As Variant
      On Error GoTo NewCollectionErr

      Dim vResponse As New Collection

      objMTSContext.SetComplete
      Set NewCollection = vResponse

      Exit Function

NewCollectionErr:
      objMTSContext.SetAbort
      Set NewCollection = RaiseError("NewCollection")

End Function
```

IMANAGEMENT—`IManagement.cls`

```
Option Base 0
Option Explicit
Implements ObjectControl


Private oDb As ADODB.Connection


Private objMTSContext As ObjectContext


Private Function ObjectControl_CanBePooled() As Boolean
    ObjectControl_CanBePooled = True
End Function


Private Sub ObjectControl_Deactivate()
    Set objMTSContext = Nothing
    Set oDb = Nothing
End Sub


Private Sub ObjectControl_Activate()
    On Error GoTo ActivateErr

    Set objMTSContext = GetObjectContext()

    Exit Sub

ActivateErr:
    Call RaiseError("ObjectControl_Activate")

End Sub


Public Function DeleteComment(ByVal vGuestBookData As Variant) As
Variant
    On Error GoTo DeleteCommentErr

    Dim lCommentId As Long
    Dim vSQL As Variant
    Dim vResponse As New Collection

    lCommentId = vGuestBookData("commentid")
```

```
    Let vSQL = "DELETE FROM Comments " & _
        "WHERE Comments.CommentId = " & lCommentId & ";"

    Set oDb = objMTSContext.CreateInstance("ADODB.Connection")

    oDb.Open vDbConn
    Call oDb.Execute(vSQL)
    oDb.Close

    vResponse.Add False, Key:="error"
    objMTSContext.SetComplete
    Set DeleteComment = vResponse

    Exit Function

DeleteCommentErr:
    objMTSContext.SetAbort
    Set DeleteComment = RaiseError("ReadComments")

End Function
```

GENERAL—general.bas

Code requires:

- An ODBC connection to the Guest Book database is defined with a DSN of **GuestBook**
- SQL Server access account with:
  - An account name of sa
  - A blank password

```
Public Const vDbConn As Variant = "DSN=GuestBook;UID=sa;PWD=;"
```

```
Public Sub Trace(vMsg As Variant)
    Dim intFileNo As Integer

    IntFileNo = FreeFile
    Open "e:\data\trace.txt" For Append Shared As #intFileNo
    Print #intFileNo, Time & " " & vMsg
    Close #intFileNo

End Sub
```

```
Public Function RaiseError(ByVal vName As Variant) As Variant
    Dim vErrorInfo As Variant
    Dim vResponse As Collection

    vErrorInfo = "GuestBook System Failure: " & Hex(Err.Number) & " "
& Err.Source & "->" & vName & " " & Err.Description

    Err.Clear

    Set vResponse = New Collection
    vResponse.Add True, Key:="error"
    vResponse.Add vErrorInfo, Key:="errorinfo"

    Trace (vErrorInfo)

    Set RaiseError = vResponse

End Function
```

GuestBook Database Schema

COMMENTS TABLE

```
CREATE TABLE [dbo].[Comments] (
        [commentid] [int] IDENTITY
                    (1, 1) NOT NULL ,
        [fullname] [char] (40) NULL ,
        [email] [char] (40) NULL ,
        [company] [char] (30) NULL ,
        [city] [char] (20) NULL ,
        [country] [char] (15) NULL ,
        [timedate] [char] (20) NOT
                            NULL ,
        [comment] [varchar] (1000)
                        NOT NULL ,
        CONSTRAINT [PK_Comments]
          PRIMARY KEY NONCLUSTERED
            (
            [commentid]
            )
        )
GO
```

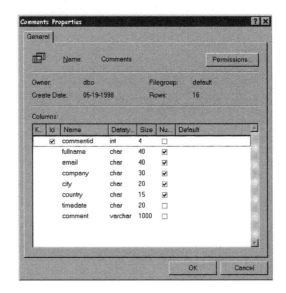

■ Summary

In this chapter we have seen how to use MTS to apply a simple security strategy that enforces strong protection of our database. Hopefully, after working through our example, the differences between programmatic and declarative security will have been clarified.

The key points in this chapter are:

- A good approach is to configure the database such that only one user account exists and has the privilege to directly access the database. Preventing direct access to the database eliminates any risk of someone using a database query/manipulation tool to hack the contents.

- All Web access to the database functionality must be done via MTS components enabling us to apply appropriate MTS role security restrictions to the various components and interfaces.

- Role security restrictions can either be configured using the MTS Explorer or programmed into the executable logic.

- MTS encourages role-based security, as opposed to having the component impersonate the client.

Now that we are confident in the knowledge that we can secure our software components, we shall put MTS security to one side and move on to another interesting security topic, Directory Services.

Directory Services

A major challenge of today's complex networked environments, such as the Internet or a large corporate Intranet, is the need to identify and locate resources, such as users, printers, and documents. For example, the use of e-mail may be rapidly expanding, but for users to exploit the advantages of electronic communications, they must be able to efficiently locate the e-mail addresses of their target correspondents. What makes this difficult is when there is a mixture of software technologies and hardware platforms.

A solution to this problem is the implementation of **Directory Services**. These enable information about a resource to be looked up and retrieved by specifying its name. This is very similar to the way we use a telephone book. While systems that do this have existed for a long time, they have been proprietary or focused on a single resource. The new generation of Directory Services addresses these two drawbacks.

In this chapter we shall study the fundamentals of Directory Services. We shall build on this initial discussion in the next two chapters and see how Directory Services can be used to manage the users of our Web services.

Specifically, we shall discuss:

- Some of the challenges posed by today's distributed computing environments

- The standard requirements for which a Directory Service is needed and the advantages that such an implementation provides

- Industry standards with regard to Directory Services; in particular, the increasingly popular Lightweight Directory Access Protocol used for accessing Directory Services over a TCP/IP network

- A simple programmatic mechanism called Active Directory Service Interfaces that makes it easy for application programmers to support a multiple directory environment within their applications

- Microsoft's strategy to use Directory Services to help integrate Windows platforms to a variety of different environments; in addition, Microsoft's future plans for Directory Services with the Windows 2000 (NT 5.0) Active Directory.

So first some basics, let us see what a Directory Service is.

What Is a Directory Service?

A universal requirement of distributed computing environments is the ability to store information such that it can easily be queried, amended, added to, and deleted by users and their applications. Some types of information are very frequently read and only occasionally altered; examples include user accounts, e-mail addresses, software component identifiers, file servers, printer locations, Web pages, digital certificates, etc. This information needs to be located in a data store that has been optimized for this type of operation. Such a data store is called a Directory Service.

Additional requirements of a Directory Service include:

- Managed centrally—but data can be distributed and replicated for performance and redundancy reasons

- Accessible—contents must be available from anywhere at any time; users may be distributed geographically across buildings, cities, or continents

- Scalable—from the smallest business to very large corporate enterprises

- Secure—access controls can be applied when necessary to certain parts of the data store
- Robust—high availability and data integrity are vital due to the mission-critical nature of the data
- Flexible—can store different types and combinations of information; formats are extensible to accommodate future requirements
- Open—accessible using industry (Internet) standard protocols
- Interoperable—can share information with other directories from different vendors

Most organizations already have many directories in place. Consider, for example, a company using an IT infrastructure based on Microsoft technologies; it may have:

- Users stored in the Windows NTDS (SAM) database
- Users stored in the Exchange e-mail system database
- Users stored in the SQL Server database
- Users stored in a customized application database
- User's configuration information stored in the Windows registry

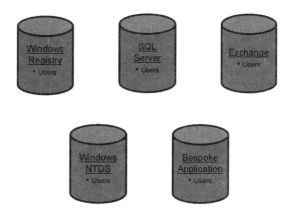

Any given user could have his attributes duplicated in several different directories. Having numerous directories can cause problems, including data duplication/synchronization, added costs (both administration and development), and poor usability (e.g., users face multiple log-ons).

The ideal solution would be to have a single Directory Service, so that all of the above information would be stored in a single data store. Microsoft sees Directory Services as a critical component for distributed computing and intends to address this with the **Active Directory** that will be a fundamental part of Windows 2000.

Considering the above example, where we saw the user's information distributed over multiple directories—with Windows 2000 all of this information would be located in the single Active Directory.

A single entry for each user would exist in the Active Directory. This object could store the complete set of information about the user required by all systems/applications. So for a user it could include: name, address, phone, e-mail address, digital certificates, photograph, skills, and so on. The schema for items stored in the Active Directory can easily be extended, so if a new system is introduced that needs a different piece of information about the user, a new attribute could easily be added to the user's information object.

Of course a Directory Service is much more than just users. It can store information about any resource in the enterprise. To accommodate these resources, the Directory Service must be able to model an organization, and it has been found that storing the entries (or objects) in a hierarchical tree structure does this best. Using a tree structure means that each object in the directory can be uniquely identified by a name based on its path in the tree. (This is similar to the way we can identify a file in the file directory structure.)

Each object in the directory stores information by means of a series of attribute and value pairs. This will be clarified shortly.

Industry Standards

Until recently, the most generally accepted solution for Directory Services was **X.500**. This is a standard produced by ITU/ISO and defines the protocols and services at a level that is platform- and network-independent. X.500 provides a global distributed directory that contains hierarchically named objects. The model encompasses a set of servers called **Directory System Agents** (DSAs), each holding a section of the directory in its **Directory Information Base** (DIB).

The DSAs cooperate such that applications can connect to any server to issue queries for data resident anywhere in the global directory. The actual location of the information is transparent to the requesting application. X.500 defines how the information is structured/distributed in the directory, the security mechanisms to protect the contents, and the protocols (called DAP, **Directory Access Protocol**) used to access this information.

X.500 is a model designed for the OSI protocol stack. This is a layered architecture that separates network communications into the seven layers shown. These layers are clearly defined and operate by passing information to the layers above and below. In effect, each layer is communicating with the equivalent layer on the remote machine.

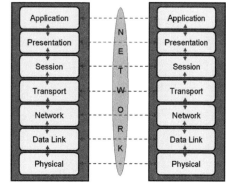

The lowest layers are responsible for putting data bits onto the network cable. The highest layers are responsible for defining how an application accesses the communication services.

However, since the definition of the OSI protocol stack, TCP/IP has fast become the industry standard for communications in heterogeneous environments like the Internet and the corporate enterprise. In Chapter 3 we mentioned that TCP/IP does not map neatly onto the OSI seven-layer model. Furthermore DAP is a large and complex protocol; it needs a full implementation of the OSI stack that provides extensive functionality, but most of it is not normally used. DAP therefore needs a substantial amount of computing resources to operate, and so is not suitable for the thin client computing of today's Internet systems.

In 1993, the University of Michigan introduced the **Lightweight Directory Access Protocol** (LDAP) for accessing Directory Services over a TCP/IP network. Since LDAP avoids the resource overhead demands of DAP, it is an ideal choice for use on the Internet with low-cost machines. Many Internet software vendors have developed their own solutions for Directory Services, but the vast majority have now adopted the LDAP standard as their strategic protocol for accessing directory contents.

Lightweight Directory Access Protocol

LDAP is a simplification of the X.500 Directory Access Protocol (DAP) and provides a mechanism to query and manage an arbitrary hierarchical database of objects each containing attribute/value pairs. LDAP operates over TCP/IP and normally uses port 389 or port 636 (for secured sockets). However, it is important to remember that LDAP is only a protocol and does not specify the actual Directory Service model or how it should function.

Many LDAP servers can combine to provide a global directory structure. If a client makes a request to an LDAP server, and the information is not stored locally, the LDAP server can connect to another server to satisfy the request. This referral activity occurs transparently to the client.

> Readers familiar with TCP/IP name servers will note that this referral activity works in a similar manner.

Various vendors have implemented their own LDAP compliant directory services in a similar manner to X.500, but these are often not fully compliant to the standard and so have problems when trying to inter-operate with offerings from other vendors.

Directory Model

The basic unit of information stored in the directory is an **attribute**. An attribute has an **attribute type** associated with it and can store one or more string **values**.

Attribute types are typically mnemonic strings, such as:

cn   . . . common name
mail   . . . e-mail address
ou   . . . organization unit
o   . . . organization
c   . . . country

The values assigned to the attribute are dependent on the type. For example, the mail attribute might store **rich@cyberdude.com**. The syntax of the information stored for a particular type is the responsibility of the directory and not the LDAP protocol.

Attributes associated to a particular entity (e.g., a user) are combined together to form a directory entry (or object). Directory entries are then organized in a hierarchical fashion to model the directory. Each entry can have many branches leading to child entries but will only have one parent entry.

One special attribute type is objectclass. This is used to define, for an entry, which attributes are allowed and which are mandatory.

Each entry in the directory is identified relative to its parent by its **Relative Distinguished Name** (RDN), which is chosen using one or more attributes from the entry. By concatenating the RDNs of all the parent entries up to the root of the tree, we get the unique identifier for the entry. This is called the **Distinguished Name** (DN) for the entry.

As an example, consider: DN = "cn=RichardHarrison, ou=HQ, o=HarrisonAssociates, c=US"

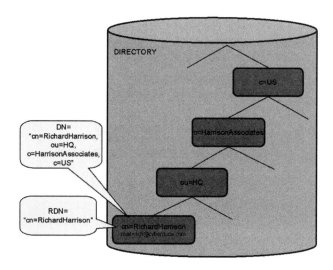

An example URL for this entry might be:

ldap://ad.harrison.net/c=US/o=HarrisonAssociates/ou=HQ/cn=Richard Harrison

where **ad.harrison.com** is the domain name of the machine where the LDAP-compliant Directory Service is located.

Operation

An LDAP client connects to a LDAP server using TCP/IP. The client can then query and modify the contents of the directory. The operations provided by LDAP include:

- Bind/unbind to the directory
- Add an entry to the directory
- Delete an entry from the directory
- Modify an existing entry in the directory
- Query for an entry in the directory that matches some supplied criterion

Binding to the directory includes authenticating the user to ascertain which entries in the directory can be made available to the user. An anonymous user may only access those entries in the directory that have been marked for public access.

The LDAP specification includes a number of APIs for use with the "C" programming language that enables the above operations to be supported in our application programs. However, in the next section we shall meet an alternative and simpler mechanism called ADSI.

LDAP supports a number of different authentication mechanisms, but one of the more popular is the **Kerberos Authentication Protocol** discussed in Chapter 2.

Active Directory Service Interface

While Microsoft is committed to LDAP, it believes that this is just a small part of the larger problem of providing interoperability between systems, and insulating administrators and developers from the complex variations between the different systems in a heterogeneous computing environment.

As we have already seen, many different directories are often deployed within the corporate enterprise. While having a single directory like the Microsoft Active Directory is beneficial, it is likely to be some time before organizations can migrate their complete infrastructures to accommodate this.

While LDAP is becoming a standard interface for directories, there are many others that have their own proprietary API. Software vendors thus have many interfaces to learn and often have to maintain multiple versions of their products, one for each directory supported.

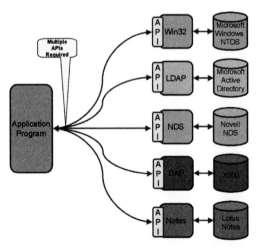

Many developers find that it is not easy to implement the low-level LDAP API for "C". In order to address this issue, Microsoft has implemented a single set of well-defined interfaces designed accessing Directory Services. This is called the Open Directory Services Interface (ODSI).

ODSI is part of the Windows Open Services Architecture (WOSA) APIs. It is a middleware-like layer that enables software developers to write applications independent of the underlying infrastructure. Furthermore, with WOSA an organization's investment in its systems is protected, since any changes to its infrastructure will typically have minimal impact on the application layers. Other examples of WOSA APIs include:

• ODBC (Open Database Connectivity)—for accessing databases
• TAPI (Telephone API)—for accessing telephone equipment
• MAPI (Messaging API)—for accessing messaging systems

With WOSA, application programmers and the vendors of supported resources both write to published interface specifications:

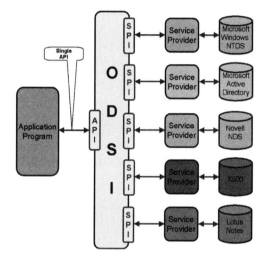

• Application programmers access the functionality by invoking API functions
• Resource vendors support the functionality by providing functions that support the Service Provider Interface (SPI)

One component of ODSI is **Active Directory Service Interfaces** (ADSI). ADSI provides a COM object model for managing the resources in a Directory Service and makes it easy for application programmers to support directories within their applications. Applications that exploit ADSI can easily operate in a multiple directory environment.

Microsoft products that support ADSI include:

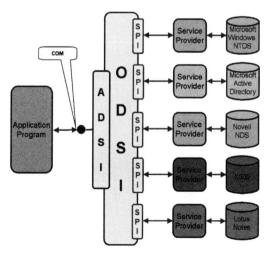

• Windows NTDS (from Windows NT 4.0 SP3)

• Active Directory (from Windows 2000)

• Exchange (from version 5.5)

- IIS (from version 4.0)
- Site Server (from version 3.0)

. . . and more will be on the way!

Now, with one learning curve to master, we can easily develop applications to access the configuration and application data stored on the Microsoft Active platform.

ADSI will work against any LDAP server that is compliant to version 2 or higher. ADSI can support the same functionality that is provided by the native LDAP "C" programming language API. The advantages of ADSI over this API include:

- ADSI is not restricted to "C"; it can be used with any high-level language or scripting language that supports COM
- ADSI is simpler to understand and use than the low-level "C" API
- ADSI is not restricted to LDAP-compliant Directory Servers

ADSI Object Model

An ADSI object hosts a number of COM objects that represent an entry within a Directory Service (e.g., a user, a printer, a file, and so on). The ADSI object, and its associated entry in the Directory Service, is manipulated by using methods on an interface that is exposed by a COM object.

There are two types of ADSI objects:

- Directory Service leaf object
- Directory Service container object

A container object may contain other ADSI objects, whereas a leaf object cannot.

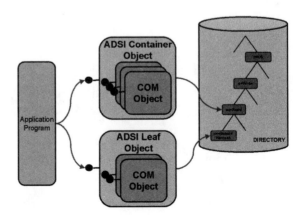

The COM objects within the ADSI object represent a logical grouping of properties and methods.

ADSI Schema

Standard ADSI objects that represent the common objects found in Directory Services include:

Container Objects	Leaf Objects
Namespaces	User
Country	Group
Locality	Alias
Organization	Service
Organization Unit	Print Queue
Domain	Print Device
Computer	Print Job
	File Service
	File Share
	Session
	Resource

A Directory Service might also contain entries that require functionality not defined by ADSI. In addition, some Directory Services are extensible and can allow their entries to be modified to include additional information. The root-node container objects found in each Directory Service include an ADSI Schema Container object that defines the objects and object relationships for the Directory Service. ADSI Schema Management objects exist and can be used to extend an ADSI implementation.

We shall see below how to inspect the schema for the IIS: namespace and display all of the properties configured in the IIS4 metabase.

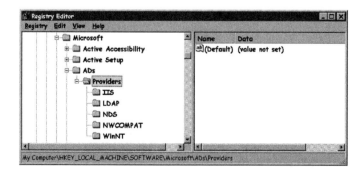

A list of ADSI namespaces (types of Directory Services, such as **WinNT:**, **LDAP:**) that have been installed can be inspected by looking at the following Registry key:

HKLM\Software\Microsoft\Ads\Providers

Active Directory Browser

Another useful tool for understanding the ADSI object model is the Active Directory Browser, which is available from Microsoft as part of the ADSI SDK. This can be used to browse all of the ADSI objects in a namespace and to inspect/amend their properties. The reader is encouraged to use this tool to discover how the numerous ADSI objects relate to each other.

> Take care not to amend any values or you could end up with a corrupted system.

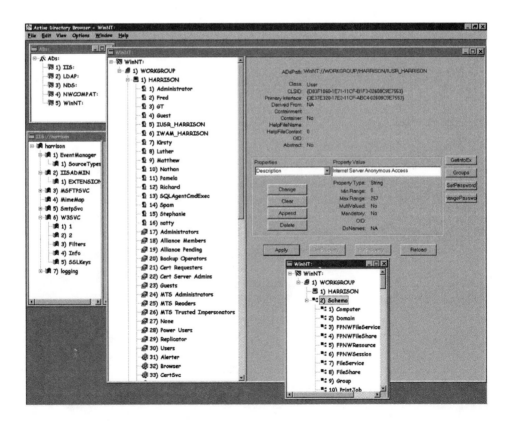

ADSI in Action

Let us now look at a couple of simple examples to inspect and manipulate ADSI objects from ASP. A more sophisticated ADSI example will follow in the next chapter.

First we shall show an ASP page that uses ADSI to front the IIS Administration Objects (IISAO) and display all the properties that have been configured in the metabase (we discussed IISAO in Chapter 3).

Following this, we shall use ADSI to examine and amend the properties for a user account in the Windows NTDS.

For these examples to work, you must secure the Web site so that you are forced to log on with a security context of the administrator. In other words, apply Windows NT file permissions to the ASP files so that only administrators are granted read access.

Trawling the IIS4 Metabase

To scan through the IIS metabase, we must first obtain an object reference to the ADSI object for the IIS namespace.

Since an instance of the ADSI object already exists, we must call the **GetObject** function rather than use the more normal **Server.CreateObject**. The parameter that is passed is the name of the ADSI object. The naming convention used is dependent on the type of Directory Service; for our example use the name of the IISAO object (IIS namespaces were discussed in Chapter 3):

```
Set objWeb = GetObject("IIS://localhost/W3SVC/1")
```

Each IISAO object has a unique identifier that resembles an URL. It consists of **IIS://** followed by the machine name followed by the path object in the IIS configuration. In our example, the object identifier for the first (default) Web server is:

IIS://localhost/w3svc/1

If we wished to operate on a remote machine, we would replace **localhost** with the name of the networked computer.

Having obtained the ADSI object reference, we can look at the generic properties applicable for all ADSI objects. All objects have a **Name**, **Parent**, **Schema** (object definition), **Class** (type of object), **GUID** (unique identifier), and **ADSPath** (full path name):

```
Response.Write "<P><B>Web Service</B><BR>"
Response.Write "Name: " & objWeb.Name & "<BR>"
Response.Write "Parent: " & objWeb.Parent & "<BR>"
Response.Write "Schema: " & objWeb.Schema & "<BR>"
Response.Write "Class: " & objWeb.Class & "<BR>"
Response.Write "GUID: " & objWeb.GUID & "<BR>"
Response.Write "ADSPath: " & objWeb.ADSPath & "<BR>"
```

As we have seen above, the schema contains the definition of the ADSI object. We can now retrieve the generic properties of the schema object:

```
Response.Write "<P><B>Web Service Schema</B><BR>"
Response.Write "Name: " & objSchema.Name & "<BR>"
Response.Write "Parent: " & objSchema.Parent & "<BR>"
Response.Write "Schema: " & objSchema.Schema & "<BR>"
Response.Write "Class: " & objSchema.Class & "<BR>"
Response.Write "GUID: " & objSchema.GUID & "<BR>"
Response.Write "ADSPath: " & objSchema.ADSPath & "<BR>"
```

The schema defines those properties that are mandatory and those that are optional. As we can see in the screenshot below, the IIS schema defines all of its parameters to be optional (even though many of these properties are in fact mandatory and cause severe problems if they are missing!). By examining the **MandatoryProperties** and **OptionalProperties** of the schema we get a collection containing all of the names of the ADSI object's properties:

```
vaProps = objSchema.MandatoryProperties
```

```
vaProps = objSchema.OptionalProperties
```

We have used a simple utility function called **DumpProperties** to examine a collection of property names and display the property value:

```
Call DumpProperties(vaProps)
```

This function examines the collection and considers each property in turn:

```
For Each vProp In vaProps
    Response.Write vProp & ": "
```

Finally, to get the property value, we use the Get method on the ADSI object and pass the property name as the parameter.

```
Response.Write objWeb.Get(vProp)
```

How it was done—for our eyes only!

We have seen odd snippets of the code; here it is in its entirety:

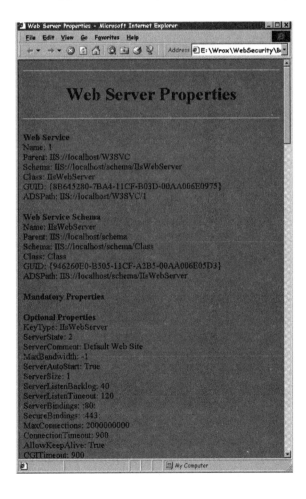

Optional Properties
KeyType: IisWebServer
ServerState: 2
ServerComment: Default Web Site
MaxBandwidth: -1

ServerAutoStart: True

ServerSize: 1

ServerListenBacklog: 40

ServerListenTimeout: 120

ServerBindings: :80:

SecureBindings: :443:

MaxConnections: 2000000000

ConnectionTimeout: 900

AllowKeepAlive: True

CGITimeout: 900

MaxEndpointConnections: -1

CacheISAPI: True

MimeMap:

AnonymousUserName: IUSR_HARRISON

AnonymousUserPass: Xzaz%OoipJaF3f

FrontPageWeb: True

AnonymousPasswordSync: True

DefaultLog onDomain:

AdminACL: Object

IPSecurity: Object

DontLog: False

Realm:

EnableDirBrowsing: False

DefaultDoc: Default.htm,Default.asp

HttpExpires:

HttpPics:

HttpCustomHeaders:

HttpErrors: 400,*,FILE,C:\WINNT\help\common\400.htm401,1,FILE,C:\WINNT\help\common\401-1.htm401,
2,FILE,C:\WINNT\help\common\401-2.htm401,3,FILE,C:\WINNT\help\common\401-3.htm401,
4,FILE,C:\WINNT\help\common\401-4.htm401,5,FILE,C:\WINNT\help\common\401-5.htm403,
1,FILE,C:\WINNT\help\common\403-1.htm403,2,FILE,C:\WINNT\help\common\403-2.htm403,
3,FILE,C:\WINNT\help\common\403-3.htm403,4,FILE,C:\WINNT\help\common\403-4.htm403,
5,FILE,C:\WINNT\help\common\403-5.htm403,6,FILE,C:\WINNT\help\common\403-6.htm403,
7,FILE,C:\WINNT\help\common\403-7.htm403,8,FILE,C:\WINNT\help\common\403-8.htm403,
9,FILE,C:\WINNT\help\common\403-9.htm403,10,FILE,C:\WINNT\help\common\403-10.htm403,
11,FILE,C:\WINNT\help\common\403-11.htm403,12,FILE,C:\WINNT\help\common\403-12.htm404,
,FILE,C:\WINNT\help\common\404b.htm405,,FILE,C:\WINNT\help\common\405.htm406,
,FILE,C:\WINNT\help\common\406.htm407,,FILE,C:\WINNT\help\common\407.htm412,
,FILE,C:\WINNT\help\common\412.htm414,,FILE,C:\WINNT\help\common\414.htm

EnableDocFooter: False

DefaultDocFooter:

HttpRedirect:

Log onMethod: 0

NTAuthenticationProviders: NTLM

AuthBasic: False

AuthAnonymous: True

AuthNTLM: True

AccessSSL: False

AccessSSL128: False

AccessSSLNegotiateCert: False

AccessSSLRequireCert: False

AccessSSLMapCert: False

AccessRead: True

AccessWrite: False

AccessExecute: False

AccessScript: False

AccessNoRemoteRead: False

AccessNoRemoteWrite: False

AccessNoRemoteExecute: False

AccessNoRemoteScript: False

AspBufferingOn: False

AspLogErrorRequests: True

AspScriptErrorSentToBrowser: True

AspScriptErrorMessage: An error occurred on the server when processing the URL. Please contact the system administrator.

AspAllowOutOfProcComponents: False

AspScriptFileCacheSize: -1

AspScriptEngineCacheMax: 30

AspScriptTimeout: 90

AspEnableParentPaths: True

AspAllowSessionState: True

AspScriptLanguage: VBScript

AspExceptionCatchEnable: True

AspCodepage: 0

AspSessionTimeout: 20

AspMemFreeFactor: 50

AspQueueTimeout: -1

AppRoot:

AppFriendlyName:

AppIsolated: False

AppPackageID:

AppPackageName:

AppOopRecoverLimit: 4

AppAllowDebugging: False

AppAllowClientDebug: False

NetLog onWorkstation: 0

UseHostName: False

CacheControlMaxAge: 0

CacheControlNoCache: False

CacheControlCustom:

CreateProcessAsUser: True

PoolIdcTimeout: 0

PutReadSize: 8192

RedirectHeaders:

UploadReadAheadSize: 49152

PasswordExpirePrenotifyDays: 0

PasswordCacheTTL: 600

PasswordChangeFlags: 1

MaxBandwidthBlocked: -1

UNCAuthenticationPassThrough: False

AppWamClsid:

DirBrowseFlags: 1073741854

AuthFlags: 5

AuthPersistence: 128

AccessFlags: 1

AccessSSLFlags: 0

ScriptMaps:

.asa,C:\WINNT\System32\inetsrv\asp.dll,1,PUT,DELETE.asp,C:\WINNT\System32\inetsrv\asp.dll,1,PUT,DELETE.
cdx,C:\WINNT\System32\inetsrv\asp.dll,1,PUT,DELETE.cer,C:\WINNT\System32\inetsrv\asp.dll,1,PUT,DELETE.ht
r,C:\WINNT\System32\inetsrv\ism.dll,1.htw,C:\WINNT\System32\webhits.dll,3.ida,C:\WINNT\System32\idq.dll,3.idc,
C:\WINNT\System32\inetsrv\httpodbc.dll,1.idq,C:\WINNT\System32\idq.dll,3.shtm,C:\WINNT\System32\inetsrv\ssin
c.dll,1.shtml,C:\WINNT\System32\inetsrv\ssinc.dll,1.stm,C:\WINNT\System32\inetsrv\ssinc.dll,1

SSIExecDisable: False

EnableReverseDns: False

CreateCGIWithNewConsole: False

EnableDefaultDoc: True

DirBrowseShowDate: True

DirBrowseShowTime: True

DirBrowseShowSize: True

DirBrowseShowExtension: True

DirBrowseShowLongDate: False

LogType: 1
LogPluginClsid: {FF160663-DE82-11CF-BC0A-00AA006111E0}
LogFileDirectory: %WinDir%\System32\LogFiles
LogFilePeriod: 1
LogFileTruncateSize: 20480000
LogExtFileDate: False
LogExtFileTime: True
LogExtFileClientIp: True
LogExtFileUserName: False
LogExtFileSiteName: False
LogExtFileComputerName: False
LogExtFileServerIp: False
LogExtFileMethod: True
LogExtFileUriStem: True
LogExtFileUriQuery: False
LogExtFileHttpStatus: True
LogExtFileWin32Status: False
LogExtFileBytesSent: False
LogExtFileBytesRecv: False
LogExtFileTimeTaken: False
LogExtFileServerPort: False
LogExtFileUserAgent: False
LogExtFileCookie: False
LogExtFileReferer: False
LogExtFileProtocolVersion: False
LogExtFileFlags: 1414
LogOdbcDataSource: HTTPLOG
LogOdbcTableName: InternetLog
LogOdbcUserName: InternetAdmin
LogOdbcPassword: sqllog
ProcessNTCRIfLoggedOn: True
AllowPathInfoForScriptMappings: False

```
<%@LANGUAGE="VBSCRIPT" %>

<% Option Explicit %>

<HTML>
<HEAD>
```

(continued)

```
<TITLE>Web Server Properties</TITLE>
</HEAD>
<BODY bgColor=aqua>
<CENTER>
<HR>
<H1>Web Server Properties</H1>
<HR>
</CENTER>
<SCRIPT LANGUAGE=vbscript RUNAT=Server>
    Sub DumpProperties(vaProps)
        Dim vProp, vItem

        For Each vProp In vaProps
            Response.Write vProp & ": "
            Select Case (Typename(objweb.get(vProp)))
            Case "Variant()"
                For Each vItem in objweb.get(vProp)
                    Response.Write vItem
                Next
            Case "Object"
                Response.Write "Object"
            Case Else
                Response.Write objWeb.Get(vProp)
            End Select
            Response.Write "<BR>"
        Next
    End Sub
</SCRIPT>

<%
    Dim objWeb, objSchema, vaProps

    Set objWeb = GetObject("IIS://localhost/W3SVC/1")
    Set objSchema = GetObject(objWeb.Schema)

    Response.Write "<P><B>Web Service</B><BR>"
    Response.Write "Name: " & objWeb.Name & "<BR>"
    Response.Write "Parent: " & objWeb.Parent & "<BR>"
    Response.Write "Schema: " & objWeb.Schema & "<BR>"
    Response.Write "Class: " & objWeb.Class & "<BR>"
    Response.Write "GUID: " & objWeb.GUID & "<BR>"
    Response.Write "ADSPath: " & objWeb.ADSPath & "<BR>"
```

```
Response.Write "<P><B>Web Service Schema</B><BR>"
Response.Write "Name: " & objSchema.Name & "<BR>"
Response.Write "Parent: " & objSchema.Parent & "<BR>"
Response.Write "Schema: " & objSchema.Schema & "<BR>"
Response.Write "Class: " & objSchema.Class & "<BR>"
Response.Write "GUID: " & objSchema.GUID & "<BR>"
Response.Write "ADSPath: " & objSchema.ADSPath & "<BR>"

vaProps = objSchema.MandatoryProperties
Response.Write "<P><B>Mandatory Properties</B><BR>"
Call DumpProperties(vaProps)


vaProps = objSchema.OptionalProperties
Response.Write "<P><B>Optional Properties</B><BR>"
Call DumpProperties(vaProps)

%>


</BODY>
</HTML>
```

User Objects with Windows NTDS

By using the ADSI provider for Windows NTDS, we can read and manipulate the security database. In the following example we shall look at the properties for an existing user and show how we can programmatically change a property.

So first, we must get reference to the ADSI object for the user:

```
Set objUser = GetObject("WinNT://HARRISON/richard")
```

In this example, the user's account name is `richard` and the machine name is `HARRISON`. If you try it, amend the values appropriately.

Next we amend two of the property values. Using the **Put** method on the user's ADSI object achieves this. The parameters are the name of the property and the new value. The properties are not written back to the directory until the **SetInfo** method is invoked.

```
Call objUser.Put("Description", "HELLO")
Call objUser.Put("FullName", "rich@cyberdude.com")
Call objUser.SetInfo
```

As with our previous ADSI example, we get a list of properties by examining the schema:

```
Set objSchema = GetObject(objUser.Schema)
vProps = objSchema.OptionalProperties
```

To get the property values we use the property name as the parameter to the **Get** method on the user's ADSI object. Some of the property values are objects and cannot be displayed as strings. To avoid the errors that might occur, we use an **On Error** clause to ignore such problems and continue processing.

```
On Error Resume Next
For Each vProp In vProps
    Response.Write vProp & ": " & objUser.Get(vProp) &
"<BR>"
Next
```

How it was done—for our eyes only!

Here is the code, in its entirety.

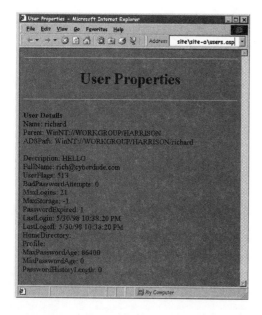

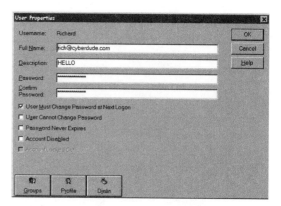

In the User Manager dialog for the user we can see the details have been updated.

```
<%@LANGUAGE="VBSCRIPT" %>

<% Option Explicit %>

<HTML>
<HEAD>
<TITLE>User Properties</TITLE>
</HEAD>
<BODY bgColor=aqua>
<CENTER>
<HR>
<H1>User Properties</H1>
<HR>
</CENTER>

<%
    Dim objUser
    Dim objSchema
    Dim vProps
    Dim vProp

    '
    ' Machine name: HARRISON, member of Workgroup: WORKGROUP
    '
    Set objUser = GetObject("WinNT://HARRISON/richard")

    Call objUser.Put("Description", "HELLO")
    Call objUser.Put("FullName", "rich@cyberdude.com")
    Call objUser.SetInfo

    Response.Write "<P><B>User Details</B><BR>"
    Response.Write "Name: " & objUser.Name & "<BR>"
    Response.Write "Parent: " & objUser.Parent & "<BR>"
    Response.Write "ADSPath: " & objUser.ADSPath & "<BR><BR>"

    Set objSchema = GetObject(objUser.Schema)
    vProps = objSchema.OptionalProperties
    On Error Resume Next
    For Each vProp In vProps
        Response.Write vProp & ": " & objUser.Get(vProp) & "<BR>"
    Next

%>
</BODY>
</HTML>
```

■ Summary

In this chapter we have discussed the challenges posed by today's distributed computing environments and seen how Directory Services provides a solution to many of the problems.

The key points in this chapter are:

- LDAP is gaining rapid momentum and becoming the method of choice for accessing a Directory Service.
- Microsoft's strategy for Directory Services is the Active Directory; it will be available with Windows 2000.
- ADSI is an abstraction layer that addresses many of the problems posed by the deployment of multiple directories in an organization and provides a simple programmatic interface to access/amend the entries within a directory.

Now that we have set the scene for ADSI, let us move on to see how we can use this to implement a Web membership system by managing the users in the Windows NTDS.

Implementing Membership with ADSI

We have progressed, step by step, through various discussions of ASP, MTS, and ADSI, and seen numerous examples of combining application-level security with the core security features provided by Windows NT to provide controls and assurances over access to our system resources.

It is now time to put all of these pieces together and study a comprehensive example. We shall be investigating the implementation of a Web site designed for a mythical company that wishes to allow its "Alliance" business partners to access a "members only" area of its site.

As with many of our examples, the site provides a framework that readers can use as the basis for their own sites. The key features of the site will be:

- Authentication using standard Windows NT Security

- Access controls based on the identity of the user

- Registration facility allowing a user to apply for membership by submitting his personal details
- Membership-approval facility for use by management personnel
- Allowing users to administer their own personal information (e.g., password), thus avoiding putting the burden of mundane administration on the central organization's own personnel
- E-mail messages will be automatically generated and sent to a visitor when his application has been accepted or rejected

In addition, the example will illustrate how to manipulate the contents of the Windows NT Directory Services using the ADSI WinNT provider.

> The code for the example can be found on the CD-ROM included with this book.

The "Alliance" Application

The Web application will allow three types of site visitors:

- A Web site user (anonymous) who may:
  - make an application to request membership in the "Alliance"
- A Web site visitor (authenticated) who has been approved for "Alliance" status and may :
  - access the restricted area of the site
  - change his password
- A Web site manager (authenticated) who may:
  - list all applications for membership in the "Alliance"
  - approve or reject applicants

Application Strategy

The site is designed such that the Web contents and application logic are partitioned around three distinct subdirectories:

- Anonymous area—the home directory (or virtual directory) containing the files that can be accessed by anyone
- Alliance area—the subdirectory containing the files that combine to form the restricted area of the site
- Manager's area—the subdirectory containing the files that combine to form the control area of the site

Rather than create a separate database of users, it is the intention of the "Alliance" application to store the user details within the standard NTDS user database.

The information that we wish to capture about the user and store for future use is:

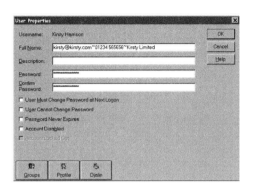

- User Name
- E-mail Address
- Phone Number
- Company Name

The User Name is used as the account name within the NTDS database. The remaining items are concatenated together with "~" delimiters and stored in the Full Name field of the NTDS user properties.

By storing the information in this fashion, we can inspect the user's details with the User Manager.

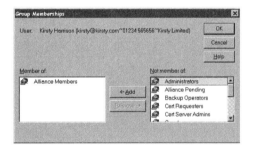

IIS controls access to three distinct areas of the Web site by applying appropriate NT Security permissions to the three directories. On accessing the two restricted areas, users are authenticated with the standard IIS authentication mechanisms that we discussed in Chapter 4.

Furthermore, security business logic using ADSI is implemented as a single software component and deployed to execute within the MTS environment, as discussed in Chapter 10.

Component Architecture

The directories and the ASP logic implemented are as follows:

The Anonymous area:

- **default.asp**—handles the main menu

- **enteralliance.asp**—handles entrance into the "Alliance" Web site
- **register.asp**—handles the capture of user details when applying for membership in the "Alliance"

The "Alliance" area:

- **default.asp**—handles the main menu
- **changepw.asp**—handles a change in a user's password details

This area would also be the home for all pages of a sensitive nature that are to be restricted to business partners.

The Manager's area:

- **default.asp**—handles the main menu
- **pending.asp**—handles the manager's process of accepting or rejecting applicants for "Alliance" membership

The example uses a single VB component called **UserManager**. The interfaces and their methods that are exposed by this component are as follows:

- IOpen
  - **CreateUser**—function to create an entry in the Windows NTDS database with the user's details that were submitted
  - **ChangePassword**—function to change a user's password
  - **NewCollection**—function that creates a VB collection object and returns a reference to it

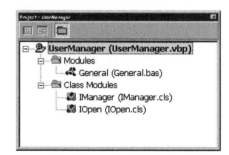

- IManager
  - **ApplyDecisions**—function that updates a list of applicants' applications for membership status
  - **GetPending**—function that gets a list of applicants that are awaiting their applications for membership to be approved

Let us look at a diagram to clarify what we have discussed so far. The interactions between the different components and the navigation between the ASP files are illustrated below:

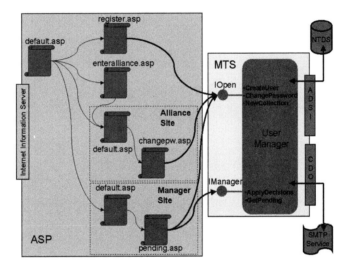

Security Configuration

This section describes the security configuration required by the "Alliance" application.

WINDOWS NT SECURITY

As we know, IIS restricts access to the various areas using standard Windows NT Security. Our application will be designed around the following user groups:

- Administrators—the group of users that can perform all actions on the server; e.g., the managers who can authorize membership in the "Alliance"
- Everyone—the group of users that includes all users of the system; contains the **IUSR_sysname** user which is the security context that anonymous execute under

- Alliance Members—the group of users who have been granted membership in the "Alliance"
- Alliance Pending—the group of users who have requested membership in the "Alliance" and are awaiting approval by the manager

The first two are standard groups that are configured when Windows NT is installed. The other two must be added to the NTDS database using the User Manager, as was discussed in Chapter 2.

> Note that by using the **Administrators** group we are saying that anyone who can authorize users also has to have full control over the entire machine not just over the "Alliance" application. An alternative approach would be to create a separate new group called **Alliance Managers** that only has the permissions needed to perform its functions in the Web site.

The file permissions are applied to the Web content so that the **Administrators** are given free access to all areas of the Web site. Further security permissions that must be applied are as follows:

No restrictions are enforced on the main Web site. Thus **Read** access is granted to the Anonymous user (i.e., the **Everyone** group) for all files in this site subdirectory.

Access to the "Alliance" site is for members only. Thus **Read** access is granted to members of the **Alliance Members** group for all files in this site subdirectory.

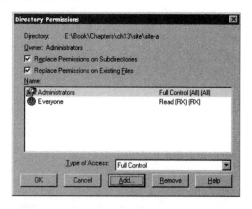

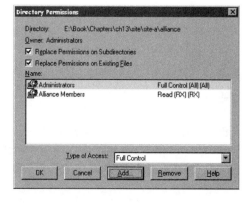

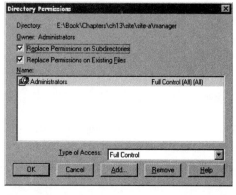

Access to the "Alliance" site is for administrators only. No further permissions are applied to the contents of the manager's site subdirectory.

MTS DECLARATIVE SECURITY

The **IManager** interface must be protected so that only Administrators can invoke its methods. The application achieves this by using MTS declarative security, as discussed in Chapter 10.

Two MTS Roles are created: Visitors and Managers.

The user group Everyone is assigned to the Visitors role, while the local Administrators group is assigned to the Managers role.

Access to the IOpen interface is given to both roles.

Access to the IManagement interface is restricted to the Managers role.

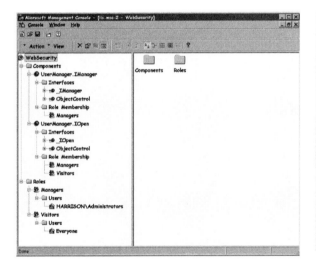 

Enable authorization checking must be enabled for the package's properties. This turns on the roles-based security checking in MTS.

The package must be configured to run under the security context of the Administrator.

If we try to access the Windows NT Domain by using ADSI from logic running under the identity (security context) of a non-administrator, then we will get a "Permission failure." In our case, the MTS software component would fail with a VB error 70 (Permission denied).

This configuration illustrates how we can run an MTS package under the Administrator identity so as to expose powerful functions to external Web users who have minimal privileges.

Components run under the security context of the Administrator must undergo a stringent review process to ensure that the code can only perform exactly what is required and does not allow the user to invoke alternative actions.

IIS AUTHENTICATION METHODS

IIS must be configured to enable user authentication using either Basic Authentication or Windows NT Challenge/Response. We discussed in Chapter 4 the differences between the two options and when each type should be enabled.

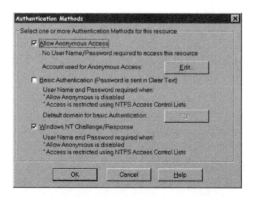

Briefly, Windows NT Challenge/Response has two key advantages:
• It does not send the password over the wire
• A user who is already logged on to a Windows NT domain need not log on again

Application Logic

Let us now look at the main points of interest in the application. First we shall look at the common issues applicable throughout the "Alliance" application and then we shall drill into the following key areas of the application:

- How a user applies for membership by registering his details
- How a user is authenticated when entering the Alliance Members site
- How a user changes his password

Common Processing Issues

Much of the software plumbing used in this application is similar to that used in Chapter 10. Please refer back to the earlier example for an explanation of the following topics:

- **Project References** (note that only Microsoft Transaction Server Type Library need be specified)
- **Parameter Passing**
- **Error Handling**
- **MTS Plumbing**

Home Menus

Each of the three Web site areas has a default page (**default.asp**) used to provide a menu allowing access to the different items of functionality within that area.

A hyperlink to the manager's area is not given from the main site. This area is strictly private and irrelevant to the Web visitor. Furthermore, we would not want to reveal its existence to a potential hacker. A manager will navigate to this page by entering the URL into the browser address field and navigating to it directly.

Register Details to Request Membership

To obtain membership in the Alliance, a user must first register his details. This is implemented using **register.asp** (ASP) and **CreateUser** (VB method).

ASP SCRIPT PROCESSING ... **register.asp**

register.asp conforms to the usual approach found in this book of handling multiple related processing stages within the same ASP file. The logic is driven into the subsequent stages by passing a parameter called **state** with an appropriate value.

```
<%
   If Not Request.QueryString("state") = "" Then
      vState = Request.QueryString("state")
   Else
      vState = 1
   End If
%>
```

When **state** is **1**, the ASP generates the HTML form enabling the user to enter his details. When the form is submitted, the same ASP page is requested, but the URL includes a **state** parameter with a value of **2**.

When **state** is **2**, the **UserManager** is first created, using the form contents, and then finally the **CreateUser** function is invoked.

```
Set objUsrMgr = Server.CreateObject("UserManager.IOpen")

Set objParams = objUsrMgr.NewCollection

objParams.Add Request.Form("username"),"username"
objParams.Add Request.Form("password"),"password"
objParams.Add Request.Form("email"),"email"
objParams.Add Request.Form("phone"),"phone"
objParams.Add Request.Form("company"),"company"

Set objResponse = objUsrMgr.CreateUser(objParams)
```

If any errors occur, the **state** variable is amended to 1 and the logic drops through to redisplay the form. Any values previously entered are redisplayed.

MTS COMPONENT PROCESSING . . . CreateUser

The VB **CreateUser** function first validates the user's details. If the required conditions are satisfied, an ADSI object for the Windows NTDS is created. In this case the name of the ADSI object is "**WINNT://**" plus the domain name.

```
Set objDomain = GetObject("WinNT://" & strDomainName)
```

We then scan down each object stored within the domain and check that no object exists within the domain that has the same name as the account name we wish to add.

```
For Each vItem In objDomain
    If LCase(vItem.Name) = LCase(Trim(vUserName)) Then
        bError = True
        vResponse.Add "User already exists", Key:="errorinfo"
        Exit For
    End If
Next
```

Subject to the user account not already existing, the new user can then be added to the Windows NTDS database. First the user object is created using the **Create** function on the ADSI Domain object.

```
Set objUser = objDomain.Create("user", vUserName)
Call objUser.SetInfo
```

Then the password details are set:

```
Call objUser.SetPassword(vPassword)
Call objUser.SetInfo
```

Next, the user details are formatted and stored in the **Fullname** field:

```
vDetails = vEmail & "~" & vPhone & "~" & vCompany

Call objUser.Put("FullName", CStr(vDetails))
Call objUser.SetInfo
```

Finally, the user is added to the Alliance Pending group.

```
Set objGroup = objDomain.GetObject("group", "Alliance Pending")
objGroup.Add ("WinNT://" & strMachineName & "/" & vUserName)
```

Remember that the MTS package has been configured to run under the security context of the Administrator. That is how a low-privilege user can invoke such potentially high-risk ADSI logic. We must always take care when configuring our software to act in this manner. It is vital that we be confident that the application logic is so tight that only the required functionality can get invoked.

Enter Alliance Members Site

The main menu contains a hyperlink to enter the "Alliance" site. This link navigates to the **enteralliance.asp** file.

ASP SCRIPT PROCESSING ... **enteralliance.asp**

This ASP file gets called twice: first to force authentication, and second to decide if the visitor has been approved membership in the "Alliance".

We force authentication using a technique that we met earlier in Chapter 8. Returning a Status code of 401 in the HTTP Response informs the browser to provide information to identify the user.

```
<%
rem      If Request.ServerVariables("LOGON_USER") Then 'See chapter text
    If Session("enterstate") = 0 Then
        Session("enterstate") = 1
        Response.Status = "401 Unauthorized"
        Response.Addheader "WWW-Authenticate", "BASIC
realm=""HARRISON"""
        Response.End
    Else
        Session("enterstate") = 0
    End If
%>
```

Depending on the Authentication Mechanisms enabled within the IIS configuration and the capabilities of the Web browser, the following actions can occur:

- For Windows NT Challenge/Response authentication only, if the user is already logged on to a Windows domain, the user account name and password hash will be transmitted (transparently to the user) to the server
- If the above operation fails, or for Basic Authentication, a dialog is displayed prompting the user for an account name and password, and the details are transmitted to the server

Authentication of the user is only required once per site visit. Two possible mechanisms were considered for deciding when the authentication process was required:

- Use a **Session** variable called **enterstate** which can toggle between two values to indicate whether this is the first or second time the page has been called
- Check the **LOGON_USER** SessionVariable—if this is empty, then the user has not supplied any credentials and the authentication process is required

With the first mechanism, the authentication process is undertaken every time the "Alliance" site is entered. On development of this example we found it had one advantage. When the manager approves "Alliance" membership, the first mechanism recognizes the change in membership status immediately, while the second mechanism needs the browser session to be terminated and restarted before access is allowed. This is due to the internal workings of a component called the **PermissionChecker**.

PERMISSION CHECKER

Once the user has been authenticated, we need to decide if it has the appropriate credentials to access the "Alliance" site. Remember that this has been secured such that only users with accounts in the Administrators or Alliance Members groups will be permitted to access the site.

To perform this test we use a server-side component from Microsoft called the **PermissionChecker**. This uses the authentication protocols provided by IIS to determine whether a Web user has been granted permission to read a file. While this component is included in the Windows NT 4.0 Option Pack documentation, it is not actually installed or even included on the CD. It is available in the Microsoft IIS Resource Kit, the Microsoft MSDN Platform SDK, or downloadable from the Microsoft Web site at:

**http://www.microsoft.com/windows/downloads/contents/
AdminTools//IISPermissionCk/default.asp**

Note that depending on where you get this component, the ProgId may be either **IISSample.PermissionChecker** or **MSWC.PermissionChecker**.

Once this component is created, it exposes a single method called **HasAccess**, which accepts a single parameter specifying a path and filename. This may include either a physical or a virtual path. The method returns **True** if the security context for the ASP session has Read access to the file. Otherwise it returns **False**.

In our example, we check that the authenticated user had Read access to the default page in the "Alliance" site. If the user's membership application has been approved, then he will be a member of the Alliance Members group and his credentials will allow Read access. In this case the HTTP sessions is redirected to the "Alliance" site.

If the user has not yet been approved, he will be a member of the Alliance Pending group and his credentials will not be allowed Read access. In this case ASP logic drops through and displays a message informing the user that his application is still awaiting consideration.

```
<%
    Dim objCheck
    Set objCheck = Server.CreateObject("IISSample.PermissionChecker")
    If objCheck.HasAccess("alliance/default.asp") Then
        Response.Redirect("alliance/default.asp")
    End If
%>
```

Change Password

Once he has been authenticated and entered the Alliance site, the user may change his password. This is implemented using **changepw.asp** (ASP) and **ChangePassword** (VB method).

ASP SCRIPT PROCESSING ... changepw.asp

The changepw.asp logic is another process that is controlled by a **state** variable.

When **state** is **1**, the ASP generates the HTML form enabling the user to enter his new password details. Once the form is submitted, the same ASP page is invoked, passing in the URL a **state** parameter with a value of **2**.

When **state** is **2**, the VB component is created, a parameter collection is created using the form contents, and the **ChangePassword** function is invoked.

```
Set objUsrMgr = Server.CreateObject("UserManager.IOpen")

Set objParams = objUsrMgr.NewCollection

objParams.Add Request.Form("newpassword"),"newpassword"
objParams.Add Request.Form("newpassword2"),"newpassword2"
Set objResponse = objUsrMgr.ChangePassword(objParams)
```

MTS COMPONENT PROCESSING . . . `ChangePassword`

The `ChangePassword` method first validates the user's details. If the required conditions are satisfied, an ADSI object for the user in the Windows NT domain is created and the user's password amended.

```
Set objUser = GetObject("WinNT://" & strMachineName & "/" & vUser)

Call objUser.SetPassword(vNewPassword)
Call objUser.SetInfo
```

We could have had the user specify his name and passed this to the component as an entry in the parameter collection. However, since the user already keyed this information when he was authenticated, we have taken a better approach that avoids the unnecessary duplication of keystrokes. To achieve this we have used the **MTS SecurityProperty** object.

MTS `SecurityProperty` OBJECT

The MTS `SecurityProperty` object is used to determine the security context of either:

- The client logic that created the MTS component (e.g., using `CreateObject`)
- The client logic that called the method within the MTS component

> It is possible to pass object references between logic such that the caller need not be the same as the creator.

We obtain a reference to an MTS component's `SecurityProperty` object by calling `Security` on the MTS `ObjectContext`. We then get the user name of the authenticated ASP session by calling `GetDirectCallerName` on the `Security` object. The user name is preceded by the Domain and so we remove the characters up to the "\" character.

```
vUser = objMTSContext.Security.GetDirectCallerName
iPos = InStr(1, vUser, "\")
If iPos > 0 Then
    vUser = Mid(vUser, iPos + 1)
End If
```

The MTS **SecurityProperty** object provides the following methods:

Method	Description
GetDirectCallerName	Gets security context associated with process that called the method
Get DirectCreatorName	Gets security context associated with process that created object containing the method
Get OriginalCallerName	Gets security context associated with base process that initiated transaction causing current method to be called
Get DirectCreatorName	Gets security context associated with base process that initiated transaction causing current object to be created

Handle Pending Requests for Membership

A manager can obtain a list of waiting applicants; and for each pending request the e-mail address, the phone number, and the company name is given. By inspecting this information, the manager can mark each applicant to be either Accepted or Rejected. Alternatively, the applicant can be left pending while further investigations are made (perhaps by phoning or e-mailing the applicant).

This logic is implemented using **pending.asp** (ASP) plus the **GetPending** and **ApplyDecisions** (VB methods).

ASP SCRIPT PROCESSING ... **pending.asp**

As usual, the ASP logic operates in multiple stages using a **state** variable to control which route through the script is taken.

When **state** is **1**, the VB component is created, a parameter collection is created, and a list of pending applicants is retrieved using the **GetPending** function.

```
Set objParams = objOUsrMgr.NewCollection
Set objResponse = objMUsrMgr.GetPending(objParams)
```

A successful response will contain a collection of applicants. Each entry will represent a user's request for membership, and there will be another collection containing his details.

The logic then generates a form containing a list of pending applicants along with their user details and a dropdown menu allowing the manager to select whether to allow membership or not. Once the form is submitted, the same ASP page is invoked, passing in the URL a **state** parameter with a value of **2**.

```
            <FORM method=post action=pending.asp?state=2>
            <TABLE>
<%          For Each vApplicant In vApplicants %>
                <TR>
                <TD> <% =vApplicant("username") %>
                   (<% =vApplicant("company") %>) </TD>
                <TD><A href="mailto:<% =vApplicant("email") %>">
                   <% =vApplicant("email") %></A></TD>
                <TD> <% =vApplicant("phone") %></TD>
                <TD><SELECT name="<% =vApplicant("username") %>">
                       <OPTION>Pending</OPTION>
                       <OPTION>Reject</OPTION>
                       <OPTION>Accept</OPTION>
                    </SELECT>
                </TD>
                </TR>
<%          Next %>
            </TABLE>
            <INPUT type=submit value=Submit id="butSub" name="~~butSub">
            </FORM>
```

When **state** is **2**, the VB component is created, a parameter collection is created using the HTML form contents (except the Submit button), and the **ApplyDecisions** function is invoked to update the NTDS database appropriately.

```
Set objParams = objOUsrMgr.NewCollection
Set objApplicants = objOUsrMgr.NewCollection
For Each vItem in Request.Form
    Set objApplicant = objOUsrMgr.NewCollection
    If Not vItem = "~~butSub" Then
        objApplicant.Add vItem,"username"
        objApplicant.Add Request.form(vItem),"decision"

        objApplicants.Add objApplicant
    End If                                              (continued)
```

```
Next
objParams.add objApplicants,"applicants"

Set objResponse = objMUsrMgr.ApplyDecisions(objParams)
```

MTS COMPONENT PROCESSING ... `GetPending`

The `GetPending` function builds a list of users who are pending membership approval by retrieving all users who are members of the Alliance Pending group.

We first create a Group object for the required NT user group.

```
Set objGroup = GetObject("WinNT://" & strMachineName & _
                "/Alliance Pending")
```

From the ADSI Group object we can get access to all members of the group using the `Members` method.

```
For Each objMember In objGroup.Members
    If objMember.Class = "User" Then
```

For each member encountered, a collection is created. This will be populated with the user's details that are to be returned to the caller.

```
Set vApplicant = New Collection
```

The user's name is the name of this object. The other user details were stored in the `FullName` property. These items are then extracted. Remember that we are using the "~" character as a delimiter for the different items.

```
vFullName = objMember.Get("FullName")
iPos1 = InStr(1, vFullName, "~")
iPos2 = InStr(iPos1 + 1, vFullName, "~")

vEmail = Mid(vFullName, 1, iPos1 - 1)
vPhone = Mid(vFullName, iPos1 + 1, iPos2 - iPos1 - 1)
vCompany = Mid(vFullName, iPos2 + 1)
```

The user's details are then stored in the collection.

```
vApplicant.Add objMember.Name, Key:="username"
vApplicant.Add vEmail, Key:="email"
vApplicant.Add vCompany, Key:="company"
vApplicant.Add vPhone, Key:="phone"
```

This collection is then appended to the main collection (containing all users) that is returned to the caller.

```
        vApplicants.Add vApplicant


    End If
Next
```

MTS COMPONENT PROCESSING ... `ApplyDecisions`

The `ApplyDecisions` function processes a list of usernames and any decisions a manager may have made about their membership status.

The applicant details are nested within a series of collections. At the top level, the function receives all its parameters within a collection. This is our normal approach for passing parameters. The only entry in the "parameter collection" is the collection of applicants, and each entry within this is another collection containing the individual's details (i.e., the user name and the manager's decision for that user).

```
Set objApplicants = vParams("applicants")

For Each objApplicant In objApplicants

    vUserName = objApplicant("username")
    vDecision = objApplicant("decision")
```

For each application we switch on the manager's decision:

```
Select Case vDecision
```

If the manager rejects the applicant, the user must be deleted. This will also automatically remove the user from the Alliance Pending user group.

First we get the Domain object and the User's object:

```
Case "Reject":
    Set objDomain = GetObject("WinNT://" & strMachineName)
    Set objUser = GetObject("WinNT://" & strMachineName & _
                    "/" & vUserName)
```

We then extract the e-mail address from the Users object. This was stored at the start of the **FullName** field and was delimited by the "~" character.

```
vEmail = Mid(objUser.Get("FullName"), 1, _
        InStr(1, objUser.Get("FullName"), "~") - 1)
```

Next we delete the User from the Domain:

```
Call objDomain.Delete("user", vUserName)
```

Finally an e-mail message can be sent to the applicant informing him of the bad news. We shall discuss further on how the e-mail logic functions.

If the manager accepts the applicant, the user must be transferred from the Alliance Pending user group to the Alliance Members user group.

First we get the Group object for Alliance Pending and the User object:

```
Case "Accept":
    Set objGroup = GetObject("WinNT://" & strMachineName & _
                    "/Alliance Pending")
    Set objUser = GetObject("WinNT://" & strMachineName & _
                    "/" & vUserName)
```

As before, we extract the e-mail address from the User object:

```
vEmail = Mid(objUser.Get("FullName"), 1, _
        InStr(1, objUser.Get("FullName"), "~") - 1)
```

Next we remove the User from the Group, using the **Remove** method:

```
objGroup.Remove ("WinNT://" & strMachineName & "/" & vUserName)
```

And now we shall add the user to the Alliance Pending group. First we get the Group object and add the user to it.

```
Set objGroup = GetObject("WinNT://" & strMachineName & _
            "/Alliance Members")
objGroup.Add ("WinNT://" & strMachineName & "/" & vUserName)
```

And finally, we can send the e-mail to the user.
If the manager leaves the application pending, no changes are made.

```
    Case "Pending":
        ' No change

    End Select
Next
```

E-MAIL AND COLLABORATION DATA OBJECTS

E-mail is sent to the applicant using the SMTP service and Collaboration Data Objects for NT Server (CDONTS) that we met in Chapter 9.

Recapping, to send an e-mail message we first create the CDO **NewMail** object and then use the **Send** method. This completes the e-mail operation in just a few lines of code.

```
Set objMail = CreateObject("CDONTS.Newmail")
Call objMail.send("manager@harrison.net", vEmail, _
    "Application to the Alliance", _
    "We are sorry but your application has been rejected")
Set objMail = Nothing
```

How it was done—for our eyes only!

The application code for the "Alliance" Site, in its entirety, is as follows:

Web Site Code

default.asp

```
<%@LANGUAGE="VBSCRIPT" %>

<% Option Explicit %>

<HTML>
<HEAD>
<TITLE>ADSI Example</TITLE>
</HEAD>
<BODY bgColor=lightgreen>
<CENTER>
<HR>
<H1>Home Page</H1>
<HR>
</CENTER>
<A href="register.asp">Register for Alliance</A><BR>
<A href="enteralliance.asp">Enter Alliance Site</A><BR>
</BODY>
</HTML>
```

`register.asp`

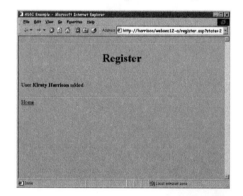

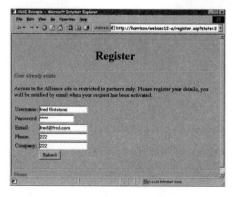

```
<%@LANGUAGE="VBSCRIPT" %>

<% Option Explicit %>

<%
    Dim vState
    Dim objUsrMgr
    Dim objParams
    Dim objResponse
%>

<%
    If Not Request.QueryString("state") = "" Then
        vState = Request.QueryString("state")
    Else
        vState = 1
    End If
%>
<HTML>
<HEAD>
<TITLE>ADSI Example</TITLE>
</HEAD>
<BODY bgColor=lightgreen>
<CENTER>
<HR>
<H1>Register</H1>
<HR>
</CENTER>
<%  If vState = 2 Then %>

<%
    Set objUsrMgr = Server.CreateObject("UserManager.IOpen")

    Set objParams = objUsrMgr.NewCollection

    objParams.Add Request.Form("username"),"username"
    objParams.Add Request.Form("password"),"password"
    objParams.Add Request.Form("email"),"email"
    objParams.Add Request.Form("phone"),"phone"
    objParams.Add Request.Form("company"),"company"

    Set objResponse = objUsrMgr.CreateUser(objParams)
    If objResponse("error") Then
```

(continued)

```
            Response.Write "<FONT color=red>" & _
                objResponse("errorinfo") & _
                "</FONT><BR>"
        vState = 1
    Else
        Response.Write "<P>User <B>" & Request.Form("username") &
"</B> added</P>"
    End If

%>


<%  End If %>

<% If vState = 1 Then %>
<P>Access to the Alliance site is restricted to partners only.
Please register your details, you will be notified by email
when your request has been activated.
<FORM method=post action=register.asp?state=2 id=form1 name=form1>
<TABLE>
<TR><TD>Username:</TD>
    <TD><INPUT id=username name=username
            size=20 maxlength=20
        value="<% =Request.Form("username") %>"></TD></TR>
<TR><TD>Password:</TD>
    <TD><INPUT type="password" id=password name=password
            size=14 maxlength=14
        value="<% =Request.Form("password") %>"></TD></TR>
<TR><TD>Email:</TD>
    <TD><INPUT id=email name=email
            value="<% =Request.Form("email") %>"></TD></TR>
<TR><TD>Phone:</TD>
    <TD><INPUT id=phone name=phone
            value="<% =Request.Form("phone") %>"></TD></TR>
<TR><TD>Company:</TD>
    <TD><INPUT id=company name=company
            value="<% =Request.Form("company") %>"></TD></TR>
<TR><TD></TD>
    <TD><INPUT type=submit value=Submit id=butSub
name=butSub></TD></TR>
</TABLE>
```

```
</FORM>
<%  End If %>


<HR>
<A href="default.asp">Home</A><BR>


</BODY>
</HTML>
```

enteralliance.asp

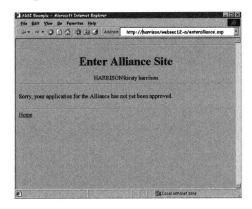

```
<%@LANGUAGE="VBSCRIPT" %>

<% Option Explicit %>

<%
rem If Request.ServerVariables("LOGON_USER") Then 'See chapter text
    If Session("enterstate") = 0 Then
        Session("enterstate") = 1
        Response.Status = "401 Unauthorized"
        Response.Addheader "WWW-Authenticate", "BASIC
realm=""HARRISON"""
        Response.End
    Else
        Session("enterstate") = 0
    End If
%>
```

(continued)

```
<%
    Dim objCheck
    Set objCheck = Server.CreateObject("IISSample.PermissionChecker")
    If objCheck.HasAccess("alliance/default.asp") Then
        Response.Redirect("alliance/default.asp")
    End If
%>

<HTML>
<HEAD>
<TITLE>ADSI Example</TITLE>
</HEAD>
<BODY bgColor=lightgreen>
<CENTER>
<HR>
<H1>Enter Alliance Site</H1>
<% =Request.ServerVariables("AUTH_USER") %>
<HR>
</CENTER>
<P>Sorry, your application for the Alliance has not yet
been approved.</P>
<HR>
<A href="default.asp">Home</A><BR>
</BODY>
</HTML>
```

`alliance/default.asp`

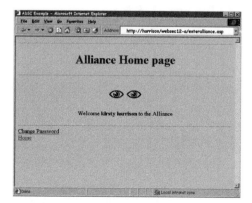

```
<%@LANGUAGE="VBSCRIPT" %>

<% Option Explicit %>

<%
    Dim vUserName
    Dim iPos

    VUserName = Request.ServerVariables("AUTH_USER")
    iPos = instr(1,vUserName,"\")
    if ipos > 0 then
        vUserName = mid(vUserName,ipos+1)
    end if
%>

<HTML>
<HEAD>
<TITLE>ADSI Example</TITLE>
</HEAD>
<BODY bgColor=pink>
<CENTER>
<HR>
<H1>Alliance Home page</H1>
<HR>

<P><FONT face=Webdings size=7>NN</FONT></P>
<P>Welcome <B><% =vUserName %></B> to the Alliance</P>

</CENTER>
<HR>
<A href="changepw.asp">Change Password</A><BR>
<A href="..\default.asp">Home</A>
</P>
</CENTER>

</BODY>
</HTML>
```

alliance/changepw.asp

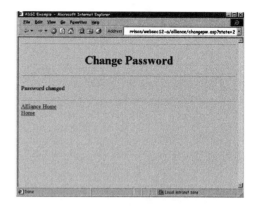

```
<%@LANGUAGE="VBSCRIPT" %>

<% Option Explicit %>

<%
    Dim vState

    If Not Request.QueryString("state") = "" Then
        vState = Request.QueryString("state")
    Else
        vState = 1
    End If
%>

<%
    Dim vUserName
    Dim iPos

    vUserName= Request.ServerVariables("AUTH_USER")
    iPos = instr(1,vUserName,"\")
    if ipos > 0 then
        vUserName = mid(vUserName,ipos+1)
    end if
%>

<HTML>
<HEAD>
```

```
<TITLE>ADSI Example</TITLE>
</HEAD>
<BODY bgColor=pink>
<CENTER>
<HR>
<H1>Change Password</H1>
<HR>
</CENTER>
<%  If vState = 2 Then %>

<%
    Dim objUsrMgr
    Dim objParams
    Dim objResponse

    Set objUsrMgr = Server.CreateObject("UserManager.IOpen")

    Set objParams = objUsrMgr.NewCollection

    objParams.Add Request.Form("newpassword"),"newpassword"
    objParams.Add Request.Form("newpassword2"),"newpassword2"

    Set objResponse = objUsrMgr.ChangePassword(objParams)
    If objResponse("error") Then
        Response.Write "<FONT color=red>" & _
                objResponse("errorinfo") & _
                "</FONT><BR>"
        vState = 1
    Else
        Response.Write "<P>Password changed</P>"
    End If
%>

<%  End If %>

<%  If vState = 1 Then %>
<P>Please enter the password details:
<FORM method=post action=changepw.asp?state=2 id=form1 name=form1>
<TABLE>
<TR><TD>Username:</TD>
    <TD><% =vUserName %></TD></TR>
```

(continued)

```
<TR><TD>New Password:</TD>
    <TD><INPUT type="password" id=newpassword name=newpassword
            size=14 maxlength=14
        value="<% =Request.Form("newpassword") %>"></TD></TR>
<TR><TD>Confirm Password:</TD>
    <TD><INPUT type="password" id=newpassword2 name=newpassword2
            size=14 maxlength=14
        value="<% =Request.Form("newpassword2") %>"></TD></TR>
<TR><TD></TD>
    <TD><INPUT type=submit value=Submit id=butSub
name=butSub></TD></TR>
</TABLE>
</FORM>
<%  End If %>

<HR>

<A HREF="default.asp">Alliance Home</A><BR>
<A HREF="..\default.asp">Home</A>

</BODY>
</HTML>
```

manager/default.asp

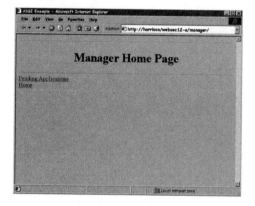

```
<%@LANGUAGE="VBSCRIPT" %>

<% Option Explicit %>
```

```
<HTML>
<HEAD>
<TITLE>ADSI Example</TITLE>
</HEAD>
<BODY bgColor=lightblue>
<CENTER>
<HR>
<H1>Manager Home Page</H1>
<HR>
</CENTER>
<A HREF="pending.asp"> Pending Applications</A><BR>
<A HREF="..\default.asp">Home</A><BR>


</BODY>
</HTML>
```

manager/pending.asp

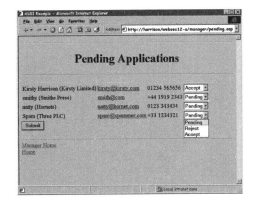 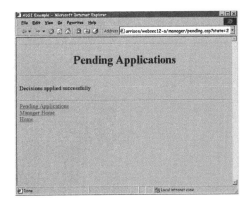

```
<%@LANGUAGE="VBSCRIPT" %>


<% Option Explicit %>


<%
    Dim vState
    Dim objOUsrMgr
    Dim objMUsrMgr
    Dim objParams
    Dim objResponse
    Dim objApplicants
```

(continued)

```
    Dim objApplicant
    Dim vItem
%>


<%
    If Not Request.QueryString("state") = "" Then
       vState = Request.QueryString("state")
    Else
       vState = 1
    End If
%>


<HTML>
<HEAD>
<TITLE>ADSI Example</TITLE>
</HEAD>
<BODY bgColor=lightblue>
<CENTER>
<HR>
<H1>Pending Applications</H1>
<HR>
</CENTER>
<%
    Set objOUsrMgr = Server.CreateObject("UserManager.IOpen")
    Set objMUsrMgr = Server.CreateObject("UserManager.IManager")
%>


<%  If vState = 2 Then %>


<%
    Set objParams = objOUsrMgr.NewCollection
    Set objApplicants = objOUsrMgr.NewCollection
    For Each vItem in Request.Form
        Set objApplicant = objOUsrMgr.NewCollection
        If Not vItem = "~~butSub" Then
            objApplicant.Add vItem,"username"
            objApplicant.Add Request.form(vItem),"decision"

            objApplicants.Add objApplicant
        End If
    Next
    objParams.add objApplicants,"applicants"
```

```
        Set objResponse = objMUsrMgr.ApplyDecisions(objParams)
        If objResponse("error") Then
            Response.Write "<FONT color=red>" & _
                  objResponse("errorinfo") & _
                  "</FONT><BR>"
        Else
            Response.Write "<P>Decisions applied successfully</P>"
        End If
%>


<%  End If %>


<%  If vState = 1 Then %>


<%
    Set objParams = objOUsrMgr.NewCollection
    Set objResponse = objMUsrMgr.GetPending(objParams)
    If objResponse("error") Then
        Response.Write "<FONT color=red>" & _
              objResponse("errorinfo") & _
              "</FONT><BR>"
    Else
        Dim vApplicants
        Dim vApplicant

        Set vApplicants = objResponse("applicants")
%>

        <FORM method=post action=pending.asp?state=2>
        <TABLE>
<%      For Each vApplicant In vApplicants %>
            <TR>
            <TD> <% =vApplicant("username") %>
              (<% =vApplicant("company") %>) </TD>
            <TD><A href="mailto:<% =vApplicant("email") %>">
              <% =vApplicant("email") %></A></TD>
            <TD> <% =vApplicant("phone") %></TD>
            <TD><SELECT name="<% =vApplicant("username") %>">
                  <OPTION>Pending</OPTION>
                  <OPTION>Reject</OPTION>
                  <OPTION>Accept</OPTION>
              </SELECT>
```

(continued)

```
            </TD>
            </TR>
<%      Next %>
        </TABLE>
        <INPUT type=submit value=Submit id="butSub" name="~~butSub">
        </FORM>

<%      End If %>

<%  End If %>
<HR>
<% If vState = 2 Then %>
<A HREF="pending.asp">Pending Applications</A><BR>
<% End If %>
<A HREF="default.asp">Manager Home</A><BR>
<A HREF="..\default.asp">Home</A><BR>

</BODY>
</HTML>
```

VB Software Component Code

IOPEN—IOpen.cls

```vb
Option Explicit

Implements ObjectControl

Private objMTSContext As ObjectContext

Private Function ObjectControl_CanBePooled() As Boolean
    ObjectControl_CanBePooled = True
End Function

Private Sub ObjectControl_Deactivate()
    Set objMTSContext = Nothing
End Sub

Private Sub ObjectControl_Activate()
    On Error GoTo ActivateErr
```

```
    Set objMTSContext = GetObjectContext()
    Exit Sub

ActivateErr:
    Call RaiseError("ObjectControl_Activate")

End Sub
```

```
Public Function ChangePassword(vUserDetails As Variant) As Variant
    On Error GoTo ChangePasswordErr

    Dim vResponse As New Collection
    Dim bError As Boolean
    Dim vNewPassword As Variant
    Dim vNewPassword2 As Variant
    Dim objUser As Object
    Dim vUser As Variant
    Dim iPos As Integer

    vUser = objMTSContext.Security.GetDirectCallerName
    iPos = InStr(1, vUser, "\")
    If iPos > 0 Then
        vUser = Mid(vUser, iPos + 1)
    End If

    vNewPassword = Trim(vUserDetails("newpassword"))
    vNewPassword2 = Trim(vUserDetails("newpassword2"))

    bError = False

    If Not bError Then
        If vNewPassword <> vNewPassword2 Then
            bError = True
            vResponse.Add "Mismatch in passwords", Key:="errorinfo"
        End If
    End If

    If Not bError Then
        If Len(vNewPassword) < 4 Or Len(vNewPassword) > 14 Then
            bError = True
```

(continued)

```
            vResponse.Add "Password must be between 4 and 14
characters", _
                    Key:="errorinfo"
        End If
    End If

    If Not bError Then

        Set objUser = GetObject("WinNT://" & strMachineName & "/" &
vUser)

        Call objUser.SetPassword(vNewPassword)
        Call objUser.SetInfo

    End If

    If bError Then
        vResponse.Add True, Key:="error"
        objMTSContext.SetAbort
    Else
        vResponse.Add False, Key:="error"
        objMTSContext.SetComplete
    End If

    Set ChangePassword = vResponse
    Exit Function

ChangePasswordErr:
    objMTSContext.SetAbort
    Set ChangePassword = RaiseError("ChangePassword")

End Function
```

```
Public Function CreateUser(vUserDetails As Variant) As Variant
    On Error GoTo CreateUserErr

    Dim vResponse As New Collection
    Dim vUserName As Variant
    Dim vPassword As Variant
    Dim vEmail As Variant
    Dim vPhone As Variant
    Dim vCompany As Variant
```

```
    Dim vItem As Variant
    Dim vDetails As Variant
    Dim objDomain As Object
    Dim objGroup As Object
    Dim objUser As Object
    Dim bError As Boolean

    vUserName = Trim(vUserDetails("username"))
    vPassword = Trim(vUserDetails("password"))
    vEmail = Trim(vUserDetails("email"))
    vPhone = Trim(vUserDetails("phone"))
    vCompany = Trim(vUserDetails("company"))

    bError = False

    If Not bError Then
        If vUserName = "" Or vPassword = "" Or vEmail = "" Or _
            vCompany = "" Or vPhone = "" Then
            bError = True
            vResponse.Add "Fields must not be blank", Key:="errorinfo"
        End If
    End If

    If Not bError Then
        If Len(vPassword) < 4 Or Len(vPassword) > 14 Then
            bError = True
            vResponse.Add "Password must be between 4 and 14
characters", _
                    Key:="errorinfo"
        End If
    End If

    If Not bError Then
        If InStr(1, vPassword, " ") <> 0 Then
            bError = True
            vResponse.Add "Password must not contain spaces",
Key:="errorinfo"
        End If
    End If

    If Not bError Then
```

(continued)

```
            Set objDomain = GetObject("WinNT://" & strMachineName)

            For Each vItem In objDomain
                If LCase(vItem.Name) = LCase(Trim(vUserName)) Then
                    bError = True
                    vResponse.Add "User already exists", Key:="errorinfo"
                    Exit For
                End If
            Next
        End If

        If Not bError Then

            Set objUser = objDomain.Create("user", vUserName)
            Call objUser.SetInfo

            Call objUser.SetPassword(vPassword)
            Call objUser.SetInfo

            vDetails = vEmail & "~" & vPhone & "~" & vCompany

            Call objUser.Put("FullName", CStr(vDetails))
            Call objUser.SetInfo

            Set objGroup = objDomain.GetObject("group", "Alliance
Pending")
            objGroup.Add ("WinNT://" & strMachineName & "/" & vUserName)

        End If

        If bError Then
            vResponse.Add True, Key:="error"
            objMTSContext.SetAbort
        Else
            vResponse.Add False, Key:="error"
            objMTSContext.SetComplete
        End If

    Set CreateUser = vResponse
    Exit Function
```

```
CreateUserErr:
    objMTSContext.SetAbort
    Set CreateUser = RaiseError("CreateUser")

End Function


Public Function NewCollection() As Variant
    On Error GoTo NewCollectionErr

    Dim vResponse As New Collection

    objMTSContext.SetComplete
    Set NewCollection = vResponse

    Exit Function

NewCollectionErr:
    objMTSContext.SetAbort
    Set NewCollection = RaiseError("NewCollection")

End Function
```

IMANAGEMENT—IManager.cls

```
Option Explicit

Implements ObjectControl

Private objMTSContext As ObjectContext


Private Function ObjectControl_CanBePooled() As Boolean
    ObjectControl_CanBePooled = True
End Function


Private Sub ObjectControl_Deactivate()
    Set objMTSContext = Nothing
End Sub


Private Sub ObjectControl_Activate()
    On Error GoTo ActivateErr
```

(continued)

```
    Set objMTSContext = GetObjectContext()
    Exit Sub

ActivateErr:
    Call RaiseError("ObjectControl_Activate")

End Sub
```

```
Public Function ApplyDecisions(vParams As Variant) As Variant
    On Error GoTo ApplyDecisionsErr

    Dim vResponse As New Collection
    Dim vUserName As Variant
    Dim vDecision As Variant
    Dim vEmail As Variant
    Dim objApplicants As Object
    Dim objApplicant As Object
    Dim objDomain As Object
    Dim objGroup As Object
    Dim objMail As Object
    Dim objUser As Object

    Set objApplicants = vParams("applicants")

    For Each objApplicant In objApplicants

        vUserName = objApplicant("username")
        vDecision = objApplicant("decision")

        Select Case vDecision
        Case "Reject":
            Set objDomain = GetObject("WinNT://" & strMachineName)
            Set objUser = GetObject("WinNT://" & strMachineName & _
                            "/" & vUserName)

            vEmail = Mid(objUser.Get("FullName"), 1, _
                    InStr(1, objUser.Get("FullName"), "~") - 1)

            Call objDomain.Delete("user", vUserName)

            Set objMail = CreateObject("CDONTS.Newmail")
```

```
        Call objMail.send("manager@harrison.net", vEmail, _
            "Application to the Alliance", _
            "We are pleased that your application has now been
accepted")
        Set objMail = Nothing
        Case "Accept":
            Set objGroup = GetObject("WinNT://" & strMachineName & _
                            "/Alliance Pending")
            Set objUser = GetObject("WinNT://" & strMachineName & _
                            "/" & vUserName)

            vEmail = Mid(objUser.Get("FullName"), 1, _
                    InStr(1, objUser.Get("FullName"), "~") - 1)

            objGroup.Remove ("WinNT://" & strMachineName & "/" &
vUserName)

            Set objGroup = GetObject("WinNT://" & strMachineName & _
                            "/Alliance Members")
            objGroup.Add ("WinNT://" & strMachineName & "/" &
vUserName)

            Set objMail = CreateObject("CDONTS.Newmail")
            Call objMail.send("manager@harrison.net", vEmail, _
                "Application to the Alliance", _
                "We are sorry but your application has been rejected")
            Set objMail = Nothing

        Case "Pending":
            ' No change

        End Select
    Next

    vResponse.Add False, Key:="error"

    objMTSContext.SetComplete
    Set ApplyDecisions = vResponse

    Exit Function
```

(continued)

```
ApplyDecisionsErr:
    objMTSContext.SetAbort
    Set ApplyDecisions = RaiseError("ApplyDecisions")


End Function
```

```
Public Function GetPending(vParams As Variant) As Variant
    On Error GoTo GetPendingErr

    Dim vResponse As New Collection
    Dim vApplicants As New Collection
    Dim vApplicant As Collection
    Dim objGroup As Object
    Dim vFullName As String
    Dim objMember As Object
    Dim vEmail As Variant
    Dim vPhone As Variant
    Dim vCompany As Variant
    Dim iPos1, iPos2 As Integer

    Set objGroup = GetObject("WinNT://" & strMachineName & _
                "/Alliance Pending")

    For Each objMember In objGroup.Members

        If objMember.Class = "User" Then

            Set vApplicant = New Collection
            vFullName = objMember.Get("FullName")
            iPos1 = InStr(1, vFullName, "~")
            iPos2 = InStr(iPos1 + 1, vFullName, "~")

            vEmail = Mid(vFullName, 1, iPos1 - 1)
            vPhone = Mid(vFullName, iPos1 + 1, iPos2 - iPos1 - 1)
            vCompany = Mid(vFullName, iPos2 + 1)
            vApplicant.Add objMember.Name, Key:="username"
            vApplicant.Add vEmail, Key:="email"
            vApplicant.Add vCompany, Key:="company"
            vApplicant.Add vPhone, Key:="phone"


            vApplicants.Add vApplicant
```

```
      End If
   Next

   VResponse.Add False, Key:="error"
   vResponse.Add vApplicants, Key:="applicants"

   objMTSContext.SetComplete
   Set GetPending = vResponse

   Exit Function

GetPendingErr:
   ObjMTSContext.SetAbort
   Set GetPending = RaiseError("GetPending")
End Function
```

GENERAL—general.bas

Machine name set to HARRISON—amend for your own environment.

```
Public Const strMachineName As String = "HARRISON"
```

```
Public Sub Trace(vMsg As Variant)
   Dim intFileNo As Integer

   intFileNo = FreeFile
   Open "e:\data\trace.txt" For Append Shared As #intFileNo
   Print #intFileNo, Time & " " & vMsg
   Close #intFileNo

End Sub
```

```
Public Function RaiseError(ByVal vName As Variant) As Variant
   Dim vErrorInfo As Variant
   Dim vResponse As Collection

   vErrorInfo = "UserManager System Failure: " & Hex(Err.Number) & _
           " " & Err.Source & "->" & vName & " " & Err.Description

   Err.Clear                                              (continued)
```

```
Set vResponse = New Collection
vResponse.Add True, Key:="error"
vResponse.Add vErrorInfo, Key:="errorinfo"


Trace (vErrorInfo)


Set RaiseError = vResponse

End Function
```

■ Summary

In this chapter we have seen how to use a combination of ASP, MTS, and ASDI to implement a Web site with an area that has been restricted to a community of known users.

The key points in this chapter are:

- ASP can easily manipulate the Windows NTDS database using the ADSI WinNT provider.

- By running the components in the security context of the administrator it is possible for low-privilege users to invoke powerful functionality. But care must be taken not to allow access to more functionality than is intended.

- By allowing Web users to manage their own 'personal information' attributes located within the central security database, we remove this burden from the administrative personnel.

- The PermissionChecker component can be used from ASP to determine whether a Web user has been granted permission to read a file.

- The MTS SecurityProperty object can be used to determine the security context of a caller or creator.

- E-mail can be sent from ASP using CDONTS; however, from this discussion, we saw how easy it is to send forged e-mail and impersonate another source.

One of the problems with using the Windows NTDS database is that it cannot scale to handle millions of users. The solution comes from the Membership Server components that are part of Microsoft Site Server. This will be our topic in the next chapter.

Membership Server

The subject matter that we shall now focus on is Membership, using Microsoft Site Server. As the latest component of the Microsoft BackOffice family of products, Site Server provides a huge amount of Internet functionality that is complementary to what is provided by the core IIS and ASP Web infrastructure.

Site Server is available in two versions. The base version is designed to provide the tools for the advanced management and targeted delivery of information. The Commercial Edition also includes Microsoft Commerce Server, which enables Web sites for the secure trading of goods and services over the Internet.

Site Server provides a structured framework for publishing Web content and addresses the complete process, including the development, approval, and deployment of information. Information can be retrieved from a variety of sources, including documents (e.g., HTML, Microsoft

Office), databases (e.g., SQL Server, those that are ODBC/OLE DB-compliant), and ADSI data stores (e.g., Active Directory, those that are LDAP compliant). The product also provides comprehensive facilities that allow Web site administrators to analyze the site's usage to monitor activity and trends for both marketing and capacity-planning reasons.

Site Server provides a large number of facilities. While we could write them ourselves, using ASP and COM components, they all come out of the box ready-built, fully tested, and designed to provide a large number of configurable alternative options. Even if we only wanted to use a small subset of the provided functionality, the cost of rolling out our own versions would by far outweigh the relatively small license costs of Site Server.

One of the compelling functions that Site Server provides is in the area of **Membership and Personalization,** and this topic fits in nicely with the scope of this book.

In this chapter we shall discuss how to use the provided Membership facilities to:

- Track and profile millions of users—the authentication mechanisms based on NT security that we have discussed so far cannot scale to anywhere near this size
- Automate the identification of users by means of cookies
- Protect areas of the site that have:
  - premium/subscription-only content
  - information that is private or sensitive

We shall then build on this in the next chapter, where we discuss how to capture and manage information about the user to control access to information. We can also use this information to make Web content more relevant by personalizing pages and establishing a channel for targeted marketing.

The Membership Server

The Microsoft Membership Server is an integral part of Site Server. It provides the functionality to address the key issue that many Web sites need membership. The main components are:

- **Membership Directory**—a central repository for organization and personal profile information; it has been designed with scalability in mind and can support millions of users
- **LDAP Service**—provides the industry-standard interface LDAP to access the contents of the Membership Directory

- **Authentication Service**—validates user credentials and creates user-security context to support access controls
- **Active User Object** (AUO)—a unified access mechanism for all user-profile information from a variety of sources; typically used from ASP

The diagram below shows these key components and illustrates how the IIS Web Server and ASP interact with the various parts of the product.

It is recommended that the reader frequently refer back to this diagram as the various components are introduced and discussed in detail.

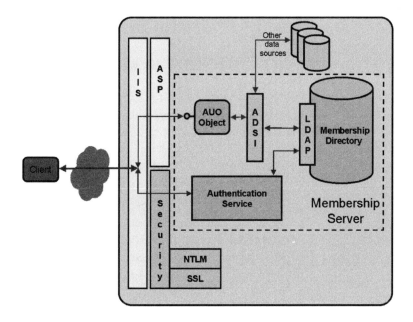

Multiple instances of the Membership Server can exist on the same machine. If you have several Web sites on the same box, they can each have their own Membership Server instance. Alternatively, Web sites can share information by using the same Membership Server instance.

Protecting the Membership Web Site

When designing a security strategy for a site, we must decide on the level of access controls we wish to impose and the mechanisms we wish to use to identify the users. Let us investigate the choices that are available.

Levels of Access

There are four levels of access controls that we can apply to our Web site:

- **Public**—content that has no access restrictions
- **Restricted**—content that requires a user to register some personal details before we allow access; however the user does not have to be authenticated and can run under the security context of an anonymous user
- **Secured** (two types, subtly different):
  - **Private**—content any authenticated user can have access to
  - **Premium**—content restricted to a subset of authenticated users (e.g., only those who have subscribed and paid for a service)

Types of Users

The types of Web site visitors that we need to handle are:

- **Anonymous Users**—they are not tracked in the Membership Directory.
- **Cookie-Identified Users**—their real identity can remain anonymous, but they are still tracked in the Membership Directory and their activity is profiled by using a unique identifier planted as a cookie on the client computer.
- **Registered Users**—they are known and identified using one of the available authentication mechanisms. As part of the registration process, the user can be prompted for various items of information (e.g., age, sex, e-mail address, address, interests, digital certificate, password, etc.) that can be stored in the Membership Directory and used for personalization and marketing purposes.

Membership Authentication

Registered users must be authenticated, and Membership Server provides a number of standard mechanisms that can be used to perform this:

- **Basic Authentication**—as discussed in Chapter 4
- **HTML Forms Authentication**—standard Web pages that request the user's credentials
- **Client-side digital certificates**—as discussed in Chapter 5
- **Distributed Password Authentication** (DPA)—a derivative of the Windows NT Challenge/Response authentication protocol that is used by some of the large ISPs (e.g., MSN and CompuServe)

Cookie-Identified Users do not have any user-security context created. This means that they can access restricted content but cannot access secured content. It is important to appreciate that this use of cookies is not secure; it should be used as an identification mechanism, not as an authentication mechanism.

Getting Started with Membership Server

Membership Server is an optional component installed during the Site Server setup process. We shall now see how to configure our Web site to utilize Membership Server; this is controlled using a number of snap-ins for the MMC.

There are three stages that we must perform:

- Create an instance of Membership Server
- Point the Membership Directory Manager at the LDAP Service
- Configure IIS to use Membership Authentication for security

Creating a Membership Server Instance

From the Personalization and Membership snap-in, right-click on the machine name and select the menu option New|Membership Server Instance. This invokes the wizard to assist us through a number of steps.

On the first screen specify that a Custom Configuration is required; i.e., we want to specify which portions of the Membership Server we require.

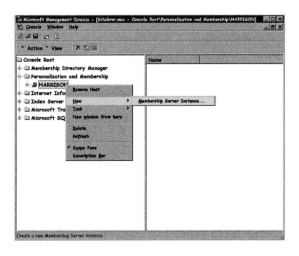

For the Configuration options we specify that we require Active User Objects (AUO) and the LDAP Service.

These items will provide our ASP logic with an easy-to-use access mechanism to the user-profile information stored in the Membership Directory.

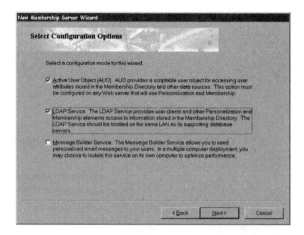

On the following dialog, we specify that we require a new Membership Directory to be created.

Recall from above that our Web site can either share an existing Membership Directory or use its own; we shall take the second option.

User accounts and administrative groups can be stored either in the Windows NTDS database or the Membership Directory. The latter is designed to scale to millions of users and should be selected for large-scale sites.

We shall take the scalable option and choose Membership Authentication.

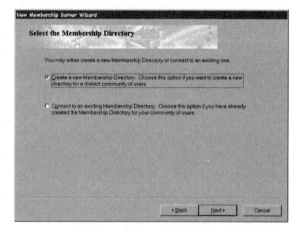

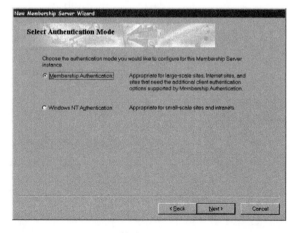

Next we give a name to our Membership Directory and specify the password for the Membership Server administrator.

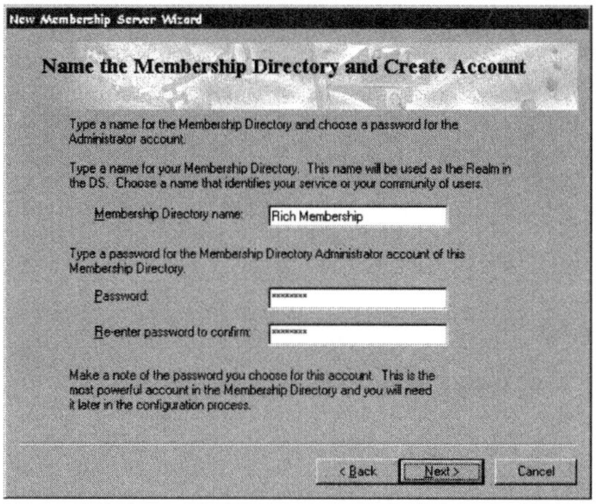

The Directory can be stored either in an Access database or a SQL Server database. The nature of the latter means that it should be chosen for large-scale sites.

Depending on the option selected, the subsequent screen requests either an Access database filename or the database connection information for the SQL Server database.

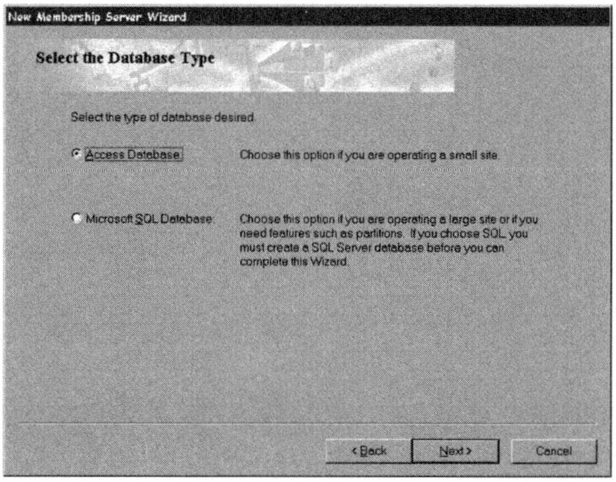

The next screen requests the IP address and Port number for the LDAP service.

The "well-known" Port number for LDAP is 389.

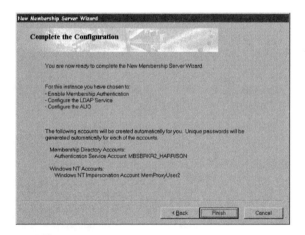

After this information has been captured, the wizard creates the Membership Server instance.

At this point we have:

- Installed a Membership Directory to store the organization and user-profile information
- Installed an LDAP Service
- Configured AUO

We have not yet told our Web server to use this Membership Server instance. This operation comes later.

The instance of Membership Server in MMC will have a bland name like Membership Instance #1.

This can be renamed something more meaningful to us. In our screen-shots we have renamed it Rich Membership

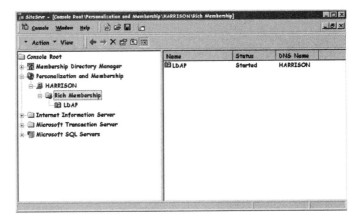

We can examine the properties of the Membership Instance and the LDAP service by right-clicking on the entry and selecting the Properties menu item.

Membership Directory Manager

Recapping from above, the Membership Directory is a central repository for organization and personal-profile information that will be used by our Web site.

We can inspect the contents of the Membership Directory using the Membership Directory Manager snap-in.

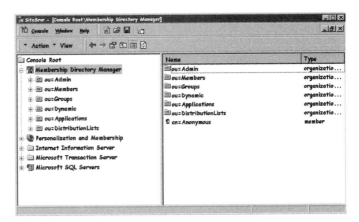

The properties for this item must specify the machine name and the Port number of the LDAP service.

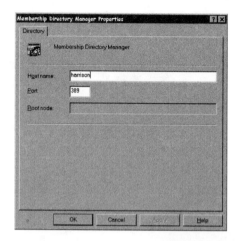

We are then prompted for a user
name and password. To examine the
entire directory, we specify the administrator and the password that was used
when the Membership Server instance
was created.

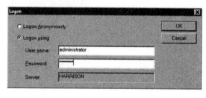

The hierarchical structure of the Membership Directory is then revealed for us to peruse. This organization, called the **Directory Information
Tree**, will be discussed shortly.

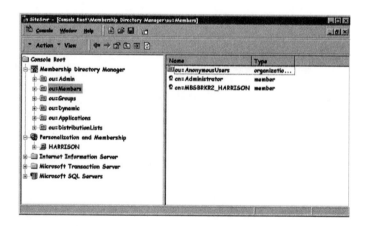

Mapping IIS to Membership Authentication

Our final task is to configure IIS to use the Membership Server Authentication, as opposed to its normal IIS/NT authentication mechanisms, discussed
back in Chapter 4 and then used in the subsequent chapters.

By right-clicking on the Web site in the Internet Service Manager (MMC,) we will see that the familiar context properties menu has a new option, Task|Membership Server Mapping.

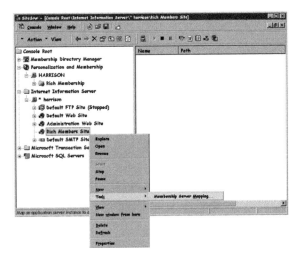

Selecting this menu option presents us with a dialog listing all Memberships Server instances (plus an option to disable mapping, i.e., return to normal IIS/NT authentication). We can select the required mapping to our new Membership Server instance.

By selecting properties for the Web site, we see the standard property sheets that we are familiar with for configuring IIS.

However, note now that a new property sheet, with a tab titled Membership Authentication, has been added. It is using this property sheet that the authentication mechanism details for the site are specified.

Remember that IIS authentication is normally configured using the Anonymous Access and Authentication Control section on the Directory Security property sheet. If you switch to this tab, you will see that the Edit button has been disabled. However, enabling SSL is still done from this property sheet.

Membership Directory

The Membership Directory is the central repository for organization and personal-profile information. It has been optimized for heavy read access, designed to scale to millions of users, and provides an extensible schema. It has many uses, such as handling Internet-scale authentication, personalization, subscription/membership tracking, managing communities, white pages, and online friends/colleagues locator. It can be used to store users, groups, credentials, permissions, roles, preferences, account status, buddy lists, and so on. When multiple communities/Web sites are hosted on the same machine, they can either share a Membership Directory or each have one of their own.

Earlier we saw that the Membership Directory is created to operate in one of two alternative modes. This dictates where the security credentials, user names, and group memberships are stored:

- **Membership Authentication Mode**—security information is stored in the Membership Directory
- **Windows NT Authentication Mode**—security information is stored in the Windows NTDS database

The Membership Directory can store two types of data:

- **Persistent Data**—this information is safe-stored in either an Access or SQL Server database; the latter is far more suitable for a high-performance, large-scale site
- **Dynamic Data**—this information is temporarily stored in memory; it only exists for users who are connected, so when no user activity is detected for a configurable timeout period, the information is deleted

Dynamic Data can be used in a similar fashion to the ASP `Session` object. The advantage of the Dynamic Data approach comes when a site is distributed over multiple Web servers for performance and redundancy reasons. Using a common Membership Directory, it could share session-context information across all of the Web servers. In contrast, the Web servers would have their own independent ASP **Session** objects that could not easily share the same session context.

Directory Information Tree

The membership's Persistent Data is structured in a hierarchical fashion as a Directory Information Tree (DIT), and this can be perused using the Membership Directory Manager mentioned earlier. The following diagram shows the top levels of the hierarchical structure found for the default DIT.

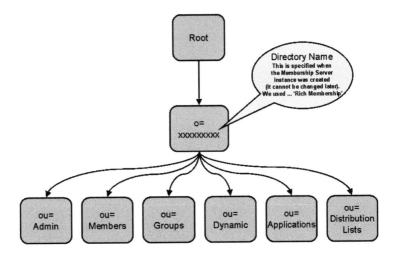

The mnemonics for the elements in the DIT conforms to the LDAP naming conventions met in Chapter 12.

o	organization
ou	organization unit (which can contain other ou containers)
cn	common name

The top-level organization units installed by default in the Membership Directory are:

- ou = Admin—one container object for the schema that defines the directory structure; also container objects for admin items, such as data sources, content indexing, and replication
- ou = Members—one leaf object for each site user that stores associated attributes (persistent); Cookie-Identified Users are in the container object called ou = AnonymousUsers

- ou = Groups—one leaf object for each administrative group, this is the basis for controlling access to data and content—stores users associated with the group as attributes (persistent); NT groups are in the container object ou = NTGroups
- ou = Dynamic—one leaf object for each user that stores associated attributes (dynamic; although this is not persistent data, it is still exposed in the DIT)
- ou = Applications—one container object for each application (e.g., Net-Meeting) and contains information used by the application
- ou = DistributionLists—one leaf object for each distribution list and stores list of e-mail addresses as attributes

Because this chapter focuses on Membership, the organization units that we shall investigate further in this book are the **Members** and the **Groups**. The following sections on Members and Groups organization units are only applicable when using Membership Authentication mode. Users and groups in Windows NT Authentication mode are stored in the Windows NTDS database and controlled in the normal manner, using the User Manager administration utility.

ou = Members

One of the key objectives of a membership system is to store information about the user base and then use it at some point in the future for maximum business benefit. The user information is stored in the Membership Directory within the **Members** organization unit.

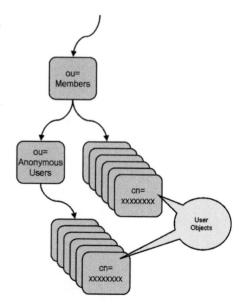

There will be one user object for each user known to the membership system. These are stored either in the container ou=Members or, if they are Cookie-Identified Users, one level down in the container ou=AnonymousUsers.

Each user object can store information associated with the user. This will be a series of attribute name/value pairs.

Using the MMC Membership Directory Manager, we can inspect

the attributes assigned to the user by right-clicking on the object and selecting the Properties menu option. This shows the Attributes property sheet.

Every Membership Directory object has a Security property sheet. This sets the security ACLs on the object; i.e., specifies those users who have permission to access/amend the object.

The Groups property sheet shows the administrative groups the user has been assigned to.

It is possible to set an expiration time for how long the user is to remain a member of the group. When the expiration date is reached, the user is not automatically deleted from the group. Instead, this is done by the site administrator, invoking a Microsoft-supplied script. More on this later.

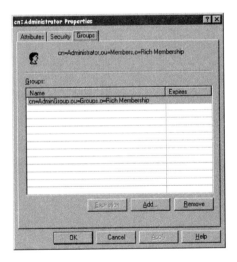

ou = Groups

For administrative purposes, members may be organized into groups. When permissions are applied to a resource, it is far more manageable to specify a single group name rather than a long list of user names.

There will be one group object for each group known to the membership system. These are stored either in the container ou=Groups or, if they are a standard Membership Administrative group, one level down in the container ou=NTGroups.

Each group object can store information associated with the group. This will be a series of attribute name/value pairs.

Using the MMC Membership Directory Manager, we can inspect the attributes assigned to the group by right-clicking on the object and selecting the Properties menu option. This shows the Attributes property sheet:

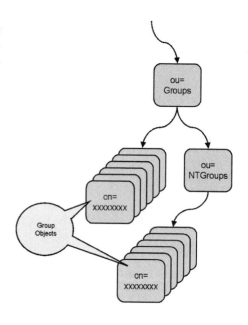

The Members property sheet shows the users or other groups associated with the group:

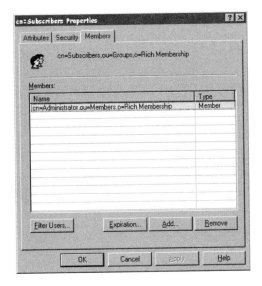

Mapping Members onto Windows NT Security

It is a fundamental concept of Windows NT security that all resources are protected by ACLs, and that a user can only perform an action on such a resource if he has the appropriate permissions granted.

But how does Membership Server, using Membership Authentication, handle this, since the users do not have real Windows NT user accounts?

Once a member has been identified by Membership Authentication, a user-security context is created that is part of the Windows NT security. This is achieved by mapping the Membership member onto Windows NT users/user groups.

Every member who is authenticated runs under the security context of MemProxyUserN, where N is a number that identifies the Membership Server instance.

However, since this account is used for all members, it does not offer a granular level of control. As we shall now see, a much better approach is to use Membership groups.

When a site is using Membership Authentication mode, each group defined in the Membership Directory will automatically have a corresponding group entry created in the Windows NTDS database.

The name of the Windows NT group is Site_directoryname_groupname

For example, the Membership group

cn=Subscribers,ou=Groups, o=Rich Membership

would map to a Windows NT group called

Site_Rich Membership_ Subscribers

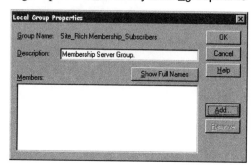

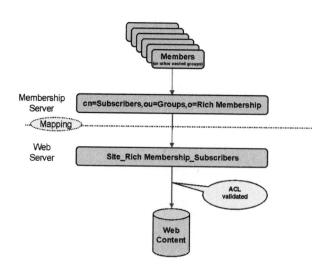

Identifying a member and mapping him onto a Windows NT group to obtain an ACL is the basis for establishing what content a user can access.

Membership Authentication

There are two areas within Membership Server that are protected using ACLs (access permissions), and the user must be authenticated in order to provide appropriate access controls. The two areas are:

- The Web Site—Web content is protected by ACLs
- The Membership Directory—the membership objects are protected by ACLs

We shall now see how to enable the different types of authentication available to each.

Web Site Authentication

We saw earlier in this chapter that there are several different types of authentication mechanisms available, using Membership Authentication, to identify a Web user. Recapping, these are:

- Basic Authentication
- HTML forms
- Client-side digital certificates
- Distributed Password Authentication (DPA)

The type of Membership Authentication to be applied is configured at a directory level, whether a home directory, a subdirectory, or a virtual directory. It is permissible to configure different directories for the same Web site to use different authentication mechanisms.

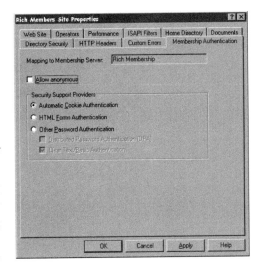

We configure the type of authentication that we require our Web site to impose using the Internet Service Manager (MMC). This is done by selecting the Properties dialog for the directory and selecting the Membership Authentication property sheet.

We shall see later in this chapter how the different options available are used.

In addition, handling client digital certificates using SSL is enabled from the Directory Security property sheet.

SSL can also be used in conjunction with the other authentication methods. This enables us to encrypt the information transmitted and ensure that no message tampering occurs.

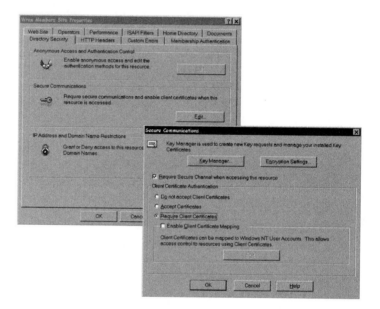

Membership Directory Authentication

When we explored the Membership Directory, we saw that every membership object has a Security property sheet, and this is where the ACLs are specified.

Enabling anonymous access and specifying the authentication mechanisms to be employed are done through the Membership Directory Security property sheet found from the LDAP Service properties dialog.

An anonymous user accessing the Membership Directory will run under the following user-security context:

- For Windows NT Authentication mode: LDAP_Anonymous
- For Membership Authentication mode: cn=Anonymous

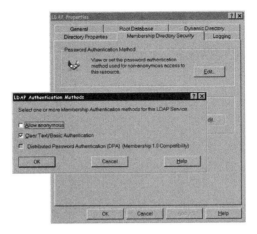

Using the same Membership Directory Security property sheet, we can force the information to always be transmitted over a secured channel.

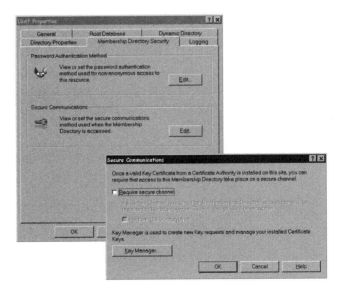

Membership Users

Recapping from above, three types of users are handled by Membership Server:

- Anonymous Users
- Cookie-Identified Users
- Registered Users

We shall now investigate each of these in greater depth and consider further the different membership-authentication mechanisms available. We start with the anonymous user.

Anonymous Users

Even in a site that implements a Membership area, we will frequently require that some of our Web pages be available for public access, such as marketing information or a registration page.

Using the Membership Authentication property sheet within the Internet Service Manager (MMC), we can enable anonymous users by turning on the Allow Anonymous checkbox.

The Allow Anonymous checkbox works in tandem with the ACLs applied on the Web content to decide whether authentication is required:

- Authentication is not performed (i.e., the user is logged on anonymously) if the Allow Anonymous checkbox is enabled and the Web content is secured such that the Everyone group has access
- Authentication is performed (i.e., the user is logged on anonymously) if either:
  - the Allow Anonymous checkbox is turned off
  - the Web content is secured such that the Everyone group does not have access

An anonymous Web site visitor will run under the user security context of `IUSR_sysname` (where `sysname` is the computer name of the Windows NT system). When IIS accesses Web content under the anonymous user, it will ensure that the `IUSR_sysname` user has been granted permission to retrieve the resource. This is the same as the standard IIS authentication that we met in Chapter 4.

Cookie-Identified Users

Cookie-Identified Users are site visitors that can remain anonymous (i.e., run under the security context of `IUSR_sysname`) but are tracked and profiled by using cookies. We have already met cookies several times in the book. As was explained, they are a general mechanism used by a Web server to store attribute/value pairs at the Web browser and then, much later, retrieve and use these values. We shall now discuss how Membership Server handles Cookie-Identified Users and see the processing that occurs.

Automatic Cookie Authentication is enabled using the Membership Authentication property sheet within the Internet Service Manager (MMC). It is done by turning on the Automatic Cookie Authentication checkbox.

When Automatic Cookie Authentication is enabled and a user accesses the site for the first time, the Membership Authentication (an ISAPI filter) intercepts the request and detects that the user has not yet been identified.

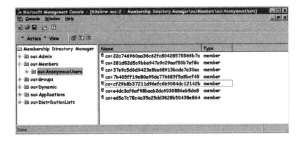

A globally unique identifier (GUID) is then generated and an entry is created in the Membership Directory; an HTTP response is then made with a cookie called SITE-SERVER containing the GUID.

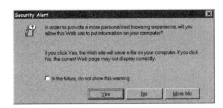

Hopefully the user will have set his browser to automatically accept cookies. If not, and the user decides to reject the cookie, the user will be redirected to a page stating that he must accept cookies.

When the SITE-SERVER cookie is accepted, the Web browser

will automatically request the original URL from the Web server. It will also send the SITESERVER cookie.

When the Membership Authentication detects an HTTP request with the SITESERVER cookie, a user-security context for **IUSR_sysname** is created for the session. Access will be permitted to all Web content that is secured for access by the Everyone group.

Remember that a Cookie-Identified User can access "restricted content" but not "secured content."

Automatic Cookie Authentication in Action

Let us test this out and navigate to a page that has been secured for Automatic Cookie Authentication. The ASP logic on the page will display the SITESERVER cookies and the REMOTE_USER server variable.

First we must use the MMC to configure the directory for Automatic Cookie Authentication. This is enabled at the directory level using the Membership Authentication property sheet.

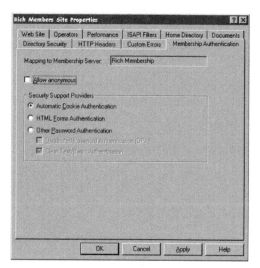

Next we must apply permissions to the appropriate Web content so that the Everyone group has read access.

TESTING IT OUT

We can see from the browser output that a GUID has been generated. This is stored in the SITESERVER cookie. Furthermore, a user object corresponding to this cookie value is created in the Membership Directory.

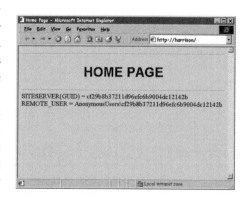

If we examine the Attributes property sheet for the user object, we see that no attributes exist at this stage. We shall see in the next chapter how to programmatically store attribute information in the user object for personalization, site analysis, or marketing purposes.

The source for this example is very simple and given in full below. The main logic for displaying all of the cookies in an HTTP request has

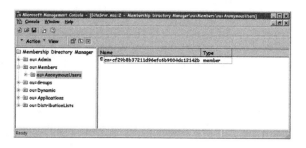

been separated into its own file, **dumpcookies.asp**, and included into the main logic. (You may find this logic useful elsewhere when debugging your Web applications.)

default.asp

```
<%@LANGUAGE="VBSCRIPT" %>
<% Option Explicit %>

<HTML>
<HEAD><TITLE>Home Page</TITLE>
</HEAD>

<BODY bgcolor="pink">
<HR>
<H1 align="center">
<FONT face="Arial">HOME PAGE</FONT></H1>
<HR>

<!-- #include file="dumpcookies.inc" -->
<% Response.Write "REMOTE_USER = " %>
<% = Request.ServerVariables("REMOTE_USER") %>

</BODY>
</HTML>
```

dumpcookies.inc

```
<%
    Dim vItem, vSubItem

    For Each vItem In Request.Cookies
        If Request.Cookies(vItem).HasKeys then
            For Each vSubItem In Request.Cookies(vItem)
                Response.Write vItem & "(" & vSubItem & ") = " & _
                    Request.Cookies(vItem)(vSubItem) & "<BR>"
            Next
        Else
            Response.Write vItem & " = " & Request.Cookies(vItem) &
"<BR>"
```
(continued)

```
        End If
    Next
%>
```

Registered Users

Registered Users are site visitors identified by a username and authenticated by much stronger security mechanisms than the cookie identification processes we have just considered. By assigning Registered Users into administrative groups, we can selectively give access to various items of secured Web-site content.

With Membership Server, users can be authenticated using the Basic Authentication or Distributed Password Authentication. When a user navigates to secured Web content, the Web server requests user credentials before proceeding. This protocol causes the Web browser to display a dialog for the user to enter his username and a password.

An alternative and much more flexible mechanism is the HTML Forms Authentication provided by Membership Server.

Like the standard IIS authentication we have already met, the HTML Forms Authentication is another mechanism where a Registered User's identity is validated by his submitting his user name/password when prompted. However, with this process the information is entered into a standard HTML form on a Web page that can be fully customized and branded as required.

When HTML Forms Authentication is enabled and a user accesses a protected page for the first time, the Membership Authentication (an ISAPI filter) intercepts the request and detects that the user has not yet been identified. The user is then redirected to the Web page that allows his credentials to be submitted for authentication.

If the details prove to be valid, a session cookie containing a hashed version of the user's credentials and timestamp is planted on the client machine and the user is redirected on to the original requested URL.

Membership Authentication validates all subsequent requests by checking the contents of the session cookie. If no activity occurs for a period of time (configurable), the session cookie will expire and the user must reenter his credentials into the same HTML log on form. Because this session cookie is vulnerable to interception over the Internet, it is recommended that for high-risk sites all pages should be protected by SSL.

Membership Sample Pages

When a Web site gets mapped on to using Membership Authentication, a virtual root called _mem_bin is added to the Web site.

This points to a physical directory containing a number of ASP Web pages and software components that can be used to handle the Membership logic. For example, to capture the user's credentials in the scenario described above, the Web browser gets redirected to the **formslogin.asp**.

The virtual root _mem_bin contains a

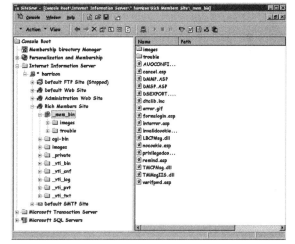

subdirectory called trouble. This contains a set of pages used to help a site visitor troubleshoot a problem when he has problems with Membership Authentication. These get invoked automatically by the Membership Authentication or can be called by our own logic.

As an alternative, all of these pages can be used as the basis for our own membership ASP pages and can be amended, as we feel fit, to take on the same look and feel as the rest of our site. In this case, we just point the virtual root to a physical directory that contains our customized versions.

HTML Forms Authentication in Action

It's again time to test this all out. We shall navigate to a page that has been secured for HTML Forms Authentication. The ASP logic on the page will display the cookies and the REMOTE_USER server variable.

First we must use the MMC to configure the directory for HTML Forms Authentication. This is enabled at the directory level, using the Membership Authentication property sheet.

Next we shall create two members called Fred and Bert, and a user group called Rich Managers.

Then we shall make Fred a member of Rich Managers.

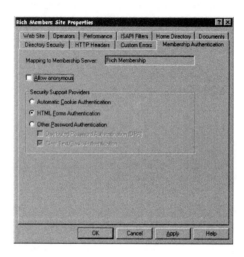

CREATING A USER GROUP

We create a user group by right-clicking on the organization unit called ou=groups and selecting the menu option New|User. This invokes a wizard to:

- Create and name a new group
- Add attributes for the group
- Add members to the group

The first item requested is the name of the group. In our example we shall call it Rich Managers.

Next, we can optionally add a description attribute. Attributes are selected from a list given by clicking on the Add Attributes button.

Finally, we can add members. However, in our example we have not yet added Fred and Bert. A list of members to select from is given by clicking on the Add button.

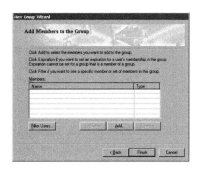

This will create a corresponding user group called Site_Rich Membership_Rich Managers in the Windows NTDS database. We must secure our Web content, using the Security property sheet in Windows Explorer, so that this user group has read access.

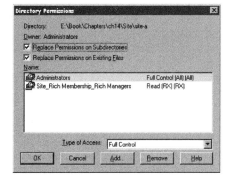

Remember that a Membership Directory group called **groupname** maps on to a Windows NT group called **Site_directoryname_groupname**.

CREATING A USER

We create a user by right-clicking on the organization unit called ou=Members and selecting the menu option New|User. This invokes a wizard to:

- Create and name a new member
- Add attributes for the member
- Add group membership for the member

The first item requested is the name of the member. In our example we shall call him Fred (and the subsequent time Bert).

Next, we must add:

- An **account-status** of 1 (see below)
- **User-password** with a value that we must remember

Attributes are selected from a list given by clicking on the **Add Attributes** button.

Finally, we can assign the member to a group. With **Fred** only, we add him to the **Rich Managers** group. A list of groups to select from is given by clicking on the **Add** button.

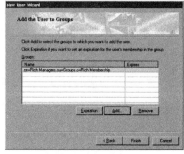

All membership accounts in the Membership Directory must have the attribute **account-status**; the values are:

1. . . active—this is the only value that Membership Authentication will successfully authenticate
2. . . pending—used while a background check is being undertaken
3. . . disabled—used to temporarily suspend account activity.
4. . . to be deleted

It is possible to set an expiration date for the user being a member of a group. When this expires, **account-status** automatically gets set to a value of 4. The administrator can remove all expired users from the groups by invoking a Microsoft-supplied script.

Another Microsoft-supplied script enables the **account-status** attribute to be changed to 4 for all users who have not visited the site for a certain period of time and thus can be assumed unlikely to return. This could be useful where a large number of Cookie-Identified Users has been accumulated.

TESTING IT OUT

When we try to navigate to our secured site, Membership Authentication intercepts our request and processes the ASP file called **Forms Login.asp**.

If we try to access with Fred's credentials, we are successfully authenticated and redirected to the original URL requested.

The ASP code for this is the same as in the above Cookie-Identified User example. However, note the difference in the cookies used.

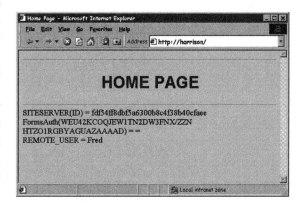

However, if we try to access with Bert's credentials (he is not a Rich Manager), our request is rejected and we are redirected to PrivilegedContent.asp

If we amend Fred's account-status to 3 and try to log on as Fred, we also get redirected to this page.

■ Summary

This concludes the first part of our investigation into Microsoft Membership Server, which provides comprehensive functionality for building a Web community with a scalable management solution. In this chapter we have looked at the main components of the membership architecture and seen the various options available for membership authentication.

The key points in this chapter are:

- Membership Server can scale to track and profile millions of users, protect restricted areas of a Web site, and automate the identification of users by using cookies.

- The main components of the membership architecture are the Membership Directory, the LDAP Service, the Authentication Service, and Active User Objects.

- The Membership Directory is a central repository for organization and personal-profile information that will be used by our Web site.

- Security information can be stored in either the Membership Directory (Membership Authentication Mode) or Windows NTDS database (Windows NT Authentication Mode).

- Web content may be secured (users must be authenticated), restricted (users need not be authenticated but are tracked/profiled), or public (no access restrictions).

- Web visitors may be registered users (authenticated), cookie identified users or anonymous users.

- Registered users can be authenticated using Basic Authentication, HTML Forms Authentication, Client-side digital certificates, or Distributed Password Authentication.

- Identifying a Member and mapping him onto a Windows NT group to obtain an ACL is the basis for establishing what content a user can access. A Membership Directory group called groupname maps on to a Windows NT group called Site_directoryname_groupname.

We shall now proceed to see how Active User Objects can be used to programmatically store attribute information about the Web visitor. This can be used for personalization, site analysis, or marketing purposes.

Active User Objects

In the previous chapter we introduced a major element of Microsoft Site Server (Membership and Personalization) called Active User Objects (AUO). We mentioned briefly that it provided a unified access mechanism and single interface to all user-profile information coming from a variety of sources. Now is the time to investigate AUO in greater depth and see how it combines with ADSI to provide an invaluable tool in our membership solutions.

In this chapter we shall see how to use ASP to interface with AUO to:

- Automatically identify a Web user and provide access to their associated personal attributes. Such information about the user could be located in a number of different datastores.

- Allow users to register their details and update their profiles online. This avoids the need for the user to contact central administration whenever any changes are required. Furthermore, the

519

captured information can be used to establish a channel for targeted marketing. Many companies have found this an effective tool to help focus their limited resources in the most cost effective manner

• Intelligently use the information in the user's profile in order to make the information more fitting by providing personalized pages. With the vast amount of information the Internet now provides, it is important to help the user to avoid an overload of irrelevant data

But first, let us delve a little deeper into how AUO actually operates.

AUO . . . A Container of ADSI Objects

Put simply, AUO provides us with a simple and convenient mechanism for ASP script logic to interface with all information that might be associated with a Web-site visitor. Such information might even be distributed across an enterprise and located in a number of data stores such as Membership Server, a mail system, a database, and so on.

AUO provides a single interface by extending ADSI to consolidate the user attributes into a single namespace. Furthermore, it insulates the ASP script logic from the following complexities:

• The actual location of the data—this could be located on the same machine as the Web server, on the same LAN, or distributed halfway around the world on the Internet

• The mechanisms used to access the data—AUO supports any data store that can be accessed by ADSI

• How to identify/authenticate the user—this is done by AUO impersonating the currently logged-on user, who is identified either by the **SITESERVER GUID** cookie (Cookie-Identified Users) or by his user name (Registered Users); such authentication was discussed in the previous chapter.

As an example, consider the diagram below that illustrates a possible scenario where ASP interfaces with user-profile information stored in a number of different locations.

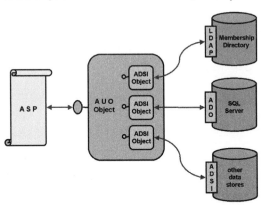

We can see that AUO acts as a container of ADSI objects—one for each target location. But providing just a single interface makes life much simpler for the ASP script developer.

The ADSI objects contained by the AUO object are configured by means of the **AUO Providers** property sheet. Selecting properties on the Membership Server instance in MMC accesses this dialog.

Additional AUO providers can be configured by means of the **Add** button.

We can inspect the default entry, which is always the Membership Directory, by selecting **Edit**.

When the AUO object is instantiated, it represents the current Web user; the ADSI objects it creates must run under the security context associated with that user.

Recapping from when we introduced ADSI in Chapter 12, an ADSI object is obtained by specifying the **ADsPath** name. In the above screenshot showing the **AUO Provider Properties**, we can see that the ADSI object name is specified. In fact, this is only part of the full **ADsPath** name that is actually used. Appended to this name is a suffix item that makes the actual ADSI object name user-specific. The options available for the suffix are:

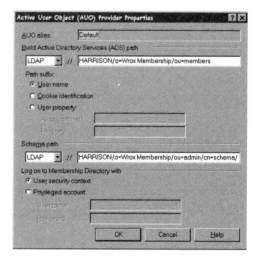

- The user name taken from the **REMOTE_USER** server variable
- The **SITESERVER GUID** (cookie identifier)
- A user property (attribute) from the directory

For example, if we have

a prefix = LDAP://HARRISON/o=Rich Membership/ou=members

and a REMOTE_USER = harrison\richard

then our full ADsPath name would be

**LDAP://HARRISON/o=Rich Membership/ou=members/ou=harrison/
cn=richard**

Dealing with User Directory Attributes

An AUO instance is created using the **Membership.Userobjects** progid.
Once it has been instantiated, it provides an interface into the user properties (attributes) stored in the default provider plus any number of secondary
providers.

> The default provider is always the Membership Directory. Secondary
> providers are any data source accessible using ADSI.

The AUO should only be created once for each ASP page invoked.
When the logic to handle each attribute needs to be encapsulated—in an
"include" file, for example, or a Design Time Control (explained below)—
we can conditionally test for its existence before creation as follows:

```
<%
    If Not isObject(User) Then      ' User is a page level variable
        Set User = Server.CreateObject("Membership.UserObjects")
    End If
%>
```

Reading Attributes: Default Provider

We can access the user properties using the ADSI methods such as **get**. As
an example, the following code would extract the user's first name and sur-
name, and display a personalized welcome message:

```
Welcome <B><% = User.get("givenName") %> <% = User.get("sn") %>
</B>
```

This would required the `givenName` and `sn` attributes to exist in the user's entry in the Membership Directory (the default provider). Properties can take on any name, provided they have been defined in the Directory schema. We shall meet the **User Attribute Editor** later in this chapter and see how these attributes are defined.

Alternatively, the properties can be accessed as direct properties (using the **dynamic property syntax**) on the object, as illustrated here:

```
Welcome <B><% = User.givenName %> <% = User.sn %></B>
```

Attributes that contain a "-" character cannot be used with the dynamic property syntax. The Microsoft Directory Manager does not allow us to create attributes that contain the "-", so this is only an issue when using other AUO providers.

There is an exception with the dynamic property syntax that needs to be noted: to access the user's unique id (the cookie GUID), we must use the ADSI methods as below. Using **User.GUID** retrieves the GUID of the User object's Class definition.

```
Users GUID = <% = User.get("GUID") %>
```

Reading Attributes: Secondary Providers

We saw above that AUO could encompass multiple AUO providers. If the attributes were in a secondary AUO provider called, for example, **custdb**, the above code would become:

```
Welcome <B><% = User("custdb").givenName %>
     <% = User("custdb").sn %></B>
```

Setting Attributes

We can set a value in the AUO provider by assigning a value to the relevant property in the **User** object and then calling the **SetInfo** method. The following example shows setting the **mail** attribute located in the AUO default provider:

```
<%
    User.mail = "rich@cyberdude.com"
    User.SetInfo
%>
```

Attributes can have multiple values. These can be set and retrieved using arrays. As an example, consider the following code that shows how to set a multi-value attribute and then retrieve/display its contents:

```
<%
    User.TechInterests = Array("VB","ASP","IIS","DHTML")
    User.SetInfo
%>
```

```
<%

    Interests = User.TechInterests
    For Each Interest in Interests
        Response.Write Interest & ", "
    Next
%>
```

In the above examples, the processing to access and update an attribute is relatively simple. Things get a little trickier when handling some types of attributes. For example, special validation processing should be done for items such as passwords or those that can take multiple values from a defined list of acceptable values. We shall be tackling these later in the chapter by using Design Time Controls to assist us.

Site Vocabulary

The Site Vocabulary is a set of key terms and values that a Web application can call upon and utilize within the script logic processing. Rather than hard-code such values in the Web application, it is better to retrieve and use items stored in the central Site Vocabulary. If a change is required, it is easier to amend this single location rather than hack through numerous ASP source files.

The Site Vocabulary is located at:

```
modelName=default, ou=Tag Terms, ou=Other, ou=Admin
```

For example, item lists can be stored in the Site Vocabulary in an area called **Enumerated Lists.** Lists can be managed using the directory management tools and various APIs.

We shall see how to do this later in the chapter when we set up a fixed list of Technical Interests . . . as shown in the screenshot.

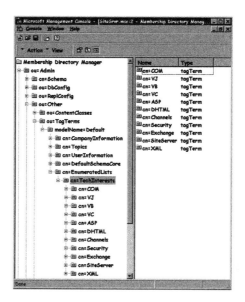

We shall now discuss a mechanism called **Design Time Controls** that provides a very simple method of generating complex or lengthy script logic by means of setting a few configuration parameters. Site Server includes a number of Design Time Controls that make the handling of AUO and user attributes simpler.

Design Time Controls

A Design Time Control (DTC) is a special type of ActiveX control that is used exclusively when a page is authored (i.e., at design time). Each control is designed to automate the generation of HTML and ASP logic for a specific task.

A DTC provides an easy-to-understand user interface that captures the author's requirements and then processes the specified options to insert appropriate HTML and ASP into the file currently being edited. The generated code is then used later at run-time (either on the client-side or the server-side). At this time the DTC has no involvement. The information about the

DTC is included in the file but wrapped within an ASP/HTML comment so as not to be processed at run-time.

The use of DTCs insulates the developer from any complex or lengthy functionality. This can obviously save a lot of time and reduces the likelihood of any bugs.

By using ActiveX technologies, DTCs can be invoked by any DTC compliant editor. Obviously, the latest Microsoft FrontPage and Visual InterDev development tools support DTCs.

When using Visual InterDev, a list of DTC Controls is displayed in the ToolBox under the Design-Time Controls tab. This list can be customized to only show those that the developer frequently uses. To see the complete list available and choose what is shown in the Toolbox, select the Tools|Customize Toolbox menu option.

A DTC can be inserted within a page at the current cursor position, by clicking on the DTC in the Toolbox. The control then appears on the page being edited. The actual interface to the control will differ from one DTC to another. Typically, they provide an interface allowing the main options to be selected directly in the editor by the page author. Additionally, the complete set of properties can be changed via the Properties window or by right-clicking on the control and selecting the Properties menu option.

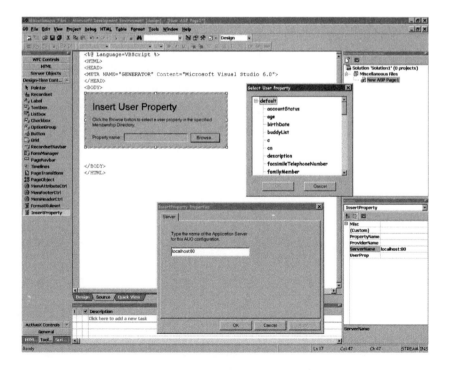

Once all of the page author's selections have been made, we can look at the script logic that the control has generated by right-clicking on the control and selecting the Show Run-time Text menu option.

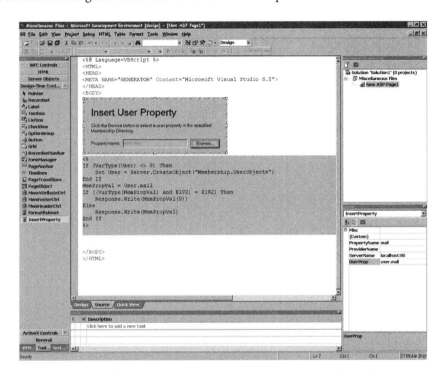

It is possible to manually edit the generated text; but if we change the text and then reinstantiate the DTC, our amendments will be lost.

If we want to amend the DTC-generated text, the best approach is to first delete the information about the DTC and just leave the text that the control generated. This can be done by right-clicking on the control and selecting the Convert to Run-time Text menu option.

The above screenshots show the **Insert User Property DTC**. The code it generates achieves similar functionality to that described in our discussion above on creating the AUO and reading a user attribute. We shall now take a more in-depth look at this DTC and then follow up with a look at the other DTCs provided for handling membership.

INSERT USER PROPERTY DTC

The Insert User Property DTC, as its name would suggest, inserts a user property in the Web page.

The property is pulled from the directory (AUO provider) specified in the ProviderName property (or if not set, then from the default AUO provider).

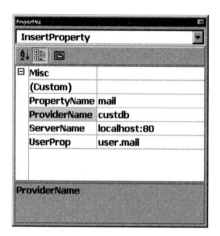

From the screenshot above, where we showed the ASP code that this DTC generates, we can see that if the user property is a multi-value attribute, then only the first value is displayed.

We would have to manually edit the script logic if we required the other values to be displayed.

Membership Design Time Controls

There are three Membership DTCs that are designed to assist in the development of HTML forms for ASP pages handling user registration/profile capture tasks, such as obtaining user information for the first time or allowing a user to update his details. Web sites should ideally be designed to allow users to maintain their own information so that this relieves one's own staff of any administration burden.

The three Membership DTCs are:

- Membership Header DTC
- Membership Attribute DTC
- Membership Footer DTC

These controls must be used together, in the above order, on the ASP page to create an HTML form. There will be one Membership Attribute DTC for each user property in the form. However, there can only be one Membership Header DTC and one Membership Footer DTC present.

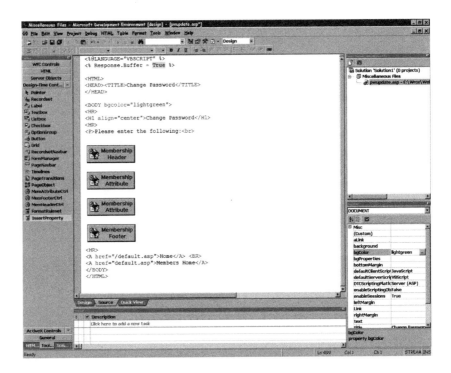

In addition, the following statement must be present at the top of the ASP page:

```
<% Response.Buffer = True %>
```

This prevents the HTTP Response (in particular the HTTP Response Headers) from being sent until the DTC-generated script logic has completed its processing.

MEMBERSHIP HEADER DTC

The Membership Header DTC will generate the HTML for the start of the form and must be positioned before the other membership DTCs. Its mechanics are specified via the following property sheets.

The General property sheet allows us to specify the task for the Web page. The options available are dependent on what authentication mode we are using:

- When operating in Membership Authentication mode, we can either Create a new user and ensure that it is unique or Update an existing user.

- When operating in Windows NT Authentication mode, the user must already exist as an NT account and so we can only use the Update an existing user option.

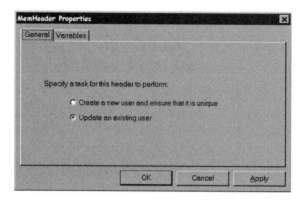

The Variables property sheet allows us to specify certain items to insert into the Web page.

The ScriptID must be set when operating in "Create a new user" mode. It must be a user present in the Membership Directory that has sufficient privilege to create new users.

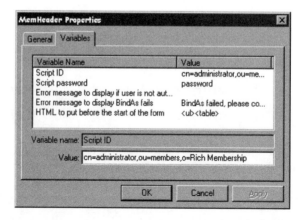

The Script Password must be a valid password for the ScriptID user.

HTML to put before the start of the form allows us to insert some HTML. This often contains the `<TABLE>` tag to start a table so that the latter attribute text legends and fields can be smartly formatted.

We can also configure several error messages:

- If a user is not authenticated
- If BindAs fails ("bind" is the name of the operation where we request that the AUO function under the security context of the ScriptID user)

MEMBERSHIP ATTRIBUTE DTC

The Membership Attribute DTC is included once for each user property required in the page.

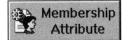

The Attribute property sheet allows us to specify the user property.

A full list of attribute types that the AUO provider(s) supports (i.e., the attribute schema) can be retrieved using the Get Attributes button. This then populates the tree on the right-hand side from which the required AUO provider and attribute can be selected. We shall see shortly how to manage the attribute schema.

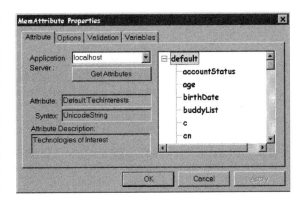

The Options property sheet allows us to specify the type of user interface that will be used in the Web page.

The options in the dropdown-list box for the UI type will be dependent on the attribute type. For example, single text line, drop down list

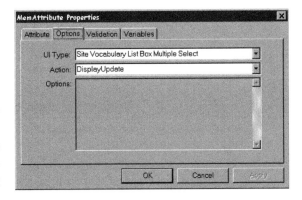

box, radio buttons, etc. Certain options become available for those attributes that require special processing, e.g., username and passwords.

The Action option specifies whether the attribute is to be display, updated, or both.

Items used for UI types that require selection from a list are specified in the Options box.

The Validation property sheet allows us to specify the specific field validation.

If Input Required is enabled, the client-side run-time processing will not complete unless this attribute has been entered.

Integer values can be restricted to be within a certain range. Likewise, the length of strings can be restricted to be within a certain range.

The Vocab option enables an attribute to be restricted to values in a list specified in the Site Vocabulary. The Site Vocabulary can be displayed on the right-hand side by means of the View Site Vocabulary button. The node containing the required values can then be selected.

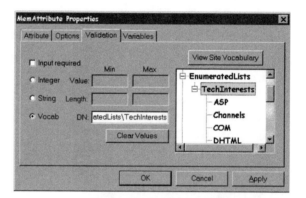

The Variables property sheet allows us to specify any values to format the screen. It allows us to include any HTML that we required to be inserted before and after the field.

Depending on the UI type, additional vari-

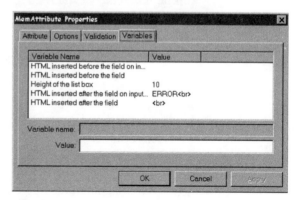

ables may be included to control the interface. In the example screenshot, there is the option to specify the height of the list box.

MEMBERSHIP FOOTER DTC

The Membership Footer DTC adds the Submit button and completes the HTML form.

As before, the Variables property sheet allows us to specify any values to format the screen. It allows us to include any HTML that we required to be inserted.

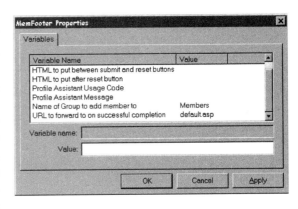

In addition, we can enable the Profile Assistant (discussed in Chapter 11) so that information can be transferred from the user profile to the form, thereby avoiding any tedious keystrokes. A non-blank Profile Assistant Usage Code will enable this facility.

The Name of Group to add member to specifies a Directory group that you wish the user to become a member of.

The URL to forward to on successful completion specifies the page which gets called next.

We shall see an example of the Membership DTCs in action later in the chapter.

Editing User Attributes

Up to now we have administered the Membership services using snap-ins for the MMC.

An alternative mechanism is the Web-based Administration (**WebAdmin**) interface that is accessed via a Web browser and enables the administration tasks to be done remotely. The URL for WebAdmin

http://harrison:7486/SiteServer/Admin/

This is for my machine called **harrison** with the administration Web running on port 7486. Replace machine name and port number appropriately.

Some tasks that are quite complex to undertake via the MMC snap-ins have been simplified in the WebAdmin interface by providing a wizard. This

takes the administrator through a series of dialogs to determine the requirements and then completes the request.

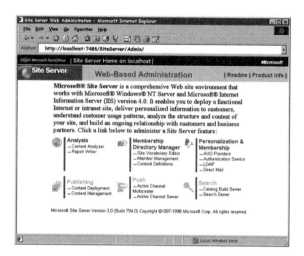

An example of a task that is handled more easily via the WebAdmin interface is "Editing User Attributes."

User Attribute Editor

We can edit the list of User Attributes (in the Membership Schema) by
means of the WebAdmin User Attribute Editor, accessed via the Membership
Directory Manager.
This facility is available
from the main WebAd-
min menu screen.

When entering
this facility, we have to
select the Membership
Server instance and pro-
vide a suitable username
and password (the
membership adminis-
trator's credentials will
give us full access).

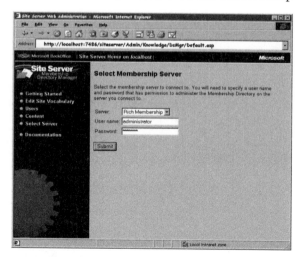

The User Attribute Editor is available from the Users menu option.

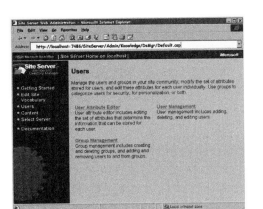 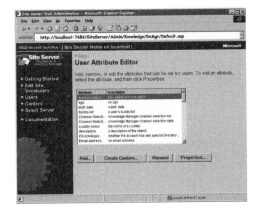

The User Attribute Editor displays the full list of available user attributes defined in the Membership Schema.

By means of the Properties button we can inspect the:

- Attribute name (this can be amended)
- Attribute description (this can be amended)
- Attribute syntax
- Attribute constraints (these can be set/amended)

Earlier, when discussing the Membership Attribute DTC, we saw a screenshot that included an attribute called Tech-Interests that is not a standard attribute installed by default. We shall now see how this is added to the Membership Schema.

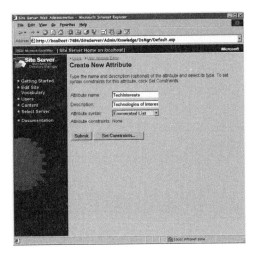

We create new attributes by means of the Create Custom button.

In this example, we have set up a multi-value attribute called TechInterests that can store the Technical Interests of a user in the Membership Directory.

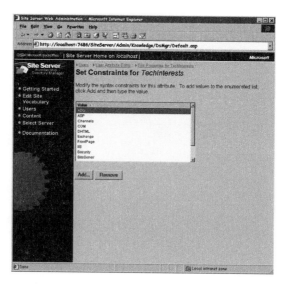

We shall see below how to create a Web page that enables a user to select whichever of the available values are appropriate to him and store them in the TechInterests attribute located in his Membership Directory entry.

We can then specify the details for the attributes and set any constraints for the attribute value.

The 'Members' Application

We shall now demonstrate a Web site for an organization that wishes to establish a channel for targeted marketing through profiling the users by collecting their personal information and interests. Many companies have found that building a Web community is an effective tool in helping to establish customer loyalty.

The application allows two types of site visitors:

- Anonymous users who may:
  - visit a subset of the site including a registration page
- "Registered" members who may:
  - visit the members site
  - administer their personal details
  - change their passwords
  - provide information about their main interests
  - cancel their membership

Application Strategy

The site is designed such that the Web contents and application logic are partitioned around two distinct subdirectories:

- The Anonymous area—the home directory (or virtual directory) containing the files that can be accessed by anyone
- The "Members" area—the subdirectory called "restricted" containing the files that combine to form the restricted area of the site

The Anonymous area has NT permissions applied such that the Everyone user group has read access.

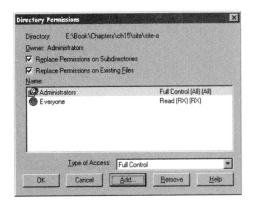

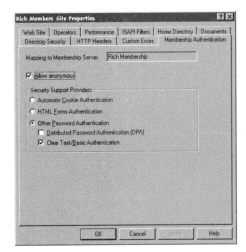

The Membership Authentication for this directory is set to **Allow Anonymous** access.

We require the Restricted area to be limited to those members of a group in the Membership Directory called **Members**.

This is achieved by applying Windows NT file permissions such that read access is limited to the Site_Rich Membership_Members user group (our Membership Directory is called Rich Membership). Note too that we allow the site administrators full access for development reasons.

The Membership Authentication for this directory is set to HTML Forms Authentication.

A user who navigates to the restricted area of the site will be redirected to the **formslogin.asp** page where his credentials will be requested.

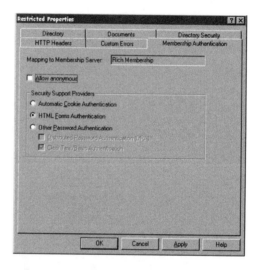

We met **formslogin.asp** in the previous chapter; an example is provided as part of Membership Server; but in this example, we shall customize it to our exact requirements.

On submitting the details, the user will be authenticated and if identified to be a valid member of the Members group will be then redirected onto the originally requested page.

Application Architecture

The directories and the ASP logic implemented are as follows:
The Anonymous area:

- **default.asp**—handles the main screen/menu options.
- **register.asp**—handles the capture of user details when applying for membership.
- **complete.asp**—handles the processing when a user's registration details are successfully accepted; this is configured in the Membership Footer DTC.

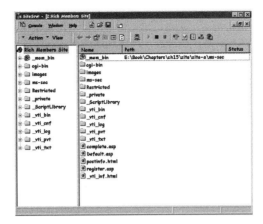

The other files and directories are for configuration information used by the FrontPage Server Extensions (we discussed these in Chapter 4).

When a Web site gets mapped onto a Membership Server Instance, a virtual root called **_mem_bin** is added to the Web site. This points to a physical directory containing a number of ASP Web pages and software components that can be used to handle the Membership logic.

We have taken a copy of these standard ASP pages and amended the virtual root so that it points to the physical directory where our version resides. This allows us to customize their look and feel to fit in with our own site.

In particular, this directory contains:

- **formslogin.asp**—handles the capture of the user's authentication credentials

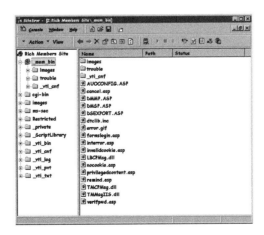

The Members' area:

- **default.asp**—handles the main screen/menu options
- **membership.asp**—handles the menu options for membership administration
- **detupdate.asp**—handles the updating of user details
- **pwupdate.asp**—handles the change of user password
- **preferences.asp**—handles the setting of user preferences; in our example we allow the user to specify his technical interests (stored in the new TechInterests attribute created earlier)
- **cancel.asp**—handles a user canceling their membership

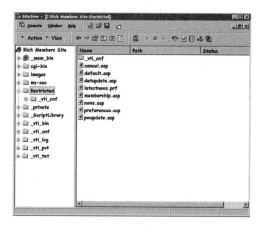

The other two files, **news.asp** and **latestnews.prf,** are used to demonstrate personalized content and will be discussed later in the chapter.

Application Logic

Let us now look at the main points of interest in the application.

Register Details for Membership

Registering the user's details is implemented using **register.asp**. This page is built using the Membership DTCs and will capture the following attributes:

- Username
- Password (twice to ensure no typos)

- Password reminder (a phrase that helps the user remember his password; should be personal and cryptic so that no one else would be able to determine the password from this information)
- Name (First name and Last name)
- E-mail address
- Address (Street, City, State, Zip Code, and Country)

In the Membership Footer DTC we:

- Enable the Profile Assistant so that many of the attributes do not have to be keyed in by the user
- Set the next page for successful completion to `complete.asp`
- Specify that on successful completion the user will be added to the Members group.

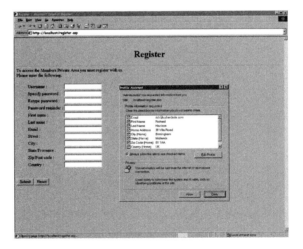

Authentication

The main menu contains a hyperlink to enter the 'Members' site. This link navigates to the `restricted/default.asp` file. However, the membership authentication filter will intercept the request and, to handle the authentication process, will route the user to the `_mem_bin/formslogin.asp` page.

Our version of this ASP file is based on the standard example supplied by Microsoft but has been customized to look consistent with the rest of our site. We have also implemented a variable in the `Session` object that counts how many times authentication has been attempted. A user who issues wrong credentials three times is locked out completely for that session.

```
<% Session("log oncount") = Session("log oncount") + 1 %>
<% If Session("log oncount") > 3 then %>
   <P>Maximum number of log on attempts has been exceeded.<BR>
   Return to <A href="/default.asp">Home</A>
<% Else %>
```

Provided that this count has not been exceeded, an HTML form is displayed to request the user's name and password. These details are submitted to the Microsoft-supplied **verifpwd.asp** for authentication. Provided that the credentials are accepted, the user is then redirected to the originally requested URL.

For high-risk sites, this form should be accessed using SSL so that this private information is transmitted in an encrypted form. With HTML Forms Authentication, only this page needs to be encrypted.

> This contrasts with Clear Text Authentication, where every subsequent HTTP request includes the password credentials, and so for complete confidence, we must apply encryption for every page in the session— very inefficient!

Attribute Maintenance

The attribute maintenance has been split into three distinct pages:

- Change password
- Update details
- Specify preferences

Each of these pages is built using the Membership DTCs to display and capture the user attributes.

Cancel Membership

The cancel membership page is used to allow users to cancel their memberships. We discussed this in the previous chapter and saw that an attribute called account-status is amended to indicate that the user is awaiting deletion. A script invoked by the administrator does the actual deletion.

The ASP page is called twice: first to display a message requesting the user to confirm the request, and second to process the cancellation. The page is forced into the second stage by passing a parameter state with a value of 2.

To amend the account-status attribute for a member, we must invoke the action under the user-security context of the Membership Administrator. We saw earlier in this chapter that the **BindAs** method is used to request that the AUO function under the security context of a particular user.

```
<%
    vMemUserScriptID = "cn=administrator,ou=members,o=Rich Membership"
    vMemUserPassword = "password"
%>
```

```
<%
    Set objUser = Server.CreateObject("Membership.UserObjects")
    objUser.BindAs "", vMemUserScriptID, vMemUserPassword
    objUser.accountStatus = 4
    objUser.SetInfo
%>
```

Note that the actual schema name for the attribute is **accountStatus**; the hyphen is only present in the display name of this attribute.

How it was done—for our eyes only!

The application code for the "Members" Site, in its entirety, is as follows:

Web Site Code

default.asp

```
<%@LANGUAGE="VBSCRIPT" %>
<% Option Explicit %>

<HTML>
<HEAD><TITLE>Home Page</TITLE>
</HEAD>

<BODY bgcolor="lightblue">
<HR>
<H1 align="center">Home Page</H1>
<HR>
<A href="restricted/default.asp">Members Area</A><BR>
<A href="register.asp">Register</A>
</BODY>
</HTML>
```

register.asp

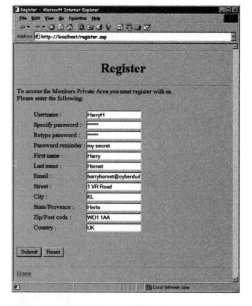

```
<%@LANGUAGE="VBSCRIPT" %>
<% Response.Buffer = True %>

<HTML>
<HEAD><TITLE>Register</TITLE>
</HEAD>
```

```
<BODY bgcolor="lightblue">
<HR>
<H1 align="center">Register</H1>
<HR>
To access the Members Private Area you must register with us.<BR>
Please enter the following:<br>
```

Membership Header	Task : Create a new user and ensure that it is unique Script ID : cn=administrator,ou=members,o=Rich Membership Script password : password
Membership Attribute	Attribute : cn (common name) UI type : Username Action : Update
Membership Attribute	Attribute : userPassword (password) UI type : Specify password Action : Update Validation : String 1 to 16 characters
Membership Attribute	Attribute : passwordReminder (reminder phrase) UI type : Single Line Text Action : Update
Membership Attribute	Attribute : givenName (firstname) UI type : Single Line Text Action : Update
Membership Attribute	Attribute : sn (surname) UI type : Single Line Text Action : Update
Membership Attribute	Attribute : mail (e-mail address) UI type : Single Line Text Action : Update
Membership Attribute	Attribute : street (address) UI type : Single Line Text Action : Update

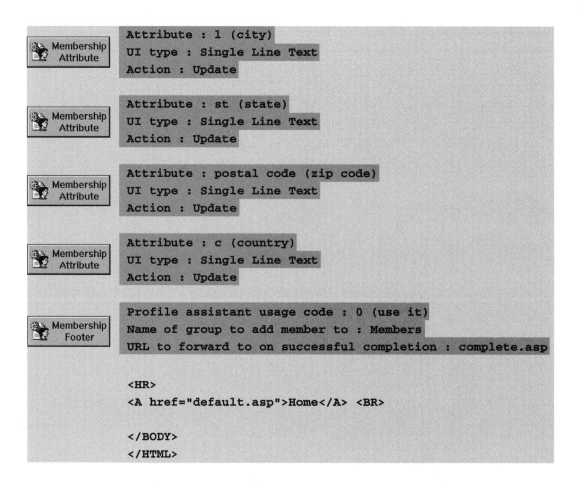

```
Membership    Attribute : 1 (city)
Attribute     UI type : Single Line Text
              Action : Update

Membership    Attribute : st (state)
Attribute     UI type : Single Line Text
              Action : Update

Membership    Attribute : postal code (zip code)
Attribute     UI type : Single Line Text
              Action : Update

Membership    Attribute : c (country)
Attribute     UI type : Single Line Text
              Action : Update

Membership    Profile assistant usage code : 0 (use it)
Footer        Name of group to add member to : Members
              URL to forward to on successful completion : complete.asp


<HR>
<A href="default.asp">Home</A> <BR>

</BODY>
</HTML>
```

complete.asp

```
<%@ LANGUAGE="VBScript" %>
<% Response.Buffer = True %>
```

```
<HTML>
<HEAD><TITLE>Successful Registration</TITLE>
</HEAD>

<BODY bgcolor="lightblue">
<HR>
<H1 align="center">Registration Successful</H1>
<P>
<HR>
<P>Thank you for registering - you can now access the members private
area.<P>
<HR>
<A href="default.asp">Home</A> <BR>
<A href="/restricted/default.asp">Members Home</A>
</BODY>
</HTML>
```

_mem_bin/formslogin.asp

```
<%@LANGUAGE="VBSCRIPT" %>
<% Option Explicit %>

<% Dim OriginalUrl %>
<% OriginalUrl = Request.ServerVariables("QUERY_STRING") %>

<HTML>

<HEAD><TITLE>Authentication</TITLE>
</HEAD>
```

(continued)

```
<BODY BGCOLOR="lightblue">
<HR>
<H1 align="center">Restricted Access</H1>
<HR>

<% Session("log oncount") = Session("log oncount") + 1 %>
<% If Session("log oncount") > 3 then %>
    <P>Maximum number of log on attempts has been exceeded.<BR>
    Return to <A href="/default.asp">Home</A>
<% Else %>
    <P>The Members Area is for registered users only.</P>
    <FORM METHOD="post" ACTION="/_mem_bin/verifpwd.asp" NAME="xyz">
        <INPUT TYPE=hidden NAME=URL VALUE="<% =OriginalUrl %>">
    <P><B>Username:</B> <BR>
    <INPUT NAME="Username" SIZE="30" ><BR>
    <B>Password:</B> <BR>
    <INPUT TYPE="password" NAME="Password" SIZE="30"></P>
    <INPUT TYPE="submit" VALUE="Login" id=submit1 name=submit1>
    </FORM>
    <HR>
    <P>If you do not have an account then you will need to
    register. Registration is available from the <A
    href="/default.asp">home</A> page.</P>
<% End If %>
</BODY>
</HTML>
```

restricted/default.asp

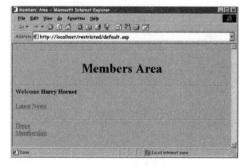

```
<%@LANGUAGE="VBSCRIPT" %>
<%
    Session("log oncount") = 0
%>
<HTML>
<HEAD><TITLE>Members Area</TITLE>
</HEAD>

<BODY bgcolor="lightgreen">
<HR>
<H1 align="center">Members Area</H1>
<P>
<HR>
Welcome <B>
```

Insert User Property

Click the Browse button to select a user property in the specified Membership Directory.

Property name: [   ] Browse...

```
Property name : user.givenName
Application Server : localhost
```

```
 
```

Insert User Property

Click the Browse button to select a user property in the specified Membership Directory.

Property name: [   ] Browse...

```
Property name : user.sn
Application Server : localhost
```

```
</B>

<P><A href="news.asp">Latest News</A>
<P>
<HR>
<A href="/default.asp">Home</A><BR>
<A href="membership.asp">Membership</A>

</BODY>
</HTML>
```

restricted/membership.asp

```
<%@LANGUAGE="VBSCRIPT" %>
<% Option Explicit %>


<HTML>
<HEAD><TITLE>Members Administration</TITLE>
</HEAD>


<BODY bgcolor="lightgreen">
<HR>
<H1 align="center">Members Adminstration</H1>
<P>
<HR>
<P><A href="detupdate.asp">Update Details</A>
<P><A href="pwupdate.asp">Change Password</A>
<P><A href="preferences.asp">Preferences</A>
<P><A href="cancel.asp">Cancel Membership</A>
<P>
<HR>
<A href="/default.asp">Home</A>  <BR>
<A href="default.asp">Members Home</A>


</BODY>
</HTML>
```

`restricted/detupdate.asp`

```
<%@LANGUAGE="VBSCRIPT" %>
<% Response.Buffer = True %>

<HTML>
<HEAD><TITLE>Update Details</TITLE>
</HEAD>

<BODY bgcolor="lightgreen">
<HR>
<H1 align="center">Update Details</H1>
<HR>
<P>Please enter the following:<br>
```

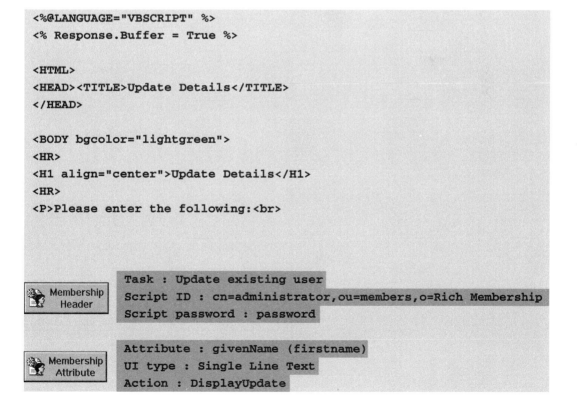

```
Task : Update existing user
Script ID : cn=administrator,ou=members,o=Rich Membership
Script password : password
```

```
Attribute : givenName (firstname)
UI type : Single Line Text
Action : DisplayUpdate
```

Membership Attribute	Attribute : sn (surname) UI type : Single Line Text Action : DisplayUpdate
Membership Attribute	Attribute : mail (e-mail address) UI type : Single Line Text Action : DisplayUpdate
Membership Attribute	Attribute : street (address) UI type : Single Line Text Action : DisplayUpdate
Membership Attribute	Attribute : l (city) UI type : Single Line Text Action : DisplayUpdate
Membership Attribute	Attribute : st (state) UI type : Single Line Text Action : DisplayUpdate
Membership Attribute	Attribute : postal code (zip code) UI type : Single Line Text Action : DisplayUpdate
Membership Attribute	Attribute : c (country) UI type : Single Line Text Action : DisplayUpdate
Membership Footer	Profile assistant usage code : (don't use it) URL to forward to on successful completion : default.asp

```
<HR>
<A href="/default.asp">Home</A>  <BR>
<A href="default.asp">Members Home</A>
</BODY>
</HTML>
```

`restricted/pwupdate.asp`

```
<%@LANGUAGE="VBSCRIPT" %>
<% Response.Buffer = True %>


<HTML>
<HEAD><TITLE>Change Password</TITLE>
</HEAD>


<BODY bgcolor="lightgreen">
<HR>
<H1 align="center">Change Password</H1>
<HR>
<P>Please enter the following:<br>
```

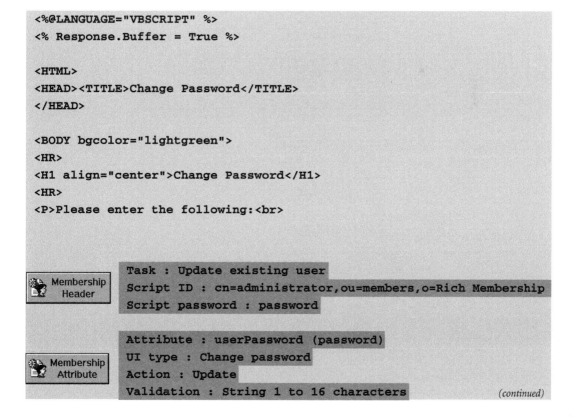

Membership Header

```
Task : Update existing user
Script ID : cn=administrator,ou=members,o=Rich Membership
Script password : password
```

Membership Attribute

```
Attribute : userPassword (password)
UI type : Change password
Action : Update
Validation : String 1 to 16 characters
```

(continued)

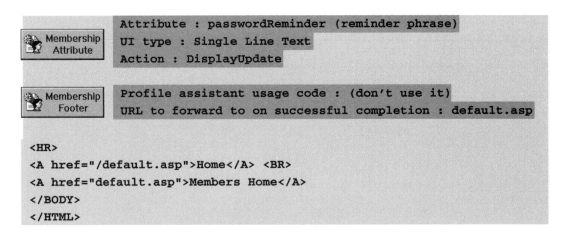

```
Membership          Attribute : passwordReminder (reminder phrase)
Attribute           UI type : Single Line Text
                    Action : DisplayUpdate

Membership          Profile assistant usage code : (don't use it)
Footer              URL to forward to on successful completion : default.asp
```

```
<HR>
<A href="/default.asp">Home</A> <BR>
<A href="default.asp">Members Home</A>
</BODY>
</HTML>
```

restricted/preferences.asp

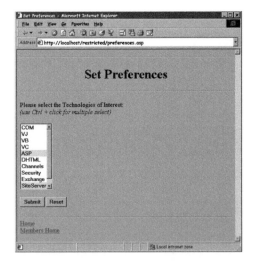

```
<%@LANGUAGE="VBSCRIPT" %>
<% Response.Buffer = True %>

<HTML>
<HEAD><TITLE>Set Preferences</TITLE>
</HEAD>

<BODY bgcolor="lightgreen">
<HR>
<H1 align="center">Set Preferences</H1>
<HR>
```

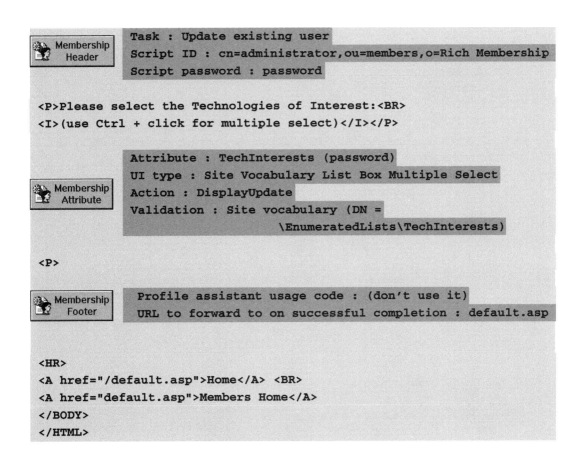

Membership Header	Task : Update existing user Script ID : cn=administrator,ou=members,o=Rich Membership Script password : password

```
<P>Please select the Technologies of Interest:<BR>
<I>(use Ctrl + click for multiple select)</I></P>
```

Membership Attribute	Attribute : TechInterests (password) UI type : Site Vocabulary List Box Multiple Select Action : DisplayUpdate Validation : Site vocabulary (DN = \EnumeratedLists\TechInterests)

```
<P>
```

Membership Footer	Profile assistant usage code : (don't use it) URL to forward to on successful completion : default.asp

```
<HR>
<A href="/default.asp">Home</A> <BR>
<A href="default.asp">Members Home</A>
</BODY>
</HTML>
```

restricted/cancel.asp

```
<%@LANGUAGE="VBSCRIPT" %>
<% Option Explicit %>
```
(continued)

```
<%
    Dim vMemUserScriptID
    Dim vMemUserPassword
    Dim vState
    Dim objUser

    vMemUserScriptID = "cn=administrator,ou=members,o=Rich Membership"
    vMemUserPassword = "password"

    If Not Request.QueryString("state") = "" Then
      vState = Request.QueryString("state")
    Else
      vState = 1
    End If
%>


<HTML>
<HEAD><TITLE>Cancel Membership</TITLE>
</HEAD>

<BODY bgcolor="lightgreen">
<HR>
<H1 align="center">Cancel Membership</H1>
<HR>

<% If vState = 2 Then %>

<%
    Set objUser = Server.CreateObject("Membership.UserObjects")
    objUser.BindAs "", vMemUserScriptID, vMemUserPassword
    objUser.accountStatus = 4
    objUser.SetInfo
    Response.Write "<P>You request for cancellation has been accepted.
</P>"
%>

<% Else %>
        <P>Are you sure you want to cancel your membership?</P>
    <FORM method="post" action="cancel.asp?state=2" id=form1 name=
form1>
```

```
            <INPUT type=submit value="Yes" id=submit1 name=submit1>
      </FORM>
<% End If %>


<HR>
<A href="/default.asp">Home</A> <BR>
<A href="default.asp">Members Home</A>
</BODY>
</HTML>
```

`restricted/news.asp`

The contents of this file will be explained as we discuss the generation of personalized content.

Personalized Content

Having discussed Membership, we shall now address its sidekick, Personalization, and see how to deliver customized Web content based on the identity of the user established by AUO.

With Site Server, we can achieve personalized content without having to use the complex query languages used by SQL Server and Index Server. Instead, we have at our disposal a high-level tool called the **Rules Manager** which enables us to define a prioritized set of content-delivery rules based on the results of a sequence of conditions.

The stages in delivering Personalized Content are:

- Define the Content Sources
- Define the Delivery Rules
- Implement the Web page using the Rule Set DTC

In the remainder of this chapter we discuss how to extend our "Members" application to implement a "Latest News" facility. This will deliver News Headlines (plus hyperlinks) for only the topics that the user has expressed an interest in.

The News Headlines will be stored in a SQL Server database. How this is populated will not be discussed here, but one suggestion is to create a protected area of the site that denies access to anyone but the site authors. This area could provide a series of simple Web database facilities to maintain the NewsItems table.

Content Sources

Content sources provide the location and structure of Web content and allow it to be retrieved for personalization. The Content Source configuration is available from the WebAdmin Contents menu option. First we must log on to the Membership Instance and then select the Content Sources menu option.

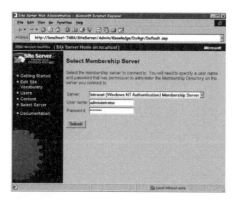

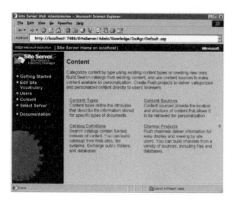

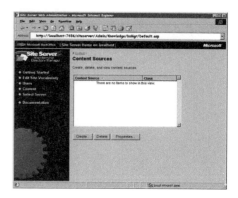

A Content Source can be any of the following:

- Search Server Source
- Index Server Source
- ODBC Data Source

Index Server and Search Server are both search engines. Index Server is targeted at searching documents (HTML, Office) and supplied as part of the Windows NT 4.0 Option Pack. Search Server is supplied as part of Site Server and provides more sophisticated facilities with the ability to crawl a variety of information sources, including files, databases, e-mail systems, newsgroup systems, and so on.

For our News example, we shall create an ODBC Data Source. We invoke the **Create Content Source Wizard** and follow the instructions:

First we create a name and description for our Content source. We shall set:

- Content Source Name = mstechnews
- Description = Latest news from Microsoft

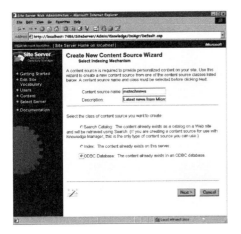 

We then set the ODBC DSN (Data Source Name) and the user credentials for an account that can access the data source.

We shall set:

- ODBC data source = mstechnews
- User name = sa
- Password = <blank>

The **ODBC DSN for a data source is configured using the ODBC Data Source Administrator. This is available from the Control panel.**

ODBC

Next we specify the name of the table in the data source that the information will be retrieved from. Optionally, when multiple tables are specified, a SQL join clause may be specified.

We shall set:

Tables = mstechnews

Join clause = <blank>

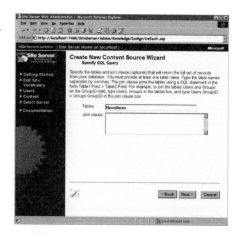

The next screen displays the fields found in the data store. Those not required may be removed from the list.

We shall leave the list of fields unchanged.

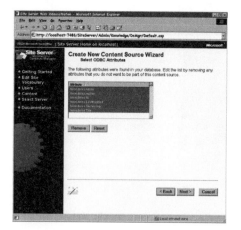

Finally the complete settings for the data source is displayed.

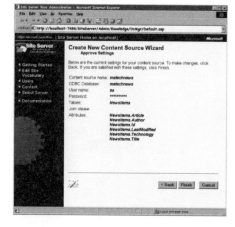

The Content Sources screen now includes our News data source.

Our News feed is now available to deliver personalized Web content.

The Rule Manager

The Rule Manager is a Site Server tool that specifies the criteria for the selection of data from defined Content Sources. The selected information is then made available for insertion into a personalized Web page or e-mail message.

A rule is one or more conditions that, if met, will trigger one or more actions. Exception conditions may also be specified, and if these are met, the actions will not be triggered even if the primary conditions are met.

For our example we shall define two rules:

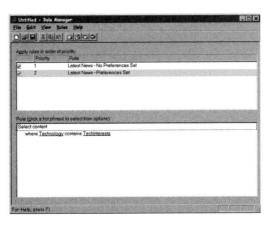

- Rule One—if the user has not set any preferences, output a suitable message informing him that he needs to do so

- Rule Two—output all news items applicable to a technology in which the user has expressed an interest

A series of rules built with the Rule Manager are saved as a Rules Set in a file with a **.prf** suffix. Each Rules Set is associated with an Application Server and a Content Source.

The name of the Application Server is requested when we enter the Rules Manager. It can also be selected from the View| Options menu option.

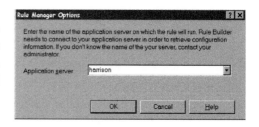

We add a rule to the Rule Set by selecting the Rules|Add New Rule menu option. For the first rule the name of the Content Source is requested

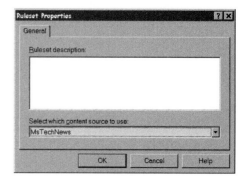

Each rule that we add produces the Rule Builder dialog. This provides a series of tabbed dialogs plus a description of the built rule. Each tab allows us to specify:

- General—this captures the rule name plus a priority value
- Conditions—all must be met for the rule to be fired
- Content—the items from the Content Source to be selected if the rule is fired
- Actions—VBScript code that gets invoked if the rule is fired
- Exception conditions—if any exception is true, then the rule will not be fired, irrespective of the primary conditions

The rule priority indicates the order in which the rule conditions are checked. A rule does not fire if a higher-priority rule has already fired.

To illustrate the Rule Builder, let us see how to define the two rules outlined above.

RULE ONE: USER HAS NOT SET ANY PREFERENCES

If the user has not set any preferences, then we want to output a suitable message.

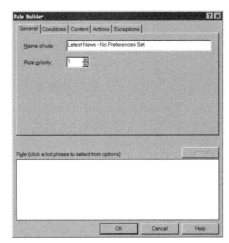

First we give the rule a title and assign it the highest priority (i.e., 1) so that it is invoked first.

We want Rule One to be fired if the user's entry in the membership directory does not have the TechInterests attribute set.

This is done by selecting the condition

<u>user property</u> has not been set

which then appears in the rule description

The items underlined are **hot phrases.** This can be replaced by an item from the attribute schema, a value from the Site Vocabulary, a hard-coded value, or an item of VB-Script.

By clicking on user property we get a list of items from the attribute schema and can select the TechInterests attribute.

The user property in the Rule Description is then replaced with the chosen attribute (i.e., TechInterests)

If the rule is fired, we wish to invoke some script logic to output our message.

This is done by selecting the action

Run <u>VB Script</u>

which then appears in the rule description.

Note that JavaScript is not supported.

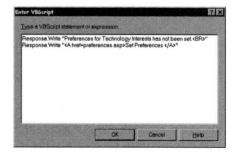

By clicking on the hot phrase, a dialog appears in which we can specify the script logic. Our message is generated using the ASP **Response.Write** method.

The definition of Rule One is now complete.

RULE TWO: OUTPUT ITEMS APPLICABLE TO USER

Our second rule is to display all news items applicable to a technology in which the user has expressed an interest.

First we give the rule a title and assign it a priority of 2.

If Rule One has not fired, we can assume that the user has set a preference. In cosnequence, we always want Rule Two to be fired.

The default condition is **always execute**. This means that we do not need to specify a condition.

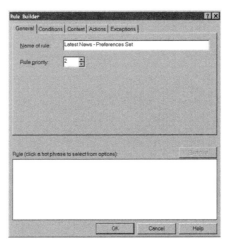

We now need to define the content to be selected, i.e., all news items associated with a technology in which the user has stated an interest.

This is done by selecting the content

<u>content property</u> contains <u>user property</u>

which then appears in the rule description.

By clicking on content property we get a list of items from the Content Source and can select the Technology property.

By clicking on user property we get a list of items from the attribute schema and can select the TechInterests attribute.

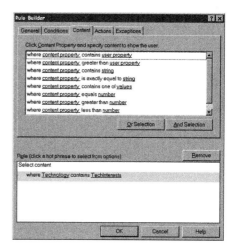

The Rule Description is then replaced with the chosen attribute (i.e., TechInterests) and content property (i.e., Technology).

Finally save the Rule Set as a file called latestnews.prf and locate this in the Restricted area of the "Members" Web site.

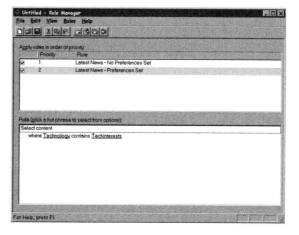

The definition of Rule Two is now complete.

Our final task is to use this Rule Set in a Web page to generate personalized content. This can be achieved using our own script logic, but rather than develop this code, a far simpler method is to use the Rule Set DTC.

Format Rule Set DTC

Rule Set Formatting

You may only use the browse button if you are currently working in a Visual Interdev project.

Rule set .prf site: Browse...

Instructions: You can
display any
properties of the
object returned by
the rule set. Specify
which properties to
display for each row
in the record set.   Help

The Format Rule Set DTC creates the ASP logic that at run-time uses a Rule Set file (`.prf` file) in a Web page to generate personalized content.

Using Visual InterDev, we insert the DTC into an ASP file by selecting the FormatRuleset DTC from the Toolbox.

We select the property sheet for the DTC by right-clicking on the control and selecting the Properties menu option.

The Selection property sheet enables us to specify which items from the Content Source we shall display. This can either be the first item, a random item, or all items. For our example, we shall select all items, i.e., display to the user all news items relevant to his stated interests.

There is also an option allowing us to write the selected content to the IIS log files. We shall leave this disabled.

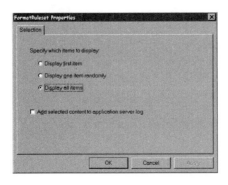

On the control we specify the name of the `.prf` file. We can use the Browse button to select the file.

Finally, on the control we specify the properties from the content we want to display and wrap this up in <HTML> formatting statements. The Insert Field button displays a list of content properties from which we can select one; selecting a field inserts the ASP code `<% = MemRecordSet("`*`fieldname`*`")%>`.

For our example, we insert the following HTML/ASP instructions.

```
<P><B>
<% = MemRecordSet("Title") %></B>
<BR>
<% = MemRecordSet("Article") %>
<HR width=30%>
```

The `Article` field in the record includes the summary text of the article plus the HTML hyperlink to the full article.

We can now save this page in our "Members" Web site as the ASP file `restricted/news.asp`. We are now ready to see Personalization in action.

Because the Rule Sets are driven by user attributes, pages using rule sets must be resident in directories that do not allow anonymous access. This is so that the user is identified and an AUO can be created to operate under the user's security context. We have satisfied this in our example because our "Latest News" page is situated within the restricted area of the site.

How it was done—for our eyes only!

`restricted/news.asp`

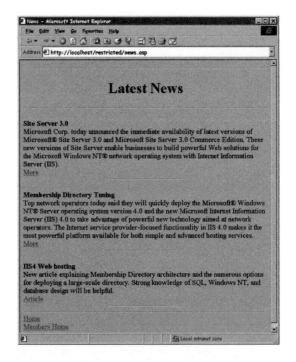

```
<%@LANGUAGE="VBSCRIPT" %>


<HTML>
<HEAD><TITLE>News</TITLE>
</HEAD>


<BODY bgcolor="lightgreen">
<HR>
<H1 align="center">Latest News</H1>
<HR>
<P>
```

Selection : Display all items

Rule Set .prf :
http://127.0.0.1:80/Restricted/
latestnews.prf

Instructions :
<P><B><% = MemRecordSet("Title")
%></B>
% = MemRecordSet("Article") %><HR
width=30%>

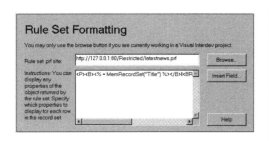

Rule Set Formatting

You may only use the browse button if you are currently working in a Visual Interdev project.

Rule set .prf site: `http://127.0.0.1:80/Restricted/latestnews.prf`   Browse...

Instructions: You can display any properties of the object returned by the rule set. Specify which properties to display for each row in the record set.   `<P><B><% = MemRecordSet("Title") %></B><BR>`   Insert Field...

Help

```
<HR>
<A href="/default.asp">Home</A> <BR>
<A href="default.asp">Members Home</A>
</BODY>
</HTML>
```

NEWSITEMS TABLE

The definition of the NewsItems table in SQL Server is as follows:

```
CREATE TABLE dbo.NewsItems (
    Id int IDENTITY (1, 1) NOT NULL ,
    LastModified char (10) NOT NULL ,
    Title char (30) NOT NULL ,
    Author char (20) NOT NULL ,
    Technology char (50) NOT NULL ,
          Article text NOT NULL )
GO
```

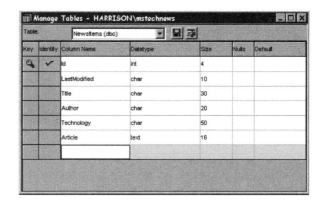

Manage Tables - HARRISON\mstechnews

Table: NewsItems (dbo)

Key	Identity	Column Name	Datatype	Size	Nulls	Default
🔑	✓	Id	int	4		
		LastModified	char	10		
		Title	char	30		
		Author	char	20		
		Technology	char	50		
		Article	text	16		

■ Summary

In this final chapter, we have seen how to build a Web application that uses AUO to automatically identify the Web user and provide access to information associated with the user that could be distributed over a number of different data stores.

The key points in this chapter are:

- AUO identifies the Web user and provides access to his associated personal attributes. It provides a single interface by extending ADSI to consolidate the user attributes into a single namespace.

- The Site Vocabulary is a set of key terms and values that a Web application can call upon and utilize within its processing.

- Design-Time Controls provides a very simple method of generating complex or lengthy script logic. Site Server provides several DTCs to simplify Web applications that need to identify the Web user and use the Membership and Personalization facilities.

- The WebAdmin User Attribute Editor provides facilities to add new user attributes to extend the Membership Directory Schema.

- The Rules Manager makes it possible to define a prioritized set of content-delivery rules based on the results of a sequence of conditions and the personal information known about the identified Web user. This avoids the need to use complex SQL and Index Server query statements.

We have now come to the end of the book, and with it our exploration of Web Security using the powerful array of software technologies from Microsoft.

A huge amount of work has been put into this book, and we hope that it has lived up to your expectations. Please let us know both the good and bad things about this book, so that future editions can take your thoughts and suggestions on board.

Support for this book and e-mail addresses can be obtained at:

http://surf.to/harrison

Microsoft and the Active Platform

This book focuses on the Microsoft platform, and we have assumed that the reader understands Microsoft's Internet strategy and has a reasonable grasp of its software products. This Appendix is provided for those readers who are not fully up to speed on this topic, and it acts as a reference guide to the key Microsoft software products and tools used to build multi-tier Internet and Intranet applications.

Microsoft and the Internet

In 1980, Bill Gates gave a keynote speech called "Information at Your Fingertips." In it he described his vision of a future in which information technology would touch many areas of everyday life. Four years later, he gave another speech updating this original theme. While software and hardware technology had undergone rapid change within the short period of time between the two speeches, he still made no reference to what would cause the biggest revolution in the IT industry since the PC, i.e., the Internet.

It was not until December 1995 that Microsoft publicly acknowledged the importance of the Internet and announced its overall strategy. Microsoft then declared that it would embrace Internet standards to deliver a comprehensive set of products and services that would seamlessly integrate desktops, LANs, legacy systems, GroupWare applications, and the public Internet to provide a more effective computing environment for the corporate enterprise.

While Microsoft joined the Internet game relatively late, it rapidly gained momentum and has since released an incredible range of innovative Internet products, all embracing various industry standards. These products have provided users with rich Internet experiences and organizations with the mechanisms to develop business-critical Internet solutions.

Exploiting Internet technologies has become the trump card in Microsoft's response to the emergence of the low-cost Network Computer (NC) and Java, which threatened its domination of the desktop. The NC/Java functions by automatically downloading any required executable logic in small chunks from a central file server. It is suggested that much lower administration costs can be achieved by minimizing the complexity of the NC hardware and limiting the client-installed software.

Windows NT

To continue its impressive growth curves, Microsoft needed to conquer the server market. Until recently, organizations had taken the traditional best-of-breed approach for their server solutions, such as Novell NetWare for a file and printer server, UNIX machines for communication gateways, Oracle or Sybase for relational databases, Lotus for e-mail and GroupWare, Sun or Netscape for the Internet, and so on. Because this approach typically results in a complex hodgepodge of technologies within the organization and increases the range of staff skills needed to support the enterprise, it obviously increased the running costs of the IT infrastructure.

The Microsoft answer for enterprise infrastructures is **Windows NT**, a single robust and high-performance multipurpose network operating system that can act with the following personalities:

- file server
- print server
- application server
- communication server
- database server

Windows NT was first conceived by Bill Gates in 1988 when he elected that Microsoft would develop its next-generation operating system. The key objectives were that the operating system was to be portable, secure, scaleable, extensible, compatible, and internationalizable.

These goals meant that Windows NT can easily be migrated to run on a number of different hardware platforms and operate in a number of languages and character sets, all with minimal changes to the core code. In addition, it can provide support for symmetric multiprocessing (SMP), i.e., run on machines with multiple CPUs.

Windows NT extensions can be developed by writing applications that conform to a well-defined application programming interface (API) called **WIN32**. In addition, it provides support for DOS, OS/2, and POSIX applications.

Strong levels of security were built into the core of Windows NT in order to meet and exceed a certifiable security standard, i.e., the C2 security guidelines required by the U.S. Department of Defense's security evaluation criteria. Compliance with the C2 security standard was originally only required for government agencies, but many commercial organizations have demanding corporate security needs and recognize the value of the enhanced security that such systems offer.

To design Windows NT, Microsoft hired David Cutler, who had worked on a number of operating systems, including the PDP-11 and VAX, at Digital Equipment Corporation. The ideal operating system initially dreamed of by Bill Gates and David Cutler was code-named Cairo. The nirvana has proven to be very difficult and tormenting, and the Cairo idea has recently changed from being an actual product release to just a philosophy.

After five years of development, Windows NT was released. It was delivered in two versions, NT 3.1 and NT Advanced Server 3.1. The 3.1 tag indicated that the roots of its user interface were from Windows 3.1; but that is where the similarities stopped.

In late 1994, Microsoft clarified the roles of the two versions by changing their names to give a clear indication of their purpose. Windows NT became Windows NT Workstation 3.51 and Windows NT Server 3.51. While based on the same core code, the internal scheduling of tasks was optimized so that one functions best as a desktop operating system and the other as a robust enterprise-level multipurpose network operating system. In 1996, NT version 4.0 (Workstation and Server) was released. It included many new features, and in addition adopted the same acclaimed user interface from Windows 95.

Windows 2000 (NT 5.0), Microsoft's next step toward Cairo, will bring many advantages in the areas of system management, application infrastructure, networking and communications, and information sharing and publishing.

ActiveX/COM

ActiveX has to be one of the most misunderstood and ambiguously used expressions in the Internet technology arena. Many people get confused because ActiveX actually encompasses a number of technologies and is not just one thing.

When Microsoft released its first set of Internet tools in March 1996, it announced **ActiveX** technology—which in all truth was just a new marketing name for its existing **OLE** technology. ActiveX (or third-generation OLE technology) is a framework that allows software components to cooperate even if they have been written by different vendors, at different times, using different tools, and if the objects are located in the same process, the same machine, or distributed over multiple machines. Put simply, ActiveX provides the *software plumbing* between software objects and insulates the component developer from such complexities.

ActiveX encompasses an ever-growing series of technologies, each of which defines the interfaces between the objects to implement the particular technology. For the Internet, examples include:

- ActiveX Scripting—enables script logic to be included in the downloaded Web page or used on the server to generate the page content
- ActiveX Controls—enables client components to be incorporated within a Web page and dynamically downloaded as needed
- ActiveX Documents—enables the browser to support non-HTML documents (such as Microsoft Office documents)
- ActiveX Server Components—enables the Web Server to interface to other server software components

To most users, ActiveX is transparent, and they just see the effects of these technologies; it is irrelevant to them whether ActiveX or "black magic" is operating behind the scenes. However, it is different for the developer—these technologies enable Microsoft's powerful environment for creating dynamic Web content.

Component Object Model

Underneath ActiveX is the generic **Component Object Model** (COM) which defines the binary interface between objects. The original specification of COM always allowed for cooperating objects to be located on different machines, but this was not implemented until Windows NT 4.0 and was then called **Distributed COM** (DCOM). Because of this, in reality DCOM and

COM are now the same animals. DCOM is layered on top of the DCE (Distributed Computing Environment) RPC (**Remote Procedure Call**) specifications. The following diagram shows how objects use COM/DCOM to cooperate even across process and machine boundaries.

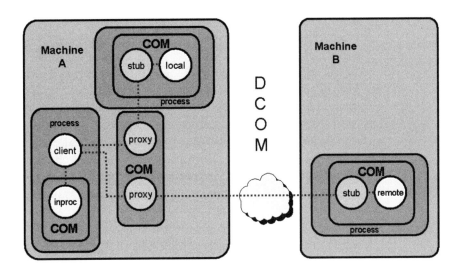

While ActiveX and COM were not originally committee-driven standards, they have since become open market–driven technologies that are fully published from the lowest-level communications protocols to the highest-level API functions. In addition, Microsoft has donated ownership of the technology's specifications to an open industry association working under the auspices of The Open Group to promote the common adoption of ActiveX core technologies. COM is now ubiquitous and available on a number of platforms, including Sun Solaris, Digital Unix, Digital Open VMS, IBM MVS, IBM OS/400, IBM AIX, HP/UX, Siemens Nixdorf, Linux 2.0 (Intel), and SCO UnixWare.

The Need for Software Components

Making effective use of information technology has become critical for companies as a means of lowering the cost of doing business and obtaining competitive advantage. Until recently, however, the software industry was frequently drowning in complexity and failing to deliver many projects on time or to budget. Furthermore, organizations were finding the new generation of advanced software costly to support and difficult to enhance. Code was frequently written in a monolithic fashion such that completely different bits of logic were intertwined, and this made it risky to make changes. Even what might appear to be a minor amendment could easily, and unknowingly, cause severe repercussions to ripple throughout the system.

IT managers recognized that new software techniques were required to overcome the problems of complexity, increase the production rate of robust software, and reuse existing proven code. One powerful technique that delivers this goal is **component-based software,** and this is fundamental when building solutions with Microsoft products.

Component-based software is a development process that emulates the construction processes used by many more established industries. For example, the majority of today's car manufacturers build vehicles from hundreds of component parts supplied by a vast number of external companies. Each individual part has been designed, manufactured, and passed through quality checks as a separate isolated process undertaken by the part supplier. By delegating responsibility for many of these low-level complexities, a car manufacturer can concentrate on its core business—designing and building cars that are more reliable and brought to market quickly due to a short development cycle.

In the early 1980s, IBM needed to quickly enter the microcomputer market to compete with the powerful desktop personal computers, such as Apple. However, since IBM did not have the experience at this low end of the computer spectrum to develop its own proprietary product quickly and from scratch, it decided to break with tradition by declaring that its new machine would adopt an open architecture. The new "IBM Personal Computer" would use "off the shelf" components, such as the microprocessor, memory, hard disks, etc., that were standard technology in the marketplace, and this enabled the company to construct a competitive machine in a very short time.

Unfortunately for IBM, many other vendors soon realized that they could follow suit, and as a result numerous "IBM PC Compatibles" became available. Compaq, for example, released its first PC-compatible machine in 1983 and was a Fortune 500 company within three years. Furthermore, a huge industry was swiftly generated to develop and manufacture these vital PC components. If you look in a PC today, you will see numerous components from a vast range of suppliers: perhaps the microprocessor is from Intel, the hard disk from Western Digital, the graphics card from ATI, the CD-ROM Drive from Mitsumi, the modem from US Robotics, the sound card from Creative Labs, the network card from 3Com, and so on. Such component suppliers are able to concentrate on their areas of expertise and can develop low-cost, technologically advanced versions of their products.

This leaves PC manufacturers the task of building machines by "cherry picking" the most cost-effective components available and integrating them together to create a computer system. Communication standards exist to ensure that the components can interact with each other or be exchanged for similar components from an alternative vendor. The PC manufacturer can avoid the internal complexities and technologies of such components; all it needs to know is the external standards to which the component conforms.

The software industry is now at a point where it can build systems in a similar manner by selecting a number of items of software that each perform a specific item of functionality and "gluing them together" (using ActiveX and COM) to form a single integrated solution. Such components can either be developed by one's own staff or purchased from the many software vendors that specialize in this market. The system designers and integration team must have confidence that the functionality of the component behaves as published, but they do not need to worry about the complexities of the internal processing logic.

Software Component Characteristics

A software component can be defined as a combination of data and of code acting on that data which together can be considered as a single unit. An **object**, of which there may be many, is a created instance of a software component.

The data and code associated to the component define everything that the component represents (state) and what it can do (behavior). These characteristics are specified by the software component's definition, which consists of:

- **Properties**—the attributes of the object that are available for access, update, or both from outside the object
- **Methods**—functions that can be invoked from outside the object; sometimes methods will take arguments
- **Events**—signals which are fired when a specific action or interesting state occurs; these signals are detected and acted upon from outside of the object

Properties and Methods that operate together to perform a specific task are often grouped together and referred to as an object's **ingoing interface**. Events that occur are grouped in an object's **outgoing interface**. An object can support more than one interface.

Some interfaces are standard and are published by software vendors; for example, Microsoft's ActiveX specifications define many standard interfaces. Published interfaces are set in stone and cannot be changed. If software developers write their software to conform to standard interfaces, their software can successfully cohabit within environments comprising software from multiple developers.

The Active Platform

Active Platform is the name Microsoft applies to the architecture that addresses its seamless integration strategy, plus the dynamic delivery of applications and rich content. This encompasses both the client (**Active Client**) and server (**Active Server**) technologies to achieve the company's goal. Microsoft's complete support for ActiveX and Internet standards enables developers to integrate HTML, scripting, components, and transactions to build powerful, scaleable, and highly available applications that run across the enterprise. This architecture frees developers from the complexity of programming infrastructures and allows them to concentrate on delivering business solutions. The Active Platform is illustrated below.

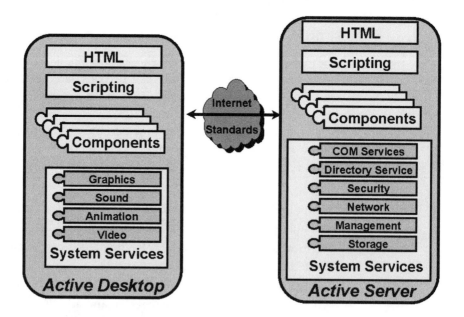

The foundation of the Active Server is Windows NT Server's security, network, and data components augmented by BackOffice (discussed shortly). Remember that ActiveX and COM provide the software glue that integrates these different items and allows the components to be deployed over multiple clients and servers. This provides a great set of tools for the creation of distributed applications where different parts of a solution can reside on separate machines to form an optimum multi-tier client server architectural solution.

The Active Client is Microsoft's operating system independent client support for HTML and ActiveX technologies, and is a set of components included with Internet Explorer 4.0. Since it is component-based, it can easily be incorporated into any client application. Microsoft has provided Active Client support for Windows NT, Windows 95/98, Windows 3.1, Macintosh, and UNIX.

Active Server Products

Microsoft has made available a number of products and components that work together with Windows NT to provide a comprehensive Active Server solution. The methods of licensing these products frequently change, and the reader is referred to the Microsoft Web site to see the options currently available; these may include:

- Licensing as part of Windows NT 4.0.
- Licensing as part of Windows NT 4.0 Option Pack.
- Licensing as part of Windows NT 4.0 Enterprise Edition.
- Licensing as part of BackOffice.
- Licensing individually.

The Microsoft Active Server products include:

- **Internet Information Server** (IIS)—provides Internet services, including Web (HTTP), File Transfer (FTP), News Groups (NNTP), and e-mail (SMTP)
- **Active Server Pages** (ASP)—provides server-side scripting mechanism to implement extensions to the IIS Web services
- **Transaction Server** (MTS)—provides infrastructure needed for multi-tier client server solutions; includes facilities to share resources, manage transactions, and administrate component deployment
- **Message Queue Server** (MSMQ)—provides assured-delivery message switching; handles network outages and heterogeneous networking architectures
- **Index Server**—provides search engine facilities to identify documents which contain specific text
- **Exchange Server**—provides integrated system for e-mail, personal and group scheduling, electronic forms, and groupware applications
- **SQL Server**—provides large-scale relational database management system designed specifically for distributed client-server computing

- **Systems Management Server** (SMS)—provides centralized management tool for software distribution, hardware/software inventory, and diagnostic facilities.
- **SNA Server**—provides facilities for interfacing with legacy IBM and other host systems using SNA communication protocols.
- **Proxy Server**—provides Internet access to corporate desktop in a secure manner; also enables caching of popular Web pages to improve performance.
- **Commercial Internet System**—provides facilities for Internet communities; includes servers for membership, personalization, billing, white pages, chat, mail, newsgroups, user locator, content replication, information retrieval.
- **Site Server**—provides Web site environment for deployment, implementation, and analysis of business-critical and electronic commerce sites.
- **NetShow Server**—provides streaming media services for video and audio broadcasting.
- **Cluster Server**—provides clustering facilities allowing multiple NT nodes to combine to provide high availability and scaleability.
- **Terminal Server**—provides Windows applications to diverse desktop hardware through terminal emulation.

These products integrate together to form a single infrastructure. The consistent approach found throughout Windows NT and these products considerably reduces training and support costs.

Windows DNA

At the Professional Developers Conference in September 1997, Microsoft unveiled its future strategy with an architectural framework for creating modern, open, scaleable, multi-tier distributed Windows applications using both the Internet and client/server technologies. This is to be known as the **Windows Distributed interNet Applications Architecture,** or Windows DNA. It builds on current investments in technology, hardware, applications, and skills.

Microsoft has recognized that developers frequently waste a huge amount of time building infrastructure-type software in their applications. The objective of Windows DNA is to lay down foundations ensuring that all this infrastructure-type software will be developed, once and for all, by Microsoft, and built into the software base of the next versions of Windows

NT. This means that developers can concentrate on innovative application logic rather than worry about software plumbing.

Windows DNA addresses the requirements for all tiers of a distributed application, i.e., the user interface, the business process logic, and the data storage. In addition, it provides a rich set of application services and a wide range of development tools. At the heart of Windows DNA is COM, which provides the integration of the various components. A further evolution of COM called **COM+** is planned to make it simpler to build and reuse components. COM+ avoids much of the infrastructure-type work currently needed when developing COM components by providing default implementations for most of the common scenarios.

Many of the services detailed in Windows DNA have been around for several years. However, Windows DNA is a formalization of the framework and a roadmap for the future. The key to Windows DNA is Windows 2000 (NT 5.0), which is not targeted for delivery until late 1999; some of the components, including IIS, MTS, ASP, and MSMQ, are available for use now with the Windows NT 4.0 Option Pack.

Development Tools

The Active Platform allows developers to use their familiar tools and programming languages to create the various software components, including Microsoft's Visual Basic, Visual C++, Visual J++, and Visual FoxPro, plus numerous offerings from other software vendors. Since staff costs are the most expensive part of any software development, it is generally accepted that the best development tool is simply the one for which your organization has the most staff trained. In our view, the choice of language is immaterial, so long as it includes facilities to build components with DCOM compliant interfaces. This will ensure that your software can readily cooperate with other components residing within the Active Platform.

Visual Studio 6.0, the latest development tool release from Microsoft, includes the development languages Visual Basic 6.0, Visual C++ 6.0, Visual J++ 6.0, and Visual FoxPro 6.0 in a single package. Also bundled in Visual Studio is Visual InterDev 6.0, which provides an environment for the development of HTML and ASP pages. An alternative for the development of HTML pages is Microsoft FrontPage, which is designed for Web authors who want to create simple Web pages with minimal scripting.

INDEX

Enterprise Systems, 18
Entrust, 168, 194
Entry Module, 309–310
Enumerated Lists, 525
Error Handling, 387
Essage Queue Server, 581
Ethernet, 68
Events, 49, 579
  application, 40
  security, 40
  system, 40
Excessive security, 11
Exchange, 102, 421, 427
Exchange Server, 581
Exit Module, 309–310
Explorer Control, 210
Export restrictions, 166
Extensibility, 20
Extranets, 83, 296, 318

False certificate, 158
FAT, 45
Fault Tolerance, 11
Fault-tolerant disk systems, 12
Fiber optic links, 11
File Allocation Table, 45
File auditing, 49
File permissions, 140, 431, 448, 455, 537
File System, 45
File Transfer Protocol (FTP), 68, 72, 151
FileSystemObject, 326
Financial stability, 217
Firewall, 80, 84, 87, 98
Format Rule Set DTC, 568
FrontPage, 123, 140, 526, 583
FrontPage Express, 223
FrontPage Server Extensions, 140, 539

Global unique identifier (GUID), 223, 370, 431, 509, 523
Global.asa file, 359
Gopher, 72
Groups, 501
Guest account, 28
Guest Book application, 380

Hacker, 14
Hash functions, 156
Hashing algorithms, 299
High availability, 11
High-performance, 16
Home directory, 118
Host address, 69
Hostname, 70
Hot fixes, 22
Hot phrases, 563
HTML forms, 505

HTML Forms Authentication, 490, 512-513, 538, 542
HTTP Request Headers, 243
HTTPS, 68, 72, 178
HTTP_AUTHORIZATION, 258
HyperText Transfer Protocol (HTTP), 68, 72, 85, 88, 90, 118, 125, 128, 151, 193, 195-196, 232, 234, 237-238, 240, 242, 254, 256, 270, 312, 361, 454, 509, 529

IDEA, 154
Identification, 491
Identity, 449
IEAK Profile Manager, 192
IIS Administration, 102
IIS Administration Objects (IISAO), 108, 431
IIS configuration, 103
IIS Log Format, 137
IIS logging, 123, 137, 195, 278, 568
IIS Metabase, 113
IIS Security, 101
IIS4 metabase, 429
IISCA, 306
IISNamespace, 110
Impersonation, 126, 182, 209
Impersonator, 158, 162
Impersonators, 13
Impostor, 13
Index Server, 102, 557–558, 581
Individual SPC, 217
Inexperienced users, 14
"Information at Your Fingertips," 573
Ingoing interface, 579
Insert User Property DTC, 527
Integrity, 16, 81, 151, 210
Interface, 579
Internet Assigned Numbers Authority (IANA), 70
Internet Connection Services for RAS (ICS), 79
Internet Control Message Protocol (ICMP), 68
Internet Explorer Administration Kit (IEAK), 190, 220
Internet Explorer deployment, 190
Internet Information Server (IIS), 19, 25, 101, 231
Internet Protocol (IP), 66
Internet Protocol Security (IPSec), 84
  Tunnel Mode, 84
Internet Protocol Suite, 16, 65
Internet Relay Chat (IRC), 72
Internet Security Framework, 20
Internet Server Applications Programming Interface (ISAPI), 232
Internet Service Manager (MMC), 102, 105, 120, 165, 317
Internet Service Provider (ISP), 76
Internet Transfer Control, 243
Internet zone, 187
Intrinsic objects, 236
IP address, 68, 118, 124, 188, 193, 201, 254–255, 493
IP Controls, 123
IP Forwarding, 86
IP Network, 69

LICENSE AGREEMENT AND LIMITED WARRANTY

READ THE FOLLOWING TERMS AND CONDITIONS CAREFULLY BEFORE OPENING THIS DISK PACKAGE. THIS LEGAL DOCUMENT IS AN AGREEMENT BETWEEN YOU AND PRENTICE-HALL, INC. (THE "COMPANY"). BY OPENING THIS SEALED DISK PACKAGE, YOU ARE AGREEING TO BE BOUND BY THESE TERMS AND CONDITIONS. IF YOU DO NOT AGREE WITH THESE TERMS AND CONDITIONS, DO NOT OPEN THE DISK PACKAGE. PROMPTLY RETURN THE UNOPENED DISK PACKAGE AND ALL ACCOMPANYING ITEMS TO THE PLACE YOU OBTAINED THEM FOR A FULL REFUND OF ANY SUMS YOU HAVE PAID.

1. **GRANT OF LICENSE:** In consideration of your payment of the license fee, which is part of the price you paid for this product, and your agreement to abide by the terms and conditions of this Agreement, the Company grants to you a nonexclusive right to use and display the copy of the enclosed software program (hereinafter the "SOFTWARE") on a single computer (i.e., with a single CPU) at a single location so long as you comply with the terms of this Agreement. The Company reserves all rights not expressly granted to you under this Agreement.

2. **OWNERSHIP OF SOFTWARE:** You own only the magnetic or physical media (the enclosed disks) on which the SOFTWARE is recorded or fixed, but the Company retains all the rights, title, and ownership to the SOFTWARE recorded on the original disk copy(ies) and all subsequent copies of the SOFTWARE, regardless of the form or media on which the original or other copies may exist. This license is not a sale of the original SOFTWARE or any copy to you.

3. **COPY RESTRICTIONS:** This SOFTWARE and the accompanying printed materials and user manual (the "Documentation") are the subject of copyright. You may not copy the Documentation or the SOFTWARE, except that you may make a single copy of the SOFTWARE for backup or archival purposes only. You may be held legally responsible for any copying or copyright infringement which is caused or encouraged by your failure to abide by the terms of this restriction.

4. **USE RESTRICTIONS:** You may not network the SOFTWARE or otherwise use it on more than one computer or computer terminal at the same time. You may physically transfer the SOFTWARE from one computer to another provided that the SOFTWARE is used on only one computer at a time. You may not distribute copies of the SOFTWARE or Documentation to others. You may not reverse engineer, disassemble, decompile, modify, adapt, translate, or create derivative works based on the SOFTWARE or the Documentation without the prior written consent of the Company.

5. **TRANSFER RESTRICTIONS:** The enclosed SOFTWARE is licensed only to you and may not be transferred to any one else without the prior written consent of the Company. Any unauthorized transfer of the SOFTWARE shall result in the immediate termination of this Agreement.

6. **TERMINATION:** This license is effective until terminated. This license will terminate automatically without notice from the Company and become null and void if you fail to comply with any provisions or limitations of this license. Upon termination, you shall destroy the Documentation and all copies of the SOFTWARE. All provisions of this Agreement as to warranties, limitation of liability, remedies or damages, and our ownership rights shall survive termination.

7. **MISCELLANEOUS:** This Agreement shall be construed in accordance with the laws of the United States of America and the State of New York and shall benefit the Company, its affiliates, and assignees.

8. **LIMITED WARRANTY AND DISCLAIMER OF WARRANTY:** The Company warrants that the SOFTWARE, when properly used in accordance with the Documentation, will operate in substantial conformity with the description of the SOFTWARE set forth in the Documentation. The Company does not warrant that the

SOFTWARE will meet your requirements or that the operation of the SOFTWARE will be uninterrupted or error-free. The Company warrants that the media on which the SOFTWARE is delivered shall be free from defects in materials and workmanship under normal use for a period of thirty (30) days from the date of your purchase. Your only remedy and the Company's only obligation under these limited warranties is, at the Company's option, return of the warranted item for a refund of any amounts paid by you or replacement of the item. Any replacement of SOFTWARE or media under the warranties shall not extend the original warranty period. The limited warranty set forth above shall not apply to any SOFTWARE which the Company determines in good faith has been subject to misuse, neglect, improper installation, repair, alteration, or damage by you. EXCEPT FOR THE EXPRESSED WARRANTIES SET FORTH ABOVE, THE COMPANY DISCLAIMS ALL WARRANTIES, EXPRESS OR IMPLIED, INCLUDING WITHOUT LIMITATION, THE IMPLIED WARRANTIES OF MERCHANTABILITY AND FITNESS FOR A PARTICULAR PURPOSE. EXCEPT FOR THE EXPRESS WARRANTY SET FORTH ABOVE, THE COMPANY DOES NOT WARRANT, GUARANTEE, OR MAKE ANY REPRESENTATION REGARDING THE USE OR THE RESULTS OF THE USE OF THE SOFTWARE IN TERMS OF ITS CORRECTNESS, ACCURACY, RELIABILITY, CURRENTNESS, OR OTHERWISE.

IN NO EVENT, SHALL THE COMPANY OR ITS EMPLOYEES, AGENTS, SUPPLIERS, OR CONTRACTORS BE LIABLE FOR ANY INCIDENTAL, INDIRECT, SPECIAL, OR CONSEQUENTIAL DAMAGES ARISING OUT OF OR IN CONNECTION WITH THE LICENSE GRANTED UNDER THIS AGREEMENT, OR FOR LOSS OF USE, LOSS OF DATA, LOSS OF INCOME OR PROFIT, OR OTHER LOSSES, SUSTAINED AS A RESULT OF INJURY TO ANY PERSON, OR LOSS OF OR DAMAGE TO PROPERTY, OR CLAIMS OF THIRD PARTIES, EVEN IF THE COMPANY OR AN AUTHORIZED REPRESENTATIVE OF THE COMPANY HAS BEEN ADVISED OF THE POSSIBILITY OF SUCH DAMAGES. IN NO EVENT SHALL LIABILITY OF THE COMPANY FOR DAMAGES WITH RESPECT TO THE SOFTWARE EXCEED THE AMOUNTS ACTUALLY PAID BY YOU, IF ANY, FOR THE SOFTWARE.

SOME JURISDICTIONS DO NOT ALLOW THE LIMITATION OF IMPLIED WARRANTIES OR LIABILITY FOR INCIDENTAL, INDIRECT, SPECIAL, OR CONSEQUENTIAL DAMAGES, SO THE ABOVE LIMITATIONS MAY NOT ALWAYS APPLY. THE WARRANTIES IN THIS AGREEMENT GIVE YOU SPECIFIC LEGAL RIGHTS AND YOU MAY ALSO HAVE OTHER RIGHTS WHICH VARY IN ACCORDANCE WITH LOCAL LAW.

ACKNOWLEDGMENT

YOU ACKNOWLEDGE THAT YOU HAVE READ THIS AGREEMENT, UNDERSTAND IT, AND AGREE TO BE BOUND BY ITS TERMS AND CONDITIONS. YOU ALSO AGREE THAT THIS AGREEMENT IS THE COMPLETE AND EXCLUSIVE STATEMENT OF THE AGREEMENT BETWEEN YOU AND THE COMPANY AND SUPERSEDES ALL PROPOSALS OR PRIOR AGREEMENTS, ORAL, OR WRITTEN, AND ANY OTHER COMMUNICATIONS BETWEEN YOU AND THE COMPANY OR ANY REPRESENTATIVE OF THE COMPANY RELATING TO THE SUBJECT MATTER OF THIS AGREEMENT.

Should you have any questions concerning this Agreement or if you wish to contact the Company for any reason, please contact in writing at the address below or call the at the telephone number provided.

PTR Customer Service
Prentice Hall PTR
One Lake Street
Upper Saddle River, New Jersey 07458

Telephone: 201-236-7105

About the CD-ROM

The CD-ROM included with *ASP/MTS/ADSI Web Security* contains all of the source code examples in the book organized by chapter. Various Microsoft programs referred to in the book must be obtained directly from Microsoft or an authorized reseller.

You can obtain a 90-day evaluation version of Microsoft Site Server 3.0 by going to:

http://backoffice.microsoft.com/downtrial/moreinfo/siteserver3.asp

You can obtain the Windows NT 4.0 Option Pack by going to:

**http://www.microsoft.com/windows/downloads/contents/wurecommended/
s_wuservicepacks/nt4optpk/default.asp**

System Requirements

The CD-ROM is a standard ISO 9660 CD. The various source code and data files on the CD are organized into the following directories:

ch06
ch07
ch08
ch09
ch10
ch11
ch12
ch13
ch14
ch15

License Agreement

Use of the *ASP/MTS/ADSI Web Security* CD-ROM is subject to the terms of the License Agreement and Limited Warranty on p. ???.

Technical Support

Prentice Hall does not offer technical support for any of the programs on the CD-ROM. However, if the CD is damaged, you may obtain a replacement copy by sending an email that describes the problem to:

disc_exchange@prenhall.com